lonely planet

Kaua'i

Brett Atkinson, Greg Ward

PLAN YOUR TRIP

ON THE ROAD

DUKE'S BAREFOOT BAR P98

PALI KE KUA (HIDEAWAYS)
BEACH P155

Contents

COVID-19

We have re-checked every business in this book before
publication to ensure that it is still open after 2020's
COVID-19 outbreak. However, the economic and social
impacts of COVID-19 will continue to be felt long after
the outbreak has been contained, and many businesses,
services and events referenced in this guide may
experience ongoing restrictions. Some businesses may
be temporarily closed, have changed their opening hours
and services, or require bookings; some unfortunately
could have closed permanently. We suggest you check
with venues before visiting for the latest information.

**NA PALI COAST WILDERNESS
STATE PARK, P179**

4

Right: Na Pali
Coast Wilderness
State Park (p179)

WELCOME TO
Kaua'i

I always love arriving at one of the world's most laid-back airports – an island-enforced transition to a state of unhurried relaxation. Picking up super-fresh poke at a local market or chatting with easygoing food-truck owners only magnifies my serene vibe, and I'm soon ready to jump into active adventures exploring Kaua'i's improbably scenic landscapes. Salty spray enlivens catamaran trips along the Na Pali Coast, while the island's heritage and rugged interior combine on a tubing trip on historic irrigation channels. Sunset beers and pau hana happy hour snacks reinvigorate me for another supremely relaxing itinerary the following day.

By Brett Atkinson, Writer

🐦 @travelwriternz 📷 travelwriternz
For more about our writers, see p288

MNSTUDIO/SHUTTERSTOCK ©

Kaua'i

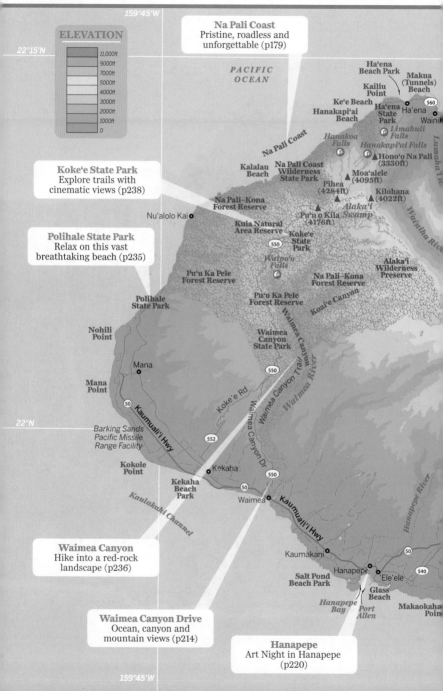

ELEVATION

11,000ft
9000ft
7000ft
5000ft
4000ft
3000ft
2000ft
1000ft
0

Na Pali Coast
Pristine, roadless and
unforgettable (p179)

Koke'e State Park
Explore trails with
cinematic views (p238)

Polihale State Park
Relax on this vast
breathtaking beach (p235)

Waimea Canyon
Hike into a red-rock
landscape (p236)

Waimea Canyon Drive
Ocean, canyon and
mountain views (p214)

Hanapepe
Art Night in Hanapepe
(p220)

PACIFIC
OCEAN

Ha'ena
Beach Park
Makua
(Tunnels)
Beach
Kailiu
Point
Ke'e Beach
Ha'ena
State
Park
Ha'ena
560
Waini
Hanakapi'ai
Beach
Limahuli
Falls

Hanakoa
Falls
Hanakapi'ai Falls
Hono'o Na Pali
(3330ft)

Kalalau
Beach
Na Pali Coast
Wilderness
State Park
Moa'alele
(4095ft)
Pihea
(4284ft)
Kilohana
(4022ft)

Na Pali–Kona
Forest Reserve
Pu'u o Kila
(4176ft)
Alaka'i
Swamp

Nu'alolo Kai
Kuia Natural
Area Reserve
Koke'e
State
Park

550
Waipo'o
Falls
Alaka'i
Wilderness
Preserve

Pu'u Ka Pele
Forest Reserve
Na Pali–Kona
Forest Reserve

Polihale
State Park
Pu'u Ka Pele
Forest Reserve
Koaie Canyon

Nohili
Point
Waimea
Canyon
State Park

Mana
550

Mana
Point
Koke'e Rd
Waimea Canyon Dr
Waimea Canyon Trail
Waimea River

50
Kaumuali'i Hwy
Barking Sands
Pacific Missile
Range Facility

552

Kokole
Point
Kekaha
Beach
Park
Kekaha
550

Waimea
Kaumuali'i Hwy

50
Kaulakahi Channel

Kaumakani
Hanapepe River

Salt Pond
Beach Park
Kaumakani
Hanapepe
Ele'ele
50
540

Glass
Beach
Hanapepe
Bay
Port
Allen
Makaokaha
Poin

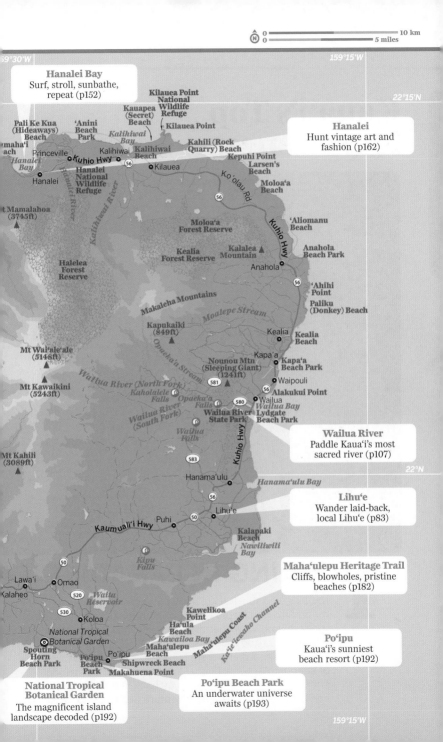

| 0 | 10 km |
| 0 | 5 miles |

Hanalei Bay
Surf, stroll, sunbathe, repeat (p152)

Hanalei
Hunt vintage art and fashion (p162)

Wailua River
Paddle Kaua'i's most sacred river (p107)

Lihu'e
Wander laid-back, local Lihu'e (p83)

Maha'ulepu Heritage Trail
Cliffs, blowholes, pristine beaches (p182)

Po'ipu
Kaua'i's sunniest beach resort (p192)

Po'ipu Beach Park
An underwater universe awaits (p193)

National Tropical Botanical Garden
The magnificent island landscape decoded (p192)

159°30'W
159°15'W
22°15'N
22°N

Kilauea Point National Wildlife Refuge
Kauapea (Secret) Beach
Kilauea Point
Pali Ke Kua (Hideaways) Beach
'Anini Beach Park
Kalihiwai Bay
Kahili (Rock Quarry) Beach
Kepuhi Point
Larsen's Beach
-maha'i ach
Princeville
Kalihiwai
Kalihiwai Beach
Moloa'a Beach
Hanalei Bay
Kuhio Hwy
56
Kilauea
Ko'olau Rd
'Aliomanu Beach
Hanalei
Hanalei National Wildlife Refuge
Kuhio Hwy
t Mamalahoa (3745ft)
Kalihiwai River
Anahola Beach Park
Moloa'a Forest Reserve
Kalalea Mountain
Halelea Forest Reserve
Kealia Forest Reserve
Anahola
56
'Ahihi Point
Paliku (Donkey) Beach
Makaleha Mountains
Moalepe Stream
Kapukaiki (849ft)
Kealia
Kealia Beach
Mt Wai'ale'ale (5148ft)
Opaeka'a Stream
Nounou Mtn (Sleeping Giant) (1241ft)
Kapa'a
Kapa'a Beach Park
Mt Kawaikini (5243ft)
Wailua River (North Fork)
581
Waipouli
56
Alakukui Point
Kaholalele Falls
Opaeka'a Falls
580
Wailua
Wailua Bay
Wailua River (South Fork)
Wailua River State Park
Lydgate Beach Park
Wailua Falls
Kuhio Hwy
583
Mt Kahili (3089ft)
Hanama'ulu
Hanama'ulu Bay
56
Puhi
Lihu'e
50
Kaumuali'i Hwy
Kalapaki Beach
Nawiliwili Bay
50
Lawa'i
Omao
Kipu Falls
Kalaheo
520
Waita Reservoir
530
Koloa
Kawelikoa Point
National Tropical Botanical Garden
Ha'ula Beach
Maha'ulepu Coast
Kawailoa Bay
Ka'ie'ie'eaho Channel
Spouting Horn Beach Park
Po'ipu Beach Park
Maha'ulepu Beach
Po'ipu
Shipwreck Beach
Makahuena Point

Kaua'i's Top Experiences

1 HIKING IN PARADISE

Kaua'i's versatile Pacific trails meander through lush mountains and fertile valleys or plummet deep into a red-rock canyon. View-friendly trails take in clifftop vistas from remote and roadless coastlines, while other routes through primordial forests feature the natural surprise of spectacular waterfalls. Hiking opportunities include shorter routes that will have you back in time for a sunset cocktail, or the overnight adventure of a two-day hike.

Above: Hanakapi'ai Falls (p137)

Kalalau Trail

Kaua'i's most popular trail traverses the unforgettable Na Pali Coast. Grab an early start from the cafes of Hanalei to kick off the 22-mile two-day round trip at Ke'e Beach. Look forward to remote beaches, the spectacular Hanakapi'ai Falls, and the vertiginous lava rock cliffs of the Kalalau Valley. p136

Right: Kalalau Trail

Maha'ulepu Heritage Trail

This trail segues from the popular beaches of Po'ipu to a far wilder stretch of coast, full of secluded coves, snorkeling reefs, blowholes and sea cliffs. Experienced South Shore surfers and kitesurfers carve the shallow reef break offshore. p182

Above: Maha'ulepu Heritage Trail

Kuilau Ridge & Moalepe Trails

A wonderful exploration of Wailua's fertile highlands, the highlights of this scenic and beautiful trail include moss-cloaked glades, tropical ferns, and keyhole views onto Mt Wai'ale'ale. p104

Above: Bridge between Kailua and Moalepe trails

MATT MUNRO/LONELY PLANET ©

Above: Hanakapi'ai Falls (p137)

BEACHES FOR ALL

When it comes to finding that ideal stretch of sand, Kaua'i offers an embarrassment of riches. Whether you crave the rugged and all-natural, or something more easygoing and family-friendly, the island is a spectacular example of the paradox of choice. Thankfully, with time and judicious planning, you can explore many of Kaua'i's best. Relaxing, bodyboarding, or the underrated art of beachcombing all await.

Lydgate Beach Park

A fun-filled playground for the kids, plus bathrooms, lifeguards, and two safe pools protected by a breakwater make Lydgate Beach a great option for families. p109

Hanalei Bay

Kaua'i's preeminent horseshoe bay is the ultimate destination for many travelers, and the global gods of surfing built their reputations on its half-dozen surf breaks. The beach superbly combines a wide sweep of white sand with jade mountain views. p152

Above top: Hanalei Bay

Polihale Beach

Ancient Hawaiians thought Polihale was a spiritual beach, and nothing has changed. Sprawled at the base of the Na Pali cliffs, this is the perfect spot to relax and reflect after a lengthy hike or a busy trip. Suitably, it's at the end of a long, bumpy dirt road. p235

Above: Polihale Beach

3 WATERBORNE ISLAND FUN

You've explored the land, you've chilled on the beach, now it's time to get your aquatic adventure on. From boating to paddling, diving to surfing, Kaua'i offers a multitude of ways to get wet and be happy. And as it's such a compact island, it's very practical to schedule a week of exciting adventures at diverse locations.

Sea kayaking

For experienced kayakers, the 12-hour, 17-mile paddle along the Na Pali Coast is a scenic blast of mind-boggling beauty. Beginners can learn to paddle on the more benign waters around Po'ipu. p44

Below: Sea kayaking, Na Pali Coast (p179)

MICHAEL RUNKEL/GETTY IMAGES ©

FATCAMERA/GETTY IMAGES ©

River kayaking

An essential Kaua'i experience is paddling up the sacred Wailua River to secret waterfalls. Getting away in the quiet of early morning is the perfect way to start. p44

Above: Kayaking, Wailua River (p107)

Surfing

Kaua'i is a great place to learn how to surf, especially on the more sheltered breaks of the South Shore. Small group sizes and free practice time make Po'ipu a good choice. p52

Right: Going surfing

4 NO ONE'S GOING HUNGRY

Above: *Poke* bowl (cubed raw fish mixed with *shōyu*, sesame oil, salt, chili pepper, *'inamona* or other condiments; p36)

You're sure to be eating local on Kaua'i, an island with dozens of organic farms, grass-fed beef aplenty and a fishing fleet plying the waters offshore. Establishments across the island range from affordable and convenient food trucks to restaurants that pamper and plate with elegance. Factor in local coffee roasters, Kaua'i's very own kombucha and craft beer, and freshly squeezed juices for the ultimate in ongoing island sustenance.

The freshest of seafood

Poke, sushi and sashimi are all delicious staples on Kaua'i. The in-store kitchen at Makai Sushi serves up some of the finest, and spiciest, *poke* on the island p201

A diverse culinary menu

Asian culinary influences fuse with traditional Hawaiian food around the island. The brilliant flavors at Saimin Dojo reflect the island's social jigsaw. p121

Farmers' market bounty

Self-catering is easy with the freshest of seasonal produce. Stock up at popular events like Saturday morning's Kaua'i Community Market. p96

5 ART & DESIGN

Kaua'i has plenty of art galleries and stores with all manner of collectibles. Surprises to discover include 1950s Japanese fishing buoys, heritage maps from all around the Pacific, and contemporary photography. Modern sculpture, oil paintings and carved woodwork all reinforce diverse and contrasting styles, while a new breed of artisan makers are repurposing and reinventing amid compact workshops.

Warehouse 3540

This converted warehouse has an eclectic array of out-of-the-ordinary arts and crafts stores – interesting clothing, jewelry and stationery all feature along with a tasty park-up of food trucks. p207

Above top: Food truck, Warehouse 3540

Browsing in Hanalei

Head north to Hanalei for interesting shopping, including retro surprises at the Yellowfish Trading Company and stunning collectibles from around Asia and the Pacific. p173

Above: Hanalei (p162)

Hanapepe's Art Night

Every Friday night, the heritage town of Hanapepe keeps its shops and art galleries open late. There's also the added attraction of the best book store on the island. p221

Above: Talk Story Bookstore (p224)

6 ACTIVE ADVENTURES

MATTHEW MICAH WRIGHT/GETTY IMAGES ©

EVERETT ATLAS/SHUTTERSTOCK ©

Kipu Ranch Adventures

Drive an ATV around the ranch from *Jurassic Park* and learn about other Hollywood blockbusters filmed on the island. If it's been raining, the slippin' and slidin' action on red dirt tracks is even more fun. p93

Left top: Quad biking, Kipu Ranch Adventures

Ke Ala Hele Makalae

Rent a mountain bike, tandem or beach cruiser to negotiate this shared-use path along the island's east coast. Kapa'a's cafes are a great post-ride treat. p126

Left bottom: Paliku (Donkey) Beach, Ke Ala Hele Makalae Trail

Kaua'i Backcountry Adventures

Drift in an inner tube through tunnels and former irrigation channels amid the forested mountains inland from Lihu'e. Look forward to a combination of gentle thrills and easygoing relaxation. p92

Discover Kaua'i's landscapes on a variety of action-packed adventures. Local guides are easygoing but professional, and always equipped with an entertaining sense of humor. It's a great way to discover the island's rugged hinterland, and most of the activities are also ideal for adventurous traveling families. You may also learn about the island's history of movie-making along the way.

7 SPELLBOUND BY SPECTACLE

From the soaring pinnacles and waterfall-adorned valleys of the Na Pali Coast to the red-dirt depths of the Waimea Canyon, Kaua'i's reputation as just maybe Hawaii's most spectacular island is gloriously intact. Opportunities to experience what makes the archipelago's oldest island so special include catamaran sailing trips, sightseeing by helicopter, or negotiating a Jeep through the twists and turns of a landscape dubbed the Grand Canyon of the Pacific.

Hit the Road

The island's signature scenic drive is a long ascent that takes you from one end of Waimea Canyon to another. En route, stretch your legs on a number of spectacular short hikes. p214

Below: Waip'o Falls (p240)

Sky-high waterfall views

There's nothing like seeing Kaua'i by air. Twisting through tropical valleys, landing at remote waterfalls, and soaring over the stunning coastline are all possible. p73

Above: Walua Falls (p85)

Cruising the coast

The Na Pali Coast rises out of the sea with its knife-edge pinnacles and alluring valleys. For a spectacular view, board a comfortable catamaran. A refreshing mai tai is always included. p179

Right: Cruise along Na Pali Coast (p43)

8 FESTIVALS & CULTURE

BOYKOV/SHUTTERSTOCK ©

Above: Hula performance (p257)

The people of Kaua'i love a good festival, and attending one is a great way to learn about traditional Hawaiian culture. There's usually a decent array of good-value food stalls serving up *ono grindz* (local food), so it's a good way to score a well-priced and authentic lunch or dinner. Most festivals run through spring and summer, and popular events focus on traditional music, dance and games.

Hawaiian Slack Key Guitar Festival

The Hawaiian musical style of slack key guitar *(ki ho'alu)* is performed by masters at this free annual event. The music's creative tunings were traditionally secrets only known to extended family. p95

Koloa Plantation Days

A *paniolo* (Hawaiian cowboy) rodeo, traditional Hawaiian games, and Polynesian dancing all reinforce the island's culture and history at this annual family-friendly South Shore festival. p189

Hula Competition

The three-day Kaua'i Mokihana Festival Hula Competition provides the opportunity to see dancers perform authentic and traditional routines beyond the sometimes touristy confines of a luau. p95

Need to Know

For more information, see Survival Guide (p269)

Currency
US dollar ($)

Language
English, Hawaiian

Visas
Rules for entry to the US keep changing. Confirm current visa and passport requirements for your country at the US Department of State website (www.travel.state.gov).

Money
ATMs are available in all major towns. Visa and MasterCard are widely accepted. American Express and Discover are hit or miss.

Cell Phones
Cell reception is good except in remote locations. All multi-band GSM phones will work in the US.

Time
Hawaiian Standard Time (GMT/UTC minus 10 hours)

When to Go

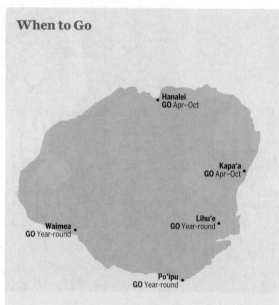

Hanalei
GO Apr–Oct

Kapa'a
GO Apr–Oct

Lihu'e
GO Year-round

Waimea
GO Year-round

Po'ipu
GO Year-round

Tropical climate, wet & dry seasons

High Season
(Jun–Sep)

➡ Accommodations prices are the year's highest.

➡ Beaches are busy with visiting families.

➡ North Shore seas are calm and good for swimming.

Shoulder
(Dec–Mar)

➡ Winter surf conditions are way up on the North Shore and Westside.

➡ Whales arrive and are visible from the land and sea.

➡ Prices are highest around the annual holidays.

Low Season
(Apr–May, Oct–Nov)

➡ Visitor numbers and accommodations prices are lower.

➡ Festivals abound across the island, with popular music festivals in November.

➡ Beaches are less crowded, even though the weather is often perfect.

Useful Websites

Lonely Planet (www.lonely planet.com/usa/hawaii/kauai) Destination information, hotel bookings, traveler forum and more.

Kaua'i Surfrider (https://kauai. surfrider.org) Insights on the state of Kaua'i's waters and the chance to volunteer with local riders to clean up beaches.

The Garden Island (www.the gardenisland.com) Good coverage of local events and island-specific issues and current affairs.

Kaua'i Explorer (www.kauai explorer.com) Great site for ocean reports, trail information and beach tips.

County of Kaua'i (www.kauai. gov/visitors) Information on buses, camping, hiking, public safety and links to products uniquely made on the island (www.kauaimade.net).

Important Numbers

Hawaii's area code (⏣808) is optional for local calls and compulsory when calling between islands. Dial ⏣1 before toll-free or long-distance calls, including to Canada (for which international rates apply).

USA's country code	⏣1
International access code	⏣011
Emergency (ambulance, fire & police)	⏣911
Directory assistance	⏣411

Exchange Rates

Australia	A$1	$0.68
Canada	C$1	$0.75
Europe	€1	$1.11
Japan	¥100	$0.92
New Zealand	NZ$1	$0.64
UK	UK£1	$1.29

For current exchange rates, see www.xe.com.

Daily Costs

Budget: Less than $200

➡ B&B or inn within a town: $100–125

➡ Grocery shopping and farmers markets: $30–40

➡ Kaua'i Bus: $4–8

Midrange: $200–350

➡ Hotel room, condo or B&B: $125–300

➡ Meals at midrange restaurants: $40–50

➡ Rental car: $50–60

Top End: More than $350

➡ Hotel, resort or vacation rental: from $300

➡ Fine dining with three-course meals: from $50

➡ Diving, golf, spa, helicopter tour, sunset cruises: from $200

➡ Rental car: $50–60

Opening Hours

Banks 8:30am–4pm Monday to Friday, some to 6pm Friday, and 9am–noon or 1pm Saturday

Bars & Clubs To midnight daily, some to 2am Thursday to Saturday

Businesses 8:30am–4:30pm Monday to Friday, some post offices 9am–noon Saturday

Restaurants Breakfast 6–10am, lunch 11:30am–2:30pm, dinner 5–9:30pm

Shops 9am–5pm Monday to Saturday, some also noon–5pm Sunday

Arriving in Kaua'i

Lihu'e Airport (p278) Almost all visitors to Kaua'i rent cars from car-rental companies located at the airport.

Taxis can be found curbside outside the baggage-claim area during the day but can be expensive; book ahead if arriving at night.

In almost all cases, you are better off renting a car. Average taxi fares are $15 to Lihu'e, $30 to Kapa'a, $50–60 to Po'ipu and $100–125 to Princeville.

Uber is available in Kaua'i, but there the number of drivers is very limited. For families or groups, it may be more economical to book an airport shuttle with Speedi Shuttle (p278).

Kaua'i Bus (p279) makes limited runs from 6am–8pm from the airport to Lihu'e and west to Kalaheo, Waimea and Hanapepe ($2).

Language & Etiquette

The island's locals are a laid-back and friendly bunch and appreciate the use of a few common phrases.

Aloha! Literally translates to 'love,' but used for 'hello,' 'welcome' and 'goodbye.'

Mahalo! 'Thank you' – can be used to show gratitude one-on-one, for example, '*Mahalo* for the delicious food,' but also with groups: 'A big *mahalo* to all of the guides today.'

For information on **getting around**, see p279

What's New

There are many exciting new reasons to visit Kauaʻi. The island's flavor-packed food scene is growing in diversity, art and design stores are showcasing an increased focus on local influences, and the North Shore's new parking-permit system has ensured that one of Kauaʻi's best beaches is protected from overcrowding.

Haʻena State Park Permits

Closed following heavy rain and devastating floods on the island's North Shore in April 2018, Haʻena State Park was reopened in June 2019. A parking permit system – limited to 900 visitors per day – has now been introduced. Available up to one month in advance, the permits are often booked up as soon as they come online at www.gohaena.com, but the new system does mean visitor numbers at glorious Keʻe Beach (p178) are now limited.

New Tours & Experiences

Exploring beyond the island's stunning beaches and scenery, new tours by Tasting Kauaʻi (p38) visit farmers markets, food trucks, restaurants and small-scale producers all around the island. Expect a strong focus on local and sustainable food experiences, such as the 'Jam Tasting Room' at Monkeypod Jam (p207). Another new experience is Kauai Safaris (p92) combination of rum tasting and a 4WD tour around Kilohana Plantation. And if you prefer four legs to 4WD, try spending an afternoon exploring with one of the shelter dogs from the Kauai Humane Society (p87) near Lihuʻe.

Marketplace Makeover

The Eastside's Coconut Marketplace (p117) reopened in 2019 after the completion of a multi-year renovation, and soon became the new home of some well-established restaurants. Nom Kauai (p116) specializes in gourmet spins on burgers and waffles, while Sushi Bushido (p117) is an energetic fusion eatery. Other marketplace highlights include regular hula shows and live music (p119), and a

---

LOCAL KNOWLEDGE

WHAT'S HAPPENING IN KAUAʻI

Brett Atkinson, Lonely Planet writer

Chat with another friendly customer at one of Kauaʻi's juice shacks, beaches or *poke* spots, and eventually the conversation will turn to how the island is changing. That morning and afternoon tangle of Eastside traffic wasn't on their minds when they decamped here a decade ago, and they'll definitely have an opinion on how big land purchases by billionaire island-fans like Facebook's Mark Zuckerberg are impacting on access to the land and beaches.

They're probably juggling a few gigs – perhaps balancing painting or sculpture with working on an organic ginger and turmeric farm – and also considering renting a spare room on Airbnb. Housing's getting pretty expensive on the island, you see, and they definitely understand why the number of homeless people on Kauaʻi is increasing. Visitors are still welcome though, and just before your ginseng-infused acai bowl arrives, they'll be enthusiastically telling you all about that great new Sri Lankan food truck up at Hanalei.

twice-weekly farmers market. Future plans include Munchology, a lounge and eatery specializing in shared plates, to be opened by the switched-on owners of Nom Kauai.

Stylish Shopping

Don't worry, Baby Shark toddler onesies, Barack Obama dashboard dolls and Kaua'i red-dirt T-shirts are all still available, but the island's shopping scene also includes hip havens selling interesting locally made art and design. The funky lineup at Warehouse 3540 (p207) at Lawa'i on the South Shore features fashion, jewelry and handmade stationery, while Blü Umi (p225) in Hanapepe offers apparel and cool retro graphic prints.

Food Trucks to Follow

A tasty and inexpensive option for dining around the island, a number of new food trucks have recently opened to complement old favorites like Al Pastor (p127) and Scorpacciata (p127). Check out Kickshaws (p206) at Warehouse 3540 in Lawa'i for upscale takes on comfort food like mac n' cheese or tuna melts, followed by a dessert of organic artisan shave ice from nearby Fresh Shave (p206). For super-fresh seafood, head north to Hanalei Poke (p171), or east to Lihu'e for Kikuchi's (p96) ahi (yellowfin tuna) wraps.

New Restaurants

Local, sustainable and fusion flavors all feature in the island's parade of recent restaurant openings. Saimin Dojo (p121) on the Eastside combines Hawaiian, Japanese and Korean flavors, while Ama (p171) in Hanalei is a similarly well-priced spot for Asian-inspired noodles and soups. Kaua'i Ono (p160) in Princeville offers five-course alfresco gourmet feasts featuring the freshest produce from Kaua'i's farms, while Kiawe Roots (p202) barbecue restaurant in Po'ipu is one of the island's best-value eateries. For great baking, there's Midnight Bear Breads (p223) in Hanapepe.

Accommodations Options

There are two new standout places to stay on the island, for travelers at opposite ends of the vacation-budget spectrum. Timbers Kauai Ocean Club & Residences (p96) near Lihu'e is the island's newest and most luxurious resort, with its clifftop location

KAUAI   BIG ISLAND   O'AHU

≈ 50 people per sq km

including a spectacular infinity pool. Local and sustainable ingredients underpin the menu at the resort's Hualani's restaurant. Considerably cheaper, and definitely more mobile, are the 4WD expedition vehicles – including rooftop tents and compact kitchens – available to hire from Kauai Overlander (p279).

Drinking in Eastside Views

Until recently it wasn't really an option to combine *pau hana* (happy hour) cocktails with oceanfront Eastside views, but a couple of new bars have changed that. The Lava Lava Beach Club (p118) at Wailua's Kauai Shores (p115) hotel is a true sand-between-the-toes experience, while just down the coast at the Hilton Garden Inn (p116), Mamahune's Tiki Bar (p119) combines bay vistas with a wonderfully fake mini-volcano.

Accommodations

Find more accommodations reviews throughout the On the Road chapters (from p81)

Find more accommodations reviews throughout the On the Road chapters (from p81)

PRICE RANGES

The following price ranges refer to a high-season, double-occupancy room with private bathroom but no breakfast, unless otherwise specified. Rates do not include the 13.41% accommodations tax.

$ less than $150

$$ $150–250

$$$ more than $250

Accommodations Types

Vacation Rentals Stand-alone vacation homes to rent range from simple plantation-style cottages to spacious five-bedroom affairs.

Condos Located in larger, multiunit complexes but still featuring full kitchens and other facilities like laundries and pools. A good option for families.

Resorts & Hotels Range from hotel-style bedrooms to self-contained apartments. More on-site facilities, including pools, bars, restaurants, spas and kids' clubs.

B&Bs Surprisingly underrepresented on Kaua'i. Home-style accommodations in a private room with breakfast provided.

Hostels Focused on a younger budget-conscious market with cheaper rooms and dorms, often with shared bathroom facilities.

Cabins Basic forest cabins (p242) are available in Koke'e State Park.

Campgrounds Both state and county campgrounds are available and must be booked in advance (p59). Locations include Na Pali Coast Wilderness State Park, Koke'e State Park and various county beach parks around the island. Note that some of these parks are regularly frequented by the island's homeless population.

Best Places to Stay

Best on a Budget

Budget accommodations are relatively limited in Kaua'i, but worthwhile options include lodging on an orchard, a well-kept motel and rustic forest lodges. Private rooms listed on Airbnb are also often well priced.

➡ Green Acres Cottages (p148), Kilauea

➡ Coco's Kaua'i (p229), Waimea

➡ Rosewood Kaua'i (p115), Wailua

➡ Koke'e State Park Cabins (p242), Koke'e State Park

Best for Families

Scattered around the island are some excellent options for families. Self-catering and stocking up at farmers markets is the recommended option – all of the following have well-equipped kitchens, and in most cases outdoor barbecues as well. Wailua and Po'ipu are conveniently located for access to good beaches and excursions.

➡ Fern Grotto Inn (p115), Wailua

➡ Nihilani (p158), Princeville

➡ Kiahuna Plantation Resort Kaua'i by Outrigger (p200), Po'ipu

➡ River Estate (p176), Wainiha

Best Hotels & Resorts

On Kaua'i, many bigger hotels and resorts also offer spas, water parks, multiple restaurants and children's programs. On-site amenities could also include a golf course, beachfront barbecues and lazy days hammocks. Many Kaua'i properties offer beachfront views, but swimming in their manicured and often extravagant pool complexes is usually preferable to the ocean.

→ Timbers Kauai Ocean Club & Residences (p96), Lihu'e

→ Grand Hyatt Kauai Resort & Spa (p200), Po'ipu

→ Hanalei Colony Resort (p177), Ha'ena

→ Hotel Coral Reef (p127), Kapa'a

→ Waimea Plantation Cottages (p230), Waimea

Best Vacation Rentals

Vacation rentals are the best option to fully transition into an island-vacation frame of mind. Smaller properties, often a stand-alone house or a scattering of cottages, reinforce a local vibe, and there are usually lush gardens to relax and recharge in. Amenities include kitchens for self-catering.

→ 17 Palms (p115), Wailua

→ Hanalei Dolphin Cottages (p169), Hanalei

→ Hanalei Surfboard House (p169), Hanalei

→ Kauai Paradise House (p176), Wainiha

→ Anini Lani Kai (p154), 'Anini

Timbers Kauai Ocean Club & Residences (p96)

CLAUDINE VAN MASSENHOVE/SHUTTERSTOCK ©

PLAN YOUR TRIP ACCOMMODATIONS

Booking

Be sure to book Kaua'i accommodations well in advance, especially during the peak season of June to September. A good time to come is from April to May or October to March, when beaches are quieter, the weather is often excellent and many festivals take place.

Lonely Planet (lonelyplanet.com/hotels) Find independent reviews, as well as recommendations on the best places to stay – and then book them online.

Kaua'i Vacation Rentals (www.kauaivacation rentals.com) Condo-rental listings across the island.

Garden Island Properties (www.kauaiproperties. com) A locally owned, island-wide rental agency with affordable condos and houses for rent.

Parrish Collection Kaua'i (www.parrishkauai. com) Good collection of house and condo rentals.

Po'ipu Beach Resort Association (www. poipubeach.org/places-to-stay/condominium-resorts) Overview of South Shore rental options.

Where to Stay

→ Lihu'e (p83) Most skip this commercial hub and head to the North or South Shore.

→ Kapa'a & the Eastside (p103) Anahola and Kapa'a have some nice places, fun beach scenes and good snorkeling, but it lacks the drama of the scenery further north. Good restaurants are a plus.

→ Hanalei Bay & the North Shore (p135) It rains more up north, but it's also more verdant. The areas around Hanalei are the accommodations center.

→ Po'ipu & the South Shore (p181) The beaches are gorgeous, and you'll get way more sun than up north, as the area around Po'ipu is the driest on Kaua'i.

→ Waimea Canyon & the Westside (p209) There are a few good beach houses and inns in towns like Waimea and Kekaha. There are fewer restaurants, practically no nightlife and a cool zen quiet here that may just be perfect.

Getting Around Kaua'i

For more information, see Transportation (p278)

How to Get Around

Car Rental Recommended, unless on a very tight budget. Well-maintained highway provides access to most of the island. Free parking widely available.

Bus Goes through all major towns; limited runs, especially on weekends.

Taxi Flag-fall fee is $3.50, plus 35¢ per additional 0.1 miles or up to 45 seconds of waiting. Plan on calling for a taxi.

Resort Shuttle Complimentary; run regularly within most major resort areas.

Bike Good option if staying in one town. In general, if on the Eastside or North Shore expect some rain.

Traveling by Car

➡ Renting a car often costs more on Kaua'i than on the other major Hawaiian Islands. Normally, a rock-bottom economy car from a major rental company will cost you around $250 per week, with rates doubling during the peak periods. Rental rates will generally include unlimited mileage.

➡ To minimize costs, comparison shop; differences of 50% between suppliers are not unheard of.

➡ Cars are sometimes prohibited by contract from traveling on dirt roads. That said, most roads are passable by regular car, if you go slow.

➡ Another strategy for cost saving is to use a local rental agency. These mom-and-pop firms, which generally operate from home, rent used vehicles

RESOURCES

American Automobile Association (AAA; ☑808-593-2221, from Neighbor Islands 800-736-2886; www.hawaii.aaa.com; 1130 N Nimitz Hwy, Honolulu; ⊕9am-5pm Mon-Fri, to 2pm Sat) Provides 24-hour emergency roadside assistance, free maps and discounts on car rentals and accommodations. AAA has reciprocal agreements with automobile associations in other countries, so bring your membership card from home. The Hawaii office is in Honolulu.

Department of Transportation (https://hidot.hawaii.gov/highways/roadwork/kauai) Updates on traffic conditions and roadworks around the island.

GuideofUS Hawaii (www.hawaii-guide.com/kauai/kauai-driving-times) Estimates on how long trips around the island could take. Note that morning and afternoon rush-hour traffic on the Eastside will impact on these estimates.

that may be 10 years old, but can be had for around $25 per day.

➡ For motorcycle rentals, the go-to place is Kaua'i Harley-Davidson (p280), which has a 20-bike fleet in Puhi, just outside Lihu'e. For smaller scooters and mopeds contact **Kauai Mopeds** (☑808-652-7407; www.kauai-mopeds.com; per day from $90).

➡ Rates for 4WD vehicles average $70 to $100 per day (before taxes and fees). Agencies prohibit driving off-road; if you get stuck they'll slap a penalty on you.

No Car?

Bus

The county's Kaua'i Bus (p279) stops approximately hourly on weekdays in towns along major highways, with limited services on Saturdays, Sundays and holidays. Routes run islandwide,

but don't reach the Na Pali Coast Wilderness, Waimea Canyon or Koke'e State Parks. Schedules are available online. Check the website for where to buy monthly passes ($40).

Buses are air-conditioned and equipped with bicycle racks and wheelchair ramps. A few caveats: drivers don't give change; surfboards (except for boogie boards), oversized backpacks and luggage aren't allowed on board; stops are marked but might be hard to spot; and schedules do not include a map.

Bicycle

Cycling all the way around the island isn't much fun, due to heavy traffic and narrow road shoulders. But it's a convenient way of getting around beach resorts, and the Eastside has a recreational paved bicycle path running through Kapa'a. The best

bike ride on the island is down the winding road of Waimea Canyon.

Bicycles can be rented in Waipouli, Kapa'a, Po'ipu and Hanalei. Tourist resort areas and specialty bicycle shops rent beach cruisers, hybrid models and occasionally high-end road and mountain bikes. Rental rates average $25 to $40 per day (easily double that for high-tech road or mountain bikes).

Generally, bicycles are required to follow the same rules of the road as cars. Bicycles are prohibited on freeways and sidewalks. State law requires all cyclists under the age of 16 to wear helmets. For more bicycling information, including downloadable cycling maps, search the website of the Hawaii Department of Transportation (http://hidot.hawaii.gov/highways).

PLAN YOUR TRIP GETTING AROUND KAUA'I

DRIVING FAST FACTS

➡ Drive on the right.

➡ All vehicle occupants must wear a seatbelt.

➡ The maximum speed limit is 50mph (25mph in built-up areas).

➡ The minimum age for a full license is 18 years.

➡ Blood alcohol limit of 80mg per 100mL (0.08%) for drivers 21 years and older.

Road Distances (miles)

	Lihu'e	Kapa'a	Hanalei	Po'ipu
Kapa'a	11			
Hanalei	31	24		
Po'ipu	14	23	44	
Waimea	24	33	56	19

Don't–Miss Drives

Kuhio Highway This road trip on the island's North Shore begins at the Kilauea Point National Wildlife Refuge and travels for 15 miles via Princeville and Hanalei to Ha'ena State Park and Ke'e Beach. To park at Ha'ena State Park, apply for a parking permit up to a month in advance. (p140)

South Shore Driving Tour Excellent beaches, good eating and drinking, and the heritage plantation architecture of Old Koloa Town are all highlights on this meandering 30.7-mile

exploration of the island's South Shore. Along the way, book for a guided tour of the National Tropical Botanical Garden. (p184)

Waimea Canyon Drive This most spectacular drive on the island follows the entire length of Waimea Canyon into Koke'e State Park, ascending 19 miles from the coast to Pu'u o Kila Lookout. Stop at scenic lookouts and take short hikes along the way for the quintessential Kaua'i driving adventure. (p214)

Month by Month

January

As the mercury dips a bit and the holidays float into the rearview, Kaua'i experiences a mild tourist exodus and hotel prices drop, even as humpback whales continue to dazzle.

🎉 Art Night in Hanapepe

Hanapepe's deservedly popular weekly Art Night is held every Friday of the year. Galleries and shops keep their doors open late, food vendors descend and there is music in the air. It's the best time and place to experience this historic little town. (p221)

☆ Kapa'a Art Walk

On the first Saturday of every month from 5pm to 8pm, Old Town Kapa'a celebrates and showcases island artists and artisans during the Kapa'a Art Walk. Expect live music, food trucks and a block-party atmosphere. (p126)

🎉 Princeville Night Market

The first monthly Princeville Night Market offers original art and handicrafts, tasty snacks, locally roasted coffee and live music. It's held on the second Sunday of every month. (p158)

February

Winter means nights cool enough to cuddle up, big surf, and whales still blowing offshore. Hotels and restaurants book up well in advance of Valentine's Day. Presidents' Weekend brings a tourist influx too.

🎉 Waimea Town Celebration

The Westside comes alive during the annual Waimea Town Celebration in mid-February. There are food, craft and game booths, a beer garden, a canoe race, a *paniolo* (Hawaiian cowboy) rodeo, and lei-making and hula-dancing competitions. It's the perfect time for a family visit. (p229)

☆ E Pili Kakou I Ho'okahi Lahui

Featuring instruction from some of Hawaii's top *kumu hula* (teachers of hula), the E Pili Kakou I Ho'okahi Lahui (www.epilikakou.com) is a two-day retreat held in late February.

March

High-surf season winds down on the North Shore, though wind and rain can still taunt and bring heavy swells. Mainland USA's spring break brings families to Kaua'i's beaches en masse.

🎉 Prince Kuhio Celebration

Po'ipu's two-week-long Prince Kuhio Celebration honors Prince Jonah Kuhio Kalaniana'ole, known for his efforts to revitalize Native Hawaiian culture during his lifetime. Events include hula, an outrigger-canoe race, lei and poi making, a rodeo, as well as Hawaiian spiritual ceremonies. (p199)

May

May is a wonderful time to experience Kaua'i, as tourist season hits a short lull in advance of the busy summer season. North Shore waters are more serene and the weather is often perfect.

⭐ May Day Lei Contest & Fair

Simple strings of plumeria (frangipani) are mere child's play next to the floral masterpieces entered in Lihu'e's annual May Day Lei Contest. (p94)

⭐ Banana Poka Round-Up

Part invasive eradication effort, part handicraft fair, folks gather in gorgeous Koke'e State Park to remove the South American banana poka vine, which they weave into baskets. Come for live music, a rooster-crowing contest and the 'Pedal to the Meadow' bicycle race. (p241)

June

Summer is here, the beaches are packed and the north and west shores are placid as can be. It's a great time to swim, snorkel and dive on Kaua'i.

🍴 Taste of Hawaii

Known as the 'Ultimate Brunch Sunday,' Wailua's Taste of Hawaii is a casual affair showcasing 40 chefs from around Hawaii serving endless samples from gourmet food booths. Ample live music too. (p115)

July

High surf rolls onto the South Shore, while the whole island generally sees consistent sunshine. Summertime is sweet on the Garden Island.

⭐ Fourth of July Concert in the Sky

Enjoy island food, live entertainment and the grand finale fireworks at the Fourth of July Concert in the Sky at Vidinha Stadium. (p94)

⭐ Koloa Plantation Days

Koloa Plantation Days is a family-friendly, nine-day fair celebrating the history of the South Shore with a parade, *paniolo* rodeo, traditional Hawaiian games, Polynesian dancing and plenty of 'talk story' about old times. (p189)

August

Summer crowds are at their most populous, but there's plenty of ocean and beach space and lots of parties, too.

☆ Heiva I Kaua'i Ia Orana Tahiti

Imagine dance troupes from as far away as Tahiti and Japan joining mainland US and local Hawaiian dancers for a Tahitian dancing and drumming competition at Kapa'a Beach Park. Yeah, best to plan your schedule accordingly. (p127)

🍴 Music & Mango Festival

A late-summer celebration of locally harvested food (yes, the mango looms large) and live music on the nonprofit Waipa Foundation's farmlands on the outskirts of Hanalei. (p168)

⭐ Kaua'i County Farm Bureau Fair

An old-fashioned county fair blooms at Vidinha Stadium in late August. There are carnival rides and games, livestock shows, a petting zoo, hula performances and lots of local food. (p95)

September

Summer crowds dissipate and ideal weather conditions usually prevail. When they don't, double rainbows will cheer you up.

🏃 Kauai Marathon

(http://www.thekauaimarathon.com)A popular road race on the South Shore, the Kauai Marathon also features a short-course half marathon. Locals pack the streets to cheer on (or heckle) their (suffering) friends.

☆ Kaua'i Composers Contest & Concert

Encouraging the island's up-and-coming talent to show their skills, the Kaua'i Composers Contest & Concert is the signature event of the Kaua'i Mokihana Festival in mid- to late September.

⭐ Kaua'i Mokihana Festival Hula Competition

Three days of serious hula competitions are staged at the Kaua'i Beach Resort & Spa. If you want to watch dancers perform without the luau kitsch, this is your best option. (p95)

⭐ Kaua'i Folk Festival

This two-day celebration of roots and Americana music is held at Grove Farm near Lihu'e. (p95)

October

The best month of the year to travel almost anywhere, and especially here. The weather is lovely, crowds are thin on the ground and hotel prices drop significantly.

🎆 Fall Festival

Since 2001, the Kauai Christian Academy has hosted Kilauea's Fall Festival fundraiser, featuring local food and art vendors, a huge silent auction, live music, carnival games, a corn maze, and pony and hay rides. (p148)

🍴 Kaua'i Chocolate & Coffee Festival

The Hanapepe-based Kaua'i Chocolate & Coffee Festival offers tastings, demonstrations, live entertainment and farm tours. (p222)

⭐ Eo e Emalani I Alaka'i

A one-day outdoor dance festival at Koke'e Museum commemorating Queen Emma's 1871 journey to Alaka'i Swamp. The festival includes a royal procession, hula dancing, live music and more. (p241)

November

High surf arrives in the north and west, and heavy (or shall we say heavier) rain marks the 'unofficial' start of winter.

⭐ Hawaiian Slack Key Guitar Festival

Watch masters of the Hawaiian slack key guitar *(ki ho'alu)* blend styles (and strings) for this free event. Check the website for this year's location. (p95)

December

Humpback whales have arrived and are ready to reveal themselves to the holiday crowds. Hold your breath, dive down and listen to their song.

🍴 Kalo Festival

Enjoy demonstrations on growing taro and pounding poi, traditional Hawaiian games for kids, local food vendors and live music at the Kalo Festival in Waipa. (p168)

🎆 Lights on Rice Parade

Illuminated floats deliver the Christmas spirit to Rice St in downtown Lihu'e on the first Friday evening of December. Ideal for families. (p95)

Itineraries

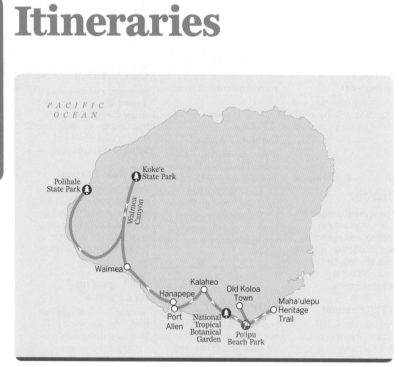

 Po'ipu Beach Park to Koke'e State Park

The South Shore and Westside of Kaua'i offer beaches, great food and good hiking.

Start your first day in **Kalaheo** at Kalaheo Café & Coffee Co, before an early tour of the **National Tropical Botanical Garden**. At nearby **Po'ipu Beach Park**, two sheltered lagoons are ideal for kids and beginner snorkelers. Adjacent Brennecke's Beach has an outside reef good for experienced ocean swimmers and freedivers. On the other flank is a consistent reef break ideal for surfers. Afterwards, head to **Old Koloa Town** for live Hawaiian music at the Garden Island Grille.

On day two, stretch your legs on the scenic **Maha'ulepu Heritage Trail**. Head for lunch at Koloa Fish Market (bring cash). Drop by Po'ipu Beach Park for another sunset, then explore the Shops at Kukui'ula. Kiawe Roots is a good choice for dinner.

On day three join a Na Pali catamaran tour in **Port Allen** before strolling **Hanapepe** town. Friday night is Art Night. Eat at Japanese Grandma.

On your last day pack a picnic from **Waimea's** Ishihara Market, then drive Hwy 550 through the **Waimea Canyon** and into **Koke'e State Park**. Negotiate the Awa'awapuhi Trail with stunning coastal views before a final end-of-the-road sunset in **Polihale State Park**.

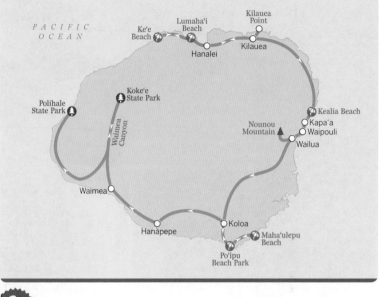

8 DAYS Dream Week

You have one week to explore, taste and experience the best of the Garden Island. Ready, set...go!

Check into your chosen lodgings in **Kilauea** and make your way into **Hanalei**. Park near Hanalei Beach Park, take a dip or maybe have a surfing lesson, then hit luscious **Lumaha'i Beach** for sunset. Grab a casual dinner and drinks at nearby Tahiti Nui. After morning coffee and breakfast, head to primordial Limahuli Garden, then hike the Kalalau Trail from **Ke'e Beach** to Hanakapi'ai Beach. Catch a Technicolor sunset on Ke'e Beach, then take the slow drive back to Hanalei for dinner at Bar Acuda. Wake up in time for a yoga class at Metamorphose Yoga Studio, then visit the lighthouse at **Kilauea Point** before spending the rest of the day at Kauapea (Secret) Beach or Kahili (Rock Quarry) Beach. Dine at the Bistro in Kilauea.

On day four check into Fern Grotto Inn in **Wailua**, then paddle the Wailua River. Book dinner at the JO2 in **Waipouli**. The following morning, breakfast at Java Kai in **Kapa'a**, then ride the bike path to **Kealia Beach**. That evening hit Hukilau Lanai in Wailua for island-style fine dining before craft beers at Avalon Gastropub. Wake up with a hike up **Nounou Mountain**, then pack up and drive to **Koloa**, pick up lunch at the fish market and spend the day at **Po'ipu Beach Park**. Check into your short-term rental in Po'ipu. Wake up and go scuba diving with Seasport Divers if you're certified; otherwise, hit the Maha'ulepu Heritage Trail and spend the morning at rugged and beautiful **Maha'ulepu Beach**. Land in **Hanapepe** by early evening for a bit of gallery hopping, especially if it's Friday Art Night.

Day eight is all about the trails. Stop at Ishihara Market in **Waimea** to pack a picnic, then drive Hwy 550 as the road rises to the rim of **Waimea Canyon**. Venture into **Koke'e State Park** and onto Awa'awapuhi Trail with views overlooking the Kalalau Valley and the stunning Na Pali Coast, before driving on toward the western end of the road for a final Kaua'i sunset in **Polihale State Park**.

MAUIPHOTOS/SHUTTERSTOCK ©

Top: Waterfall, Waimea Canyon (p233)

Bottom: Na Pali Coast (p179)

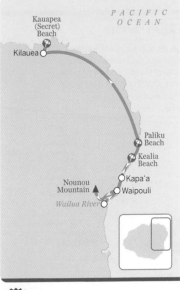

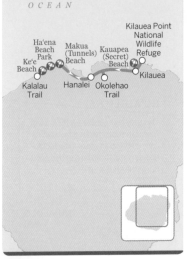

2 DAYS — Wailua to Kilauea

From one of the state's most sacred rivers to one of the island's most spectacular beaches, with all kinds of beauty and flavor in between.

Start your day with a serene paddle up the **Wailua River**. Whether you choose to join a tour group or blaze your own wake, you will either hop in a kayak or rent an SUP board, glimpse heiau (ancient temples) and explore a hidden waterfall. Next fuel up with coffee and breakfast at Java Kai, a **Kapa'a** classic. When you're ready to keep moving, rent a bike and cruise the 5-mile Ke Ala Hele Makalae path. It stretches from the south end of Kapa'a Beach Park to **Paliku Beach**, 5 miles away. Grab a nap at **Kealia Beach**, then spend the rest of the afternoon and early evening exploring the shops in Old Town Kapa'a. At night travel south to **Waipouli** for a tasty local dinner at Saimin Dojo.

The next morning, climb **Nounou Mountain** then grab some Tiki Tacos in Waipouli and hit one of Kilauea's sublime beaches. We suggest **Kauapea (Secret) Beach**. Take a quick dip, plant your body in the sand, repeat as necessary. Dine at the Bistro in **Kilauea**.

2 DAYS — Kilauea to Na Pali Coast State Park

Explore the North Shore from Kilauea Point to the mythic end of the road.

Wake up in **Kilauea** with coffee at Kilauea Bakery, a local staple, and a yoga class at Metamorphose. Then drive to **Kilauea Point National Wildlife Refuge** and check out the stately lighthouse. Back in Kilauea, grab lunch at Kilauea Fish Market, and then hit **Kauapea (Secret) Beach**. Rinse off and hit the shops and galleries of **Hanalei**, enjoy an exquisite dinner at Bar Acuda and then step over to Tahiti Nui for drinks and laughs until the music stops.

You'll need another hike to get your blood flowing again, so after coffee and a bite at Hanalei Bread Company, and a strategic snack stockpile at Harvest Market, hit the **Okolehao Trail** for a steep, quick one or drive to the end of the road and get a taste of the **Kalalau Trail**. Be sure to book a permit well in advance. Next hit **Ha'ena Beach Park** or, if you surf, **Makua (Tunnels) Beach** for another well-spent, lazy afternoon. Wake up in time to drive to a **Ke'e Beach** sunset, then hit the sushi bar at the Dolphin restaurant for dinner in dear, sweet Hanalei.

Kaua'i: Off the Beaten Track

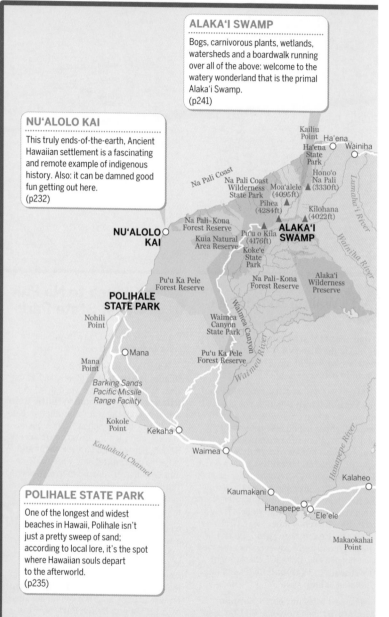

ALAKA'I SWAMP

Bogs, carnivorous plants, wetlands, watersheds and a boardwalk running over all of the above: welcome to the watery wonderland that is the primal Alaka'i Swamp.
(p241)

NU'ALOLO KAI

This truly ends-of-the-earth, Ancient Hawaiian settlement is a fascinating and remote example of indigenous history. Also: it can be damned good fun getting out here.
(p232)

POLIHALE STATE PARK

One of the longest and widest beaches in Hawaii, Polihale isn't just a pretty sweep of sand; according to local lore, it's the spot where Hawaiian souls depart to the afterworld.
(p235)

Kailiu Point
Ha'ena
Ha'ena
State
Park
Wainiha
Hono'o
Na Pali
Na Pali Coast
Na Pali Coast
Wilderness
State Park
Moa'alele
(4095ft)
Kilohana
(4022ft)
Pihea
(4284ft)
Na Pali-Kona
Forest Reserve
Pu'u o Kila
(4176ft)
ALAKA'I
SWAMP
Kuia Natural
Area Reserve
Koke'e
State
Park
Na Pali-Kona
Forest Reserve
Alaka'i
Wilderness
Preserve
NU'ALOLO
KAI
Pu'u Ka Pele
Forest Reserve
POLIHALE
STATE PARK
Nohili
Point
Waimea
Canyon
State Park
Mana
Pu'u Ka Pele
Forest Reserve
Mana
Point
Barking Sands
Pacific Missile
Range Facility
Kokole
Point
Kekaha
Kaulakahi Channel
Waimea
Kalaheo
Kaumakani
Hanapepe
'Ele'ele
Makaokahai
Point
Lumaha'i River
Wainiha River
Waimea Canyon
Waimea River
Hanapepe River

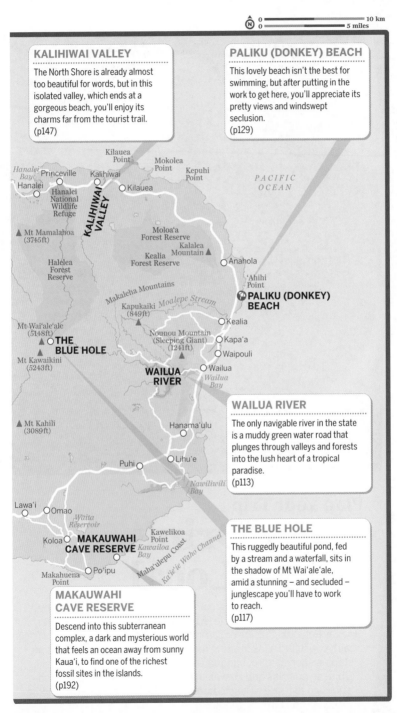

N
0 —————— 10 km
0 —————— 5 miles

KALIHIWAI VALLEY

The North Shore is already almost too beautiful for words, but in this isolated valley, which ends at a gorgeous beach, you'll enjoy its charms far from the tourist trail. (p147)

PALIKU (DONKEY) BEACH

This lovely beach isn't the best for swimming, but after putting in the work to get here, you'll appreciate its pretty views and windswept seclusion. (p129)

Kilauea Point
Mokolea Point
Kepuhi Point

PACIFIC OCEAN

Hanalei Bay
Princeville
Kalihiwai
Hanalei
Hanalei National Wildlife Refuge
Kilauea

KALIHIWAI VALLEY

▲ Mt Mamalahoa (3745ft)

Moloa'a Forest Reserve
Kalalea Mountain ▲
Kealia Forest Reserve
Anahola

Halelea Forest Reserve

'Ahihi Point

Makaleha Mountains
Kapukaiki (849ft)
Moalepe Stream

PALIKU (DONKEY) BEACH

Mt Wai'ale'ale (5148ft)
▲ ○ THE BLUE HOLE
▲
Mt Kawaikini (5243ft)

Kealia

Nounou Mountain (Sleeping Giant) (1241ft)
▲

Kapa'a
Waipouli

WAILUA RIVER
Wailua
Wailua Bay

WAILUA RIVER

The only navigable river in the state is a muddy green water road that plunges through valleys and forests into the lush heart of a tropical paradise. (p113)

▲ Mt Kahili (3089ft)

Hanama'ulu

Puhi
Lihu'e

/ Nawiliwili Bay

Lawa'i
○ Omao
Waita Reservoir
Koloa
MAKAUWAHI CAVE RESERVE
Kawelikoa Point
Kawailoa Bay
Po'ipu
Maha'ulepu Coast
Makahuena Point
Kaie'ie Waho Channel

THE BLUE HOLE

This ruggedly beautiful pond, fed by a stream and a waterfall, sits in the shadow of Mt Wai'ale'ale, amid a stunning – and secluded – junglescape you'll have to work to reach. (p117)

MAKAUWAHI CAVE RESERVE

Descend into this subterranean complex, a dark and mysterious world that feels an ocean away from sunny Kaua'i, to find one of the richest fossil sites in the islands. (p192)

Spam *musubi*

Plan Your Trip

Eat & Drink Like a Local

Island-caught fish. Island-grown produce. Island-casual setting. Kaua'i likes to keep it simple. Whether you're savoring four-star Hawaii Regional Cuisine or sampling that curious Spam *musubi* (rice ball), you'll find a fascinating fusion of flavors – from Polynesian staples such as taro, banana and coconut to Japanese teriyaki, Chinese noodles and Hawaiian *kalua* (earth oven) pig. The real spoils go to those willing to hunt down the best fish markets, indie bakeries and farmers markets.

Regional Treats

Taro Chips

Try homemade taro chips at Taro Ko Chips Factory (p223) in Hanapepe.

Saimin

Enjoy steaming noodle soups and fusion eats at Saimin Dojo (p121) in Waipouli.

Laulau

Feast on delicious *kalua* pork cooked in taro leaves at the family-owned Pono Market (p127) in Kapa'a.

Poke

Makai Sushi (p201) in Po'ipu serves excellent *poke* and sushi.

Barbecue

Barbecue excellence with a distinctive island flavor at Kiawe Roots (p202) in Po'ipu.

Shave Ice

Fresh Shave (p206) in Kalaheo serves artisan shave ice made from organic ingredients.

Food Experiences

The Basics

Dining in Kaua'i is casual – even when it is elegant. Top tourist restaurants require reservations (sometimes several days in advance).

Fish markets Taking a *bentō* box, *poke* or sushi roll to go is a local tradition, and most towns have a worthwhile fish market (and rotating farmers markets) worth checking out. Increasingly, supermarkets and delis also offer a wide range of fresh *poke*.

Joints Be they taco stands, noodle spots, hamburger places or juice bars, the small-time joints are the lifeblood of island cuisine. Look for lines out the door at lunchtime to pick a top spot.

Food trucks There's an increasing range of food trucks offering everything from Mexican eats through to fusion gourmet flavors and artisan shave ice.

Restaurants There are plenty of fancy tourist restaurants, often with live entertainment.

The Island Diet

The island diet is more than just a meal. It's a window on the island itself. But defining it is no simple matter. It's multi-ethnic, yet distinct from classic fusion cooking. It's got a full-fledged highbrow cuisine, yet its iconic dishes are lowbrow local *grinds* (akin to street food). The only way to understand the island diet is to partake of its pleasures.

➡ The primary starch in Hawaii is sticky, medium-grain white rice. Jasmine rice is tolerated with Thai food, but flaky rice is considered haole (Caucasian) food.

➡ The top condiment is soy sauce (ubiquitously called by its Japanese name, *shōyu*), which combines well with sharp Asian flavors, such as ginger, green onion and garlic.

➡ Meat, chicken or fish is often integral to a dish. For quick, cheap eating, locals devour anything tasty, from Portuguese sausage to hamburger steak to corned beef. But the dinner-table highlight is always seafood, especially succulent, freshly caught ahi (tuna).

➡ Nonlocal classics (such as pizza and bagels) are usually disappointing. Also bear in mind that 'barbecue' typically means teriyaki-marinated.

➡ While Kaua'i's top restaurants can hold their own among statewide peers, you generally won't find the cutting-edge culinary creativity that you'd find on O'ahu, or even on Maui or the Big Island.

Two excellent resources on Hawaii cuisine are Edible Hawaiian Islands (https://ediblehi.com), which covers the gamut, and Hawaii Seafood (www.hawaii-seafood.org), which is all about just that.

SEAFOOD DECODER

Hawaiian seafood has some typical crowd-pleasers, plus a few unknown standouts that you'll want to try.

➡ ahi – served seared, grilled, raw, and always delicious

➡ aku – bonito or skipjack tuna is smaller and has a more robust flavor

➡ akule – big-eyed scad has a sweet, oily flavor like mackerel

➡ hapu'upu'u – noted for its delicate white meat

➡ hebi – a mild-flavored billfish

➡ kajiki – Pacific blue marlin

➡ mahimahi – delicious and everywhere

➡ monchong – medium flavor with a high fat content

➡ onaga – ruby snapper

➡ ono – local word for wahoo; can be a bit rubbery

➡ opah – moonfish; a favorite with local chefs

➡ 'opakapaka – crimson snapper served in filets

➡ shutome – swordfish

➡ tombo – albacore tuna

➡ ulua – crevalle jack

Drinks

You can learn about coffee production at the Kauai Coffee Company. (p217) The best cafes on the island are Java Kai (p129) in Kapa'a and Aloha Roastery in Lihu'e (p99) and Koloa (p191).

While fresh fruit is plentiful at farmers markets, fresh fruit juice tends to be pricey and sold mainly at health-food markets and roadside fruit stands, such as the Kalalea Juice Hale (p133), which makes tropical smoothies to order.

An offshoot of the smoothie is the frosty, an icy dessert with the texture of ice cream, made by puréeing frozen fruit in a food processor. Try it at Fehring Family Farm (p150). For good cold-pressed juices, nut milks and kombucha, visit the Kauai Juice Co's stores in Kapa'a (p129) and Kilauea (p150).

Unique to Hawaii are two fruit-juice 'tonics' nowadays marketed mainly to tourists: 'awa (kava), a mild sedative, and noni (Indian mulberry), which some consider to be a cure-all. Both fruits are pungent (if not repulsive) in smell and taste, so they are typically mixed with other juices. Try them at the Kalalea Juice Hale (p133).

Among alcoholic beverages, beer is the local drink of choice. There are a few craft breweries worth checking out too, such as Kauai Island Brewery & Grill (p220) in Port Allen and Kauai Beer Company (p98) in Lihu'e. Wine is gaining in popularity among the upper-income classes, and all top-end restaurants offer a decent selection.

Food Tours

Tasting Kaua'i (www.tastingkauai.com; per person $110) offers food-based experiences around the island, including visits to farmers markets, food trucks, restaurants and small-scale producers. Highlights include fusion Hawaiian-Asian flavors on the island's Eastside, brilliant poke and artisan jams on the South Shore, and herbal teas, kombucha and fresh island juices on the North Shore. Friday-night Hanapepe and Saturday-morning Lihu'e farmers-market tours are also available.

Interesting food-related tours are also offered at the Ho'opulapula Haraguchi Taro Farm (p168), Garden Island Chocolate (p147), Kauai Coffee Company (p217) and Lydgate Farms (p118).

Food Trucks

Food trucks are one of the best ways to eat cheaply around the island, and up-and-coming and innovative chefs are increasingly seeing it as a way to get their food to a wider group of diners.

Check out the food-truck pods in central Hanalei, the northern end of Kapa'a and at Warehouse 3540 (p207) in Lawa'i to see what's new and interesting.

Here's our top five at the time of writing.

Al Pastor (p127) Terrific fish tacos and burritos.

Kickshaws (p206) Gourmet versions of classic comfort food.

Kikuchi's (p96) Tasty ahi tuna wraps.

Scorpacciata (p127) Wood-fired pizza and parmesan fries.

Fresh Shave (p206) Artisan shave ice from a shiny retro trailer.

Traditional plate lunch – ahi *poke*, lomi lomi salmon, *tako poke*, *kalua* pig, poi, and *laulau*

Luau

In ancient Hawaii, a luau commemorated an auspicious occasion, such as births, war victories or successful harvests. Today, only commercial luau offer the elaborate Hawaiian feast and hula dancing that folks expect to experience. A $80 to $140 ticket buys you a highly choreographed Polynesian dance show and an all-you-can-eat buffet of typical luau dishes such as poi (steamed, mashed taro, *kalua* pig, steamed mahimahi, teriyaki chicken and *haupia* (coconut pudding). The food isn't great (it's usually toned down for the tourist palate), but somehow the whole slightly kitsch, totally over-the-top luau experience should make it to all but the most cynical of tourist itineraries. It's something you only have to do once.

Kilohana Plantation's Luau Kalamaku (p99) offers the most impressive show – a compelling theatrical production and professional-caliber dancers. The Tahiti Nui Luau (p173) in Hanalei is also a genuine joy, albeit with lower-key musical entertainment. The long-running luau at Smith's Tropical Paradise (p109) is a family affair and, while touristy, the multicultural performances with dancers of all ages have their appeal. Both the Grand Hyatt (p203) and Sheraton (p200) offer beachside luaus in Po'ipu.

If you want to save some bucks you can sit beachside and watch the show with a bottle of wine, but remember, by paying for the show, your money goes to local performers and local waiters.

Private luau celebrations, typically for weddings or first birthdays, are often large banquet-hall gatherings. The menu might be more daring – perhaps including raw *'a'ama* (black crab) and *'opihi* (edible limpet) – and the entertainment more low-key. No fire eaters.

The Other Pink Meat

Simply put, locals love Spam. Yes, *that* Spam. It's a local comfort food, typically eaten sliced and sautéed to a light crispiness in sweetened *shōyu*. Expect to see Hormel's iconic canned ham product served with eggs for breakfast or as a *loco moco* option. It's especially enjoyed as Spam *musubi* (rice ball topped with fried Spam and wrapped with dried seaweed,

Top: Luau performance, Sheraton (p200)

Bottom: Shave-ice dessert

or *nori*) – folks of all stripes savor this only-in-Hawaii creation that's culturally somewhat akin to an easy, satisfying PB&J sandwich.

The affinity for Spam arose during the plantation era, when canned meat was cheap and easy to prepare for *bentō* box) lunches. In Hawaii, unlike on the mainland, there's no stigma to eating Spam. If you acquire a taste for it, plan a trip to Honolulu for the annual Waikiki Spam Jam (www.spamjamhawaii.com) and go wild in your own kitchen with *Hawai'i Cooks with SPAM: Local Recipes Featuring Our Favorite Canned Meat*, written by prolific cookbook author Muriel Miura.

Vegetarians & Vegans

Although locals love their sashimi and Spam, vegetarians and vegans won't go hungry on Kaua'i. A handful of restaurants cater to vegetarian, vegan, fish-only or health-conscious diets. Notable venues include Postcards Café (p172), the Greenery (p96), Kalaheo Café & Coffee Co (p207) and EatHealthy Cafe (p117), all of which focus on vegetarian and fish dishes. The high-end Hawaii Regional Cuisine menus always have vegetarian options. Asian eateries offer varied tofu and veggie options, but beware of meat- or fish-based broths.

Habits & Customs

In most households, home cooking is integral to daily life, thanks to the slower pace, backyard gardens and obsession with food. Meals are held early and on the dot: typically 6am breakfast, noon lunch and 6pm dinner. At home, locals rarely (perhaps never) serve formal sit-down meals with individual courses. Even when entertaining, meals are typically served in a potluck style, often as a spread of unrelated dishes.

If you're invited to a local home, show up on time and bring dessert. Remove

---

THE YEAR IN FOOD

Now that agri-tourism and gourmet cuisine are trendy, food festivals are garnering much attention. The Hanalei Taro Festival, a biennial event (even-numbered years), features poi-pounding and taro-cooking contests. More extravagant is Taste of Hawaii (p115), a line-up-and-sample extravaganza dubbed the 'ultimate Sunday brunch.'

Many public festivals and events offer family-friendly outdoor food booths, serving much more than standard concession grub. The Waimea Town Celebration (p229), Koloa Plantation Days (p189) and Kaua'i County Farm Bureau Fair (p95) showcase not only local culture but also local food, from shave ice to plate lunches.

---

your shoes at the door. And don't be surprised if you're forced to take home a plate or two of leftovers.

Kaua'i restaurants typically open and close early; late-night dining is virtually nonexistent. In general, locals tip slightly less than mainlanders do, but still up to 20% for good service and at least 15% for the basics.

Except at top resort restaurants, the island dress code means that T-shirts and flip-flops are ubiquitous. The local, older generation tends toward neat and modest attire.

In top restaurants, you may consider a reservation – otherwise you are generally good to go. Takeaway picnics are an excellent option for lunch. Many hotels, condos and vacation rentals have barbecues, making grilling out and catering your own Hawaiian feasts easier than you'd think.

There's not a lot of nightlife in Kaua'i. Most places close early, with a few exceptions in the bigger tourist centers.

Ke'e Beach (p178)

Plan Your Trip
On the Water

Tucked into Kaua'i's 90 miles of coastline are more than 60 beaches. You need not drive far to find another (and yet another) gorgeous strand. North Shore and Westside beaches are most hazardous during winter (November through March) thanks to big surf, when South Shore and Eastside beaches are relatively calm. The pattern reverses in summer. Before plunging in, check out Kaua'i Explorer (www.kauaiexplorer.com), a Hanalei-based resource with info on beaches, ocean safety, marine life, ecotourism and much more.

Lifeguard-Protected Beaches

Lifeguard staffing on the island's beaches is subject to change, so check with Hawaii Beach Safety (www.hawaiibeachsafety.com) online to confirm that the following beaches still have lifeguards. The website also outlines current conditions at each beach. It's definitely worthwhile checking online before making a journey to more remote locations.

Eastside

Anahola Beach Park (p131), Kealia Beach Park (p123) and Lydgate Beach Park (p109)

North Shore

Ha'ena Beach Park (p177), Black Pot Beach Park (Hanalei Pier) (p162) and Wai'oli (Pine Trees) Beach Park (p163)

South Shore & Westside

Po'ipu Beach Park (p193), Kekaha Beach Park (p231) and Salt Pond Beach Park (p221)

Na Pali Coast Sea Tours

Glimpsing the Na Pali Coast by sea is an unforgettable experience. Primordial valleys of green not only beckon you to explore, but also to head back in time. Depending on your craft, you can paddle, snorkel, venture into sea caves or just kick back with a tropical drink, luxuriating in one of the world's great views. Assuming you can stomach the wave action, there's really no question of whether you should experience this Kaua'i highlight – the only question is how. Here's some help with sorting through the complexities.

Boat Tours

You have three types to choose from: catamarans (powered or sail), rafts (either Zodiacs or rigid-hulled inflatable boats; RIBs) or kayaks.

Catamarans are the cushiest, offering smoother rides, ample shade, restrooms and crowd-pleasing amenities, like on-board water slides and unlimited food and beverages. Some are equipped with sails (and actually use them), while others are entirely motorized. If you've only sailed monohulls before, this is a far more stable and roomy experience.

Rafts are the thrill-seeker's choice, bouncing along the water, entering caves (in mellower weather) and making beach landings, but most lack any shade, restrooms or comfy seating, so they're not for everyone (bad backs beware). The best rafts are RIBs, with hard bottoms that allow smoother rides (sit in back for less jostling but potentially more sea spray). The largest may include a canopy and even a toilet.

Kayaks are for people who want a workout with their Na Pali Coast tour. They're of the sit-on-top variety, with seat backs and pedal rudders. You don't need to be a triathlete or kayaking expert to use one, but you should be in top physical condition, as kayak tours can last 12 hours and you'll be paddling 17 miles.

Departure Point

You can access the Na Pali Coast from the North Shore or Westside. If you're visiting in the summer months, the North Shore – whether Hanalei or 'Anini – is definitely preferable, and it's the only option for kayaks, which paddle 17 miles from Ha'ena Beach Park to Polihale State Park. Kayak trips are organized by two outfitters in Hanalei.

Boat trips from Westside have to cover a lot of extra water before they reach the Na Pali Coast. As a result, they only get to see half the coastline. But in the winter months, when waves are brutal on the North Shore, tours there stop running, leaving you no other choice. Westside tours depart from Port Allen Harbor. However, winter weather still takes its toll, preventing landings at Nu'alolo Kai and limiting snorkeling opportunities.

Preparations

Book Na Pali Coast boat or kayak tours as far ahead as possible – ideally before you arrive. High surf or foul weather may cause cancellations, and repeated rescheduling.

Kayaking

River

With seven rivers, including the only navigable one statewide, river kayaking is all the rage on Kaua'i. A Wailua River tour, which includes a dip at a 130ft waterfall, is the classic. Due to the river's popularity, the county strictly regulates its use (eg no tours on Sundays). Most outfitters are located in Wailua, Hanalei and Lihu'e.

If you're seeking a solitary nature experience, you should visit Kaua'i's other rivers, smaller but perhaps more charming and leisurely. Hanalei River and Kalihiwai Stream are highly recommended. A handful of kayak tours navigate the Hule'ia River, which passes through the off-limits Hule'ia National Wildlife Refuge.

Sea

Sea kayaking off Kaua'i should be done on a tour due to rough surf. Beginners can learn in Po'ipu and Hanalei, while the fit and ambitious can challenge themselves on the grueling 17-mile Na Pali journey, possible only in summer. If you are very experienced, in summer it's possible to rent kayaks and camping gear for a Na Pali paddle under your own steam.

Stand-Up Paddleboarding

In the 1960s, Waikiki watermen developed stand-up paddleboarding (SUP) when teaching groups of beginner surfers. Standing on their boards, using a paddle to propel themselves, they could easily view their surroundings. In the early 2000s, SUP emerged as a global sport when big-name pros, including local boy Laird Hamilton, started doing it as a

Stand-up paddleboarding

substitute when waves were flat or when they wanted to catch especially big surf outside the main lineup. Companies that provide rentals and lessons have popped up beside beaches and rivers island-wide, including at Lihu'e's Kalapaki Beach, near Wailua on the Eastside, around Po'ipu on the South Shore and in Hanalei on the North Shore.

Swimming

You can find protected swimming lagoons year-round at Lydgate Beach Park (p109) and Salt Pond Beach Park (p221). Elsewhere, swimming is a seasonal sport. On the North Shore, swimming is lovely in summer, when waters are glassy at Hanalei Bay (p152) and Ke'e Beach (p178). In winter, when giant swells pound the North Shore, head to the South Shore, especially Po'ipu Beach Park. (p193)

Lap swimmers who need lanes and walls can take advantage of the Olympic-sized YMCA pool (p91) in Lihu'e.

Kayaking, Wailua River (p107)

Ocean Safety

The Hawaiian Islands don't have a continental shelf. Consequently, the ocean doesn't roll up gently to their doorstep: it strikes hard. This creates swimming conditions that are altogether different than those on the mainland. The ocean has a devastating power here, producing dangerous rip currents, rogue waves and undertows. For most visitors, the following warning applies: *you cannot think of swimming in Hawaii the way you think of swimming back home.* This is particularly true of Kaua'i, which has the highest per-capita drowning rate of all of the main Hawaiian Islands. Up to 10 tourists drown here each year. In 2018 there were nine drownings with a further 15 in 2019.

To protect yourself, heed the basic warnings:

➡ Never turn your back on the ocean.

➡ Never swim alone. If you're an inexperienced swimmer, swim only at lifeguarded beaches. At beaches without lifeguards, swim only if (and where) locals are doing so.

➡ Observe the surf for a while before entering. Look for recurring sets of waves, currents and other swimmers.

➡ Observe the wind. Windy conditions increase ocean chop.

➡ Don't walk on coastal rocks, where an unexpected wave can sweep you out. It's easy to misjudge the 'safe zone.'

➡ Don't assume that water conditions are consistent in all regions.

There is, of course, no reason why you can't have a great time swimming on Kaua'i. Just use your head, and if that little voice is warning you about something, listen to it. In Hawaii there is a saying: 'When in doubt, don't go out.' These are words to stay alive by. For current information and more advice, read the ocean report and safety tips at Hawaii Beach Safety (http://hawaiibeachsafety.com) and Kaua'i Explorer (www.kauaiexplorer.com).

GEORGE KARBUS PHOTOGRAPHY/GET TY IMAGES ©

Humpback whale

Whale-Watching

Each winter about 10,000 North Pacific humpback whales migrate to the shallow coastal waters off the Hawaiian Islands to breed, calve and nurse. Whale-watching boat tours are a hot-ticket item, especially during the peak migration season (January through March). Although it can't compete with the sheer number of whales spotted off Maui or the Big Island, Kaua'i still sees plenty of migratory whales, with some of its North Shore waters protected by the **Hawaiian Islands Humpback Whale National Marine Sanctuary** (www. hawaiihumpbackwhale.noaa.gov). Whale-watching boat tours depart mainly from Port Allen Harbor on the Westside. But if you park yourself on the Princeville cliffs, Kilauea Point (p143) or at Po'ipu Beach Park (p193) on any winter's day, you are likely to see whales spouting and breaching all day long.

Plan Your Trip

Diving & Snorkeling

Don't leave the island without donning a mask at least once. South Shore waters see most diving activity from dive boats and the shore, as there is less swell here most of the year. In the summer the North Shore also has good conditions. Snorkeling offers sheltered sites and turtles aplenty.

Diving

Note that the closest hyperbaric chambers for recompression therapy are located on O'ahu. For members, **Divers Alert Network** (DAN; ☑emergency hotline 919-684-9111, info 800-446-2671; www.diversalertnetwork. org; annual membership from $35) gives advice on diving emergencies, insurance, decompression services, illness and injury.

South Shore & Eastside

The South Shore is Kaua'i's scuba mecca, thanks to mostly smooth conditions which nurture ample visibility beneath the surface. For nine months a year it's the only place to dive, which is why it's the base of operations for all the island's dive shops, and with a dozen sites within a short boat ride of Kukui'ula Small Boat Harbor (p193), there's plenty of variety to keep you coming back. The best part is that the proximity of the dive shops to the harbor and of the harbor to the dive sites means it takes less than half a day to suck two tanks dry (unless you are lucky enough to be heading to Ni'ihau (p49) – in that case, three tanks are a must).

Koloa Landing (p197) is the best shore dive on the island, and with a maximum depth of 45ft most beginners will do at least one tank here. You'll see frog fish, leaf and devil scorpion fish,

Diving & Snorkeling Tips

Medical Kit

Ensure your travel medical kit contains treatment for coral cuts and tropical ear infections, as well as the standard problems.

Check-up

Have a dive medical before you leave home – local dive operators may not always ask about medical conditions that are incompatible with diving.

Gear

It may be a worthwhile investment to bring or buy your own high-quality mask, if you plan on snorkeling more than once or twice.

Timing

As a rule, snorkel early – morning conditions are often best, and if everyone else is sleeping, they won't be crowding the water and kicking up sand to mar visibility.

Reef Etiquette

Follow coral-reef etiquette: don't touch any coral, which are living organisms; watch your fins to avoid stirring up sand and breaking off pieces of coral; and finally, don't feed the fish.

and dragon moray eels with orange horns peeking out of rocks sprouting with new corals. You're likely to see turtles too. Koloa Landing is also where Freedive Kauai (p154) drops a line and leads students down to the ocean floor on a single breath. Often they move a bit offshore, away from the reef that the scuba divers enjoy, to get a bit more depth. Beginners will hit 66ft; intermediate students may hit 100ft on a single breath. In the summer they bring students to 'Anini Beach Park (p154) on the North Shore.

Stone House, another terrific beginner's dive, is a finger of lava jutting from the sand, ranging from 35ft to 65ft beneath the surface. Big schools of domino damsels and butterfly fish are common and look like floating walls of color. There are some octopus hiding in the lava rocks here too.

Nukumoi Point (p197) is a turtle-cleaning station stretching from 25ft to 55ft and is another great beginner's dive and ideal if you want to see turtles. There are some lovely nudibranch and tiger cowrie shells here, and in winter you'll hear whale song almost the entire dive. If you're really lucky, you might be visited by a pod of spinner dolphins. You can almost see the reef from the Po'ipū Beach Park lifeguard tower – look for where the waves break outside.

Sheraton Caverns (p197), a series of collapsed lava tubes home to giant, 100-year-old sea turtles who nap on the lava rock shelves for up to four hours at a time, is considered the best beginners' dive on the island because the visibility is so dependable and you can find a little bit of everything, including octopus, eels, adorable fingernail-sized harlequin shrimp and white-tip sharks. Maximum depth here is 65ft.

Turtle Bluffs (p197) looks like an underwater version of the cliffs you'd find above water at Salt Pond Beach Park (p221). They plummet from 55ft to 85ft and feature big sand caves where sharks are often napping or staking out prey. Lobster, crabs and big bait balls are also common.

Fish Bowl is a lava rock structure carved by water and time into a series of bowls, where big schools of blue stripe snapper and yellow goat fish can lure apex predators. Depth ranges from 35ft to 75ft and visibility and water color are almost always marvelous.

General Store (p197) is another dependable dive site with good visibility even when most sites are murky. It's centered around a (mostly decomposed) 1892 shipwreck. But nearby lava rock formations are punched with shadowy swim throughs where (harmless) sharks often lurk, and some big moray eels too.

Snorkeling

Harbor Ledges, the closest dive site to the boat dock, isn't deep but is a wonderful night dive. Turtles and sharks are common, and reports of dolphins are too numerous to count.

Advanced scuba divers have plenty of terrain to explore off the South Shore.

Zac's Pocket, a ledge that runs from north to south, set between Brennecke's Beach and the Hyatt, has arguably the best living coral reef on Kaua'i (not including Ni'ihau). The reef stretches from 80ft to 120ft and it's a drift dive. Conditions can be temperamental thanks to swirling currents that often blow divers off the reef – so it's a rare treat to be able to dive here, but if you are lucky you may glimpse Galapagos, white-tip and gray sharks, manta rays, and humpback whales in winter.

Brennecke's Ledge, another deep dive suitable for advanced-level folks, is a rock outcrop growing with pristine black coral at a depth between 65ft and 85ft. On the branches you can see rare long-nose hawkfish, sponge crabs and the odd manta ray. You'll hear whales in season, and may even see them down there.

Ice Box (p197), a horseshoe-shaped reef with boulders on either end, is another of the deeper sites (65ft to 85ft) but is suitable for intermediate

ADAM HESTER/GETTY IMAGES ©

divers. It's patrolled by white-tip reef sharks, octopus, lobsters, morays and occasional rays.

The Eastside has one notable dive site.

Ahukini Landing, a Lihu'e shore dive for all levels when conditions are calm, contains ordnance from WWII and is often home to rays, octopus and lobster. Occasional humpbacks cruise by in winter, though the water is usually too rough for beginners and visibility is hit and miss. Depth ranges from 10ft to 65ft.

North Shore & Westside

If you visit the island in summer, some of the South Shore sites may be murky and hard to access. Thankfully that's perfect timing to explore the often inaccessible north and west shore.

Tunnels (p176), the only scuba dive on the North Shore, is a reef made up of lava tubes on the inside and outside of the barrier reef that produces epic surf nine months a year. It's a shore dive, with swim throughs aplenty, common sightings of spotted eagle rays and monk seals, frequent white-tip reef sharks and occasional Galapagos sharks. Depth ranges from 5ft to 65ft. Though there is current, beginners are welcome.

Mana Crack, a huge fissure in the Na Pali Coast set more than a mile offshore between Polihale and Miloli'i, is an advanced-level drift dive with phenomenal visibility ranging in depth from 60ft to 120ft. Expect sharks, rays, eels and much more.

Ni'ihau

Undoubtedly the very best diving around Kaua'i can be found on Ni'ihau, that small island visible offshore and off-limits to visitors. This is the best place to dive with monk seals and sandbar sharks, and trip itineraries almost always include three dives.

Lehua Rock is the star of the scene. Picture an underwater, extinct volcanic crater with walls dropping down to between 200ft to 400ft on either side. You'll need good breath control to explore the walls, though there is easier diving inside the crater too. Here you may be fortunate enough to swim with wild dolphin pods and watch manta rays soar among massive schools of tropical fish.

Ni'ihau Caves, a labyrinth of archways home to ghost shrimp, moray eels, frog fish, octopus and sponge crabs, is another favorite. The big feature here is TV Cave – large and square just like your grandpa's television; some divers spend up to 30 minutes exploring that one cave alone. Neon Cave is another stunner, home to a resident monk seal and often graced by the presence of huge manta rays. Maximum depth in the caves is 70ft.

Snorkeling

OK, so scuba and freediving aren't for you; still, don't leave Kaua'i without having snorkeled. It's a wonderful introduction to a completely different, beautiful world. Almost anyone can do it and it's dirt cheap. Rental equipment is freely available, but if you're passing through Lihu'e, you can buy some for under $10 at big-box chain stores. In all locations, make sure you stay safe by snorkeling with a buddy.

The South Shore has the most snorkeling locations around Po'ipu. The twin lagoons in front of Po'ipu Beach Park (p193) offer terrific entry-level snorkeling. You're likely to see turtles and bunches of tropical fish. The same goes for the beach in front of the Sheraton. If you can make it past the break off Brennecke's Beach (p193), however, the rocks that tumble to the sea from shore on either side offer much better visibility, and there's much more life. Think: turtles, baby reef sharks and tons of fish. Further offshore, Nukumoi Point (p197) beckons, but that's a serious swim and should only be attempted by extremely strong open-water swimmers. If that's you, make sure to check in with the lifeguards before you take off. With underwater tunnels and a sizable population of eels, Koloa Landing (p197) is the best of the bunch on the South Shore.

If you're on the Westside, go to Salt Pond Beach Park (p221), with its shallow waters. On the Eastside, choose Lydgate Beach Park (p109), which has a protected lagoon perfect for kids. On the North Shore, head to 'Anini Beach Park (p154) year-round; in summer hit Ke'e Beach (p178) or Makua (Tunnels) Beach (p176). The latter can often be spectacular, but are off-limits to snorkelers when the surf's up. Snorkeling is also a key part of most Na Pali Coast boat tours (p43).

Kaua'i: Diving & Snorkeling

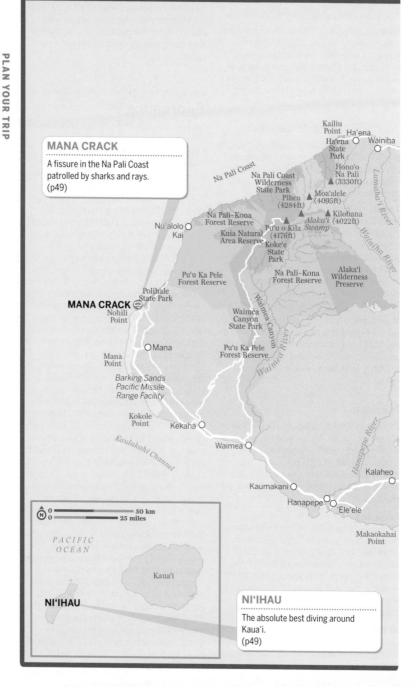

MANA CRACK

A fissure in the Na Pali Coast patrolled by sharks and rays. (p49)

NI'IHAU

The absolute best diving around Kaua'i. (p49)

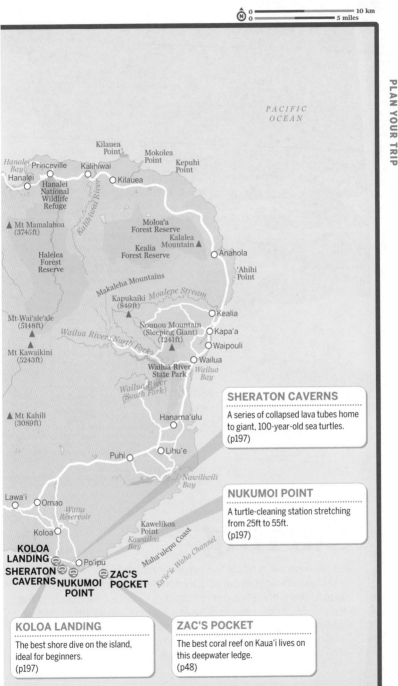

N
0 — 10 km
0 — 5 miles

PACIFIC
OCEAN

Kilauea
Point
Mokolea
Point
Kepuhi
Point

*Hanalei
Bay*
Princeville
Kalihiwai
Hanalei
Kilauea
Hanalei
National
Wildlife
Refuge

Mt Mamalahoa
(3745ft)

Moloa'a
Forest Reserve
Kalalea
Mountain
Kealia
Forest Reserve
Anahola

'Ahihi
Point

Halelea
Forest
Reserve

Makaleha Mountains

Kapukaiki
(849ft)
Moalepe Stream

Mt Wai'ale'ale
(5148ft)

Wailua River (North Fork)

Nounou Mountain
(Sleeping Giant)
(1241ft)

Kealia

Kapa'a

Waipouli

Mt Kawaikini
(5243ft)

Wailua

Wailua River
State Park
*Wailua
Bay*

*Wailua
River
(South Fork)*

Mt Kahili
(3089ft)

Hanama'ulu

SHERATON CAVERNS

A series of collapsed lava tubes home
to giant, 100-year-old sea turtles.
(p197)

Puhi
Lihu'e

*Nawiliwili
Bay*

Lawa'i
Omao

*Waita
Reservoir*

Koloa

Kawelikoa
Point
*Kawailoa
Bay*

Maha'ulepu Coast

NUKUMOI POINT

A turtle-cleaning station stretching
from 25ft to 55ft.
(p197)

**KOLOA
LANDING**

**SHERATON
CAVERNS**

**NUKUMOI
POINT**

Po'ipu

**ZAC'S
POCKET**

Ka'ie'ie Waho Channel

KOLOA LANDING

The best shore dive on the island,
ideal for beginners.
(p197)

ZAC'S POCKET

The best coral reef on Kaua'i lives on
this deepwater ledge.
(p48)

Surfer, South Shore (p198)

Plan Your Trip

Surfing

People have been riding the waves of Kaua'i for over 500 years, and there are an estimated 300 surf breaks surrounding the island. There are a few decent beginner spots – especially along the South Shore – but mostly you'll find powerful waves, tubes and reef breaks that are better suited to practiced experts. Locals rule the waves – especially on the North Shore – so check with the local surf shop before you head out.

Surf Lingo

Hawaii has a wonderful linguistic tradition, and the surfing lexicon here is fabulous. A few words you definitely want to know:

Aggro
Aggressive.

Barney
Defined in the classic 1987 surf movie *North Shore* as a 'kook in and out of the water,' it means somebody who doesn't know what they are doing.

Brah
Brother or friend.

Green room
The inside of a wave's tube.

Grom or grommet
Younger surfers (who are probably better than you).

Howlie
White person or non-Hawaiian.

Surf Beaches & Breaks

Given the steepness of the waves, short-boarders and big-wave riders will find more versatility on Kaua'i's waves. Long-boards still make their way into the lineup, especially when the waves aren't quite so big. You can also ride stand-up paddleboards, boogie boards or just head out for bodyboarding sessions. Bringing your own board can be expensive, so consider renting or buying locally (then reselling upon departure).

Water temperatures range from 78°F to 82°F (26°C to 28°C), and most people ride with just board shorts and a rash-guard. If you get cold easily, you may want to consider a light wetsuit in winter.

Staying safe here means not paddling out for waves that are too big for your abilities. Watch rip currents, know where the channel is, and think about the way the shape of the reef might just affect the shape of your head.

Surfline (www.surfline.com) reports current conditions at the best-known surf breaks, as do Surf Forecast (www.surf-forecast.com) and Kauai Explorer (www.kauaiexplorer.com). Alternatively, call the **Surf Hotline** (☏808-241-7873).

North Shore

Hanalei Bay (p162) is the nexus of Kaua'i surfing, where, you'll find both reef and point breaks. Beginners should head south of the pier to surf the gentle waves at Kiddies. The eastern point of the bay has four reef breaks (The Bowl, Flat Rock, Impossibles and Super Impossibles) that can sometimes be connected for one of Hawaii's longest rides. A quarter mile east of here, Summers is big with the SUP crowd, while still further east below the cliffs you'll find Hideaways (p155).

West of Hanalei, Waikokos (p163) is a gentle left that rarely gets above 4ft. You can find tougher reef breaks nearby at Wiapa, Chicken Wings and Middles (p163).

West of Wainiha are the twin guns of Tunnels (p176) and Cannons, sometimes referred to as the Pipeline of Kaua'i.

Check out Rock Quarry Beach (p146) on the eastern edge of Kilauea, or head west of here to Kalihiwai Beach (p147) for a killer right point break.

South Shore

There are some fun waves to be had around Po'ipu. Breaking best in the summer on south swells, spots such as PK's (p198), Acid Drop (p199) and Centers (p199) challenge even advanced surfers. First-timers can get their feet wet at Waiohai (p198), near the Marriott resort, and Donovans (p199; aka Learners), in front of the Kiahuna. Only bodyboarding and bodysurfing are permitted at Brennecke's Beach (p193).

Po'ipu Beach Park (p193) is crowded but has a really good beginner wave called Lemon Drops, while Shipwreck Beach (p195) and Maha'ulepu Beach (p196) draw experts.

Westside

Pakalas (also known as Infinities) near Waimea is the Westside's hottest break, but it's for locals only and the unprotected western waters mean winter breaks are treacherous. The Waimea Rivermouth (p228) has dirty water, but fun waves that can be suitable for beginners. For strong waves near Waimea, try Davidson (p232) or Major's Bay (p232).

In Polihale State Park (p235) you get mostly beach breaks, with the takeoff points and rides changing with the winds. On the south end, look for a reef break at Queen's Pond. On the north, hit up the beach peaks or go to Echo's, just at the start of the Na Pali Cliffs (advanced riders only). Boogie boarders have fun here.

Eastside

Transitional swells happen on the Eastside, where surfers hit Kealia Beach Park (p123) and Lihu'e's Kalapaki Beach (p85), a good spot for the SUP crowd. Eastside swells often break on distant reefs and hence get blown out except during early-morning hours and leeward wind conditions.

Unreals (p132) is a consistent right point at Anahola Bay that can work well on an easterly wind swell, when leeward winds are offshore. Locals here can be unwelcoming to outsiders.

Kalihiwai Beach (p147)

Learning to Surf

There are dozens of surf schools, primarily in Hanalei and Po'ipu, as well as at Kalapaki Beach in Lihu'e. Try for small classes to get the most out of the instruction.

Beginners don't normally require much more than an intro class. Classes usually last one or two hours, with board rental included. They include some practice on the beach, then you head to the lineup. Instructors will often push you on to the waves to help you get the hang of it.

Surfing Etiquette

Just as Hawaiian royalty had certain breaks reserved just for them, so goes it on Hawaii's surf breaks. Respect locals and local customs or you might end up with a black eye (and a bad reputation). Tourists are welcome, but deference to local riders is always recommended.

In the water, basic surf etiquette is vital. The person closest to the peak of the wave has the right of way. When somebody is already up and riding, don't take off on the wave in front of them. Don't paddle straight through the lineup. Rather, head out through the channel where the waves aren't breaking and then find your way into the lineup. When you wipe out – and you'll do this plenty – try to keep track of your board.

Also, remember you're a visitor out in the lineup, so don't expect to get every wave that comes your way. There's a definite pecking order and, frankly, as a tourist you're at the bottom. That said, usually if you give a wave, you'll get a wave in return.

As a tourist in Hawaii, there are some places you go and there are some places you don't go. For many local families, the beach parks are meeting places where generations gather to celebrate life under the sun. They're tied to these places by a sense of community and culture, and they aren't eager for outsiders to push them out of their time-honored surf spots.

Top: Hanalei Bay (p162)

Bottom: Stacked surfboards

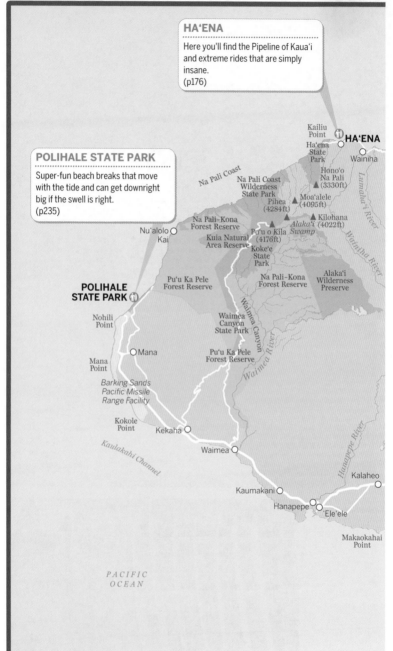

HA'ENA

Here you'll find the Pipeline of Kaua'i and extreme rides that are simply insane.
(p176)

POLIHALE STATE PARK

Super-fun beach breaks that move with the tide and can get downright big if the swell is right.
(p235)

Kailiu Point

HA'ENA

Ha'ena State Park

Wainiha

Hono'o Na Pali

Na Pali Coast

Na Pali Coast Wilderness State Park

▲ Moa'alele (3330ft)

Lumaha'i River

Pihea (4284ft)

Na Pali–Kona Forest Reserve

▲ (4095ft)

▲ Kilohana (4022ft)

Alaka'i Swamp

Wainiha River

Nu'alolo Kai

Kuia Natural Area Reserve

Pu'u o Kila (4176ft)

Koke'e State Park

Pu'u Ka Pele Forest Reserve

Na Pali–Kona Forest Reserve

Alaka'i Wilderness Preserve

POLIHALE STATE PARK

Nohili Point

Waimea Canyon State Park

Waimea Canyon

Waimea River

Pu'u Ka Pele Forest Reserve

Mana

Mana Point

Barking Sands Pacific Missile Range Facility

Kokole Point

Kekaha

Waimea

Kaulakahi Channel

Kaumakani

Hanapepe

'Ele'ele

Kalaheo

Hanapepe River

Makaokahai Point

PACIFIC OCEAN

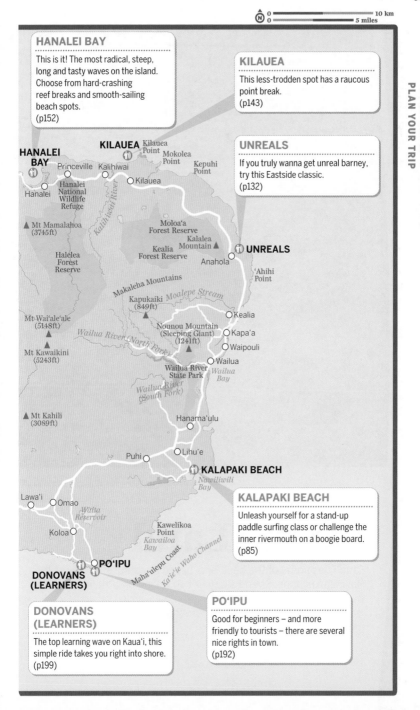

N
0 ——— 10 km
0 ——— 5 miles

HANALEI BAY

This is it! The most radical, steep, long and tasty waves on the island. Choose from hard-crashing reef breaks and smooth-sailing beach spots.
(p152)

KILAUEA

This less-trodden spot has a raucous point break.
(p143)

UNREALS

If you truly wanna get unreal barney, try this Eastside classic.
(p132)

KALAPAKI BEACH

Unleash yourself for a stand-up paddle surfing class or challenge the inner rivermouth on a boogie board.
(p85)

DONOVANS (LEARNERS)

The top learning wave on Kaua'i, this simple ride takes you right into shore.
(p199)

PO'IPU

Good for beginners – and more friendly to tourists – there are several nice rights in town.
(p192)

Map labels: HANALEI BAY, KILAUEA, Kilauea Point, Mokolea Point, Kepuhi Point, HANALEI BAY, Princeville, Kalihiwai, Kilauea, Hanalei, Hanalei National Wildlife Refuge, Kalihiwai River, Mt Mamalahoa (3745ft), Moloa'a Forest Reserve, Kalalea Mountain, Kealia Forest Reserve, Anahola, UNREALS, 'Ahihi Point, Halelea Forest Reserve, Makaleha Mountains, Kapukaiki (849ft), Moalepe Stream, Mt Wai'ale'ale (5148ft), Wailua River (North Fork), Nounou Mountain (Sleeping Giant) (1241ft), Kealia, Kapa'a, Waipouli, Mt Kawaikini (5243ft), Wailua River State Park, Wailua, Wailua Bay, Wailua River (South Fork), Mt Kahili (3089ft), Hanama'ulu, Puhi, Lihu'e, KALAPAKI BEACH, Nawiliwili Bay, Lawa'i, Omao, Waita Reservoir, Kawelikoa Point, Koloa, Kawailoa Bay, Maha'ulepu Coast, Ka'ie'ie Waho Channel, PO'IPU, DONOVANS (LEARNERS)

Ziplining

Plan Your Trip
On the Land

Kaua'i has some of the best land-based adventures of any of the Hawaiian Islands. Spend a day or two taking on a zipline, heading out for a horseback ride, cruising the back roads on an ATV, camping in lost corners of the forest or golfing on drop-dead-gorgeous golf courses.

Outdoor Adventures

Ziplining

Ziplines are popular across Hawaii, but Kaua'i's magnificent forests are hard to beat. Neither skill nor training are required, but participants must meet minimum age (generally seven years for a tandem ride) and maximum weight restrictions (ballpark no more than 280lb). Some operators offer superman flights (head first), others include rappelling through waterfalls or ATV tours.

Koloa Zipline (p189)

Skyline Eco-Adventures (p196)

Just Live! (p92)

Kaua'i Backcountry Adventures (p92)

Princeville Ranch Adventures (p157)

Tubing

Participants float through the network of plantation irrigation tunnels and channels in the remote mountainous region inland from Lihu'e. It's a family-friendly experience suitable for children five years and over, and a perfect mix of low-level thrills and relaxed serenity. It's also a good option for a rainy day, but you need to book ahead.

Kaua'i Backcountry Adventures (p92)

Camping

Kaua'i offers camping at all levels of roughin' it. Some campgrounds, such as 'Anini Beach Park, are within view of houses; others, such as the campground at Kalalau Beach, are miles from civilization.

For camping supplies and rentals, the best rental source is Pedal 'n Paddle (p165) in Hanalei. You can also buy camping gear from some outdoor outfitters, such as Da Life (p100) at Kalapaki Beach and Aloha XCHNG (p207) in Kalaheo, or from chain retailers like Kmart, Walmart and Costco in Lihu'e.

On the North Shore, try Kayak Kaua'i (p164) and Na Pali Kayak (p167) out of Hanalei to get geared up for Na Pali adventures.

Another backcountry option is to stay in rustic cabins located within state parks and preserves. Whatever you do, make sure you are not camping on private campsites. Everybody loves going to the beach at night – to look at the stars, drink wine, and make out. It's generally fine, but you should check with locals first to make sure you're going to a beach that's cool for tourists.

State Parks

State-park campgrounds can be found at the following parks.

Na Pali Coast Wilderness State Park (www.dlnr. hawaii.gov/dsp/parks/kauai/napali-coast-state-wilderness-park; end of Hwy 560) Camping at Hanakapi'ai and Kalalau Valleys is an integral part of the overnight hike here.

Koke'e State Park (p238) Drive-up and hike-in camping, and a bunch of cabins.

Waimea Canyon State Park (http://hawaii stateparks.org; $5 per day parking fee, covers all overlooks in Waimea Canyon & Koke'e state parks; 🚶) Hike-in camping only, and a few cabins worth checking out.

Polihale State Park (p235) Beachfront camping.

Permits are required from the Division of State Parks (p277), obtainable either in person in Lihu'e or online at https://camping.ehawaii.gov up to a year in advance. Fees range from $18 to $30 per night (or $20 per person per night on the Na Pali Coast). Maximum-stay limits of three to five nights are enforced.

For backcountry camping on the Westside, the Division of Forestry & Wildlife (p277) issues free permits for four backcountry campgrounds in Waimea Canyon, three campgrounds in and around Koke'e State Park, and the Waialae campground near the Alaka'i Wilderness Preserve. Apply online or in person at the Lihu'e office.

County Parks

The county maintains seven campgrounds on Kaua'i, all of which have bathrooms, cold-water outdoor showers and picnic tables.

Moving clockwise around the island:

Ha'ena Beach Park (p177; closed 10am Monday to noon Tuesday)

Black Pot Beach Park (Hanalei Pier; p162; open Friday and Saturday nights only)

'Anini Beach Park (p154; closed 10am Tuesday to noon Wednesday)

Anahola Beach Park (p131; closed 10am Thursday to noon Friday)

Lydgate Park (p109; open 7am to 6pm)

Salt Pond Beach Park (p221; closed 10am Tuesday to noon Wednesday)

Lucy Wright Park (p228; closed 10am Monday to noon Tuesday)

Note that at the time of writing, the campgrounds at Ha'ena Beach Park and Black Pot Beach Park were closed due to floods in 2018.

The best county campgrounds are the coastal parks at Ha'ena, Hanalei, Salt Pond Beach, and the particularly secluded and idyllic 'Anini Beach. The parks at Lucy Wright and Anahola tend to attract a shadier crowd and are not recommended for solo or female campers. Lydgate Park's camping is on grassy lawns with excellent coastal views. Each campground is closed one day a week for cleaning and in order to prevent people from permanently squatting there.

Camping permits cost $3 per night per adult camper (children under 18 years free) and are issued in person at neighborhood offices around the island or by mail (at least one month in advance) by the Division of Parks & Recreation (p277) in Lihu'e. For mail-in permits, only cashier's checks or money orders are accepted for payment.

Golf

Kaua'i has only nine golf courses, but there's something for every taste and budget. Pros and experts can try the Makai Golf Club (p157) in Princeville. The best course in Lihu'e is the Ocean Course at Hōkūala (p90), while the Puakea Golf Course (p90) is no slouch either. Nearby Wailua Municipal Golf Course (p112) is a cheaper alternative. Po'ipu Bay (p196) and Kiahuna golf courses (p196) in Po'ipu are a little more affordable than the northern counterparts. Probably

Golfing, Princeville Resort (p159)

the cheapest course is the Kukuiolono Golf Course (p205) on the South Shore near the village of Kalaheo. To save on resort fees, golf in the afternoon for the 'twilight' rate. All the courses rent clubs and several require carts.

For an afternoon of fun with the kiddos, check out the North Shore's Kauai Mini Golf & Botanical Gardens (p147).

Horseback Riding

Vast pastureland, exposed coastal cliffs and jungly rainforests provide ample terrain for horseback riding. A handful of stables offer tours, mainly for beginners and families. On the South Shore, CJM Country Stables (p197) rides along the Maha'ulepu Coast, while on the North Shore, Princeville Ranch Stables (p157) and Silver Falls Ranch (p147) traverse green pastures, ranch lands, streams and waterfalls.

Even though it's hot, it's recommended that you wear long pants to avoid painful riding sores on your inner thighs and ankles. It's how the cowboys do it!

Horseback riding

ATV

Kaua'i has an endless number of dirt tracks, and large expanses of unpopulated private land. This makes it an inviting playground for all-terrain vehicles (ATVs). If you've never driven one before, don't be cowed by the great big four-wheeled thing; it's a breeze, and loads of fun. Just be prepared to swallow a few bugs and get dirty. Most operations now have traditional four-wheeler ATVs, as well as more modern (and more stable) razors and other off-roaders. You have to be 16 years or older to drive, and tours generally require riders to be at least five years old.

Of the companies that specialize in ATV tours, try Kipu Ranch Adventures (p93) in Lihu'e.

Yoga, Spas & Massage

Beyond the island's many opportunities to get active in the outdoors, Kaua'i also offers chances to relax and recharge. Popular activities to restore a sense of physical and emotional balance while on the island include yoga, spa and massage services. Local Hawaiian traditions are often incorporated into spa and massage treatments.

Yoga

Kauai Yoga on the Beach (p112)

Black Coral (p164)

Bikram Yoga Kauai (p120)

Spas

Spa by the Sea (p120)

Anara Spa (p196)

Halele'a Spa (p157)

Massage

Ola Massage (p120)

Angeline's Mu'olaulani (p132)

Waimea Canyon State Park (p23

Plan Your Trip
Hiking & Biking

Kaua'i arguably has some of the best hiking and trekking of all the Hawaiian Islands. Trails can be extended over a few days, with stops at camps or cabins, and there's loads of variety (from beachfront walks to slippery treks down steep slopes). For inexperienced hikers or families with small kids, plenty of shorter trails get you close to the nature, flora and fauna of Hawaii, while historic trails in some of the older villages introduce you to a unique history. The biking is OK, but not as amazing as you might expect.

Guided Hikes

The Kaua'i chapter of the **Sierra Club** (https://sierraclubhawaii.org) leads guided hikes ranging from beach clean-up walks to hardy day-long treks. With a suggested donation of only $5 per person for nonmembers, these outings are an extraordinary bargain. All hikers must sign a liability waiver, and those aged under 18 must be accompanied by an adult. Advance registration may also be required; check the website in advance.

Kaua'i Nature Tours (p115) offers hiking tours all over the island. While their tours are expensive, the guides are full of endless tales, scientific facts, and colorful historical and cultural information about the island.

Hike Kaua'i Adventures (p240) offers bespoke hiking adventures all over the island with a friendly guide that knows the island backward and forward.

Hiking
Where to Hike

If you don't explore the island on foot, you're missing out on Kaua'i's finest (and free) terrestrial offerings. Hike up mountaintop wet forests, along steep coastal cliffs and down a colossal lava canyon – places you can't get to by car. Trails range from easy walks to precarious treks, catering to all skill levels.

For the most variety, head to Waimea Canyon (p59) and Koke'e state parks (p238). Don't miss the Pihea Trail (p240),

which connects to the Alaka'i Swamp Trail, for a look at pristine native forest filled with singing birds, or trek the Awa'awapuhi Trail (p240) or Nu'alolo Trail (p240) for breathtaking views of the Na Pali cliffs.

Along the Na Pali Coast, the wilderness Kalalau Trail (p215) is an exhilarating challenge, though as a day hike it's only realistic to attempt the round-trip to Hanakapi'ai Falls, and parking restrictions mean you'll probably have to depend on the North Shuttle bus service.

Eastside hikes head inland and upward, such as the Nounou Mountain trails (p104), which afford sweeping mountain-to-ocean views, and the Kuilau Ridge and Moalepe trails (p104). In addition to official trails, Kaua'i's vast coastline allows mesmerizing ocean walks, particularly along the cliffs of the Maha'ulepu Heritage Trail (p182) and the endless carpet of sand in remote Polihale State Park (p235). In Lihu'e, an afternoon walk out to the Ninini Point Lighthouse (p86) is a gorgeous way to spend the afternoon.

On the South Shore, the **McBryde Garden** (☑808-742-2623; www.ntbg.org; 4425 Lawa'i Rd; self-guided tours adult/child 6-12yr $30/15; ☻visitor center 8:30am-5pm, tours by reservation only; ⊛) ☙ and **Allerton Garden** (☑808-742-2623; www.ntbg.org; 4425 Lawa'i Rd; 2½hr tours adult/child 6-12yr $60/30, 3hr sunset tour $100/50; ☻visitor center 8:30am-5pm, tours by reservation only) are great spots to walk with families and friends and take in an afternoon picnic, while on the North Shore, the Limahuli Garden (p176) provides a tropical entrance to Eden and fun hikes through large gardens.

Some of the bigger hikes in the state parks will likely be too strenuous for young kids. But your tots will love running through the maze at Lydgate Beach Park (p109), or cruising the boardwalk at Ke Ala Hele Makalae (p126) on the Eastside. The short jaunt to Kilauea Point (p143) is a top spot for birdwatching. The Canyon Trail (p240) in Waimea Canyon State Park is widely considered the best kid-friendly hike on the Westside, as are the short interpretive trails out to the lookouts along the drive.

The villages of Koloa, Waimea and Hanapepe all have signed historical walks.

FOMINAYAPHOTO/SHUTTERSTOCK ©

Top: Hiking, Pihea Trail (p240)

Bottom: Cycling, Po'ipu Beach Park (p193)

Hiking Safety

People have died in Kaua'i hiking out on trails that have been closed, or out to remote beaches that see large waves. Don't be a statistic. And don't cross private property.

➡ Before you leave, tell somebody where you are going and when you expect to be back.

➡ Take enough water for your entire trip, and treat any water found along the trails.

➡ Pack first-aid supplies and snacks.

➡ Cell phones can be handy, but may lack reception in many remote areas (eg Koke'e State Park, Na Pali Coast).

➡ Wear appropriate footwear: while hiking sandals are fine for easy coastal walks, bring hiking shoes or boots for major trails.

➡ Rain is always a factor, especially on the North Shore, at Koke'e State Park and in Waimea Canyon. Trails that are doable in dry weather can become precariously slippery with mud.

➡ Flash floods are real threats wherever there are stream or river crossings. Never cross a waterway when it's raining. River fords may quickly rise to impassable levels, preventing you from returning for hours or days.

➡ If possible, hike with a companion.

➡ Don't go off-trail or bushwhack new trails.

➡ Lava terrain is frequently eroded and can be unstable, especially along cliffs.

➡ Never go beyond fenced lookouts.

➡ Note the time of sunset and plan to return well before it's dark. Be aware that daylight will fade inside a canyon long before sundown.

➡ Bring a flashlight just in case.

➡ Most accidents occur not due to a trail's inherent slipperiness or steepness, but because hikers take unnecessary risks.

➡ When hiking along the coast, be aware of rising tides, tide tables and frequent large waves. Kaua'i has more drowning deaths than any of the Hawaiian Islands. A lot of people visit beaches that should be off-limits.

Cycling & Mountain Biking

Road Cycling

It's possible to cycle along the belt highway in the Westside, South Shore and most of the Eastside, but there are no bike lanes and road shoulders can be narrow or nonexistent. Only experienced cyclists should consider cycling as transportation on Kaua'i.

Once the Eastside's coastal path, Ke Ala Hele Makalae (p126), is completed, cycling from Lihu'e all the way to Anahola will be doable by the masses. For now, the path is used only recreationally in stretches near Lydgate Beach Park and from Kapa'a Beach Park north to Paliku (Donkey) Beach. Bear in mind that cyclists share the path with pedestrians.

Cycling the North Shore beyond Hanalei is a real pleasure now that the traffic has been restricted, though there's no scope to enter the state park at the end of the road. On the Westside, cycling downhill on Hwy 550 from Waimea Canyon is so spectacular that it has been turned into a guided tour; book ahead with Outfitters Kauai (p238).

Mountain Biking

If you aren't afraid of mud and puddles, you can go wild on countless dirt roads and a few trails islandwide. The Powerline Trail (p157) is much too overgrown these days to traverse its full length between Wailua and Princeville, though it's fun to take a short ride at either end. The dirt roads near Po'ipu, above Maha'ulepu Beach, are flat but nice and dry, and you're less likely to encounter rain showers there. For a solitary ride, your best bets are the hunter roads at Waimea Canyon State Park. For more information, check online with Na Ala Hele (p275) or contact Kauai Cycle (p120), an Eastside bike rental and repair shop with a knowledgeable crew.

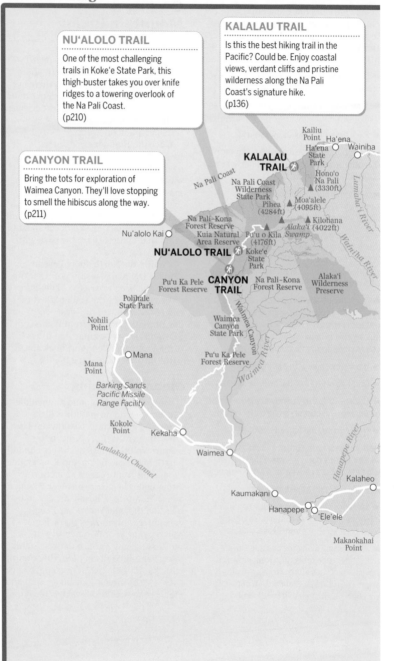

NU'ALOLO TRAIL

One of the most challenging trails in Koke'e State Park, this thigh-buster takes you over knife ridges to a towering overlook of the Na Pali Coast.
(p210)

KALALAU TRAIL

Is this the best hiking trail in the Pacific? Could be. Enjoy coastal views, verdant cliffs and pristine wilderness along the Na Pali Coast's signature hike.
(p136)

CANYON TRAIL

Bring the tots for exploration of Waimea Canyon. They'll love stopping to smell the hibiscus along the way.
(p211)

KALALAU TRAIL

NU'ALOLO TRAIL

CANYON TRAIL

Kailiu Point   Ha'ena
Ha'ena   Wainiha
Ha'ena State Park
Hono'o Na Pali
Na Pali Coast Wilderness State Park
Pihea (4284ft)   Moa'alele (4095ft)
Na Pali Coast
Na Pali-Kona Forest Reserve
Kilohana
Alaka'i (4022ft)
Nu'alolo Kai   Kuia Natural Area Reserve   Pu'u o Kila (4176ft)   Swamp
Koke'e State Park
Pu'u Ka Pele Forest Reserve   Na Pali-Kona Forest Reserve   Alaka'i Wilderness Preserve
Polihale State Park
Nohili Point   Waimea Canyon State Park
Mana   Pu'u Ka Pele Forest Reserve
Mana Point
Barking Sands Pacific Missile Range Facility
Kokole Point   Kekaha
Waimea
Kaulakahi Channel
Kalaheo
Kaumakani
Hanapepe   'Ele'ele
Makaokahai Point
Lumaha'i River
Wainiha River
Hanapepe River
Waimea River
Waimea Canyon

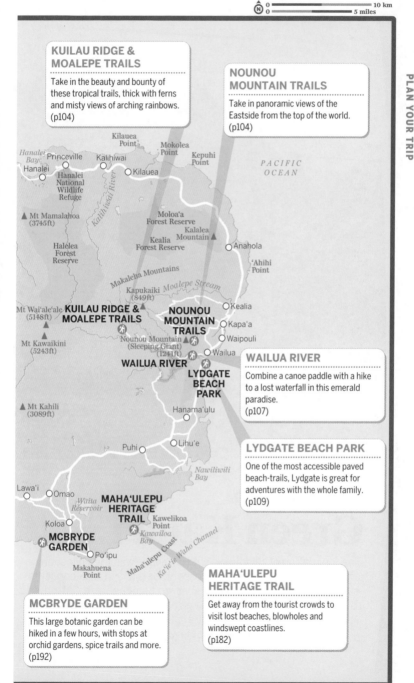

0   0   10 km
N   0   5 miles

KUILAU RIDGE & MOALEPE TRAILS

Take in the beauty and bounty of these tropical trails, thick with ferns and misty views of arching rainbows. (p104)

NOUNOU MOUNTAIN TRAILS

Take in panoramic views of the Eastside from the top of the world. (p104)

WAILUA RIVER

Combine a canoe paddle with a hike to a lost waterfall in this emerald paradise. (p107)

LYDGATE BEACH PARK

One of the most accessible paved beach-trails, Lydgate is great for adventures with the whole family. (p109)

MAHA'ULEPU HERITAGE TRAIL

Get away from the tourist crowds to visit lost beaches, blowholes and windswept coastlines. (p182)

MCBRYDE GARDEN

This large botanic garden can be hiked in a few hours, with stops at orchid gardens, spice trails and more. (p192)

Hanalei Bay
Hanalei
Princeville
Kalihiwai
Kilauea Point
Mokolea Point
Kepuhi Point
Kilauea
Hanalei National Wildlife Refuge

PACIFIC OCEAN

Kalihiwai River

▲ Mt Mamalahoa (3745ft)

Moloa'a Forest Reserve
Kealia Forest Reserve
Kalalea Mountain ▲

Halelea Forest Reserve

Anahola
'Ahihi Point

Makaleha Mountains

Kapukaiki (849ft)
Moalepe Stream

Mt Wai'ale'ale (5148ft)
KUILAU RIDGE & MOALEPE TRAILS

Kealia

NOUNOU MOUNTAIN TRAILS

Kapa'a

Mt Kawaikini (5243ft)
Nounou Mountain ▲ (Sleeping Giant) (1241ft)
Waipouli
Wailua

WAILUA RIVER

LYDGATE BEACH PARK

▲ Mt Kahili (3089ft)

Hanama'ulu

Puhi
Lihu'e

Nawiliwili Bay

Lawa'i
Omao
Koloa
Waita Reservoir

MAHA'ULEPU HERITAGE TRAIL

Kawelikoa Point
Kawailoa Bay

MCBRYDE GARDEN
Po'ipu
Makahuena Point

Maha'ulepu Coast
Ka'ie'ie Waho Channel

Limahuli Garden (p176

Plan Your Trip

Green Kaua'i

The foundation of life for ancient Hawaiians was the philosophy of *aloha 'aina* – love, care and respect for the land. Eco-concepts such as 'green' and 'sustainable' weren't catchphrases introduced by foreigners; they were principles already built into the fabric of everyday life, based upon a spiritual relationship with the land. Today those principles and that love are coming full circle on the Garden Island.

Helpful Organizations

Island Breath (www.islandbreath.org) Dig deep into local issues with its links to newspaper and independent articles on Kaua'i's hot-button sustainability topics.

Kauai Explorer (www.kauaiexplorer.com) While known mainly for its outstanding ocean-safety tips, this refreshingly concise site also contains preservation tips and a handy 'Where to Recycle' guide.

Malama Kaua'i (www.malamakauai.org) This Kilauea-based grassroots organization is the island's watchdog, dedicated to protecting the *'aina's* (land's) ecosystems and culture with a biweekly KKCR public-radio show, volunteering opportunities and more.

important and valuable industry, which drives the economy but also affects the environment and increases the cost of living.

Environmentally, the biggest impacts of tourism are from cruise ships and helicopters. Cruise ships burn diesel fuel, releasing exhaust fumes equivalent to thousands of cars into the island's atmosphere. Their discharge of ballast water and wastes can pollute the ocean, damage coral reefs and accidentally introduce invasive species. Helicopter tours are popular with visitors, but contribute to both air and noise pollution. They also diminish the enjoyment of Kaua'i's natural areas for those who choose to visit them in low-impact ways, such as by hiking or kayaking.

Luxury resorts and residential developments take up large swaths of land and incorporate sprawling, irrigation-hungry golf courses. As well as putting environmental pressure on the island, they impact the ability of locals to afford housing. The massive Kukui'ula community on the south coast targets offshore buyers, mainly from the mainland US. Price tags begin at around $1 million for the exclusive Lodge at Kukui'ula development, out of reach for most locals working in the service, retail and hospitality industries.

On the Ground

When it comes to putting green theory into practice there are definite steps you can take as a visitor to reduce further harm to the *'aina* (land) without forgoing any of its charms.

The Island Goes Green

Kaua'i can be seen as an isolated island threatened by overdevelopment, traffic, waste creation, a lack of affordable housing, and an extreme reliance on imported fuel and food. At a local level however, there is a viable community spirit working together to create future-based alternatives to the unsustainable practices impacting on the island.

Impact of Tourism

Tourism is high on the list of ecological concerns. Kaua'i locals have a love-hate relationship with the island's most

Transportation & Accommodations

Given the limited availability of bus services and safe bicycle lanes, there's no getting around the fact that you'll probably need a car on Kaua'i. But choosing a small rental car and planning excursions carefully can make a difference to how much fuel you use. Consider picking a couple of self-catering and low-key accommodations around the island. Then, at each place, keep your sightseeing to within that region. Along with saving on fuel costs this will allow you to immerse

Top: Kauai Coffee Company (p217)

Bottom: Kamokila Hawaiian Village (p112)

yourself in your immediate surroundings, which could result in a richer, more local travel experience.

Many airlines and websites allow you to estimate and pay to offset the impact of the carbon emissions generated by your flight to the island, should you wish to do so.

Camping is another way to make your vacation more green. Kaua'i offers state and county park campgrounds by the coast and in inland forests. All require getting advance permits, reservable online or available in person from government offices (most are in Lihu'e), so plan ahead.

Food

When it comes to food, where you buy is as important as what you buy. Buying locally grown produce, locally caught fish and locally made cheeses, preserves and baked goods is very easy to do. Wherever you're located on the island, it should only take a drive of around 20 minutes to reach a local weekly farmers market or daily fish market. To find unique, homegrown food and drinks made around the island, visit the Kaua'i Made website (http://kauaimade.net), or look for its purple-and-green stickers on products when you're out shopping.

Kaua'i County passed a ban on plastic bags at retail shops in 2009. Grocery stores and big-box chains now charge a small fee for recyclable paper bags, but bringing a reusable tote bag is even better. Kaua'i's garbage dumps are nearly overflowing, so it's important to minimize the amount of waste you produce. Try to patronize restaurants and food retailers who use biodegradable utensils, avoid styrofoam and feature local produce, dairy, seafood and meats as ingredients on their menus.

Activities

For the price of an ATV or helicopter tour, you could instead get an up-close and personal experience with some of the same terrain on an expert-led hike with Kaua'i Nature Tours (p115) or a low-impact tubing adventure with Kaua'i Backcountry Adventures (p92). Outrigger-canoe sailing with Island Sails Kaua'i (p157) or the Kamokila Hawaiian Village (p112) in Wailua makes for a great time on the water.

Reduce, Reuse, Recycle

Convenient island recycling centers:

North Shore (5-3751 Kuhio Hwy) At the Hanalei Transfer Station, across from the Prince Golf Course in Princeville.

Eastside (4900 Kahau Rd) In Kapa'a at the end of Kahau Rd, behind the ball field near the bypass road.

Lihu'e (4303 Nawiliwili Rd) At the back of the Kmart parking lot on the pavilion side of the store.

Nawiliwili Harbor (3343 Wilcox Rd) At Reynolds Recycling, just north of the harbor, at the corner of Kanoa Rd.

South Shore (2100 Ho'one Rd) In the Brennecke's parking lot opposite Po'ipu Beach Park.

Port Allen (4469 Waialo Rd) North of the harbor at 'Ele'ele Shopping Center.

Westside, Waimea Canyon Park (4643 Waimea Canyon Dr).

Kekaha Landfill (6900-D Kaumuali'i Hwy).

Also consider various low-impact activities that help you learn about Hawaiian history and local culture, such as Limahuli Garden (p176) on the North Shore and the Kaua'i Museum (p85) in Lihu'e. Agritourism is also big on Kaua'i, including with Ho'opulapula Haraguchi Taro Farm Tours (p168) in Hanalei and the renewable-energy-powered Kaua'i Coffee Company (p217).

Responsible Travel Tips

➡ Booking with a local activity company provides employment for locals and pumps money into the local economy.

➡ Reduce air miles by shopping for fresh in-season fruit and vegetables from local producers at the island's farmers markets.

➡ Join a food tour with Tasting Kaua'i (p38), which places a strong emphasis on visiting and supporting locally owned producers and vendors. Several of their guides are Kaua'i born and bred.

PROTECTING KAUA'I FROM ROD

First identified on the Big Island in 2014, the fungal disease Rapid Ohia Death (ROD) was also discovered on Kaua'i in 2018. Ohia trees are Hawaii's most important and sacred native species – they cover more than one million acres across the state and are one of the first plants to rise again amid fresh lava flows. Growing undetected within the tree, the fungus cuts off the flow of water over the course of a few months and eventually kills the tree.

The following actions are recommended on Kaua'i to help stem the spread of ROD. For more information visit www.rapidohiadeath.org.

➡ Clean shoes, tools and camping equipment with rubbing alcohol before and after visiting forested areas, especially if you're visiting multiple islands or adjacent forested areas. Wash clothes in hot water.

➡ Wash your vehicle's tires and undercarriage after driving off-road in forested areas.

➡ Avoid damaging the bark or roots of ohia trees, as this creates entry points for the fungus.

➡ Report any ohia trees you see with brown or yellowish leaves. See the FAQ section on www.rapidohiadeath.org for contacts.

➡ Don't transport ohia plants and wood to new areas.

➡ From January 2021, the use of coral-damaging sunscreen products is banned throughout the entire state of Hawaii. See www.hawaii.com/blog/reef-safe-sunscreen for information on which reef-safe products to purchase and use.

➡ Consider staying at smaller, standalone accommodations properties, rather than a large resort.

➡ Consider staying at accommodations with environmentally friendly features such as solar panels.

➡ Consider renting a bicycle to explore the immediate region around where you are staying. This is easier if you base yourself on the Ke Ala Hele Makalae (p126) coastal trail around Kapa'a on the Eastside, or in the leafy and relatively compact area around Po'ipu on the South Shore.

➡ A number of organizations that are working to protect Kauai's gardens, beaches and forests offer volunteering opportunities (p277).

Sustainable Agriculture

Another important issue on Kaua'i is food security. Despite the island's natural biodiversity, about 90% of its food is imported. At any given time there is only enough food on Kaua'i to feed the island for three to seven days.

Limited resources on Kaua'i mean that land, water and labor costs are comparatively high. Huge parcels of agricultural land are occupied by major multinational corporations growing genetically modified (GMO) crops, mainly corn to be exported. Opinions differ on the risks of genetic modification, but many agree that island crops should benefit residents, not multinational corporations.

A growing contingent of small-scale organic farmers argue that the old model of corporate-scale, industrialized mono-cropping (of pineapples and sugarcane, for example) enabled by chemical fertilizers, pesticides and herbicides is no longer viable on the island. Instead, family farms growing diverse crops – for the table or for sale locally, not only globally – would be sustainable.

Waipo'o Falls (p240)

Plan Your Trip
Kaua'i by Air

Seeing Kaua'i from the air is a thrilling and singular experience that may just define your trip. Though expensive, it's the only way to see much of the island, the majority of which is privately owned. Helicopter tours are by far the most popular option: while planes can fly no lower than 1000ft to 1500ft, helicopters are allowed to fly as low as 500ft and can hover. To check any tour company's flight record, consult the National Transport Safety Board (www.ntsb.gov) accident database.

Helicopter Operators

Island Helicopters (p93) offers a landing on top of Manawaiopuna Falls, more commonly known as Jurassic Falls.

Mauna Loa Helicopters (p94) is noteworthy for the chance to take the doors off...freaky but fun.

Jack Harter Helicopters (p93) Take a flight with one of the pioneers of flight tourism on the island.

Blue Hawaiian Helicopters (p93) flies high-end choppers that are said to be less noisy.

Safari Helicopters (p93) offers an ecotour with a 40-minute stop at a wildlife refuge.

Fixed-Wing Scenic Flights

With one exception, there seems to be no point in choosing a fixed-wing aircraft to tour Kaua'i, not when you can take a helicopter right to the cone of Mt Wai'ale'ale and hover there to your heart's content. The exception is an open-cockpit biplane, which flies so slowly it may as well be hovering. The combination of the romance of early aviation, the sensation of the wind and roaring engine, and the emerald tropical island sliding below, not to mention sitting side-by-side in near embrace, makes this many a honeymooner's first choice.

In fact, if it were up to passengers, biplanes would probably be as popular as helicopters on Kaua'i, but there's currently only one company that offers these scenic flights: AirVentures Hawaii (p93), based in Lihu'e. The tour leaves from Lihu'e Airport and takes you north past the Wailua River and Kilauea Lighthouse. From there, you travel up the lush Hanalei Valley, continuing over the ridge to see cascading waterfalls and 4000ft cliffs. The flight then continues north past Hanalei to the Na Pali Coast,

soaring past waterfalls and canyon drops through Waimea Canyon, and back to the South Shore, where you might just spot your hotel. They even give you the cool throwback hat and goggles!

Helicopter Tours

The most popular way to see Kaua'i from the air is to take a helicopter ride. Most helicopter tour companies depart from the airport in Lihu'e. Trips generally last 60 to 90 minutes, and start at around $229 (make internet reservations ahead of time to save money). It's worth doing some careful research before choosing an operator. You'll have to decide what kind of aircraft and tour you want (some land in neat places), and whether you want the doors on or off (some passengers like the visibility, others don't like the exposure to wind and possibly rain).

Doors-off helicopters are totally the way to go if you are an avid photographer (and suffer little from vertigo). But it's noisy and windy, and maybe just a little bit scary. On a six-seater helicopter, two people may be stuck in the middle. You can request a window, but the captain may move people around for weight balance.

You also get to choose from big window, little window and bubbles (like the ones on *MASH*). The big differences are always visibility and noise. More modern helicopters are quieter and generally have big windows. You always wear earphones so you can talk with fellow passengers and lower the noise, but even a slight reduction in sound can make your trip more pleasant. Then again, some of the older helicopters have that sweet *Magnum P.I.* feel that makes for a thrilling ride.

Make sure to check your operator's weather policy before booking. Rain delays do happen, and tour routes will vary depending on rain and winds. Cancellations or postponements by operators may happen at short notice. Consider booking early during your stay, so you can reschedule later if need be.

What should you bring? Ideally, strap everything down (hats, phones, cameras etc). It can get a little cold, so bring a

Manawaiopuna Falls, Hanapepe (p220)

jacket and long pants, plus decent shoes in case your tour includes a landing.

Always approach a helicopter from the front (never the back). The captain will generally indicate which side you should board. Put your head down and hold onto your hat (just like they do in the movies). Tours include ongoing narration from the knowledgeable pilots. Yes, you can tip them afterward, but it's not required.

From Lihu'e, expect to see the Nawiliwili Harbor and the Menehune Fishpond, Kipu Kai and the Tunnel of Trees, Manawaiopuna Falls in Hanapepe Valley, Olokele Canyon, Waimea Canyon, the Na Pali Coast, North Shore beaches like Ke'e and Hanalei, and Mt Wai'ale'ale. While the rips up impossibly steep canyons are an adrenaline junkie's dream, it's really the close proximity to waterfalls – many of which can only be seen from the air – that makes these trips amazing.

While the tours follow pretty standardized routes, you can talk with your pilot to customize your tour experience, especially if it's just you and your family or sweetheart taking the flight. This means getting closer to (or further away from) the ground, making more acrobatic banking turns or going with a more easy-breezy approach, and generally determining the way you fly.

For a really unique trip, consider a tour with **Ni'ihau Helicopters** (☑877-441-3500; www.niihau.us; per person $465), which flies over of much of Ni'ihau island (avoiding the population center of Pu'uwai), then ends with snorkeling off one of the island's beaches. Lunch, snacks and drinks are included; five-person minimum required.

Plan Your Trip
Family Travel

Welcome to an island amusement park. Instead of riding roller coasters and eating too much cotton candy, on Kaua'i keiki (kids) can snorkel amid tropical fish, eat just the right amount of shave ice, zipline in forest canopies, and enjoy sandy beaches with bodyboarding hot spots and safe toddler-friendly lagoons.

Keeping Costs Down

Self-Catering

Stay in self-catering apartments and condos. All have well-equipped kitchens and usually outdoor barbecue facilities as well. Shop at local Foodland supermarkets and purchase fresh fruit and vegetables at farmers markets.

Food Trucks

Save money by eating at food trucks. Kaua'i has a growing selection, offering everything from Mexican and Thai flavors through to artisan shave ice. Key food-truck hubs are in Hanalei, the northern end of Kapa'a, and at Warehouse 3540 (p207) in Lawa'i.

Explore the Outdoors

Many of Kaua'i's best attractions are free to access. Secure a good discount by hiring snorkeling or bodyboarding equipment for a longer period of time and then hit the beaches, or negotiate a spectacular path around popular walking and hiking trails.

Transportation

The county's Kaua'i Bus service provides adequate if relatively leisurely services to most parts of the island, and one-way fares are just $2/1 for adult/child tickets. A monthly pass ($40) is worth considering for extended stays.

Children Will Love...

Beaches & Swimming

Lydgate Beach Park, Wailua (p109) Safe swimming and good snorkeling in compact pools protected by a breakwater. There's also a terrific adventure playground.

Anahola Beach Park, Anahola (p131) Sheltered by palms and pine trees, this popular beach offers safe swimming in a sheltered cove.

Donovans, Po'ipu (p199) Also dubbed 'Learners,' this beach is the most popular on the island for surfing lessons.

'Anini Beach Park, North Shore (p154) Protected by a sweeping reef, this beach is a prime spot for family-friendly swimming and snorkeling. Also good for stand-up paddleboarding (SUP) adventures.

Eating & Drinking

Garden Island Chocolate, Kilauea (p147) Take a cacao-farm tour to learn about chocolate making and get to taste over 20 different flavors.

Kauai Juice Co, Kapa'a (p150) A refreshing and energizing range of cold-pressed juices, nut milks and zingy kombucha.

Pink's Creamery, Hanalei (p170) Fruity ingredients including liliko'i (passion fruit) and lychee are used for sorbet, popsicles and ice cream.

Fresh Shave, Kalaheo (p206) Using fresh and organic ingredients, Kaua'i's best shave ice is served from a vintage trailer amid Warehouse 3540's funky collection of food trucks.

Midnight Bear Breads, Hanapepe (p223) Picnic-ready baked goods, often made with organic ingredients. Say aloha! to the island's finest cinnamon rolls.

Kalalea Juice Hale, Anahola (p133) Definitely a healthy *hale* (house), with fresh coconuts, *liliko'i* lemonade, and and refreshing smoothies. Lots of organic produce too.

Active Adventures

Kaua'i Backcountry Adventures, Lihu'e (p92) Negotiate darkened tunnels and narrow irrigation channels while floating in an inner tube.

Just Live!, Lihu'e (p92) Adrenaline-fueled adventures aplenty including ziplining, rappelling, a climbing wall and a monster swing.

Kipu Ranch Adventures, Lihu'e (p93) Exciting and spectacular trips exploring the location of big Hollywood movies on an off-road ATV.

Princeville Ranch Stables, Princeville (p157) Horseback riding adventures including a 3½-hour trip to Kalihiwai Falls for a picnic and a swim.

Ancient River Kayak, Wailua (p113) Kids can help their parents paddle up the sacred Wailua River before taking a short hike to a 100ft waterfall.

Scenic Surprises

Coconut Coasters, Kapa'a (p126) Jump on a beach cruiser or tandem to explore the Eastside's coastal bike path. Kids' bikes and tow trailers are also available.

Captain Andy's Sailing Adventures, Port Allen (p199) Kick back on the 65ft *Southern Star* catamaran with great views of the Na Pali Coast. Raft trips include snorkeling and easier, family-friendly hikes.

Safari Helicopters, Lihu'e (p93) Sky-high views of the Waimea Canyon and the Na Pali Coast. A bucket list experience for traveling families.

Maha'ulepu Heritage Trail, Po'ipu (p182) Stretch the legs on this easy to moderate coastal hike running for 3½ miles each way between Shipwreck Beach and Ha'ula Beach.

Kauai Humane Society, Lihu'e (p87) Explore the island's beaches and walking trails in the company of a well-socialized shelter dog.

Region by Region

Lihu'e

The island's commercial hub of Lihu'e is the jumping-off point for many family-friendly adventures. Take part in an off-road ATV experience with Kipu Ranch Adventures (p93) or go tubing with Kaua'i Backcountry Adventures (p92). Check out Just Live! (p92) for ziplining, rappelling and climbing. If it's raining adjourn to the Kauai Escape Room (p87) or catch a movie at Kukui Grove (p99).

Kapa'a & the Eastside

For great oceanfront views beginning in Kapa'a, ride on two wheels along the Ke Ala Hele Makalae (p126) coastal path. There's safe snorkeling and swimming at Anahola Beach Park (p131) and Lydgate Beach Park (p109), and sheltered kayaking along the easy-flowing Wailua River (p107). A boat trip up the river with Smith's Motor Boat Service (p113) is hokey but fun, and a tasty chocolate-infused experience is available at Lydgate Farms (p118).

Hanalei & the North Shore

At Kilauea, you can play a lush, Hawaiian-themed mini-golf (p147) course or take a tour of a real-life chocolate factory (p147). Princeville offers ziplines, horseback riding and kayaking at Princeville Ranch (p157), and you can also visit the Magic Dragon (p161) toy store. Hanalei is all about the beach: several companies arrange surf or kayak lessons. Children will love snorkeling cruises along the Na Pali Coast, especially in bouncy Zodiac rafts; note that companies have varying minimum age requirements.

Po'ipu & the South Shore

Po'ipu is a hugely popular destination for families with young children. There's safe swimming from the golden sands along the shorefront, at Baby Beach (p193) in particular, plentiful opportunities to learn how to surf, a couple of child-friendly luau on the beach, and the amazing Makauwahi Cave (p192) to explore. Nearby Koloa has ziplines and ATV rides. For horseback riding, contact CJM Country Stables (p197).

Waimea Canyon & the Westside

At charming little Hanapepe, home to Disney's *Lilo & Stitch,* you can cross a river on a swaying footbridge, or swim safely at lovely Salt Pond Beach Park (p221). Neighboring Port Allen is the base for catamaran and snorkel cruises with experienced operators, including Holo Holo Charters (p219). Follow the highway up the rim of Waimea Canyon to see waterfalls and rainbows, and venture out on a breathtaking clifftop trail.

Good to Know

Look out for the 🚸 icon for family-friendly suggestions throughout this guide.

Changing facilities Sparse; plan for improvisation.

Diapers (nappies) The cheapest and best selection is at supermarkets in Lihu'e or on the Eastside.

Car booster seats Available to rent from car companies, but must be reserved in advance.

Strollers Available for rent from **Kauai Baby Rentals** (☑808-651-9269, 866-994-8886; www.kauaibabyrentals.com), along with many other items, including cribs and toys.

Breastfeeding Done discreetly or in private.

Eating out Many restaurants close following lunch service and reopen for dinner, so carrying a stash of snacks is a good strategy.

High chairs Available at most restaurants.

Kids' menus Common at most restaurants.

Resorts & hotels Sometimes allow children under 18 to stay for free with their parents and may provide rollaway beds or cribs.

Vacation rentals Rates often apply only to doubles. Children above a certain age might count as extra guests at a cost of $20 to $30 each per night.

B&Bs Generally less kid-friendly, as they tend to be host multiple guests in close proximity.

Playgrounds There's a very good adventure playground at Lydgate Beach Park (p109).

Useful Resources

Lonely Planet Kids (www.lonelyplanetkids.com) Loads of activities and family travel blog content.

Kaua'i Youth Directory (www.kauaiyouth directory.com) Extensive resource for youth and teen activities on the island.

Kauai.com (www.kauai.com/kauai-activities-for-kids) Online reference and booking portal.

Kids' Corner

Did You Know? ℹ️

- Buildings on Kaua'i can't be taller than a palm tree.
- 70 per cent of Kaua'i is not accessible by foot.

Say What?

good	maika'i
thank you	mahalo
flip flops	slippahs
delicious	'ono
bite-sized snacks	pupus

Have You Tried?

Poi
Gooey and gluggy steamed and mashed taro

Regions at a Glance

Sure, Kaua'i is an outdoor adventure destination. Try and deny it and the overwhelming evidence of sensational beaches, big waves, epic diving and snorkeling, and lush mountains laced with miles of hiking trails will beat your case. It stands to reason that each region will have a touch of the outdoor beauty you might expect, yet there's so much more to experience. The locally grown island cuisine veers from delicious to sensational, the farm tours are life-affirming, and there's an abundance of tempting art galleries and boutiques. Each specific corner of Kaua'i offers all of that in its own special way. On an island where local roots matter like nowhere else, it makes sense that each region offers something unique enough to keep you moving until you've sampled them all.

Lihu'e

History
Landscape
Food & Drink

A Fascinating History

Delve into the island's history amid heritage ambience at Grove Farm and Kilohana Plantation or at the fascinating Kaua'i Museum.

Hidden Beauty

An attractive beach with a working harbor framed by green hills and an age-old fishpond best seen from the back roads. Negotiate the walking trails of a clifftop golf course for spectacular views.

Kitchens & Bars

Innovative Mexican cuisine, plate lunches your Hawaiian auntie would love, and some of the best coffee and craft beer on Kaua'i.

p83

Kapa'a & the Eastside

Food & Drink
Art & Architecture
Festivals

Restaurant Row

Here you'll find creative Japanese burger joints, new-school food trucks, age-old steak houses and sushi bars, fusion Asian flavours and craft beer emporia; this is the best place to eat and drink on island.

Old Town Kapa'a

The pastel-brushed, clapboard storefronts of Old Town Kapa'a are filled with dreamy modern canvases and handblown glass sculpture.

Party Time

Hula, art, handicrafts, music and more are celebrated in fun-loving, up-for-anything Kapa'a.

p103

Hanalei & the North Shore

Surfing
Shopping
Food & Drink

Surfing Hanalei Bay

If you conjured a surf town from stardust, it would be populated by sun-bronzed barefoot, young-at-heart souls who descend on a beautiful blue bay surrounded by mountains weeping with waterfalls. Welcome to a surfers' and sun-seekers' Eden.

Retail Therapy

Hanalei's main drag offers evocative art, sensational mid-century antiques and tasteful fashion. You won't go home empty-handed.

North Shore Nourishment

A bakery for morning coffee and treats. Organic grocer and farmers markets. Wonderful tapas bar with a wine list to match. An all-time classic dive bar. You will be fed and watered very well here.

p135

Po'ipu & the South Shore

Diving
Beaches
Shopping

Beneath the Surface

Whether you wish to venture below with a tank of air or a single deep breath, this is where you can dive with snoozing sharks and dancing turtles, swim through lava tubes and listen to whale song reverberate in your brain.

Natural Highs

A windswept edge of wild sand, a beach park built for families, a sea beckoning for exploration and mind-blowing sunsets that are hard to match.

Ye Olde Sugar Town

Koloa's quaint, leafy throwback shopping district will take you back in time.

p181

Waimea Canyon & the Westside

Hiking
Camping
Boating

State Park Trails

Three state parks, two of which are in the mountains and laced with the most spectacular trails this side of the Na Pali Coast.

Nature's Lullaby

Pitch your tent deep in a red-rock jigsaw, in an elegant grove of Japanese spruce, or on Kaua'i's longest, wildest and arguably most beautiful beach.

Na Pali Coast

You must see Na Pali from the water. Catamarans, Zodiac and rigid-hull inflatables (RIBs) all depart from Port Allen and venture on half-day cruises along Kaua'i's roadless coast. Some vessels penetrate sea caves and off-load you onto virgin beaches; others serve mai tais.

p209

On the Road

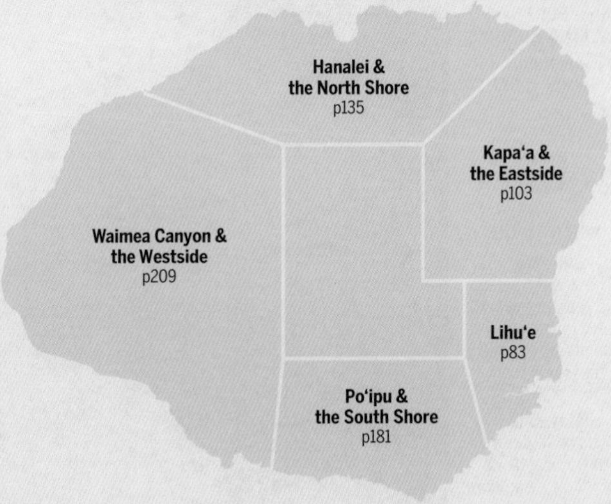

**Hanalei &
the North Shore**
p135

**Kapa'a &
the Eastside**
p103

**Waimea Canyon &
the Westside**
p209

Lihu'e
p83

**Po'ipu &
the South Shore**
p181

POPULATION
13,196

FACT
Lihu'e means 'cold chill' in the Hawaiian language. It's actually usually warm.

BEST FAMILY ACTIVITY
Kaua'i Backcountry Adventures (p92)

BEST COFFEE SHOP
Aloha Roastery (p99)

BEST WALKING BUDDIES
Kauai Humane Society (p87)

WHEN TO GO

Jun–Aug
The driest time of the year, but overall Lihu'e doesn't see as much rain as other parts of Kaua'i.

May–Sep
The best variety of tropical fruits at Lihu'e's popular farmers markets.

May–Nov
Avoids the peak cruising months of December to April.

Lihu'e shoreline
PIKAPPA51/SHUTTERSTOCK ©

Lihu‘e

L ocated near the airport and a short drive
from the attractions of both the Eastside
and the South Shore, Lihu‘e is a convenient
place to stay on the island. Established in
1849 as a thriving mill town serving nearby
sugar plantations, there's still a down-to-earth,
workaday and local ambience that's missing
in the resort areas, and the strip malls of
Lihu‘e's prosaic townscape conceal well-priced
eateries, cafes and bars.

From the array of commercial and
administrative buildings that make up Lihu‘e's
compact center, it's just a short journey down
Rice St to charming and laid-back Kalapaki
Beach, and there's good golfing and walking on
the adjacent green spaces fringing Nawiliwili
Bay. The island's most diverse shopping is on
offer at nearby malls.

The Lihu‘e area also serves as the departure
point for many helicopter excursions and
outdoor adventures like ziplining, mountain-
tubing or ATV tours.

Lihu'e Highlights

1 Kalapaki Beach (p85)
Chilling on this Kaua'i classic melds natural beauty with loads of fun for the whole family.

2 Helicopter tours (p93)
Slicing through canyons on a once-in-a-lifetime flight over the soaring cliffs of the Na Pali Coast, Mt Wai'ale'ale's rain-soaked crater and the 'Grand Canyon of the Pacific.'

3 Grove Farm (p85)
Traveling back in time in this authentically restored 19th-century sugar plantation property is like a large-scale still life.

4 Luau Kalamaku (p99)
Embracing the kitsch at the island's best luau successfully combines the traditional and the contemporary.

5 Kaua'i Museum (p85)
Learning all about the unique history of the Garden Island at this treasure trove.

History

Lihu'e's modern history is steeped in sugar. In 1849 German settlers established the first local sugarcane plantation, which struggled until the development of irrigation in 1856. Thereafter, profitability grew, attracting entrepreneur George Wilcox from Hanalei, who founded what would become the area's largest plantation, Grove Farm. Lihu'e's sugar mill (still standing south of town along Kaumuali'i Hwy) was once Kaua'i's largest.

Lihu'e's mill closed in 2000, ending more than a century of operation. But by then Lihu'e had already morphed into a very different place. The Lihu'e you see today is almost entirely a creation of the past half-century. As tourism has replaced the sugar economy, Lihu'e has had the good fortune of hosting both the island's biggest airport, and its major seaport, Nawiliwili Harbor. The result is Kaua'i's second-largest town and its commercial center. When it comes to trade, exporting sugar has now been replaced by the importation of most of the necessities of life – including sugar, if you can believe that.

◉ Sights

Grove Farm   HISTORIC SITE
(☑ 808-245-3202; http://grovefarm.org; 4050 Nawiliwili Rd; 2hr tour adult/child 5-12yr $20/10; ⊙ tours 10am & 1pm Mon, Wed & Thu, by advance reservation only) Once ranked among Kaua'i's most productive sugar companies, Grove Farm was acquired in 1864 by George Wilcox, the Hilo-born son of Protestant missionaries. The house feels suspended in time, with rocking chairs sitting still on a covered porch and untouched books lining the library's shelves. Call at least a week in advance to join a small-group tour, which includes cookies and mint tea served on the lanai (veranda). The free train ride on the second Thursday of each month is a highlight.

History buffs adore this plantation museum, but kids may grow restless.

Kalapaki Beach   BEACH
(🔄) This sandy beach and sheltered bay is tucked between a marina and the mountains. It's overlooked by the Marriott resort, which faces the bay, and by an enviable collection of houses atop a rocky ridge to the east. Its easy-access location and versatility make it popular with families, but the sandy bottom and river outlet here often make for murky water. Calmer waters toward the east are good for swimming. Swells to the west draw bodyboarders and both novice and intermediate surfers.

Kaua'i Museum   MUSEUM
(☑ 808-245-6931; www.kauaimuseum.org; 4428 Rice St; adult/child $15/free; ⊙ 9am-4pm Mon-Sat, tours 10:30am Mon-Fri) 🖋 The island's largest museum is set in two buildings – one of which was built with lava rock in 1960. Come here for a quick grounding in Kaua'i's history and ecology, and in Hawaiian history and culture in general. A smattering of Asian art is also on display. Packed with local anecdotes, the free guided tour is well worth it.

Wailua Falls   WATERFALL
(Ma'alo Rd) Made famous in the opening credits of *Fantasy Island,* these falls appear at a distance. When they are in full flow and misting the surrounding tropical foliage, it's a fantastic photo op. While officially listed as 80ft, the falls have been repeatedly measured to have a far greater drop. Heed the sign at the top that warns: 'Slippery rocks at top of falls. People have been killed.' Many have fallen while trying to scramble down the steep path beyond.

To get here from Lihu'e, follow Kuhio Hwy (Hwy 56) north. Turn left onto Ma'alo Rd (Hwy 583), which ends at the falls after 4 miles. Expect crowds and difficult parking. The alternative of seeing the falls from a helicopter is definitely the superior experience.

Ninini Beach   BEACH
Accessible from the grounds of the Ocean Course at Hōkūala (p90), this gorgeous beach is perfect for a picnic (but bad for

---

HISTORIC TRAINS

Train fans, listen up. Between the late 1880s and early 1900s, Kaua'i relied on railroads for the running of the sugar business. Workers would catch the morning train out to the fields and spend the day moving cars loaded with cut cane to the mills, or moving bags of processed sugar to the nearest ship landing. None of the trains were meant for passenger use. Grove Farm (p85) owns four of these historic plantation steam locomotives. Three have been restored to full operation, and one is fired up every second Thursday of the month for a short ride.

LIHU'E IN...

One Day

Begin with an early morning **Jurassic Falls** (p93) helicopter tour through verdant valleys. Next, adjourn to **Kalapaki Beach** (p85) for watersports, including surfing and paddleboarding, and a stroll along the harbor breakwater at nearby Nawiliwili Park. Have a relaxed lunch at **Duke's Barefoot Bar** (p98).

In the afternoon, visit the **Kilohana Plantation** (p87) to try the spiced rum at **Koloa Rum Company** (p99) and ride on the historic **Kauai Plantation Railway** (p92). Tickets can be combined with dinner and a Hawaiian luau at the popular **Luau Kalamaku** (p99). It's Lihu'e's best night-time entertainment – look forward to a compelling adventure-romance topped off by a mesmerizing fire-dance.

Two Days

Start with excellent coffee at **Aloha Roastery** (p99), before visiting **Grove Farm** (p85). Note advance reservations are needed to visit the historic former home of the Wilcox family.

For lunch, feast on local flavors at **Fish Express** (p96), before embarking on an adrenaline-fueled adventure on the tropical mountainsides near town. Try the ziplining fun offered by **Just Live!** (p92) or check out **Kaua'i Backcountry Adventures** (p92) for mountain tubing.

Relax with an afternoon beer at the **Kauai Beer Company** (p98). **Lilikoi Bar & Grill** (p98) is a fun place to dine in Harbor Mall, and it's just a short walk to **Kalapaki Beach** (p85) for a sunset stroll.

swimming because of sometimes rough water and capricious tides).

To get there, see the Lihu'e's Hidden Beaches (p88) walking tour.

Running Waters Beach   BEACH
You don't want to swim here (the surf is often too rough), but the water is pretty and there are some good tide pools nearby. Access is by a very steep trail (with no handrails) from the edge of Ocean Course at Hōkūala (p90). Follow signs that say shoreline access. There are no facilities at this compact beach.

Alekoko (Menehune)
Fishpond Overlook   VIEWPOINT
(Hulemalu Rd) This roadside overlook offers an oft-photographed vista of the Hule'ia Valley, where the Hule'ia River winds beneath a ring of verdant peaks. The river is walled off at one bend to form a 39-acre *loko wai* (freshwater fishpond). Local legend attributes construction to *menehune*, the 'little people' of Hawaiian mythology. The best time to visit is just before sunset. It's about 0.5 miles west of the entrance to Nawiliwili Harbor.

On the north side of the river lies the 240-acre **Hule'ia National Wildlife Refuge** (www.fws.gov/huleia), a breeding ground for endemic waterfowl. The refuge is closed to the public, except for guided kayaking tours.

Ninini Point Lighthouse   LIGHTHOUSE
FREE Surrounded by rugged coastal scenery, this slender whitewashed lighthouse was built in 1906. It's been automated, so alas, no lighthouse keeper. You can get here by taking the Ninini Point Trail. By car, take the road through the Hōkūala Resort, turning off near the airstrip to a dirt road headed to the point.

Kaua'i Society of Artists   GALLERY
(KSA; www.kauaisocietyofartists.org; 3-2600 Kaumuali'i Hwy, Kukui Grove Center; ⊙noon-5pm Sat-Thu, to 9pm Fri) **FREE** Island artists share gallery space at the mall and exhibit thoughtful works in oils, pencil, watercolor, sculpture materials, mixed media and photography. It's free to browse.

Lihu'e Lutheran Church   CHURCH
(www.lihuelutheranchurch.com; 4602 Ho'omana Rd; ⊙service 9am Sun) Hawaii's oldest Lutheran church is a quaint clapboard house, with an incongruously slanted floor that resembles a ship's deck and a balcony akin to a captain's bridge. The building is actually a faithful 1983 reconstruction of the 1885 original (built by German immigrants)

leveled by Hurricane Iwa. It's located just off Kaumuali'i Hwy (Hwy 50). There are Hawaiian-language classes here most Saturday afternoons at 2:30pm.

🏃 Activities

Kauai Humane Society   WALKING
(📞808-632-0610;   http://kauaihumane.org; 3-825 Kaumuali'i Hwy; donation of at least $25; ⊙11am-5pm Mon, Tue, Thu & Fri, 10am-3pm Sat & Sun; 🐾) Shelter dogs are available to accompany visitors on four- to six-hour field trips. Only well-socialized dogs are included in the program, and the Society's team can advise on which beaches and walking trails can be visited with the island's very good boys and girls.

The program is very popular, so it's advisable to arrive around 15 minutes before the start times.

Adopting cats and dogs from Kaua'i is also popular. Check out the big map at reception showing how far (even to the windswept and icy Aleutian Islands) the Society's feline and canine alumni have traveled.

Clayworks   ARTS & CRAFTS
(📞808-246-2529; www.clayworksatkilohana.com; 3-2087 Kaumuali'i Hwy, Kilohana Plantation; ⊙10am-6pm Mon-Fri, 11am-2pm Sat & Sun) This hidden pottery studio and gallery overflows with colorful vases, mugs, bowls and tiles. Potters also offer tutelage at the throwing wheel, and you'll get to take home your *raku*-fired, glazed masterpiece.

Check the website to see group and individual tuition options and call ahead to schedule a time.

Captain Terrific is the friendly feline who thinks he runs the joint.

Shoreline Trail   RUNNING
(Hōkūala Resort) This 5-mile running path encircles the golfing greens and fairways of the Ocean Course at Hōkūala (p90). It is open to the public, but you should be respectful of golfers. Along the way, you'll pass some incredible golf-course holes, and have great views of the ocean, with easy access to Ninini (p85) and Running Waters (p86) beaches.

Kauai Escape Room   LIVE CHALLENGE
(📞808-635-6957; www.escaperoomkauai.com; 4353 Rice St; per person $30-42; 🐾) Like a mystery? This escape room sets up clues for you and your team to save the world, find missing scientists or solve a Tiki Lounge mystery. It's a good diversion for families on a rainy day.

LIHU'E ACTIVITIES

GROVE FARM & KILOHANA PLANTATION

The Wilcox family were one of Kaua'i's pioneering plantation-owning families, and there are two family homes you can visit today, both situated on roughly 100-acre estates. Grove Farm Homestead is the original house of George Wilcox, and a beacon of understatement. In contrast, Gaylord Wilcox's home at Kilohana Plantation is a 16,000-sq-ft Tudor mansion, once the most expensive home on Kaua'i.

The homes also occupy opposite ends of the tourism spectrum. Grove Farm (p85) is utterly authentic, to an astonishing degree. It is as if nothing has changed in decades – because it hasn't. If you want to enter old Hawaii, then this is your first stop, and a fascinating experience.

Kilohana Plantation (📞808-245-5608; www.kilohanakauai.com; 3-2087 Kaumuali'i Hwy; admission free, attraction prices vary; ⊙10:30am-9pm Mon-Sat, to 3pm Sun) 𝗙𝗥𝗘𝗘, on the other hand, has largely been created for tourists (the Wilcox estate was never actually a plantation). Part of the original mansion has been turned into a restaurant, Gaylord's (p98). Inside the 16,000-sq-ft Tudor-style mansion, built in 1936, antique-filled rooms and ornate carpets on hardwood floors lead past cases of poi (steamed, mashed taro) pounders, koa bowls and other Hawaiiana to gallery shops.

The plantation's train is not from Hawaii, but Alaska; the tracks were laid by current employees. The enormous luau pavilion was financed by cruise line NCL, which deposits hundreds of passengers there every week. The Koloa Rum Company (p99) and Kauai Safaris (p92) both offer rum-focused activities. The end result at Kilohana is more of a well-done theme park than a historic site. Having said that, you can certainly enjoy both of these destinations equally well, it will just be for entirely different reasons.

HIKING AROUND LIHU'E

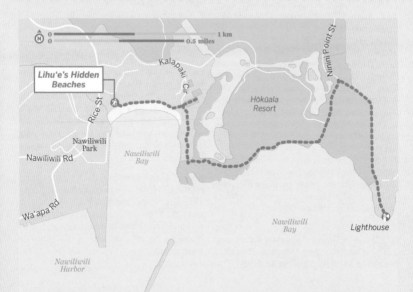

Lihu'e's Hidden Beaches

LIHU'E'S HIDDEN BEACHES

START DUKE'S

END NININI POINT LIGHTHOUSE

DURATION/DISTANCE AROUND 90 MINUTES / 2 MILES

DIFFICULTY EASY

Take an afternoon off from beach-bumming to hike to Ninini Point lighthouse on this easy walk that can be combined with a picnic lunch. Along the way, expect jets overhead, 270-degree views of Nawiliwili Bay, quiet beaches and a few glimpses of an amazing golf course. As this walk traverses beaches and across exposed lava terraces, it's only recommended at low tide and when the waters of Nawiliwili Bay are not very rough.

Start from **Duke's** (p97) on Kalapaki Beach. Walk east along the ocean for around 350yd and you'll find an elevator that takes you up to Kalapaki Circle. Turn right and follow the signs indicating 'Shoreline

Access.' Continue along Kalapaki Circle for a further 350yd, wishing you owned one of the clifftop houses with brilliant views on your right. The residential road then ends and segues into a walking path through the well-manicured expanse of the **Ocean Course at Hōkūala** (p90). Look across the fairways and lawns for a glimpse of **Kukui Point Lighthouse**. A few mornings per week – usually around 7:30am – you might see a massive cruise liner dwarfing the lighthouse as it approaches Nawiliwili Harbor.

Continue on the path for around 400yd with the sprawling and luxurious **Timbers Kauai Ocean Club & Residences** (p96) on your left. Just after the resort's spectacular infinity pool, there's another sign indicating 'Shoreline Access.' From here, a well-formed but rugged dirt track descends downhill toward the ocean. The trail is quite steep, and there are no handrails, so take your time. After rain it can also be slippery.

The capital of Kaua'i isn't the first outdoors destination most visitors associate with the island, but the treks (and beaches!) in this area are not to be missed.

The first beach you hit is **Running Waters Beach** (p86). If the waters are chill, and the tides are low, there are some incredible tide pools just before the beach. From there, hotfoot your way across lava rocks to **Ninini Beach** (p85). This is a perfect spot for an afternoon picnic, but the waters can be too rough for anything but wading. From Ninini Beach, another steep trail takes you back up onto the golf course. It's around 800yd total distance from the resort's infinity pool, down to the beaches and back uphill to the golf course again.

Stay on the assigned paths through the Ocean Course at Hōkūala. These well-marked paths (known as the Shoreline Trail) turn inland and link to Ninini Point St, which runs back south toward the ocean to segue into a final red-dirt access way to the **Ninini Point Lighthouse** (p86). This section is around 1300yd, and from Duke's you'll have walked just under 2 miles. Built in 1906, the lighthouse remains operational. Expect to see a few people living in their cars in the woods out here. Hawaiians still fish, pick *'opihi* (edible limpet) and gather *limu* (edible seaweed) nearby.

If you don't fancy the full walk and are just keen to visit the Ninini Point Lighthouse, enter at the Hōkūala Resort's main gate on Kapule Hwy around 0.5 miles south of the intersection with Ahukini Rd. Look for the Kauai Lagoons signs. Take the left fork on Ninini Point St from where it's just over 2 miles through scrubby landscape and the golf course to the lighthouse. There's no shelter from the sun, so it's best done on a bike or in a car.

Ninini Point Lighthouse (p86)

DOUG JAMES / SHUTTERSTOCK ©

LIHU'E ACTIVITIES

Lihu'e Area

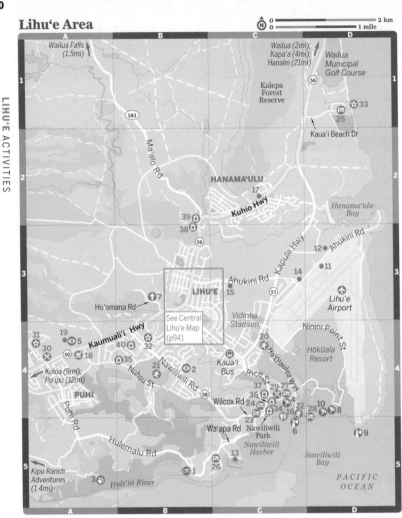

N
0 ———————— 2 km
0 ———————— 1 mile

Wailua Falls (1.5mi)

583

Ma'alo Rd

Wailua (2mi);
Kapa'a (4mi);
Hanalei (21mi)

56

Kalepa
Forest
Reserve

Wailua
Municipal
Golf Course

Kaua'i Beach Dr

25 33

HANAMA'ULU
17

Kuhio Hwy

Hanama'ulu
Bay

39
38
56

Kapule Hwy

12 Ahukini Rd
11

Ahukini Rd
15

14

51

Lihu'e
Airport

7
Ho'omana Rd

LIHU'E

See Central
Lihu'e Map
(p94)

Vidinha
Stadium

Ninini Point St

31
30
19
5
50 18
Kaumuali'i Hwy
40
32

Koloa (9mi);
Po'ipu (12mi)

35

Nuhou St

21
Nawiliwili Rd
2

Kaua'i
Bus

20

Ho'olaulea Way

Hōkūala
Resort

PUHI

Puhi Rd

Hulemalu Rd

37 29 27
36 34 4
24 16 28 10 8
23 6 7 9
Wilcox Rd

Rice St

Wa'apa Rd   Nawiliwili
Park

Nawiliwili
Harbor

Nawiliwili
Bay

PACIFIC
OCEAN

Kipu Ranch
Adventures
(1.4mi)

1
3
26
13

Hule'ia River

Golf

Ocean Course at Hōkūala   GOLF
(☎808-241-6000; www.golfhokuala.com; 3351 Ho'Olaulea Way; green fees incl cart $150-219) Designed by Jack Nicklaus, the 18-hole, par-72 Ocean Course at Hōkūala has to be one of the most beautiful golf courses in the world. There are plenty of oceanfront holes.

Book tee times up to 90 days in advance. Club and shoe rentals available. Adjacent to the course is the stunning new Timbers Kauai Ocean Club & Residences (p96).

Puakea Golf Course   GOLF
(☎808-245-8756; www.puakeagolf.com; 4150 Nuhou St; green fees incl cart $64-104) The lush cliffs of Mt Ha'upu serve as a backdrop to this Robin Nelson–designed public course. Club rental is available. Book tee times up to three months ahead. Save big after 3pm.

Watersports

Kalapaki Beach Surfing   SURFING
It's an easy 50yd paddle out to the reef, and there's no pounding shore break to get through. Most go right for a mellow,

Lihu'e Area

predictable wave, but there are more aggressive lefts, too. This is one of the most popular stand-up paddleboarding (SUP) breaks around thanks to the chill waves. Bodyboarders work the river mouth.

Kauai Beach Boys WATERSPORTS
(☏808-246-6333; https://kauaibeachboys.com; 3610 Rice St; 90min surfing or SUP lessons from $79, surfboard rental per hr/day $15/35, SUP rental per hr/day $27/70; ☺8am-6pm; ☝) On Kalapaki Beach, this concession rents snorkel gear, kayaks, surfboards and SUPs at reasonable prices, with 90-minute surfing and SUP lessons given several times daily. Call ahead for sailing lessons or to book a sailboat cruise on the bay. Exciting outrigger-canoe experiences (per person $49) negotiating the Kalapaki Bay surf are also available.

Kauai Ohana YMCA SWIMMING
(☏808-246-9090; www.ymcaofkauai.org; 4477 Nuhou St; day passes member/nonmember $5/10; ☺5:30-9am & 11am-7pm Mon-Fri, 10am-5:30pm Sat & Sun; ☝) Lap swimmers, get your fix at this open-air, Olympic-sized pool. A small weights/cardio workout room is also available, but towels and padlocks for lockers aren't provided. US mainland YMCA members should bring their card from home.

Fishing
Captain Don's Sportfishing FISHING
(☏808-639-3012; http://captaindonsfishing.com; Nawiliwili Small Boat Harbor, 2494 Niumalu Rd; 4/6hr shared charters per person $150/225, half-/full-day private charters for up to 6 passengers from $750/1250; ☺by reservation only; ☝) One of

LIHU'E FOR CHILDREN

Kalapaki Beach (p85) Set in an idyllic cove crowned by a lighthouse, this is a great beach for relaxing and also good for beginner surfers.

Kauai Plantation Railway (p92) Chug along on this vintage train that takes you through historic orchards, gardens and more.

Kaua'i Backcountry Adventures (p92) Go for the tubing tour that takes you through a sugar plantation's aqueducts.

Captain Don's Sportfishing (p91) Head out for a day trip to snorkel or whale-watch in the South Shore waters.

Kauai Humane Society (p87) Explore the island with a friendly shelter dog for the afternoon.

the many fishing charters departing from Nawiliwili Small Boat Harbor, Captain Don's gives guests creative freedom to design their own trip (fishing, whale-watching, snorkeling, a Na Pali Coast cruise) on the 39ft *Happy Ryder*. Captain Don has decades of experience on Kaua'i's waters.

State of Hawai'i Division of Aquatic Resources FISHING
(808-274-3344; http://dlnr.hawaii.gov/dar; 3060 Eiwa St, Room 306) Stop here for fishing information. There is no marine recreational fishing license in Kaua'i. Some places do prohibit fishing. This is also the place to get permits and info on collecting fish for aquariums back home.

Tours

Kauai Plantation Railway RAIL
(808-245-7245; www.kilohanakauai.com; 3-2087 Kaumuali'i Hwy, Kilohana Plantation; adult/child 3-12yr 40min ride $19/14, 4hr ride & walking tour $78.50/60; ☉ hourly departures 10am-2pm, guided tours 9:30am Mon-Fri;) If you crave a bit of historical and agricultural education, hop on this vintage-style train for a 40-minute scenic ride through a working plantation. The four-hour train and walking tour combo gets you into the fields and orchards, where you can pluck tropical fruit straight from the tree and feed the sheep, goats and wild pigs. Luau packages are available.

Kauai Safaris FOOD & DRINK
(808-652-4707; www.kauaisafaris.com; 3-2087 Kaumuali'i Hwy, Kilohana Plantation; tours $55; ☉ tours 11am, 1:30pm & 4:30pm) Journey around Kilohana Plantation in an open-sided safari vehicle for a couple of hours. Highlights include tasting Koloa Rum, a brace of robust cocktails, and saying 'Aloha!' to Kilohana's menagerie of animals, including 70 wild pigs. Safari fans need to be at least 21 years old.

Adventure Tours

Just Live! ADVENTURE
(808-482-1295; www.ziplinetourskauai.com; 3416 Rice St, Anchor Cove Shopping Center; zipline tours $79-120; ☉ tours daily, by reservation only) This outfit stands above the rest – literally – by offering Kaua'i's only canopy-based zipping, meaning you never touch ground after your first zip. The 3½-hour tour includes seven ziplines and four bridge crossings, or there's a scaled-down 'Wikiwiki' zip tour. The 'Eco-Adventure' adds a climbing wall, a 100ft rappelling tower and a heart-stopping monster swing.

Participants must be at least nine years old and weigh between 70lb and 250lb.

Da Life Outdoors ADVENTURE
(808-246-6333; www.dalifeoutdoors.com; 3500 Rice St; rappelling tours incl lunch $185; ☉ 8am Mon-Wed & Sat) Jump on a four-hour tour into Hule'ia National Wildlife Refuge (p86), where you'll learn how to wet-rappel down the 30ft Bamboo Falls, followed by the towering 60ft Papakolea Falls, and then take a lazy swim followed by a picnic lunch (minimum age 12 years). Two-hour hikes to the falls are also on offer at 2:45pm on Tuesdays and Thursdays (adult/child $49/39).

Kaua'i Backcountry Adventures ADVENTURE
(808-245-2506; www.kauaibackcountry.com; 3-4131 Kuhio Hwy; 3hr tubing/zipline tours incl lunch $116/125; ☉ tours hourly 8am-2pm, by reservation only;) This 3½-hour zipline tour features seven lines, which are elevated as high as 200ft above ground and run as far as 900ft (almost three football fields). Afterward, you can refuel with a picnic lunch at the swimming pond. The family-friendly tubing tour (for ages five and up) floats through an old sugar plantation's ditch-and-tunnel irrigation system.

Zipliners must be at least 12 years old and weigh between 100lb and 250lb.

Kipu Ranch Adventures ADVENTURE
(☑ 808-246-9288; www.kiputours.com; 235 Kipu Rd; tours adult/child from $104/49; ☺ tours daily, by reservation only; ♿) This outfit's most popular all-terrain-vehicle (ATV) tour takes you on a three-hour scenic journey around a private ranch that was used for filming *Raiders of the Lost Ark* and *The Descendants*. The four-hour tour includes a short hike to a waterfall for swimming and a picnic lunch. Expect loads of muddy-red-dirt fun if it's been raining.

Outfitters Kauai ADVENTURE
(☑ 808-742-9667, 888-742-9887; www.outfitters kauai.com; 230 Kipu Rd; zipline tours adult/child 7-14yr from $129/119, 5hr SUP tours incl lunch adult/child 12-14yr $129/99; ☺ by reservation only; ♿) Multi-activity tours offered by Outfitters Kauai combine tandem ziplines with aerial bridges, hiking, and kayaking the Huleʻia River; the weight limit for zipliners is 250lb. Experienced head-first Superman-style, the FlyLine zipline is the longest on the island. Unique SUP river tours include short hikes, swimming, a zipline and a motorized canoe ride back upstream.

Also consider doing a whale-watching sea kayak or Na Pali Coast kayak. On two wheels there's exciting downhill biking at Waimea Canyon. Main check-in location for tours is Outfitters' Poʻipu office, but dependent on activity, check-in is also possible at Kipu Ranch and the Kayak Shack at the Nawiliwili Small Boat Harbor near Lihuʻe. Check when you book.

Scenic Flights

Most 'flightseeing' tours depart from Lihuʻe Airport. Book ahead online for major discounts.

★ **AirVentures Hawaii** SCENIC FLIGHTS
(☑ 808-651-0679; https://kauaiairtour.com; 3651 Ahukini Rd, Lihuʻe Airport; 1hr tours $235; ☺ tours Mon-Fri, by reservation only) When it comes to fixed-wing aircraft, there's nothing like an open-cockpit biplane. This outfit's gorgeous YMF-5 Super can seat two people up front. Visibility may not be the same as by helicopter, but the roar of the engine and the wind makes for a memorable experience. You even get to don an old-fashioned cloth aviator's hat and goggles.

Island Helicopters SCENIC FLIGHTS
(☑ 808-245-8588, 800-829-8588; www.island helicopters.com; Ahukini Rd, Lihuʻe airpoirt;

LIHUʻE TOURS

HOW TO SPEND RAINY DAYS IN LIHUʻE

Kauaʻi Museum (p85) The best museum on the island offers well-curated exhibits.

Kipu Ranch Adventures (p93) Just as much (maybe even more) rollicking offroad ATV fun on a rainy, muddy day.

Kauaʻi Backcountry Adventures (p92) Ride an inner tube down the irrigation system of a former sugar plantation. You're going to get wet anyway.

Kukui Grove Cinema 4 (p99) Escape with a movie in this throwback Cineplex near the island's main shopping mall.

Clayworks (p87) Indulge your arty and crafty side with pottery classes.

50/75min tours $297/385) Pilots with this long-running helicopter tour company have perfect safety records, and they only fly AStar helicopters, equipped with floor-to-ceiling windows. The 'Jurassic Falls' tour includes an exclusive 25-minute landing at 350ft-high Manawaiopuna Falls, hidden deep in Hanapepe Valley.

Blue Hawaiian Helicopters SCENIC FLIGHTS
(☑ 808-245-5800, 800-745-2583; www.blue hawaiian.com/kauai/tours; 3651 Ahukini Rd; 50min tours from $229) Flies high-end Eco-Star choppers, offering more space, glass and comfort, with less noise due to quiet, enclosed tail rotors. Grab a souvenir DVD of your flight for an extra $25.

Safari Helicopters SCENIC FLIGHTS
(☑ 800-326-3356, 808-246-0136; www.safari helicopters.com; 3225 Akahi St; 60/90min tours $239/304) Flies AStar helicopters on the standard circle-island tour. The longer 'ecotour' includes a 40-minute stop at Robinson Ranch's wildlife refuge overlooking Olokele Canyon.

Jack Harter Helicopters SCENIC FLIGHTS
(☑ 808-245-3774, 888-245-2001; www.helicopters-kauai.com; 4231 Ahukini Rd; 60/90min tours $289/434) This pioneering outfit (operating since 1962) offers a standard enclosed, six-passenger AStar or a doors-off, four-passenger Hughes 500 helicopter. Longer doors-on tours are also offered.

Central Lihu'e

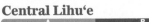

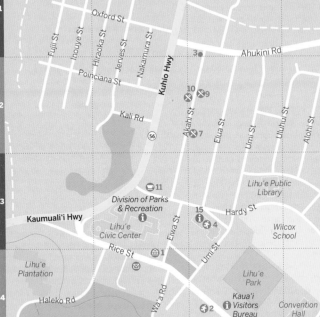

Mauna Loa Helicopters   SCENIC FLIGHTS

(☎808-245-7500; https://maunaloahelicopter tours.com; 3501 Rice St, Harbor Mall; 1hr tours from $325) Highly qualified pilots don't skimp on full 60-minute private tours for up to three passengers. Small groups allow for more-personalized interaction between pilot and passengers. You can choose to have the doors on or off, and all seats are window seats.

✨ Festivals & Events

For an up-to-date, comprehensive calendar of events, check www.kauaifestivals.com.

May Day Lei Contest   CULTURAL

(www.kauaimuseum.org; 4428 Rice St, Kaua'i Museum; ⏱May; 👪) Established in 1981, the Kaua'i Museum's annual lei contest in early May brings out legendary floral art, with do-it-yourself workshops, live music and an auction.

Fourth of July
Concert in the Sky   CULTURAL

(www.kauaihospice.org/kauai-concert-in-the-sky; Hoolako St, Vidinha Stadium; adult/child $15/7; ⏱Jul 4; 👪) Enjoy island food, live entertainment and the grand finale fireworks show set to music at Vidinha Stadium.

Central Lihu'e

Kaua'i County Farm Bureau Fair   FAIR
(www.kauaifarmfair.org; Hoolako St, Vidinha Stadium; adult/child $6/3; ⊙mid-Aug; ⊕) Old-fashioned family fun at Vidinha Stadium. The fair brings carnival rides and games, livestock shows, a petting zoo, hula performances and lots of local food.

Kaua'i Mokihana
Festival Hula Competition   CULTURAL, DANCE
(☎ 808-651-1868; www.maliefoundation.org; 4331 Kaua'i Beach Dr, Kaua'i Beach Resort & Spa; ⊙Sep) Three days of serious hula competitions are staged at the Kaua'i Beach Resort & Spa in mid- to late September. Both *hula kahiko* (ancient) and *hula 'auana* (modern) styles enchant.

Kaua'i Folk Festival   MUSIC
(www.kauaifolkfestival.com; 4050 Nawiliwili Rd, Grove Farm; 1/2 days $60/100; ⊙late Sep) Celebrating two days of folk, country, Hawaiian and Americana music, this laid-back festival combining concerts and workshops was first held in 2019. Look forward to good local foods too.

Hawaiian Slack
Key Guitar Festival   MUSIC
(⊙mid- or late Nov) FREE This opportunity to see master slack key guitarists is not to be missed. In 2019, the one-day event was staged at the Kaua'i Marriott.

Lights on Rice Parade   PARADE
(http://lightsonrice.org; ⊙Dec; ⊕) FREE A charming parade of illuminated floats takes over Rice St on the first Friday evening in December.

🛏 Sleeping

Accommodations range from the luxurious oceanfront Timbers Kauai Ocean Club & Residences to no-frills motels in the town center.

Kaua'i Palms Hotel   MOTEL $
(☎ 808-246-0908; www.kauaipalmshotel.com; 2931 Kalena St; r with/without air-con $105/95; ⊙office 7am-9pm; P@🐾) This is the most appealing motel in central Lihu'e. Inside a raggedy two-story building, the 28 rooms are small but tidy, with refrigerators and cable TV. Air-con and kitchenettes cost extra, but are definitely a necessity with a lack of ocean breezes. It's at the end of an industrial road downtown.

Kaua'i Beach Resort & Spa   RESORT $$
(☎ 866-536-7976, 808-954-7419; www.kauaibeach resorthawaii.com; 4331 Kaua'i Beach Dr; r from $159; P❄🐾🏊) Set beside its own thin ribbon of sand (no swimming), this sprawling resort sports 350 boutique-on-a-budget rooms, four pools complete with waterfalls, nightly lounge entertainment and a full-service spa. You'll pay more for a room with a view. Just north of town and the airport, it's a little isolated, but the best midrange-budget bet in the Lihu'e area.

Banyan Harbor   CONDO $$
(☎ 808-245-7333; www.vacation-kauai.com; 3411 Wilcox Rd; apt from $200; P❄🐾🏊) Sprawling Banyan Harbor is one of the island's biggest condominium complexes, but it's also a great-value accommodations option with apartments featuring full kitchens, washing machines and dryers, and spacious bedrooms. Tennis courts, barbecue facilities

and a heated swimming pool all combine to make it a great family option. Kalapaki Beach and good restaurants are a short stroll away.

Kaua'i Inn
HOTEL **$$**

(☎808-245-9000, 800-808-2330; www.kauai-inn. com; 2430 Hulemalu Rd; r from $189; P🅿️❄️@ 🛜♿) This large inn, just west of the harbor, offers a good-value home base away from traffic and crowds. The 48 plain rooms each have a refrigerator and microwave. Not all rooms come with air-con, so ask ahead if this is important.

Ground-floor rooms come with back porches; those on the 2nd floor are larger but sans lanai. Ask for a room with a mountain view.

Garden Island Inn
HOTEL **$$**

(☎800-648-0154, 808-245-7227; http://garden islandinn.com; 3445 Wilcox Rd; r from $60; P🅿️❄️ 🛜♿) This slightly run-down two-story hotel across the street from Kalapaki Beach holds its own for value and friendliness. Rooms are bright but kitschy, with murals splashed on the walls, tropical bamboo and wood furnishings, and kitchenettes. Free beach gear and DVDs to borrow.

★Timbers Kauai
Ocean Club & Residences
RESORT **$$$**

(☎808-320-7400; www.timberskauai.com; 3770 Ala'oli Way; apt from $650; P🅿️❄️🛜♿) The island's newest and most luxurious resort hugs ocean cliffs and offers stellar views from an infinity pool. Fresh, organic produce for the resort's excellent Hualani's restaurant is gathered from an on-site farm (a repurposed part of the adjacent Ocean Course at Hōkūala), while the spa and massage services are some of the best on the island.

Kaua'i Marriott
RESORT **$$$**

(☎800-220-2925, 808-245-5050; www.marriott. com; 3610 Rice St; r from $249; P🅿️❄️@🛜♿) Anyone looking for a classic Hawaii resort experience won't be disappointed here. The hotel has Kalapaki Beach, the island's liveliest oceanfront restaurant and a gargantuan pool for all-day entertainment. Hawaiian artifacts are displayed along the gleaming corridors.

Room decor and amenities are contemporary chain-hotel standard. Oceanfront units are worth it for the lanai views. Ask for a top-floor room for better views.

🍴 Eating

Eating tends toward local *grinds* – and who would want to miss that? – but there are a handful of higher-end tourist-focused restaurants near Kalapaki Beach as well.

★Kaua'i Community Market
MARKET **$**

(☎808-855-5429; www.kauaicommunitymarket. org; 3-1901 Kaumuali'i Hwy, Kauai Community College; snacks from $5; ⏰9:30am-1pm Sat; 🌱♿🚗) 🍃 One of the island's biggest and best farmers markets, in partnership with the Kaua'i County Farm Bureau, brings a bonanza of locally grown, often organic fruits and vegetables, free-range eggs and local dairy cheeses, island-grown coffee and flowers, hand-harvested honey and sea salts, Hawaiian plate lunches and poi (steamed, mashed taro), and fresh smoothies, juices, popsicles and baked goods. Don't miss it!

Kawaii Kokoro
BAKERY **$**

(☎808-320-8198; www.facebook.com/kawaii kokoro808; 3184 Akahi St; snacks from $1; ⏰6:30am-5pm Tue-Fri, from 7am Sat, from 8am Sun; P🅿️) Delicious coconut macaroons for less than a dollar are a steal at this Japanese-influenced bakery and patisserie. Also good are the cheesecakes, coconut-infused crème brûlée and matcha and green-tea profiteroles. Pop in and pick up a few sweet treats to top off a lazy beach picnic.

Fish Express
SEAFOOD **$**

(☎808-245-9918; 3343 Kuhio Hwy; mains $8-13; ⏰10am-6pm Mon-Sat, grill until 3pm; P🅿️) Fish lovers, this is almost a no-brainer. Order chilled deli items, from fresh ahi (yellowfin tuna) *poke* (cubed raw fish mixed with *shōyu*, sesame oil, salt, chili pepper, *'inamona* or other condiments) to green seaweed salad, or try a plate lunch of blackened ahi with guava-basil sauce or a gourmet *bentō* (Japanese-style box lunch). Get there early before the best *poke* runs out.

Kikuchi's
FOOD TRUCK **$**

(☎808-855-5789; 3501 Rice St; snacks $10-11; ⏰11am-4pm Wed-Sat) Hours are limited – often linked to when cruise ships are arriving at the nearby harbor – but Kikuchi's is always worth checking out for delicious ahi wraps and steamed buns crammed with pulled pork. Look for the bright-red truck.

Greenery
CAFE **$**

(☎808-246-4567; www.thegreenerycafe.com; 3146 Akahi St; mains $11-15; ⏰10:30am-3:30pm Mon-Fri; P🅿️🌱🚗) 🍃 Organic and vegetarian

THE WILCOX LEGACY

From Wilcox Memorial Hospital to Gaylord's restaurant, the face of Lihu'e is still deeply intertwined with the Wilcox family and its famous enterprise, Grove Farm Company.

The story begins in the latter part of the 19th century, when the family patriarch, George Wilcox of Hanalei, moved to Lihu'e and founded Grove Farm, just as the sugar business was beginning its long ascent. Wilcox was an innovative entrepreneur who developed new means of irrigation, planting and cultivation. He also became a power player in Hawaii politics, a community leader and a philanthropist. During his long stewardship, from 1870 to 1933, Grove Farm Company flourished. It continued to grow after his nephew Gaylord Wilcox took over the reins. By 1950, the Wilcox family was one of Kaua'i's largest landowners, with approximately 22,000 acres. The family was also highly influential in many areas of local life, including pioneering a home ownership program for workers, and donating the land for Kaua'i Community College. In 1974, sugar operations ceased, and cane lands were leased to neighboring plantations. Grove Farm Company then diversified into land development, management and licensing.

In 2001 Grove Farm Company was sold to Steve Case, of AOL fame. He has since purchased another 18,000 acres, making the company nearly twice as large as it was at the height of the sugar business. Interestingly, Case's father once worked as an accountant for Grove Farm Company.

flavors shine at this breezy garden cafe tucked away in a quiet residential street. Chicken or vegetarian wraps are served with brown rice and quinoa salads, and soul-food plates with collard greens, yams and corn bread are a hearty and filling lunch staple. Smoothies are equally healthy with the addition of kale, turmeric, ginger and honey.

Hamura Saimin NOODLES $
(☑808-245-3271; 2956 Kress St; noodles $7-11; ☺10am-10:30pm Mon-Thu, to midnight Fri & Sat, to 9:30pm Sun; ☻) An island institution, Hamura's is a hole-in-the-wall specializing in homemade saimin (local-style noodle soup). At lunchtime, expect crowds slurping noodles elbow-to-elbow at retro, U-shaped lunch counters. Save room for the other (and even more beloved) specialty, *liliko'i* (passion fruit) chiffon pie.

Tip Top Cafe DINER $
(☑808-245-2333; www.tiptop-motel.com; 3173 Akahi St; mains $6-13; ☺6:30am-2pm Tue-Sun) The austere brown-shuttered building might give you pause, but inside this retro diner teems with locals filling up on good, ol'-fashioned eats. The main draws are its famous banana-macadamia-nut pancakes, oxtail soup and *loco moco* (rice, fried egg and hamburger patty topped with gravy or other condiments)

Kukui Grove Center
Farmers Market MARKET $
(www.kukuigrovecenter.com; 3-2600 Kaumuali'i Hwy, Kukui Grove Center; snacks from $5; ☺3pm

Mon; ☑♨☺) ✐ On the garden side of the Kmart parking lot. Smaller and more focused than other island farmers markets, but still worth a visit.

Times Supermarket SUPERMARKET $
(www.timessupermarkets.com; 3-2600 Kaumuali'i Hwy, Kukui Grove Center; drinks & snacks from $5; ☺6am-11pm; ℗) Swing by this grocery store, which sells to-go salads, sandwiches, plate lunches and sushi. It has a smoothie bar and a *poke* station with 30 varieties made fresh daily.

Duke's FUSION $$
(☑808-246-9599; www.dukeskauai.com; 3610 Rice St, Kaua'i Marriott; bar mains $12-20, restaurant mains $28-32; ☺restaurant 5-10pm, bar from 11am) You won't find an evening spot more fun and lively than Duke's, which offers a classic view of Kalapaki Beach. The steak-and-seafood menu is none too innovative, but fish tacos served in the downstairs Barefoot Bar are a fave, especially on cheaper 'Taco Tuesdays.'

Hula Pie, a mound of macadamia-nut ice cream in a chocolate-cookie crust, satisfies a touristy crowd. Complimentary valet parking.

Verde MEXICAN $$
(☑808-320-7088; www.verdehawaii.com; 4454 Nuhou St, Hokulei Village; mains $12-16; ☺11am-9pm Mon-Thu, 7am-11pm Fri-Sun; ☻) Chef Joshua Stevens' Mexican, New Mexican and California-style cooking might put whatever style of tacos you've been eating

THE DUKE

When you're kicking back with your tropical drink at Duke's Barefoot Bar (p98), you may just wonder – who was Duke anyway?

Duke Paoa Kahinu Mokoe Hulikohola Kahanamoku (1890–1968) is one of Hawaii's most famous sons. In his richly varied life, he was a five-time Olympic medalist in swimming, a Hollywood actor (his film and TV credits include *Mister Roberts*), the sheriff of Honolulu for almost 30 years and the first famous beach boy, as well as being the man credited with spreading surfing to Australia. Duke was also a legitimate hero: in 1925, he used his surfboard to effect the incredible rescue of eight men from a fishing vessel that had capsized in heavy surf off Newport Beach, California; 17 others died. Duke was not really royalty, however, his name notwithstanding. He was named after his father, who was himself named after the Duke of Edinburgh, Scotland. Over the years, however, he earned many honorary titles, such as 'the Father of Surfing.'

For all his successes and international travels, Duke never forgot where he came from. He was always a traditional Hawaiian, speaking the language as much as he could, even preferring a long-board carved from koa wood. When he died of a heart attack in 1968, at the age of 77, his ashes were scattered at sea in front of Waikiki Beach.

back home to shame, at this new location on the outskirts of Lihu'e. Be sure to save room for the sopaipillas drizzled with honey or the cinnamon-churro fries for dessert. The cocktails are excellent too, and weekend brunch is very popular.

Lilikoi Bar & Grill HAWAIIAN $$
(📞 808-320-3066; www.lilikoibarandgrill.com; 3501 Rice St, Harbor Mall; mains $15-25; ⏱ 7am-9pm Mon-Fri, 8am-9pm Sat & Sun) Savvy bar staff and interesting spins on local dishes, including *poke* with kimchi and delicious coconut curry shrimp, make this breezy upstairs spot the best of the dining scene in Lihu'e's Harbor Mall. Pull a chair up to the bar and kick things off with a robust cocktail or a craft brew from the well-curated beer taps.

Pietro's PIZZA $$
(📞 808-245-2266; https://pietroskauai.com; 3501 Rice St, Harbor Mall; pizzas $18-28; ⏱ 11am-9pm Mon-Sat) This versatile spot in Harbor Mall serves takeout New York–style pizza by the slice from 11am to 9pm. From 5pm, authentic Neapolitan pizza is available for dine-in guests. In the ultimate cross-cultural mash-up, choose between the Don Corleone or the Don Ho. Pietro's pizza has been certified as authentic by the Naples, Italy-based Associazione Verace Pizza Napoletana.

Gaylord's HAWAIIAN $$$
(📞 808-245-9593; www.kilohanakauai.com; 3-2087 Kaumuali'i Hwy, Kilohana Plantation; mains lunch $15-19, dinner $21-37, Sun brunch buffet adult/child 5-12yr $32/16; ⏱ 11am-2:30pm & 5-9pm Mon-Sat, 9am-2pm Sun; 🅿) There is no doubt that the

historic Wilcox home at Kilohana Plantation provides a handsome setting, particularly on the veranda. You can daydream amid manicured lawns and white tablecloths in an open-air dining room, as you fork into a local field-greens salad, sesame-seared ahi with tempura avocado or banana-coconut cream pie. Sunday's brunch buffet has a Bloody Mary bar. Make reservations.

🍷 Drinking & Nightlife

There are a handful of bars (mostly sports bars) near Kalapaki Beach that cater to the cruise-ship set. The resorts also have bars.

★ Duke's Barefoot Bar BAR
(www.dukeskauai.com; 3610 Rice St, Kaua'i Marriott; ⏱ 11am-11pm) For a convivial, Waikiki-style tropical bar with live music every night, hurry and grab a beachside table before the nonstop evening queue. Happy hour from 4pm to 6pm daily. If you're thinking of an archetypal – and hugely enjoyable – island watering hole, look no further.

★ Kauai Beer Company BREWERY
(📞 808-245-2337; http://kauaibeer.com; 4265 Rice St; ⏱ 11am-10pm) Everyone kicks back with a hoppy Kaua'IPA, a refreshing Lihu'e Lager or a knock-your-socks-off Sleeping Giant Barley Wine at Lihu'e's beloved craft brewery. Regular seasonal brews attract loyal locals, while food trucks usually rock up on Thursday nights – check Instagram to see who's scheduled. KBC's own hearty menu stretches from poutine and pulled pork to tacos and BBQ ribs.

Aloha Roastery COFFEE
(☑808-651-4514; www.aloharoastery.com; 3-3100 Kuhio Hwy, Lihu'e Town Center; ☺6am-5pm Mon-Sat) The hippest coffee shop on the island combines cool surf-meets-Scandi decor with locally roasted beans and excellent homestyle baking that is also prepared on-site. Combine a double-shot latte with a freshly baked chocolate brioche and don't be surprised if you return the following day. And the next.

Hā Coffee Bar CAFE
(☑808-631-9241; www.hacoffeebar.com; 4180 Rice St; ☺6:30am-5pm Mon-Sat; 🛜) A popular Lihu'e haunt, this airy, high-ceilinged cafe is enlivened by retro travel prints and local art hanging on the walls. Maple-cinnamon rolls, bagels and healthy breakfast bowls round out the menu, and the big shared tables are an ideal spot to catch up on anything you need to accomplish on your electronic device of choice.

☆ Entertainment

Occasional free concerts and cultural expos are offered throughout the year. A highlight for many visitors is Kilohana Plantation's enthralling and colorful luau.

★Luau Kalamaku LUAU
(☑877-622-1780; http://luaukalamaku.com; 3-2087 Kaumuali'i Hwy, Kilohana Plantation; adult/child 12-16yr/child 5-11yr $120/80/46; ☺5-8:30pm Tue & Fri; ⓔ) Skip the same-old commercial luau and catch this dinner theater-in-the-round with a dash of Cirque du Soleil (think dancers, flashy leotards and pyrotechnics) thrown in. The stage play about one family's epic voyage to Hawaii features hula and Tahitian dancing, and show-stopping, nail-biting Samoan fire dancing. The buffet dinner is above average, despite the audience size (maximum 1000 people).

Shutters LIVE MUSIC
(4331 Kaua'i Beach Dr, Kaua'i Beach Resort & Spa; ☺5-11pm) Head over to the Kaua'i Beach Resort & Spa for live music nightly. The terrace surroundings are elegant and the entertainment kicks off around 7pm, with happy hour on food and drinks from 5pm to 6:30pm.

Kaua'i Concert Association LIVE MUSIC
(☑808-245-7464; www.kauai-concert.org; tickets from $30) Stages classical, jazz and world-music concerts at the **Kaua'i Community College (KCC) Performing Arts Center** (☑808-245-8311; www.kauai.hawaii.edu/performing-arts-center; 3-1901 Kaumuali'i Hwy), where past performers include Berklee College of Music and the Harlem String Quartet.

Kukui Grove Cinema 4 CINEMA
(☑808-245-5055; www.kukuigrovecinema.com; 4368 Kukui Grove St; tickets $7-10; ⓔ) Standard fourplex showing mainstream first-run Hollywood movies.

🛍 Shopping

Lihu'e's biggest mall is the aging, open-air **Kukui Grove Center** (☑808-245-7784; www.kukuigrovecenter.com; 3-2600 Kaumuali'i Hwy; ☺9:30am-7pm Mon-Thu & Sat, to 9pm Fri, 10am-6pm Sun; 🛜), home to department stores, sporting-goods and electronics shops, banks and more. Near Nawiliwili Harbor, the busy, low-slung **Anchor Cove Shopping Center** (3416 Rice St) and emptier two-story **Harbor Mall** (☑808-245-6255; www.harbormall.net; 3501 Rice St) draw mainly tourists from cruise ships and the nearby Marriott.

Koloa Rum Company DRINKS
(☑808-246-8900; www.koloarum.com; 3-2087 Kaumuali'i Hwy, Kilohana Plantation; ☺store 9:30am-5pm Mon, Wed & Sat, to 9pm Tue & Fri, to 6:30pm Thu, to 3pm Sun, tasting room 10am-3:30pm Mon, Wed & Sat, to 7:30pm Tue & Fri, to 5pm Thu, to 2pm Sun) Kaua'i's own rum label is a relatively new brand, which means it doesn't have a fine aged rum yet, but its dark and spiced versions win awards. Learn how to mix a classic mai tai during a free rum tasting, starting every 30 minutes daily. Combine cocktails and rum tasting with a tour of Kilohana Plantation on a Kauai Safari (p92).

Koa Store GIFTS & SOUVENIRS
(☑808-245-4871, 800-838-9264; www.thekoastore.com; 3-3601 Kuhio Hwy; ☺10am-6pm Mon-Sat, to 5pm Sun) 🌿 Here you'll find affordable and functional pieces made from koa wood, such as picture frames and jewelry boxes. Many items come in three grades, from the basic straight-grain koa to premium 'curly' koa. All items offered for sale are genuine – they're not the cheap fakes sold at tourist traps.

Edith King Wilcox Gift Shop & Bookstore GIFTS & SOUVENIRS
(☑808-246-2470; www.kauaimuseum.org; Kaua'i Museum, 4428 Rice St; ☺9am-4pm Mon-Sat) 🌿 The Kaua'i Museum's gem of a gift shop carries a variety of genuine Hawaiian crafts,

LIHU'E ENTERTAINMENT

such as Ni'ihau shell jewelry, koa woodwork and *lauhala* (a type of traditional Hawaiian leaf weaving) hats, along with collectible contemporary artworks and plenty of Hawaiiana books. Enter the shop, free of charge, through the museum lobby.

Da Life   SPORTS & OUTDOORS
(☑ 808-246-6333; www.dalifeoutdoorgear.com; 3500 Rice St; ⊙ 9am-5pm Mon-Sat, to 4pm Sun; 🖮) This outdoor outfitter and booking agent's retail shop is stuffed with sports gear for all manner of land and sea adventures on Kaua'i. If you forgot to pack it, Da Life probably stocks it.

Kapaia Stitchery   ARTS & CRAFTS
(www.kapaia-stitchery.com; 3-3551 Kuhio Hwy; ⊙ 9am-5pm Mon-Fri, to 4pm Sat) A quilter's heaven, this longtime shop features countless tropical-print cotton fabrics, plus island-made patterns and kits. Also stop here for handmade gifts and apparel, including children's clothing and aloha shirts.

Costco   FOOD
(www.costco.com; 4300 Nuhou St; ⊙ 10am-8:30pm Mon-Fri, 9:30am-6pm Sat, 10am-6pm Sun) This members-only food and goods warehouse is a good spot to stock up if you plan on self-catering.

Join in-store or online ($60) to take advantage of discounts at all Costco stores around the world.

Longs Drugs   SOUVENIRS, FOOD
(☑808-245-8871; www.cvs.com; 3-2600 Kaumuali'i Hwy, Kukui Grove Center; ⊙ 7am-10pm) So much more than a drugstore, Longs is an inexpensive place to shop for a wide selection of Hawaii-made products, from children's books to macadamia nuts and crack-seed candy.

Flowers Forever   GIFTS & SOUVENIRS
(☑ 800-646-7579, 808-245-4717; www.flowers foreverhawaii.com; 2679 Kalena St; ⊙ 8am-5pm Mon-Thu, to 6pm Fri, to 4pm Sat) Voted 'Best Kaua'i Flower Shop' for 12 years running, Forever Flowers strings together a multitude of flower, maile, *ti*-leaf and more unusual specialty lei. It will ship tropical flowers, plants and lei to the mainland too.

If you're meeting your significant other at the airport, this is where to come to pick up a welcome lei.

Tropic Isle Music & Gifts   SOUVENIRS, MUSIC
(www.tropicislemusic.com; 3416 Rice St, Anchor Cove Shopping Center; ⊙ 10am-8pm) This tiny shop is crammed with a huge selection of Hawaiiana books, CDs, DVDs, bath and body products, island-made foodstuffs – you name it. Here you can avoid mistakenly buying mass-produced knockoffs imported from Asia.

ⓘ Information

MEDICAL SERVICES

Lihu'e has the best medical services on the island, with Kaua'i's only major hospital, **Wilcox Memorial Hospital** (☑ 808-245-1100; www. wilcoxhealth.org; 3-3420 Kuhio Hwy), which has a 24-hour emergency room.

Kaua'i Urgent Care (☑ 808-245-1532; www. wilcoxhealth.org; 4484 Pahe'e St; ⊙ 8am-7pm) is a walk-in clinic for nonemergencies, and **Longs Drugs** (☑ 808-245-8871; Kukui Grove Center, 3-2600 Kaumuali'i Hwy; ⊙ store 7am-10pm, pharmacy to 9pm Mon-Fri, to 6pm Sat & Sun) is a full-service pharmacy.

For major emergencies, you may be airlifted to Honolulu.

MONEY

American Savings Bank (☑ 808-246-8844; www.asbhawaii.com; 3-2600 Kaumuali'i Hwy, Kukui Grove Center) Convenient shopping-mall branch with a 24-hour ATM.

Bank of Hawaii (☑ 808-245-6761; www.boh. com; 4455 Rice St) Downtown bank with a 24-hour ATM.

OPENING HOURS

Lihu'e works on a standard Monday to Friday work schedule. Expect slightly more regular hours here than on the rest of the island, which is on island time.

POST

Lihu'e Post Office (☑ 808-245-1628; www. usps.com; 4441 Rice St; ⊙ 8am-4pm Mon-Fri, 9am-1pm Sat)

TOURIST INFORMATION

Division of Parks & Recreation (☑ 808-241-4463; www.kauai.gov; 4444 Rice St, Suite 105, Lihu'e Civic Center; ⊙ 8am-4pm Mon-Fri) For tourist information and details about visiting local parks.

Kaua'i Visitors Bureau (☑ 808-245-3971; www.gohawaii.com/kauai; 4334 Rice St, Suite 101; ⊙ 8am-4:30pm Mon-Fri) Comprehensive online resources for visitors, with free downloadable vacation-planning kits. The office staff are helpful.

❶ Getting There & Away

AIR

Lihu'e Airport (LIH; 📞 808-274-3800; http://airports.hawaii.gov/lih; 3901 Mokulele Loop) Only 2 miles from downtown, this small airport handles all commercial interisland, US mainland and Canada flights.

BOAT

The only commercial passenger vessels docking on Kaua'i at Lihu'e's Nawiliwili Harbor are cruise ships, mainly Norwegian Cruise Line (p278) and Princess Cruises (p278).

❶ Getting Around

TO/FROM THE AIRPORT

Car rental To pick up rental cars, check in at agency booths outside the baggage-claim area, then catch a complimentary shuttle bus to the agency's parking lot. (Or go straight to the rental-car lot, where there may be less of a queue.)

Taxi Cabs are infrequently used because most visitors rent cars, but you'll usually find them waiting curbside outside the baggage-claim area (around $12 to Lihu'e). If not, use the courtesy phones to call one.

BUS

Kaua'i Bus (p279) serves Lihu'e with a shuttle that runs hourly from about 6am until 9pm.

Stops include Kukui Grove Center, Lihu'e Airport (no large backpacks or luggage allowed), Vidinha Stadium and Wilcox Memorial Hospital. There's also a lunchtime shuttle within central Lihu'e that runs at 15-minute intervals between approximately 10:30am and 2pm.

CAR & MOTORCYCLE

Most businesses have free parking lots for customers. Metered street parking is pretty easy to find.

Kaua'i Harley-Davidson (📞 808-212-9495; www.kauaiharley.com; 3-1878 Kaumuali'i Hwy; ⊙ 8am-5pm) It'll cost up to $200 per day, plus a $1000 minimum security deposit, but if you want a hog in paradise, you've got one.

Rent-A-Wreck Kauai (📞 808-245-7177; www.rentawreckkauai.com; 3148 Oihana St; ⊙ 8am-5pm) Locally owned agency rents older economy-size island cars from $25 per day, and scooters or mopeds from $35 per day, with additional taxes and fees. Younger drivers (over 21 years) and debit cardholders welcome. Book in advance; free airport pickups available.

TAXI

Kauai Taxi Company (📞 808-246-9554; http://kauaitaxico.com) Taxi service. Tours also available.

LIHU'E GETTING THERE & AWAY

Lydgate Beach Park (p109)
ABBIE WARNOCK-MATTHEWS/SHUTTERSTOCK ©

Kapa'a & the Eastside

If you look past the strip malls and highway traffic, the Eastside fascinates. Its geography runs the gamut, from mountaintop forests to pounding surf and a majestic river. In ancient times, the Wailua River was sacred and Hawaiian royalty lived along its fertile banks. Kapa'a's historic town center echoes another bygone era of sugar plantations.

Kaua'i's population is concentrated here. Stretching from Wailua to Kapa'a, the 'Coconut Coast' has a busy, workaday vibe, as opposed to the swankier resorts of Princeville and Po'ipu. Traffic can grind to a painful halt at any time of day, however. Further north and hidden away from the hubbub is down-home Anahola – a fishing and farming village where Native Hawaiians make up about half of all residents.

INCLUDES

Wailua	109
Waipouli	120
Kapa'a	123
Anahola	131
Ko'olau Road	133

HIKING, CYCLING & KAYAKING IN EASTERN KAUA'I

HIKING TOUR: NOUNOU MOUNTAIN TRAIL

START KUAMO'O-NOUNOU TRAILHEAD
END NOUNOU EAST TRAILHEAD
DURATION/DISTANCE TWO HOURS/
4 MILES
DIFFICULTY MODERATE

The Sleeping Giant is a locals' favorite hike, as it combines brevity (it can be done in a couple of hours, which makes it a doable daily workout), a steep incline that gets the heart pumping and sweeping views of the Coconut Coast from Anahola to Lihu'e.

Although there are **three trails** that converge near the summit, we suggest starting at **Kuamo'o-Nounou Trailhead** on Kuamo'o Rd. From here it's a slightly more gentle approach through the gorgeous **Norfolk Island pine grove**, with their paper bark and mossy roots, planted in the 1930s by the Civilian Conservation Corps. The drawback is that after rain, the trail can be slick and muddy. Follow it through the pines. The incline is gentle at first but you will soon be huffing and puffing as the trail winds up to the giant's shoulders. Before long you'll converge with the others and pop out onto a plateau, with a sheltered **picnic area**.

Now atop the giant's chest, only his head prevents you from getting a 360-degree view. There is a trail to the left that leads along a slender ridge to the **true summit**. Signs say that it's off-limits, but some take their chances – just know that it is risky and not recommended. If you go for it, take extreme care and be smart. You wouldn't want to be one of those newsy footnotes. You know, the one about the hiker who died falling off a cliff while taking a selfie.

From the picnic area, veer right at the fork and continue down the exposed **Nounou Mountain East Trail Junction** toward the ocean. Wear a hat, as the sun can be fierce without the shady pine grove. The trail offers sweeping views of the ocean and distant mountains as you switchback down to the East Nounou East **trailhead** on Haleilio Rd.

Call a taxi to transport you back to your car's location on Kuamo'o Rd, or pre-arrange a drop-off at Kuamo'o Rd and pickup at Haleilio Rd before you commence walking.

HIKING TOUR: KUILAU RIDGE & MOALEPE TRAILS

START KUAMO'O RD/OLOHENA RD
END KUAMO'O RD/OLOHENA RD
DURATION/DISTANCE HALF DAY/VARIES
(8.5 MILES AT THE LONGEST)
DIFFICULTY MODERATE

The **Kuilau Ridge Trail** is recommended for its sheer beauty: emerald valleys, dewy bushes, thick ferns and glimpses of misty **Mt Wai'ale'ale** in the distance. After 1 mile, you'll reach a grassy clearing with a picnic table. Continue north on descending switchbacks until you meet the mountain-view **Moalepe Trail** (2.25 miles one-way).

Both of these moderate hikes are among the most visually rewarding on Kaua'i. Remember, the trails don't complete a circuit so you must retrace your steps (8.5 miles round-trip). You might want to skip the final mile of the outbound leg, which crosses the treeless pastureland of Wailua Game Management Area.

The Kuilau Ridge Trail starts at a marked trailhead on the right just before Kuamo'o Rd crosses the stream at the **Keahua Arboretum**, 4 miles above the junction of Kuamo'o Rd and Kamalu Rd. The Moalepe Trail trailhead is at the end of Olohena Rd in the Wailua Homesteads neighborhood.

On the east side of Kaua'i, you can trek through jungle or cycle along by the ocean, then end up with to-die-for views.

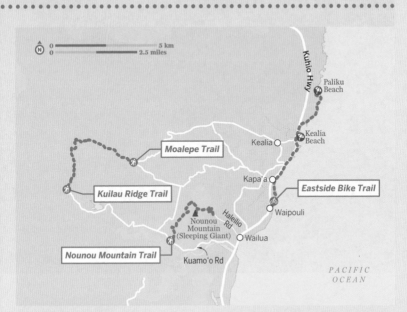

CYCLING TOUR: EASTSIDE BIKE TRAIL

START KAUAI CYCLE
END JAVA KAI
DURATION/DISTANCE TWO HOURS/10 MILES
DIFFICULTY EASY TO MODERATE

There are other places to rent a pair of wheels, but seeing as this is a cycling tour you should get yours at **Kauai Cycle** (p120) in Waipouli, the island's best bike shop. It has a range of equipment offering various degrees of comfort and speed. Grab a multigear bike as there are a few small hills to climb.

Head northeast on Kuhio Hwy. From there, make your first right on Keaka Rd, and a left on Moanakai Rd. With very little traffic you'll be pedaling along the coast without a care in the world. Follow it until you cross the canal on a footbridge, and connect with the Ke Ala Hele Makalae, the island's only dedicated bike path. When the plan for it was hatched, there were grand plans for this path

to stretch from Lihu'e to Anahola, but this 5-mile stretch is all that has been built, so use it. It is a rather pleasant strip of concrete that follows the contour of the beach, laying flat past **Kapa'a Beach Park** (p123), then rising slightly higher with the bluffs before dropping down along the stunning **Kealia Beach** (p123), with its shore break perfect for body boarders. The path rises up one more time before its terminus just before **Paliku Beach** (p129), an isolated cove set between Anahola and Kapa'a, inaccessible to cars.

Dependent on water conditions, you can cool off in the tides at Paliku or Kealia (be sure to swim in the area with lifeguards), then hop on your ride and cruise back to Kapa'a. You've earned breakfast. Indulge yourself at **Java Kai** (p129) with its tasty espresso drinks, smoothies and bagel sandwiches. Afterward walk it off with a long, slow browse among the shops and galleries in Old Town Kapa'a, before returning your trusted steed (ie your rent-a-bike).

River kayaking

KAYAKING THE WAILUA RIVER

START HOLOHOLOKU HEIAU
END HIKINA AKALA HEIAU
DURATION/DISTANCE THREE HOURS/4 MILES

DIFFICULTY EASY TO MODERATE

One of the iconic tours on the island is this pleasant, easily done yet still adventurous paddle up the sacred Wailua River. At 20 miles long, it's the longest navigable river flowing in the state of Hawaii.

Begin with a moment of pre-trip contemplation at **Holoholoku Heiau** (p113), the oldest *luakini* (temple dedicated to the war god Ku) on the island. Remember to include a simple acknowledgment of thanks to the local ancestors who built Wailua and this temple. From there grab your kayak rental from one of the operations on the Wailua River. A good option is **Wailua River Kayaking** (p113).

Now it's time to paddle upstream. If the wind kicks up or the current feels a bit strong, stay close to the edge of the river and be mindful of boats along the way. Paddle around two bends in the river before your first stop at **Kamokila Hawaiian Village** (p112). Kids will love the traditional Hawaiian-hut reproductions and gardens of guava, mango and banana trees.

When you've had your fill, continue upstream and take the north fork in the river. When you reach shore, stash your kayaks and start hiking along a jungle trail for a little under a mile. It helps to bring amphibious shoes or sandals that strap your feet in securely, as you'll be crossing streams and scrambling over slick rocks. You'll soon reach the 100ft-tall **Uluwehi Falls**. Now's the time to eat that picnic lunch you packed for your journey and sip some water.

When you're rested, double back to the river and paddle downstream toward the sea. The current will be at your back, though the wind will likely be in your face. When you reach the dock, return your kayak and follow the river mouth to **Lydgate Beach Park** (p109), where you can pay your respects once more at **Hikina Akala Heiau** (p113). It sits on a small rise overlooking the Coconut Coast.

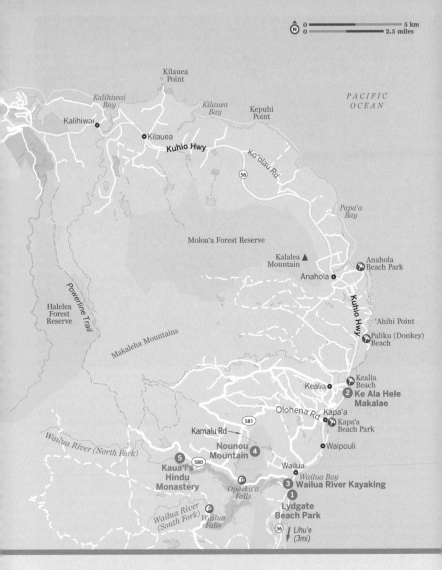

Kapa'a & the Eastside Highlights

1 **Lydgate Beach Park**
(p109) Exploring playgrounds, sheltered swimming areas and tide-line driftwood piles with the kids.

2 **Ke Ala Hele Makalae**
(p126) Running, walking or pedaling the 5 miles between Kapa'a Beach Park and Paliku (Donkey) Beach at sunrise.

3 **Wailua River Kayaking**
(p107) Feeling the mana (spiritual essence) as you paddle the sacred Wailua River into a valley that was the birthplace of kings and the abode of ali'i (high royalty).

4 **Nounou Mountain** (p104) Taking in the sweeping river, valley and coastal views of

Kaua'i's Eastside from the 'Sleeping Giant' – you'll have to climb as much as 1000ft to earn your photo op.

5 **Kaua'i's Hindu Monastery**
(p109) Finding serenity in this forest sanctuary – an intricately carved main temple surrounded by bountiful gardens, high above the Wailua River.

ℹ Getting There & Away

It's easy to get in and out of this region, where Hwy 50 arcs around the airport in Lihu'e and becomes Kuhio Hwy (Hwy 56) – the Eastside's main drag, which links Wailua to Waipouli, Kapa'a, Anahola and points north. Kuamoo Rd (Hwy 580) serves the Wailua Homesteads, where some of the island's most appealing trails sprout. The Kapa'a Bypass, looping inland from Kapa'a to just north of Wailua, will help you avoid Waipouli–Kapa'a gridlock during rush hour, though traffic can be a drag at anytime here. Most rental-car agencies are clustered around the airport, though Kapa'a has a discount agency (p131).

The Kaua'i Bus (p279) county bus system links the region with the south, west and north, and buses are equipped to carry bicycles. Taxis are pretty useless, however.

Wailua

POP 2300

Wailua has two sides. The coast belongs to strip-mall businesses and package tourists, who are packed into oceanfront condos and hotels like happy slices of a pie chart. But you can find that wild-palm-grove magic for which Kaua'i is famous here too. Just head to the languid Wailua River or follow the hiking trails that wind high into the lush forested mountains.

◉ Sights

Take a virtual tour of the Wailua Heritage Trail (www.wailuaheritagetrail.org) for an overview of historical sights and natural attractions, with a downloadable map.

★Kaua'i's Hindu Monastery   HINDU TEMPLE
(☑888-735-1619; www.himalayanacademy.com; 107 Kaholalele Rd; ◎9am-noon, inner gate open after 10:45am) FREE Serious pilgrims and curious sightseers are welcome at this Hindu monastery, set on 70 acres and surrounded by verdant forest above the Wailua River. The property was an old inn, until the monks bought it in 1966. Now it's a blend of organic and botanical gardens, cascading streams, and sacred temples and shrines devoted to Ganesha, Nandi and Shiva.

While visitors can access a limited area on their own, more detailed guided tours are offered for free once a week – call or check the website for details. Modest dress required: no shorts, T-shirts, tank tops or short dresses. If you're not dressed properly, you can borrow sarongs at the entrance.

The Kadavul Temple (which visitors may not enter, except to attend a 9am daily worship service) contains a rare single-pointed quartz crystal, a 50-million-year-old, six-sided *shivalingam* (representation of the god Shiva) that weighs 700lb and stands over 3ft tall. Monks have performed a *puja* (prayer ritual) here every three hours around the clock since the temple was established in 1973.

★Lydgate Beach Park   BEACH
(Leho Dr; ◎7am-6pm; P⊕❀) A narrow stretch of blond sand strewn with driftwood can entertain restless kids of all ages, all afternoon. Generally safe swimming can be found in two pools inside a protected breakwater, and beginner snorkeling too. Other amenities include two big playgrounds, full-size soccer fields, a paved recreational path, picnic tables and pavilions, restrooms, outdoor showers, drinking water and lifeguards. To get here, turn *makai* (seaward) on Kuhio Hwy between mile markers 5 and 6. At the park's northern end, multifeatured Kamalani Playground is a massive 16,000-sq-ft wooden castle with swings, a volcano slide, mirror mazes, an epic suspension bridge and other kid-pleasing contraptions.

Beware of the open ocean beyond the protected pool – it can be rough and dangerous, with strong currents, huge waves, sharp coral and slippery rocks. When the wind is blowing, kitesurfers put on a tremendous show. Camping is allowed at the south end of the park.

'Opaeka'a Falls Lookout   VIEWPOINT
(Kuamo'o Rd; P❀) While not a showstopper, these 150ft-high waterfalls make for an easy roadside stop, less than 2 miles up Kuamo'o Rd. For the best photographs, go in the morning. Don't be tempted to try trailblazing to the base of the falls, as the steep cliffs are perilous and have caused fatalities. Cross the road for fantastic photo ops of the Wailua River.

Smith's Tropical Paradise   GARDENS
(☑808-821-6895; www.smithskauai.com; adult/child 3-12yr $6/3; ◎8:30am-4pm; P⊕) Other gardens might have fancier landscaping, but you can't beat Smith's for value. Take a leisurely stroll along a mile-long loop trail past a serene pond, grassy lawns and island-themed gardens. The setting can seem Disney-esque, with an Easter Island *moai* statue replica, but it's as appealing as it is unpretentious.

KAPA'A & THE EASTSIDE WAILUA

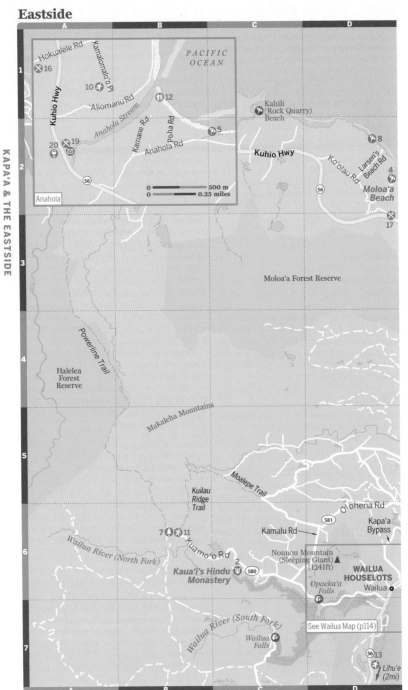

Eastside

rboretum   PARK

Rd; P ☎) FREE Sitting prettily at f Kuamo'o Rd around 7 miles from this arboretum has grassy fields, ng stream and groves of rainbow eucalyptus and other towering trees. Locals come here to picnic and to swim in the freshwater stream and pools, but be aware that the water is infected with leptospira bacteria, which can cause potentially serious infections.

Kamokila Hawaiian Village   CULTURAL CENTER

(☑ 808-823-0559; http://villagekauai.com; 5443 Kuamo'o Rd; adult/child 3-12yr $5/3; ☺9am-5pm; P ♿) This 4-acre site along the Wailua River has reproductions of traditional Hawaiian structures amid thriving gardens of guava, mango and banana trees. While not a must-see, it's a pleasant diversion, especially for kids. Kamokila also offers canoe rentals and guided outrigger canoe tours (adult/child $30/20), leaving hourly, which include paddling, hiking and waterfall swimming.

Turn south from Kuamo'o Rd, opposite 'Opaeka'a Falls. The half-mile road leading to the village is steep and narrow. You can also rent a kayak elsewhere and paddle in up the Wailua River.

🏃 Activities

Most Eastside hiking trails ascend into Kaua'i's tropical-jungle interior. Expect humidity, red dirt (or mud) and slippery patches after rains. For information on tackling the popular Nounou Mountain (Sleeping Giant) Trail, Kuilau Ridge Trail (p104) and Moalepe Trail (p104) refer to our recommended self-guided tours (p104).

Kauai Yoga on the Beach   YOGA

(☑ 808-635-6050; www.kauaiyogaonthebeach. com; 420 Papaloa Rd, Kauai Shores; drop-in classes incl mat rental $25) What could be better than doing your sun salutations on the sand as the sun actually rises (or maybe just a little later in the morning)? Classes are usually held from 8:30am beachfront at the Kauai Shores hotel. Check the website to book private sessions or join a yoga experience, also taking in the island's Hindu Monastery.

Kauai Water Ski Co   WATERSPORTS

(☑808-639-2829, 808-822-3574; www.kauaiwater skiandsurf.com; 4-356 Kuhio Hwy, Kinipopo Shopping Village; per 30/60min $100/195; ☺9am-5pm Mon-Fri, to noon Sat) Hawaii's only non-ocean water-skiing happens on the Wailua River. Rates are per trip, not per person (maximum number of riders varies by skill level; beginners welcome), and include water-skiing or wakeboarding equipment and a professional instructor as your driver. Reservations required.

Wailua Municipal Golf Course   GOLF

(☑ 808-241-6666; www.kauai.gov/golf; 3-5350 Kuhio Hwy; nonresident green fees $24-60, club rental $20-35) This 18-hole, par-72 course, designed by former head-pro Toyo Shirai, is one of Hawaii's top-ranked municipal golf courses. Plan ahead because morning tee times are sometimes reserved a week in advance. After 2pm, the regular $48 green fee drops by half and it's first-come, first-served. Cart and club rentals available. You'll pay a premium to play on weekends.

KAYAKING AROUND WAILUA

Majestic and calm, the 20-mile-long Wailua River is fed by two streams originating on Mt Wai'ale'ale. It's the only navigable river across the Hawaiian Islands, and kayaking it has become a visitor must-do. Fortunately, the paddle is a doable 4 miles for all ages.

Tours usually paddle 2 miles up the river's north fork, which leads to a mile-long hike through dense forest to Uluwehi Falls ('Secret Falls'), a 100ft waterfall. The hike crosses a stream and scrambles over rocks and roots, and if muddy it will probably cause some slippin' and slidin'. Wear sturdy, washable, nonslip watersports sandals.

Most tours last four to five hours, departing in the morning or early afternoon (call ahead for exact check-in times). The maximum group size is 12, with paddlers going out in double kayaks. The pricier tours include lunch, but on budget tours, you can store your own food in coolers or waterproof bags. Bring a hat, sunscreen and insect repellent.

Experienced paddlers might want to rent individual kayaks and go out on their own (p107). Note that not all tour companies are also licensed to rent kayaks, and no kayak tours or rentals are allowed on Sundays. Kayaking outfitters are based in Wailua or Kapa'a.

THE SACRED WAILUA RIVER

To ancient Hawaiians, the Wailua River was among the most sacred places across the islands. The river basin, near its mouth, was one of the island's two royal centers (the other was Waimea), home to the high chiefs. Here, you can find the remains of many important heiau (ancient stone temples); together they now form a National Historic Landmark.

Long and narrow Hikina'akala Heiau (Rising of the Sun Temple; Kuamo'o Rd) sits south of the Wailua River mouth, which is today the north end of Lydgate Beach Park. In its heyday, the temple (built around 1300 CE) was aligned directly north to south, but only a few remaining boulders outline its original massive shape. Neighboring Hauola Pu'uhonua (meaning 'the place of refuge of the dew of life') is marked by a bronze plaque. Ancient Hawaiian kapu (taboo) breakers were assured safety from persecution if they made it inside.

Believed to be the oldest luakini (temple dedicated to the war god Ku, often a place for human sacrifice) on the island, Holoholoku Heiau is a quarter-mile up Kuamo'o Rd on the left. It's believed to be Kaua'i's oldest heiau. Toward the west, against the flat-backed birthstone marked by a plaque reading Pohaku Ho'ohanau (Royal Birthstone), queens gave birth to future royals. Only a male child born here could become king of Kaua'i.

Perched high on a hill overlooking the meandering Wailua River, well-preserved Poli'ahu Heiau (Kuamo'o Rd), another luakini, is named after the snow goddess Poli'ahu, one of the sisters of the volcano goddess Pele. The heiau is immediately before 'Opaeka'a Falls Lookout (p109), on the opposite side of the road.

Although Hawaiian heiau were originally imposing stone structures, most now lie in ruins, covered with scrub. But they are still considered powerful vortices of mana (spiritual essence) and should be treated with respect. For a compelling history of the Wailua River's significance to ancient Hawaiians, read Edward Joesting's *Kauai: the Separate Kingdom*.

☞ Tours

Kayak Wailua KAYAKING
(☏808-822-3388; www.kayakwailua.com; 4565 Haleilio Rd; 4½hr tours $60) This small, family-owned company specializes in Wailua River tours. It keeps its boats and equipment in tip-top shape; shuttles you to the marina launch site; and provides dry bags for your belongings and a nylon cooler for your own food.

Kayak Kaua'i KAYAKING
(☏808-826-9844, 888-596-3853; www.kayak kauai.com; Wailua River Marina; double kayak rental per day $95, 4½hr tours $75-95) Reputable island-wide operator offering Wailua River tours and kayak rentals (small surcharge for dry bags and coolers). If you're renting, you'll have to transport the kayak a short distance atop your car.

Ancient River Kayak KAYAKING
(☏808-826-2505; www.ancientriverkayak.com; 440 Aleka Pl; tours adult/child $85/65; ⊘tours depart 7am & 12:30pm Mon-Sat) Rents all kinds of beach gear and runs paddling tours of the Wailua River that include a short hike to and from a 100ft waterfall. Tours include lunch. To ask about gear rental or to confirm a tour, book online or call the office.

Wailua River Kayaking KAYAKING
(☏808-821-1188; https://wailuariverkayaking.com; 169 Wailua Rd; single/double kayak rental $50/85 for 5 hours, tours $90) Located at the boat ramp on the north bank of the Wailua River, this outfit is convenient for individual rentals (no need to transport the kayak), and it offers half-day tours too.

Smith's Motor Boat Service BOATING
(☏808-821-6892; www.smithskauai.com; Wailua Marina; 80min tour adult/child $25/12.50; ⊘departures at 9:30am, 11am, 2pm & 3:30pm) If you're curious to see the once-legendary Fern Grotto, this 2-mile covered flat-bottom boat ride is hokey but homespun. Bear in mind that since heavy rains and rock slides in 2006, visitors cannot enter the grotto, but must stay on the wooden platform quite a distance from the shallow cave.

Wailua

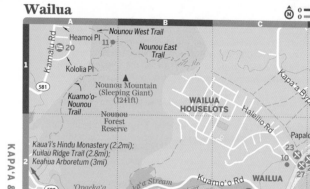

Wailua

Kaua'i Nature Tours   HIKING

(☎808-742-8305,888-233-8365; www.kauainature
tours.com; tours adult/child 7-12yr from $155/135)
Geoscientist Chuck Blay's company offers a
full-day guided hiking tour of the Waimea
Canyon – snacks, drinks and transportation
included. Guided hikes also hit the North
Shore's Na Pali Coast, Po'ipu and Koke'e
State Parks.

✨ Festivals & Events

Taste of Hawaii   FOOD & DRINK

(www.tasteofhawaii.net; per person $100; ⊙Jun)
On the first Sunday in June, the Rotary
Club of Kapa'a hosts the 'Ultimate Sunday
Brunch' at Smith's Tropical Paradise (p109),
where you can indulge in gourmet samples
by 40 chefs from around Hawaii. Dance it
off to more than 10 live-music acts. For
discounts, buy tickets online in advance.

🛏 Sleeping

⭐**Kauai Shores**   HOTEL $$

(☎808-822-4951; www.kauaishoreshotel.com; 420
Papaloa Rd; r $153-185; P ❄ 🎧 ☲) Renovated
by Hawaii's boutique-hotel-chain Aqua, this
true beachfront midranger has tidy rooms
splashed with sunny modern panache. Retro
vintage style infuses the hotel's Lava Lava
Beach Club (p118) bar and restaurant and
there's a thoroughly laid-back and easygoing
vibe. The mandatory 'hospitality fee' ($15
plus tax per night) covers continental
breakfast, morning yoga, beach chairs and
towels for borrowing.

⭐**Fern Grotto Inn**   INN $$

(☎808-821-9836; www.kauaicottages.com; 4561
Kuamo'o Rd; cottages $178-250, 3-bedroom
house $325; P ❄ 🎧) Charmingly retro yet re-
modeled, these early-20th-century plantation-
style cottages and newly built units vary in
size, but all have hardwood floors, tasteful
furnishings and a kitchen or kitchenette. A
prime location near the Wailua River dock
reduces the need to drive, and there are bikes,
beach toys and a kayak to borrow. Four-night
minimum.

⭐**Rosewood Kaua'i**   INN $$

(☎808-822-5216; www.rosewoodkauai.com; 872
Kamalu Rd; r with shared bathroom $85-95, r
with private bathroom $185, private cottage $185;
P 🎧) Budget travelers are spoiled at this
hostel-cum-B&B, located amid verdant
gardens 5 miles inland from Wailua. If you
stay in the main house, the price includes a
magnificent hot breakfast with the owners,
who are delightful company. They rent small
but tidy bunkhouse rooms with kitchenettes
and lots of light, and a smaller cottage next
door on the same property.

The main house feels warm, homey and
comfortable. Bunkhouse mattresses are thick
and plush, and the bunkhouse bathrooms
and outdoor shower are shared. Expect a
small cleaning fee. Three-night minimum.

Plantation Hale   CONDO $$

(☎808-822-49141; www.plantation-hale.com; 525
Aleka Loop; 1-bedroom units $220; P ❄ 🎧 ☲) An
older, 180-unit property, all of which have
full kitchens and are somewhat dated – as
if your vaguely hip grandma lived here. Still,
they are spacious with granite countertops
and flat-screens in the living room and
bedroom. Look forward to a central location
to explore the island and walking access to
cafes and restaurants.

Aston Islander on the Beach   HOTEL $$

(☎808-822-7417, 877-977-6667; www.aston
islander.com; 440 Aleka Pl; r $199-239; P ❄ 🎧 ☲)
It's not a resort, so don't expect frills. Still, the
rooms inside these plantation-style beach-
front buildings are contemporary, with
teak furnishings and granite counter tops, flat-
screen TVs, microwaves and mini-fridges.
A mandatory amenity fee ($18 plus tax per
night) covers parking plus DVD and video-
game rentals. Deep discounts are often
available online.

⭐**17 Palms**   RENTAL HOUSE $$$

(☎888-725-6799; www.17palmskauai.com; 414
Wailua Kai St; d $239-329; P 🎧) Tucked away
in a quiet and leafy residential enclave a
short walk from the beach, plus good eating
and drinking, 17 Palms' two cottages include
the two-bedroom Meli Meli and the one-
bedroom Hale Iki. Wooden accents enliven
the cottages' soothing neutral decor, and
both are well-equipped for an extended stay
for either couples or families. Additional
cleaning fee of $110 to $145.

Sheraton Kauai
Coconut Beach Resort   HOTEL $$$

(☎877-997-6667,808-822-3455; www.marriotthawaii.
com; 650 Aleka Loop; r from $275; P ❄ 🎧 ☲)
Rebranded under the Sheraton marque, this
polished, 300-plus-room beachside hotel has
been fully renovated, from its soaring lobby
to its ocean-view pool. Business-class suites
pamper guests with deep soaking tubs and
kitchenettes. More than half the regular

rooms have cinnamon-wood plantation shutters opening onto private lanai (veranda). The mandatory resort fee ($32 per night) covers parking and two mai tais.

Hilton Garden Inn
HOTEL **$$$**

(☑ 808-823-6000; www.hilton.com/en/hilton-garden-inn; 3-5920 Kuhio Hwy; r from $290, ste from $325; P✳🛜🏊) Choose a stand-alone Japanese-style chalet suite set in a palm grove, or more typical hotel rooms in one of the main buildings that overlook Lydgate Beach Park. The lobby is open and modern with a stylish bar front and center, and lots of cushy seating. Mamahune's Tiki Bar (p119), added in 2019, features brilliant views.

Kauai Coast at the Beachboy
RESORT **$$$**

(☑ 808-822-3441; www.shellhospitality.com/kauai-coast-resort-at-the-beachboy; 520 Aleka Loop; r from $287; P✳🛜🏊) A time-share resort that also rents extra rooms to the public. Set behind the Coconut Marketplace, rooms are spacious with private balconies overlooking an inviting pool area that spills onto a lawn that rolls toward the sand. The lobby restaurant, Hukilau Lanai (p118), is one of the island's best. Search online for discounted rooms.

🍴 Eating

Haole Girl Island Sweets
BAKERY **$**

(☑ 808-822-2253; www.haolegirlsweets.com; 4-484 Kuhio Hwy, Coconut Marketplace; pastries $4-7; ⊙9am-1pm Tue-Thu; P) Imagine banana bread, quiche with a buttery crust, croissants stuffed with goat cheese, spinach and sun-dried tomato, and the world's most decadent sticky buns, all made and sold by a sole proprietor who still gets such a kick out of doing her thing. Come in, smell the warm goodness and munch happily. Look for them at farmers markets around Kaua'i too.

Passion Bakery & Cafe
CAFE **$**

(☑808-821-0060; www.facebook.com/mcsterioff; 4-356 Kuhio Hwy, Kinipopo Shopping Village; mains $8-12; ⊙6am-2pm Mon-Sat; P) A popular cafe for good coffees and breakfasts that pair feta or vegan sausage with eggs. It also does a tofu scramble and a range of sandwiches. But the freshly baked breads – some of which incorporate taro – are the thing.

★ Nom Kauai
BURGERS **$$**

(☑ 808-635-5903; www.nomkauai.com; 4-484 Kuhio Hwy, Coconut Marketplace; mains $13-20; ⊙7am-2pm; P) Known for burgers catered to any time of day. Breakfast burgers and egg sandwiches come in a Belgian waffle bun, while traditional burgers are smothered in mushrooms, blue cheese and bacon. Excellent fried-chicken sandwiches and a well-curated selection of craft beer, wine and milkshakes too. Harnessing local Kaua'i produce and ingredients is an important part of the Nom ethos.

At the time of writing, owners Thomas and Alicia were planning on opening Munchology – a lounge and eatery specializing in shared plates – in an adjacent Coconut Marketplace location.

★ Street Burger
BURGERS **$$**

(☑808-212-1555; www.streetburgerkauai.com; 4-369 Kuhio Hwy; mains $15-23; ⊙11am-10pm Tue-Sat; P) The coolest spot in Wailua has

---

WHATEVER HAPPENED TO COCO PALMS?

Old-timers might recall **Coco Palms Resort** as Hollywood's go-to wedding site during the 1950s and '60s. Built in 1953, it was Kaua'i's first resort, and its romantic lagoons, gardens, thatched cottages, torch-lit paths and coconut groves epitomized tropical paradise. The highest-profile on-screen wedding here was when Elvis Presley wed Joan Blackman in the 1961 film *Blue Hawaii*. At its height, the Coco Palms was a playground for Hollywood stars, and the trendiest mainland couples came here to get hitched. But it was also an Old Hawaii kind of place where guests knew hotel staff on a first-name basis and returned year after year.

In 1992, Hurricane 'Iniki demolished the 396-room hotel, which then sat neglected for years. In early 2006, a new owner announced a $220 million plan to resurrect Coco Palms as a condo-hotel, but plans fell through. Since 2016, there have been further multiple attempts to redevelop the site as a hotel, but nothing has come to fruition. An alternative future as a county park open to the public has been mooted, but there is no plan for funding to make this happen.

THE MYSTERIOUS BLUE HOLE

How close can you get to Mt Wai'ale'ale by foot? If you can find the Blue Hole, located at the base of the mountain, you're there. It's not a 'hole' per se, but a pool fed by a pretty stream and waterfall.

To get here, take Kuamo'o Rd up to Keahua Arboretum. Unless you're driving a 4WD, you should park in the lot and hike in. The unpaved road is head-jarringly rough, and the mud can engulf ordinary cars. Either way, head left onto Wailua Forest Management Rd. After less than 1.5 miles, you'll reach a junction; turn right (a gate blocks the left direction). Go straight for about 2 miles. Along the way, you'll pass an otherworldly forest of false staghorn, guava, eucalyptus and native mamane and ohia. The dense foliage introduces you to a rainbow of greens, from deep evergreen to eye-popping chartreuse.

You will then reach a locked yellow gate; it is meant to keep out cars, but the state allows foot traffic (be warned: lots of mud). From here you must slosh about 0.75 miles till you reach the dammed stream, which is the north fork of Wailua River. The stream rises and falls depending on the season and rainfall. Occasionally, it is deep enough for kids to swim. Blue Hole is a quiet, secluded spot, not a tourist destination by a long shot. To avoid getting stuck or lost, hire a guide.

hammered-aluminum tabletops, a chalkboard craft-beer menu, and an open grill where gourmet burgers are made. And they are glorious. Choose a Greek burger topped with olive tapenade and feta, an Italian layered with prosciutto, buffalo mozzarella, spinach and marinara sauce, or get serious with a $23 street burger.

The street burger is topped with cured pork belly, a fried egg, arugula, blue cheese and crispy fried onions. They make their own veggie patties, and offer six flavors of fries: Parmesan and garlic, pickled peppers and sriracha, truffle and garlic, herb, chili, and sea salt.

Oyster 369   SEAFOOD **$$**
(☎808-212-1555; www.oyster369.com; 4-369 Kuhio Hwy; shared plates $11-23; ☻5-9pm Tue-Sat; ℗) Options on Oyster 369's raw bar menu include oysters on the half-shell, *poke* (cubed raw fish mixed with *shōyu*, sesame oil, salt, chili pepper, *'inamona* or other condiments), ceviche and tuna carpaccio, while shrimp, mussels, calamari and clams are all carefully oven-roasted and lightly seared in the kitchen. More than 20 beers are available, courtesy of the tap list next door at the associated Street Burger, and there's also a good seafood-friendly wine list.

EatHealthy Cafe   VEGAN **$$**
(☎808-822-7990; www.eathealthykauai.com; 4-369 Kuhio Hwy; mains $13-22; ☻8am-9pm

Tue-Sat; ℗✐❀) Asian, South American and Middle Eastern flavors infuse healthful vegan and plant-based dishes to delight both mindful eaters and gourmets at this rustic hideaway. The Tex-Mex burrito with soy 'chorizo' is a breakfast standout, while the kimchi burger is good for a leisurely lunch. No beer or wine, but smoothies and kombucha. Seating is in the garden (bring mosquito repellent).

Sushi Bushido   JAPANESE **$$**
(☎808-822-0664; www.sushibushido.com; 4-484 Kuhio Hwy, Coconut Marketplace; dishes $7-28; ☻11am-9pm Sun-Thu, to 11pm Fri-Sat) Relocated to the reopened Coconut Marketplace, this locals' favorite has pop art on the walls and serves imaginative fusion sushi, such as the yellowtail 'lollipop' roll drizzled with sweet sauce. Prices are high, portions small and waits can be long, but the social atmosphere and extensive sake list make it a fun night out.

Coconut Marketplace   MARKET **$$**
(www.coconutmarketplace.com; 4-484 Kuhio Hwy; ☻hours vary; ℗🐾) Reopened after a renovation in 2019, this mall is developing as a convenient dining hub with good res-taurants including Sushi Bushido and Nom Kauai. A tiny farmers market (snacks from $5) is held at this mall on Tuesday and Thursday mornings from 8am until noon.

CACAO: HAWAII'S NEXT BIG BEAN?

The world's chocolate comes mainly from West Africa, Brazil, Ecuador, Malaysia and Indonesia. But Kaua'i's humid tropical climate and regular rain means the prized cacao bean can be nurtured here too. It's among the specialty crops that local-agriculture proponents are touting for Hawaii's next generation of farmers. Learn more about diversified agriculture and cacao growing at **Lydgate Farms** (☑808-821-1857; https://lydgatefarms.com; 5730 Olohena Rd; 3hr tours adult/child under 12yr $95/free; ☺tours 9am-noon Mon-Fri, cafe & gift shop 9:30am-12:30pm; ⊞), which offers a unique chocolate-farm tour that includes a tasting of single-estate dark-chocolate bars from around the world, including those produced at the Big Island's 'Original Hawaiian Chocolate Factory' and O'ahu's Waialua Estate.

The owners, Will and Emily Lydgate, are the great-grandchildren of Kaua'i minister and community leader John Mortimer Lydgate, namesake of Lydgate Beach Park (p109). The property was not an inheritance, as 'JM' had no desire to acquire land or profit from the sugar industry. With this thriving example of a 'teaching farm,' meant to experiment with workable crops, the Lydgates are trying to encourage a shift away from the mono-crops and sheer capital outlays of industrial agriculture toward small-scale farming and diversified crops. The other main crops here are timber, bamboo and vanilla, but the 8-acre farm features hundreds of thriving tropical species, so it's a fantastic introduction if you're curious to see what thrives on Kaua'i, from avocados and citrus to soursop and sapodilla. Advance reservations at least one week prior are recommended for tours, but you can visit the on-site cafe and gift shop without a reservation.

Kintaro JAPANESE $$
(☑808-822-3341; 4-370 Kuhio Hwy; small plates $4-15, mains $12-28; ☺5:30-9:30pm Mon-Sat) Night after night for more than 30 years, this locals' favorite sushi bar has packed 'em in, thanks to thick slices of sashimi and creative rolls that are expertly prepared. The yellowtail sushi and sashimi are especially great. It also has a sprawling cooked-food menu and sizzling teppanyaki service, with chefs showing off at table-side grills. Make reservations.

Sleeping Giant Grill SEAFOOD $$
(☑808-822-3474; 440 Aleka Pl; mains $10-21; ☺11am-8pm Mon-Sat; ℗⊞) This friendly restaurant makes *broke da mout* (delicious) ahi (yellowfish tuna) wraps, fresh *poke*, grilled fish plates, salads with local greens, and more. Get takeout for a picnic on the beach.

★**Hukilau Lanai** HAWAII REGIONAL $$$
(☑808-822-0600; www.hukilaukauai.com; 520 Aleka Loop, Kauai Coast Resort at the Beachboy; mains $21-36; ☺5-9pm Tue-Sun; ℗⊞) One of the most consistent restaurants on the island, seafood is king here, with a half-dozen fresh-catch options, paired with locally grown vegetables and sauced differently every night. It does steaks and chops too, and hosts frequent live-music acts. Book for the great-value five-course tasting menu ($32), available for reservations up to 5:45pm. Gluten-free and kids' menus available.

🍷 Drinking & Nightlife

Imua Coffee Roasters CAFE
(☑808-821-1717; www.facebook.com/imuacoffee; 440 Aleka Pl; ☺6am-4pm Mon-Sat, to 11:30am Sun; 🛜) One of the best indie coffee roasters on the island, this friendly spot is well located for those on the northern end of the Wailua swirl. There's relaxed outdoor seating out the back on a compact patio.

Trees Lounge BAR
(☑808-823-0600; www.treesloungekauai.com; 440 Aleka Pl; ☺5pm-12:30am Mon-Sat) On the (very) short list of (semi-) reliable island nightspots. It offers fresh oysters on Tuesdays, cheap martinis at happy hour, pub grub such as po'boys and fish skewers, and frequent DJs and live music as well. Friday is especially popular for a blast of salsa. Check its Facebook page for regular events spanning everything from stand-up comedy to jazz.

Lava Lava Beach Club BAR
(☑808-241-5282; https:/lavalavabeachclub.com; 420 Papaloa Rd, Kauai Shores; ☺7am-9pm; 🛜⊞) Adjoined to the Kauai Shores hotel, the Lava Lava Beach Club offers beachside eating and drinking, so kick off those slippahs and ease into happy-hour specials

of cheaper beers, cocktails and bar snacks, including tasty flatbreads. There's live music most nights from 6pm and the colorful and fun vintage decor is a treat. Popular with families staying in nearby hotels.

Mamahune's Tiki Bar COCKTAIL BAR
(www.facebook.com/mamahuneskauai; 3-5920 Kuhio Hwy, Hilton Garden Inn; ⊙11am-10pm) With some of the Eastside's best coastal views, Mamahune's keeps things straightforward with an outdoor gazebo and wise-cracking bar staff adept at making pretty decent cocktails. Pull up a bar stool; order the *ahi* nachos from the *pupu* (bar snacks) menu; and be sure to grab a photo of the fake volcano and waterfall. Kitschy but loads of fun.

Avalon Gastropub PUB
(☑808-822-9368; www.avalongastropub.com; 4-356 Kuhio Hwy, Kinipopo Shopping Village; ⊙5-9pm Tue-Sun) This stylish recent opening pairs an interesting selection of crafty brews from Hawaii and mainland US with superior bar food. Secure a seat in the clubby interior or in the compact courtyard and team a hoppy West Coast IPA with a pork-belly Scotch egg or pan-seared duck. Craft cocktails are prepared with creativity and aplomb.

Potions TEAHOUSE
(☑808-634-6477; www.facebook.com/potions. kauai; 4-361 Kuhio Hwy; ⊙11am-11pm) All that funky, hippy energy that swirls around Kaua'i has coalesced in this psychedelic Indian kombucha bar where the often-sweet fizzy brew is on tap and flavored with dandelion and burdock, chocolate and pepper, ginger and ginseng, chamomile and spearmint. If you're hungry, it also does four kinds of vegetarian curry.

☆ Entertainment

Smith's Garden Luau LUAU
(☑808-821-6895; www.smithskauai.com; Wailua Marina, Smith's Tropical Paradise; adult/child 7-13yr/child 3-6yr $98/30/19; ⊙4:45pm or 5pm Mon-Fri Jun-Aug, Mon & Wed-Fri Feb-Oct, Mon, Wed, Fri Nov-Jan; ☉) It's a Kaua'i institution, attracting droves of tourists yet run with aloha spirit by four generations at the family's riverside gardens. Surprisingly, the highlight is the buffet food, including a roasted pig unearthed from an *imu* (underground oven). The multicultural Polynesian show of Hawaiian hula, Tahitian drum dances and Samoan fire dancing is less exciting.

Prebook online for discounts.

Coconut Marketplace DANCE, MUSIC
(☑808-822-3641; www.coconutmarketplace. com; 4-484 Kuhio Hwy; ⊙usually 5pm Wed & 1pm Sat; ☉) FREE While touristy, the Coconut Marketplace's free hula show is nevertheless fun and a good introduction to local culture. On Friday nights at 5pm there's usually live music from local musical legend Larry Rivera.

🛍 Shopping

The long-running shopping mall at the northern end of Wailua, Coconut Marketplace (p117), reopened in 2019 after a major makeover. Cafes and restaurants now feature along with souvenir shops and a few interesting local galleries.

Olivine Beach FASHION & ACCESSORIES
(☑808-742-7222; www.olivinekauai.com; 4-369 Kuhio Hwy; ⊙10am-6pm Tue-Sat) A high-end fashion boutique that feels dropped in from the Hamptons or Malibu, but looks perfectly at home in Wailua. Owned by a former Donna Karan fashion designer, it stocks Vitamin A bikinis, Stillwater T-shirts, Mother denim and many more high-end labels. There's a great vibe.

Pagoda ANTIQUES
(☑808-821-2172; www.facebook.com/PagodaKauai 4-369 Kuhio Hwy; ⊙10am-6pm Mon & Wed-Fri, noon-5:30pm Tue, 10am-4pm Sat) A treasure chest selling antique Japanese hand-blown glass fishing buoys that frequently wash up on Kaua'i's shore, vintage Japanese kimonos and tea sets, rice sacks and all manner of furniture. The price tag is the first offer, and the owners are often willing to negotiate.

ℹ Information

Longs Drugs (☑808-822-4918; www.cvs.com; 645 Aleka Loop; ⊙store 7am-10pm, pharmacy 8am-9pm Mon-Fri, 9am-5pm Sat & Sun) This pharmacy has an ATM, and also sells beach gear, snacks, drinks and souvenirs.

ℹ Getting There & Away

Don't look for a town center. Most attractions are scattered along coastal Kuhio Hwy (Hwy 56), or Kuamo'o Rd (Hwy 580) heading *mauka* (inland). Driving north, Kapa'a Bypass runs from just north of the Wailua River to beyond Kapa'a, usually skipping the Waipouli and Kapa'a gridlock. Lihue airport is around 6 miles south. There is no scheduled public transport from the airport to Wailua.

Waipouli

Waipouli ('Dark Water') and its gentle lagoons once served as a departure point for ancient Hawaiians setting sail for Tahiti and other Polynesian islands. Nowadays it's less a town than a cluster of restaurants, grocery stores and miscellaneous businesses in strip malls. This makes it a convenient place to stock up on supplies or, better yet, grab a bite to eat.

🏃 Activities

Kayak- and surf-rental outlets in Waipouli are located at a distance from the river and beaches.

Seasport Divers   DIVING

(☑ 808-823-9222,   800-685-5889;   www.seasportdivers.com; 4-976 Kuhio Hwy; dive trips $100-245; ⊘ 9am-5pm; 🚹) Eastside waters are less protected by reefs and choppier due to easterly onshore winds, so diving and snorkeling are limited. Still, this small branch of a Po'ipu-based outfit rents diving and snorkeling gear, bodyboards and surfboards, and books excellent dive trips – from beach or boat – along the South Shore.

Kauai Cycle   CYCLING

(☑ 808-821-2115; www.kauaicycle.com; 4-934 Kuhio Hwy; per day/week cruiser $30/110, mountain & road bikes $40/165, full-suspension mountain bikes $60/250; ⊘ 9am-6pm Mon-Fri, to 4pm Sat; 🚹) The best bike shop on the island, Kauai Cycle sells, services and rents cruisers, hybrids, and road and mountain bikes maintained by experienced cyclists. Rental prices include a helmet and lock.

Spa By The Sea   SPA

(☑ 808-823-1488; http://spabytheseakauai.com; 4-820 Kuhio Hwy; treatments from $140; ⊘ 9am-6pm) The resident spa at Waipouli Beach Resort offers all the treatments: hair, nails, facials, and massages lasting 50 to 80 minutes. Get local with a *lomilomi* (traditional Hawaiian massage) or a hot stone treatment. Book ahead.

Ola Massage   MASSAGE

(☑ 808-821-1100; http://kauairetreat.com; 4-971 Kuhio Hwy; treatments $53-170; ⊘ 9am-7pm Mon-Fri, 10am-6pm Sat & Sun) A humble mini-mall massage studio with a range of treatments on the menu. There's reflexology by the half-hour, standard deep-tissue massage by the hour and a *lomilomi* treatment with two therapists.

Golden Lotus Studio   MASSAGE

(☑ 808-823-9810; www.goldenlotuskauai.org; 4-941 Kuhio Hwy; ⊘ 9am-9pm Mon-Fri, 10am-5pm Sat-Sun) A massage, dance and yoga studio notable for its affordable student massages available to all comers for just $40. Dance classes and workshops are available throughout the year as well.

Bikram Yoga Kauai   YOGA

(☑ 808-823-9642; www.bikramyogakauaiikapaa.com; 4-885 Kuhio Hwy; drop-in classes $20) Come find your yogic bliss in this heated studio. Classes are offered daily, so there's plenty of opportunity to get centered. To build some serious prana, opt for the Traveling Yogi special (seven days unlimited for $59). Go online for current schedules.

Snorkel Bob's   SNORKELING

(☑ 808-823-9433; www.snorkelbob.com; 4-734 Kuhio Hwy; per week snorkel set adult/child under 13yr from $38/25, wetsuit/bodyboard from $25/32; ⊘ 8am-5pm; 🚹) Beyond the competitive rates, the cool thing about this place is that if you're island-hopping you can rent snorkel gear on Kaua'i and return it on the Big Island, O'ahu or Maui.

🛏 Sleeping

Waipouli Beach Resort & Spa   RESORT $$

(☑ 800-688-7444, 808-822-6000; www.outriggerwaipouli.com; 4-820 Kuhio Hwy; studios from $199, 1-/2-bedroom condos from $299/399; 🅿 ❄ @ 🛜 🏊) The surrounding strip malls and traffic belie the Outrigger's cachet as the Eastside's fanciest condo complex. Units are law-firm handsome with big flat-screen TVs, and kitchenettes or full kitchens with washer-dryers. There's no swimmable beach, but a saltwater 'river pool' and sand-bottom hot tubs compensate somewhat. Outrigger represents nearly half of the almost 200 rental units, but also check www.vrbo.com.

Outrigger's mandatory resort fee ($25 per night) covers parking and internet access and there's a one-time cleaning fee of at least $165 due upon checkout.

Garden Island Properties   ACCOMMODATIONS SERVICES $$

(☑ 808-822-4871; www.kauaiproperties.com; 4-928 Kuhio Hwy) A locally owned, island-wide rental agency with a solid collection of affordable condos and houses for rent. It's based in the heart of Waipouli.

✗ Eating

A couple of fast-food fusion gems and interesting fine dining make Waipouli a great place to eat.

★ Saimin Dojo   JAPANESE $

(☑808-320-3248; www.saimindojo.com; 4-733 Kuhio Hwy; mains $9-16; ⊙11am-9pm; ℗⬆) Saimin (Hawaiian-style noodle soup) is the star here – we can't go past the bowl with kimchi and garlic cilantro shrimp. But the whole menu is brilliant, including the option to add chili, short ribs or fried chicken to their great versions of *loco moco* (rice, fried egg and hamburger patty with gravy). There's a beachy vibe with wall-mounted surfboards, and kids dine free on Tuesdays.

Kenji   FUSION $

(☑808-320-3558; www.kenjiburger.com; 4-788 Kuhio Hwy; mains $9-14; ⊙11am-8:30pm Wed-Mon; ⬆) A new-school Japanese fast-food fusion joint spinning up truffle and teriyaki burgers, fried-chicken sandwiches with sriracha slaw, and a Japanese burrito – the number-one bestseller. More a hand roll than a burrito, it's nori-wrapped rice stuffed with shrimp tempura, crab meat and spicy tuna, drizzled with *unagi* (freshwater eel) sauce. More please.

VIP Treats & Sweets   BAKERY $

(☑808-635-8218; www.facebook.com/VIPtreats andsweets; 4-439 Kuhio Hwy, Kauai Village Shopping Center; snacks from $2; ⊙6:30am-4pm Mon-Sat; ℗⬆) Pop into this friendly bakery for *malasadas* (Portuguese doughnuts) fried to order from 7am to 2pm Tuesday, Thursday and Saturday, or to pick up interesting breads, like sourdough made with local taro. VIP supplies cafes and restaurants around the island, and really knows its stuff.

Tiki Tacos   MEXICAN $

(☑808-823-8226; www.facebook.com/tikitacos; 4-961 Kuhio Hwy, Waipouli Complex; mains $6-8; ⊙10am-8:30pm; ℗) This laid-back place with a reggae soundtrack offers authentic taqueria gravitas right down to the house-made tortillas. Tacos come with chicken, locally caught fish, chorizo, shrimp, Kaua'i-raised lamb, beef or pork, spicy vegetables or tofu, and they're piled high with island-grown cabbage, *queso fresco* (fresh cheese), sour cream and onion. The house-made hot sauces rock.

Shrimp Station   SEAFOOD $

(☑808-821-0192; 4-985 Kuhio Hwy; dishes $8-15; ⊙11am-3pm & 5-8:30pm; ℗⬆) This offshoot of Waimea's original Shrimp Station serves the same family recipes. With seasonings such as garlic, Cajun and Thai on the shrimp tacos, burgers and plate meals, it's hard to shoot and miss here. Some claim it has the 'Best Coconut Shrimp on the Planet.' Investigate for yourself.

Tropical Dreams   ICE CREAM $

(http://tropicaldreamsicecream.com; 4-831 Kuhio Hwy; snacks from $5; ⊙noon-9pm Sun-Thu, to 9:30pm Fri & Sat; ℗⬆) A tiny taste of ice-cream heaven, this Hawaii-born chain rotates through scores of premium flavors crafted almost entirely from Hawaii-harvested ingredients. It does soft serve as well as old-fashioned scoops. It's so good the owners have even opened a store in Austin, Texas. Try the macadamia and honey flavor.

Papaya's Natural Foods   HEALTH FOOD $

(☑808-823-0190; www.papayasnaturalfoods. com; 4-901 Kuhio Hwy; ⊙8am-8pm Mon-Sat, 10am-5pm Sun; ℗🍴) 🌿 Kaua'i's biggest health-food store carries local and organic produce, plus other island specialties such as Kilauea honey and goat cheese. Deli fixings and the salad bar make for a quick, healthy meal, while the cafe grills taro burgers, blends fresh-fruit smoothies and sells shots of Hawaiian *noni* juice (a type of mulberry with smelly yellow fruit used medicinally).

Coconut's Fish Cafe   SEAFOOD $$

(☑808-320-3138; www.coconutsfishcafe.com; 4-831 Kuhio Hwy, Safeway Shopping Center; mains $13-22; ⊙11am-9pm; ℗⬆) A Kaua'i offshoot of its locations on Maui, Coconut's is a dependable and good-value option amid Waipouli's strip-mall ambience. Standouts are the macadamia-crusted mahimahi and the Kalua pork tacos.

Monico's Taqueria   MEXICAN $$

(☑808-822-4300; www.monicostaqueria.net; 4-733 Kuhio Hwy; mains $14-22; ⊙11am-3pm & 5-9pm Tue-Sun; ℗⬆) Everything made by this Oaxaca-born chef tastes fresh and authentic, from stuffed burritos and fish-taco plates to freshly made chips, salsa and sauces. Sip something from the well-stocked tequila bar while you wait.

KAPA'A & THE EASTSIDE WAIPOULI

THE SOURCE: MT WAI'ALE'ALE

Nicknamed the Rain Machine, Mt Wai'ale'ale (translated as 'rippling water' or 'overflowing water') averages more than 450in of rainfall annually. With a yearly record of 683in in 1982, it's widely regarded as one of the wettest places on earth. Its steep cliffs cause moist air to rise rapidly and focus rainfall in one area. Believed by ancient Hawaiians to be occupied by the god Kane, it's located in the center of the island, representing Kaua'i's *piko* (navel). It's the source of the Wailua, Hanalei and Waimea Rivers, as well as almost every visible waterfall on the island.

JO2 FUSION $$$

(☑ 808-212-1627; www.jotwo.com; 4-971 Kuhio Hwy; dishes $11-36; ⊙5-9pm; P) Flavors are subtle, fresh, and familiar yet inventive at this restaurant helmed by the highly regarded chef Jean Marie Josselin. His focus is all-natural cuisine, infused with Asian and Mediterranean flavors, and crafted from the best seafood, meat and vegetables available on the island. Highlights include risotto with seared *ono* (white-fleshed wahoo) and Kauai shrimp, and the buttermilk *pannacotta* dessert.

Oasis on the Beach HAWAII REGIONAL $$$

(☑808-822-9332; www.oasiskauai.com; 4-820 Kuhio Hwy, Waipouli Beach Resort & Spa; mains $15-31; ⊙8am-9pm; P) Truly on the beach, like the name says, with unmatched ocean views, a romantic atmosphere and sophisticated cuisine featuring local ingredients. It's perfect for sharing elevated fusion dishes or hitting up one of Kaua'i's better happy hours (4pm to 6pm daily). At Sunday brunch they spike the *loco moco* with cognac and the eggs Benedict with sriracha. Make reservations for dinner. Expect slow service.

Lemongrass Grill FUSION $$$

(☑ 808-822-2288; www.lemongrasskauai.com; 4-871 Kuhio Hwy; mains $18-40; ⊙4-9pm; P) This East Shore institution dishes up solid fusion fare, mainly with a Thai and Southeast Asian spin, such as hoisin charred ribs and fresh fish steamed, seared, or macadamia-nut crusted. Surf-and-turf steak-and-shrimp combos seal the deal for really hungry diners, and there is live music most nights.

🍷 Drinking & Nightlife

There are no bars here to speak of, but you can enjoy the tasty wine list and creative cocktails at JO2 (p121), order a perfect sunset cocktail on the shore at Oasis, or try a honey-wine tasting at Kaua'i's only meadery, Nani Moon.

☆ Entertainment

Outdoor Movies OUTDOOR CINEMA

(All Saints' Episcopal Church Kaua'i; ☑ 808-822-4267; www.allsaintskauai.org/movie-nights-on-the-lawn; 4-1065 Kuhio Hwy; ⊙Sep-Oct; ♠) FREE This Waipouli church usually hosts a couple of features in September and October on its wide lawn. Bring snacks and a blanket, get comfy and enjoy family-friendly entertainment with your brood. Screenings are usually on a Saturday night. Check the Facebook page of All Saints' Episcopal Church Kaua'i for upcoming dates.

🛍 Shopping

Waipouli's two pedestrian shopping malls are **Waipouli Town Center** (4-771 Kuhio Hwy) and **Kauai Village** (4-831 Kuhio Hwy). Options include supermarkets, restaurants and cafes.

Nani Moon Meadery & Tasting Room WINE

(☑ 808-651-2453; www.nanimoonmead.com; 4-939 Kuhio Hwy; tasting flights $12, by the glass $8; ⊙noon-5pm Tue-Sat) 🍷 Nani Moon makes and pours tropical honey wine, which is arguably the oldest alcoholic beverage on earth – humans have been drinking it for 6000 years or more. It crafts a half dozen flavors of mead using only locally sourced ingredients, including tropical fruit and ginger. Most are surprisingly dry, food-forward and 'best enjoyed under moonlight.'

Marta's Boat FASHION & ACCESSORIES

(☑ 808-822-3926; www.facebook.com/martasboat kauai; 4-770 Kuhio Hwy; ⊙10am-6pm Mon-Sat) This unique boutique delights 'princesses of all ages' with original block and screen prints on silks and other soft and flowing fabrics, and some funky, fab jewelry. We especially loved her hand-knitted quilts for babies, which would make any new parent smile. A quirky art-love philosophy is at work here.

Ambrose's Kapuna Surf Gallery ART

(☑ 808-822-3926; 770 Kuhio Hwy; ⊙11am-5pm Tue-Sat) Don't miss the chance to meet longtime artist-surfer-philosopher Ambrose Curry. Originally from California, he has lived on Kaua'i since 1968 and is also an artist and board shaper. You will love rambling around his workshop and gallery, which are an extension of his whirring mind. Interesting T-shirts, prints and paintings are all for sale.

Moloa'a Bay Coffee FOOD & DRINKS
(☑ 808-821-8100; http://moloaabaycoffee.com; 943 Kipuni Way; ⊙ 8am-noon Mon-Fri) If you've missed sampling this North Shore estate-grown coffee at Kaua'i's top farmers markets, stop by the retail shop on weekday mornings to taste the hand-picked, small-batch roasted brews. Unusually, it also makes flavored teas from dried coffee-fruit husks.

ℹ Information

There are ATMs inside **Foodland** (☑ 808-822-7271; www.foodland.com; 4-771 Kuhio Hwy; ⊙ 6am-11pm) in Waipouli Town Center and, just a minute north, inside **Safeway** (☑ 808-822-2464; www.safeway.com; 4-831 Kuhio Hwy; ⊙ store 24hr, pharmacy 8am-8pm Mon-Fri, 9am-6pm Sat & Sun) in the Kauai Village shopping center.

ℹ Getting There & Away

Waipouli lies between Wailua and Kapa'a, about 7 miles north of Lihu'e airport. If you're driving, your only option is the Kuhio Hwy, which can slow to a crawl as it snakes through Old Town Kapa'a. This town is oriented toward vehicles and built out with shopping centers set up around huge parking lots. It's no pedestrian paradise.

Linking Lihu'e with Hanalei, Kaua'i Bus (p279) runs north and south through Waipouli approximately hourly from 6am to 10pm on weekdays (limited weekend service).

Kapa'a

POP 11,000

Featuring the charming heritage wooden shopfronts of Old Town Kapa'a, this is the only walkable town on the Eastside. Although it's not Kaua'i at its most beautiful, sunny Kapa'a has a more down-to-earth disposition than other tourist towns, and its eclectic population of old-timers, fresh transplants, new-age hippies and budget travelers coexists happily. A paved recreational path for cyclists and pedestrians runs along the part-sandy, part-rocky coast, the island's best vantage point for sunrises. Kapa'a's downfall? It sits right along the highway – try walking across the road during rush hour!

◎ Sights

★ **Kealia Beach Park** BEACH
(Kuhio Hwy; P ♿ 🐕) Blessed with a wild, near-pristine location, a laid-back vibe and easy access via car or the coastal path, scenic Kealia is the Eastside's best beach. Isolated from residential development, the beach begins at mile marker 10 as you head north on the Kuhio Hwy and continues for more than a mile. Outdoor showers, restrooms, lifeguards, picnic tables and ample parking are available. Natural shade is not, so sunscreen is a must.

The sandy bottom slopes offshore gradually, making it possible to walk out far to catch long rides back. But the pounding barrels can be treacherous and are not recommended for novices; it's a crushing shore break. A breakwater protects the north end, so swimming and snorkeling are occasionally possible there.

Fuji Beach BEACH
(Baby Beach; Moanakai Rd; ♿ 🐕) Nicknamed 'Baby Beach' because an offshore reef creates a shallow, placid pool of water that's perfect for toddlers, it's located in a modest neighborhood that attracts few tourists. This is a real locals' beach. Please be respectful.

Kapa'a Beach Park BEACH
(⊙ dawn-dusk; P ♿ 🐕) From the highway, you'd think that Kapa'a is beachless. But along the coast is a low-key, mile-long ribbon of golden sand. While the whole area is officially a county park called Kapa'a Beach Park, that name is commonly used only for the northern end, where there's a grassy field and picnic tables. A further 800yd north there is a public swimming pool (☑ 808-822-3842; ⊙ 7:30am-4:30pm Tue-Fri, from 10am Sat, from noon sun) FREE. The best sandy area is at the south end, informally called Lihi Beach, where you'll find locals hanging out and talking story.

Orchid Alley GARDENS
(☑ 808-822-0486; 4-1383 Kuhio Hwy; ⊙ 10am-5pm) FREE Tucked down a little path off the main drag is this orchid nursery and butterfly garden. The owners have been here for over 20 years. They sell orchids they grow themselves and invite guests to tour their netted butterfly garden, which swirls with a handful of monarchs and swallowtail butterflies, just off the main nursery courtyard. At the rear there's a good vintage clothing shop.

Kapaʻa & Waipouli

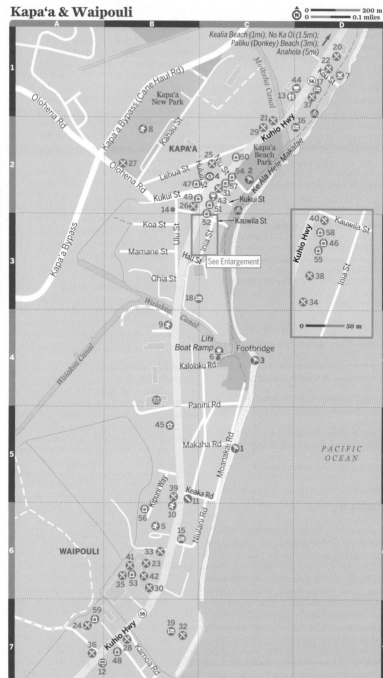

0 — 200 m
0 — 0.1 miles

Kealia Beach (1mi); No Ka Oi (1.5mi);
Paliku (Donkey) Beach (3mi);
Anahola (5mi)

Moikeha Canal

Kuhio Hwy

Kou St

Ke Ala Hele Makalae

Kapaʻa New Park

Kahau St

Olohena Rd

KAPAʻA

Kapaʻa Beach Park

Lehua St

Olohena Rd

Kapaʻa Bypass (Cane Haul Rd)

Kapaʻa Bypass

Kukui St

Ulu St

Hulumi St

Kukui St

Kauwila St

Koa St

Inia St

Kuhio Hwy

Kauwila St

Mamane St

Hau St

See Enlargement

Ohia St

0 — 50 m

Waiakea Canal

Lihi
Boat Ramp

Footbridge

Kaloloku Rd

Panihi Rd

PACIFIC
OCEAN

Makaha Rd

Moanakai Rd

WAIPOULI

Kipuni Way

Keaka Rd

Ulunui Rd

Kuhio Hwy

Kamoa Rd

Kapaʻa & Waipouli

🏃 Activities

★ **Kapaʻa Beach Shop** OUTDOORS
(☏808-212-8615; www.kapaabeachshop.com; 4-1592 Kuhio Hwy; bike rental per day $10, snorkel-set rental per day/week $7/15; ⊘8am-6pm Sun-Fri; 🚸) Located along the coastal path, this shop has loads of affordable rental options, including cruiser and hybrid comfort bikes, snorkel sets and other beach gear (chairs, umbrellas and coolers). It also sells scuba, free diving and spearfishing equipment. It is among the better connected spearfishing shops on the island.

Tamba Surf Company SURFING
(☏808-823-6942; www.tamba.com; 4-1543 Kuhio Hwy; bodyboard/surfboard rental per day from $10/25; ⊘9am-5pm Mon-Sat, 10am-3pm Sun) Along with board rentals, this fun, well-branded shop sells hip surf clothing, and new and used boards. Surf fans may recognize the name as seen on the boards, hats and T-shirts of many pro surfers, past and present, who hail from Kauaʻi.

KE ALA HELE MAKALAE

The Eastside's Ke Ala Hele Makalae (The Path That Goes by the Coast) is a paved shared-use path reserved for pedestrians, cyclists and other nonmotorized modes of transportation. Also known as the Kauai Path (www.kauaipath.org) or Kapa'a Bike Path, it has jump-started locals into daily fitness: walking, running, cycling, rollerblading and, perhaps, forgoing the habit of driving everywhere.

In Kapa'a, the path currently starts at Lihi Boat Ramp (Map p124) at the south end of Kapa'a Beach Park and ends just past Paliku (Donkey) Beach at Ahihi Point, 5 miles north. It also runs for 2 miles south from Kapa'a to Lydgate State Park, but at the time of writing, around one mile of this was along the busy Kuhio Hwy. Ask bike-rental places for an update on this stretch.

The ambitious plan calls for it to eventually extend more than 16 miles all the way from Lihu'e's Nawiliwili Harbor to Anahola Beach Park, but those dreams have been in place for many years now, with zero progress to show for it.

While a loud minority has complained about pouring concrete along the coast, most appreciate the easy access. Sunrise walks are brilliant. And for an added kick, you can head out on a cruiser bike rented in Kapa'a or Waipouli. It would be wonderful to see the path extended sooner rather than later.

Kauai Power Yoga
YOGA

(☏ 808-635-5868; www.kauaipoweryoga.com; 4-1191 Kuhio Hwy; per class $20, 30 days unlimited $50) Affiliated with Baptiste Power Yoga, a national brand of Vinyasa flow, it offers two to four classes a day within a short walk from Old Town Kapa'a. If you plan on taking more than two classes, buy a month's unlimited pass.

Coconut Coasters
CYCLING

(☏ 808-822-7368; www.coconutcoasters.com; 4-1586 Kuhio Hwy; bike rental per day from $20; ⊙9am-5pm Tue-Sat, to 4pm Mon & Sun; ⊕) Conveniently located in the heart of Kapa'a town, this outfit rents beach cruisers, road and mountain bikes, tandem bicycles, hybrid comfort bikes, kids' bikes and tow trailers. The shop, which also does repairs, is right by the bike path. With prior arrangement, bikes can be delivered to your accommodations.

Kapa'a New Park
SPORTS

(www.kauai.gov; 4536 Olohena Rd; ⊕) You'll find free tennis courts, soccer and baseball fields, and a skateboarding park here.

🍴 Tours

Duke's Kayak Adventures
KAYAKING

(☏ 808-639-2834; http://kayaktourkauai.com; 3-4684 Kuhio Hwy; per person $39; ⊙tours depart at 7am & 12:15pm Mon-Sat) Offers kayak tours up the Wailua River to Uluwehi Falls. Booking ahead for this popular tour is recommended.

Wailua Kayak Adventures
OUTDOORS

(☏guided tours 808-639-6332, rentals 808-320-0680; www.wailuakayakadventure.com; 1345 Ulu St; single/double kayak rental per day $35/70, 4½hr tours per couple $120, SUP rental per day $30) Offers good-value individual kayak and SUP rentals, but you'll have to transport your chosen vessel to Wailua River on top of your car. Rental pickup is available between 8:30am and 10:30am and returns must be in by 5pm. It also offers affordable guided kayak tours departing at 7am and 1pm that include generous snacks at your waterfall destination.

Hawaiian Style Fishing
FISHING

(☏808-635-7335; www.hawaiianstylefishing. com; Kaloloku Rd; 4hr trips per person $140, half-/full-day private charter $600/1050) Join gregarious Captain Terry, who shares the catch with you. Shared and private charters (six-passenger maximum) depart from Lihi Boat Ramp at the end of Kaloloku Rd. Book a week or more in advance.

🎉 Festivals & Events

Old Town Kapa'a comes to life on the first Saturday of every month, when the shops, cafes and restaurants stay open late and the crowds descend from all over for a bit of eating, shopping and people watching.

Kapa'a Art Walk
CULTURAL

(⊙5-8pm 1st Sat of month) Old Town businesses open their doors in celebration, showcasing island artists, live music and food. Locals and visitors alike come together in high spirits, and after-parties often keep going past 9pm. Parking is crowded, so arrive early or expect to walk into town. Bring cash.

Heiva I Kaua'i la Orana Tahiti DANCE
(www.heivaikauai.com; ⊙Aug; 🔊) FREE For two days in early August, dance troupes from as far away as Tahiti, Japan and the US mainland join groups from around Hawaii at Kapa'a Beach Park (p123) for this traditional Tahitian dancing and drumming competition.

🛏 Sleeping

Kauai Beach House HOSTEL $
(☎808-652-8162; www.kauaibeachhouse.net; 4-1552 Kuhio Hwy; dm/r with shared bathroom from $38/103; 🛜) Not the cleanest or cheapest of hostels, with ramshackle bunks and courtyard, and a relaxed hippy vibe. Private rooms tend to be better maintained than dorms, but they also share bathrooms. It's overpriced, but on the plus side, there's a communal kitchen and it's located right on the beach.

Pono Kai Resort RESORT $$
(☎808-822-9831; http://ponokairesort.com; 4-1250 Kuhio Hwy; studio/1-/2-bedroom condo from $135/150/180; P@🛜🏊) An aging three-star condo complex dominates the middle stretch of Kapa'a beach. Most of these units are not especially well maintained, offering outdated bathrooms and electronics, but they're spacious. Outside there are BBQ grills, shuffleboard tables and tennis courts. Cleaning and reservation fees vary by rental agency.

★Hotel Coral Reef HOTEL $$$
(☎808-822-4481, 800-843-4659; www.hotelcoralreefresort.com; 4-1516 Kuhio Hwy; f from $280; P❄🛜🏊) A lovely boutique hotel that provides good value for money. Rooms offer wood furnishings, recessed lighting, granite counters and flat-screen TVs, not to mention sliding shutters and glass doors that open onto the beach if you spring for an ocean view. Recently renovated 3rd-floor suites are particularly comfortable.

Delicious continental breakfasts come gratis and include freshly baked banana bread.

🍴 Eating

Roadside restaurants abound, none terrible, but some terribly touristy. There's a collection of beachside gourmet food trucks on the northern end of the Kapa'a strip.

★Pono Market DELI $
(☎808-822-4581; 4-1300 Kuhio Hwy; meals $6-14; ⊙6am-2pm Mon-Sat; 🔊) Line up for local *grinds* (food) at this longtime hole-in-the-wall serving generous plate lunches, homemade sushi rolls, spicy ahi *poke* bowls, savory seafood delicacies such as smoked marlin, and traditional Hawaiian dishes including pork *laulau* (bundle made of pork and salted butterfish, wrapped in taro and *ti* leaves and steamed). Bite into a *manju* (Japanese sweet bean-filled pastries) for dessert. It serves coffee and scoop ice cream too!

Al Pastor MEXICAN $
(☎808-652-6953; 4-1620 Kuhio Hwy; dishes $8-11; ⊙noon-5pm Tue-Sun) The most popular food truck of the bunch, this is a real-deal, authentic taco truck with fresh fish tacos and burritos, terrific *al pastor* (spit-roasted pork) and *lengua* (beef tongue) tacos, garlic shrimp, and vegetarian burritos stuffed with beans, rice and sautéed zucchini, onion and carrots. *USA Today* ranked it as a top-25 food truck in America for a reason.

Scorpacciata PIZZA $
(☎808-635-5569; www.scorpacciatakauai.com; 4-1306 Kuhio Hwy; pizzas $11-16; ⊙11am-8pm; 🔊) A permanently parked food truck, firing individually sized, thin-crust pizza pies from local ingredients. Keep it simple with an authentic margherita, or get adventurous with the fig and pig, featuring smoked bacon and fig jam. And don't skip the Parmesan fries.

> **ISLAND INSIGHTS: HULA**
>
> The intoxicating, graceful movements of hula dancing have not always been practiced solely by those with two X chromosomes. Prior to Western contact, *kane* (men) performed hula, until early-19th-century Christian missionaries discouraged its practice altogether. Today, a slow-growing revival of *kane* hula has taken shape, with much credit given to local *kumu* (teachers).

...ners Market
MARKET $

...m/kauai-farmers-markets; Kapa'a ...k, Olohena Rd; snacks from $5; ⊙ 3-...) ✔ One of the island's biggest ...tended farmers markets, this ...oor gathering is the spot to pick up local produce such as mangoes, star fruit, ginger and even fresh coconuts. Many of the vendors own organic farms on the North Shore.

Hoku Foods
HEALTH FOOD $

(☑ 808-821-1500; www.hokufoods.com; 4585 Lehua St; snacks $5-10; ⊙ 10am-6pm; ✎) ✔ This small, back-street, all-natural grocer is ideal for health-conscious types who seek a wide assortment of organic, gluten-free, bulk and raw foods. Stocks locally grown produce, locally sourced fish, and convenient snacks and drinks for hiking or the beach.

Holo Holo Paniolo Grill
BARBECUE $

(☑ 808-822-4656; http://paniolobbqkauai.com; 4-1345 Kuhio Hwy; sandwiches $9-10, plates $14-15; ⊙ 11am-2:30pm Mon, Fri & Sat, 4:30-9:30pm Mon-Sat) The grill smolders with tri-tip, chicken, burgers and ribs. This is a great opportunity to try Santa Maria–style BBQ, which hails from Central California. Order inside and pick a table on the atmospheric patio out front of the historic building. Hawaiian influences also feature with grilled fish sandwiches and shrimp broils packed with seafood, corn and potatoes.

Mermaids Cafe
FUSION $

(☑ 808-821-2026; www.mermaidskauai.com; 4-1384 Kuhio Hwy; mains $10-16; ⊙ 11am-9pm; ✎) 'No shirt, no shoes, no worry' at this walk-up counter that makes humongous burritos and wraps, curry bowls and stir-fry plates. Get the ahi nori wrap with brown rice and wasabi-cream sauce, and you'll return every day thereafter to repeat the experience – maybe adding a coconut-milk Thai ice tea. This is a Kapa'a institution for a reason.

Ono Family Restaurant
DINER $

(☑ 808-822-1710; 4-1292 Kuhio Hwy; mains $10-14, shave ice $3.75; ⊙ 7am-1pm Mon-Fri, 7am-2pm Sat) A classic diner with big breakfasts, meaty burgers and larger plate lunches built around teriyaki chicken and Portuguese-style pork mains. Grab a cute wooden booth and take in the history and the budget comfort food, or step around the corner to the service window for a blast of the beloved shave ice.

★ The Local
GASTROPUB $$

(☑ 808-431-4926; www.thelocalkauai.com; 4-1380 Kuhio Hwy; mains & snacks $10-25; ⊙ 3-9pm Wed-Sun) A farm-to-table gastropub with imaginative dishes like beer-battered tuna belly, spicy buttermilk-fried chicken, starfruit Caprese and lamb empanadas. It does wood-fired pizzas and muddled and mixed cocktails. Dinner service begins at 5pm, and the airy corner location is enlivened with colorful large-format photography of Kaua'i scenery.

Sukothai
THAI $$

(☑ 808-821-1224; https://sukhothaicafe.com; 4-1330 Kuhio Hwy; mains $12-20; ⊙ 11am-9pm; ✎) Relocated to the heart of Kapa'a, Sukothai is considered Kaua'i's best Thai restaurant. Look forward to dishes not often seen on American menus, such as *pla prig prow* (fish stir-fried with chili paste and cashews) and a tofu *larb* (spicy salad). There are no less than 10 vegetarian dishes on offer and it does all your favorite curries, noodles and rice dishes.

Art Cafe Hemingway
CAFE $$

(☑ 808-822-2250; www.art-cafe-hemingway.com; 4-1495 Kuhio Hwy; mains $13-24; ⊙ 9am-1pm daily & 6-9pm Fri-Sun; 🐾) It does creative omelets and scrambles for breakfast, veggie curries and beef bourguignon at lunch and dinner, and there is always a quiche du jour. But the desserts – think chocolate samosas and black-pepper soufflé – get most of the local buzz. Service was unfortunately haphazard on our last visit.

Chicken in a Barrel
BARBECUE $$

(☑ 808-823-0780; http://chickeninabarrel.com; 4-1586 Kuhio Hwy; meals $13-19; ⊙ 11am-8:30pm Mon-Sat, to 7pm Sun) A smoky, salty hut a block off the beach, this is the original of its three locations on the island (the others are in Hanalei and Waimea). It is a barbecue joint, pure and simple, with quarter- and half-chicken plates, pulled pork, baby-back ribs, and rib-and-chicken combos, all smothered in its signature sauce.

Kountry Kitchen
DINER $$

(☑ 808-822-3511; www.kountrystylekitchen.com; 4-1489 Kuhio Hwy; mains $9-22; ⊙ 6am-1:30pm) A good old-fashioned Hawaiian diner, with a bamboo motif on the walls, no-nonsense waitstaff and big breakfasts. Consider the Polynesian omelet with kimchi and Portuguese sausage, or the grilled fish and eggs. It also does *kalua*-pig plates, burgers and teriyaki-chicken sandwiches. This way to comfort food.

PALIKU (DONKEY) BEACH

Once unofficially known as a nude spot, this **beach** (Makanani St) is scenic but rarely swimmable. It's a place where you can escape the cars on the highway and instead amble along on foot, with rocks scattered at the water's edge, windswept ironwood trees and *naupaka* and *'ilima* flowers adding dashes of color.

Summer swells might be manageable, but stay ashore if you're an inexperienced ocean swimmer. From October to May, dangerous rip currents and a powerful shore break take over. Stick to sunbathing or sunrise beach strolls at that time.

The beach is accessible two ways. You can cycle or walk north along Kapa'a's coastal path and turn *makai* (seaward). Or you can drive the Kuhio Hwy to a parking lot with restrooms about halfway between mile markers 11 and 12. Look for the small brown parking and hiking sign.

The beach-access footpath cuts through a 300-acre planned community called **Kealia Kai** (www.kealiakai.com). Public nudity is illegal in Hawaii and the developer has cracked down on folks baring all.

Sam's
Oceanview Restaurant INTERNATIONAL $$$
(☑808-822-7887; www.samsoceanview.com; 4-1546 Kuhio Hwy; dishes $11-32; ☺4-9pm Wed-Mon, 9am-3pm Sun; ⓟ) Start with ahi *poke* nachos, followed by wild-boar and lamb sausages and Belgian fries, or move on to a flank steak with chimichurri sauce or a vegetarian island curry. California dominates the wine list and the Pacific Ocean dominates the view.

🍷 Drinking & Nightlife

★ **Java Kai** CAFE
(☑808-823-6887; www.javakai.com; 4-1384 Kuhio Hwy; ☺6am-7pm; 🕎🍴) 🧀 Always busy, this Kaua'i-based micro-roastery is best for grabbing a cup of joe or a fruit smoothie to go. The muffins, scones, banana bread and coconut-macnut sticky rolls are baked fresh, and the salads are tossed with Kailani Farms greens. Another highlight is the selection of Blair Estate shade-grown organic coffee, grown just a few minutes up the road.

If you come early, avoid the lines and head around back to **Kai Bar** in the roastery.

Kauai Juice Co JUICE BAR
(☑808-631-3893; www.kauaijuiceco.com; 4-1384 Kuhio Hwy; ☺8am-5pm; 🚲🍴) Another foot-hold in the benevolent Kauai Juice Co empire which pushes addictive green and fruit juices, freshly pressed nut milks and coconut manna. You should definitely try the manna – but everything here is good.

Small Town Coffee Co CAFE
(www.smalltowncoffee.com; 1543 Kuhio Hwy; ☺6am-4pm; 🍴) This indie coffeehouse brews organic, fair-trade coffee for the hippie-boho crowd, who also enjoy the fresh kombucha and chai tea. Good tunes perpetually play from the big red bus in the strip-mall parking lot.

Olympic Cafe BAR
(☑808-822-5825; www.olympiccafekauai.com; 4-1354 Kuhio Hwy; ☺6am-9pm Sun-Thu, to 10pm Fri & Sat) Historically, people have long packed this spacious 2nd-floor sports bar to enjoy perched views of the Coconut Coast. With a full bar, copious draft beers and decent island-style bar food, it's a popular place to grab a drink, especially during happy hour. Also a top spot the morning after for hearty scrambles and breakfast wraps.

🛍 Shopping

★ **Larry's Music** MUSICAL INSTRUMENTS
(☑808-652-9999; http://kamoaukulelecompany.com; 4-1310 Kuhio Hwy; ☺11am-4pm Mon-Fri) 🧀 This high-quality uke dealer offers starters for less than $100 and vintage and high-end ukes costing $1000 to $5000. All come with the manufacturer's warranty. Ask about ukuleles and expect a warm and thorough response from the musically talented folks doing the sales. This place is a blast. No wonder it's been around since 1952.

Shipwrecked CLOTHING
(http://shipwreckedkauai.com; 4-1384 Kuhio Hwy; ☺9am-5pm Mon-Sat, to 4pm Sun) The best clothing shop on the Eastside offers stylish casual and beachwear from mainland-, Australian- and London-based designers like Passenger and Vuori for men, and Joa

Brown, Boys and Arrows, and One Teaspoon for women. It has nice threads for kids and local skincare brands too.

Hula Girl
CLOTHING, GIFTS

(☑808-822-1950; www.facebook.com/HulaGirl Kauai; 4-1340 Kuhio Hwy; ◎10am-6pm) This family-run shop is a standout for contemporary Hawaiian clothing and gifts – shirts, dresses, jewelry, souvenirs and more, but also for fabulous reproductions of popular Aloha prints from the 1940s and 1950s. Look for the Avanti label for the best vintage reproductions. You'll pay extra for those, but it's worth it.

Aloha Images
ART

(☑808-821-1382; www.alohaimages.com; 4504 Kukui St; ◎11am-7pm) The oldest art gallery on the island is arguably its best, especially when it comes to highly regarded fine artists – folks such as Steven Valiere, who is local and traffics in fanciful large-format canvases, and Tim Nguyen, who offers surrealist Polynesian scenes with deep soul. Interest-free lay away available.

Kiko
GIFTS & SOUVENIRS

(☑808-822-5096; www.kikokauai.com; 4-1316 Kuhio Hwy; ◎10am-6pm Mon-Sat, 11am-5pm Sun) It deals in 'simple goods' including beach and shoulder bags crafted from upcycled rice sacks, saris and plastic bags; a carefully curated book table; some beautiful driftwood fish sculptures; and toys and books for kiddos. It's set back from the street. Enter through an inviting garden.

Kela's Glass Gallery
GLASS

(☑808-822-4527; www.glass-art.com; 4-1400 Kuhio Hwy; ◎10am-7pm Mon-Sat, 11:30am-4:30pm Sun) Glowing pendants, glass vases and sculpture, platters and bowls, globes and animals, even waves! The glass comes in many striking colors and forms at this one-of-a-kind gallery representing dozens of artists and artisans. Even if you're not in the mood to buy, it's a fun shop to browse in.

a.ell atelier
FASHION & ACCESSORIES

(www.aelldesign.com; 4-1320 Kuhio Hwy; ◎10am-6pm Mon-Sat, 11am-5pm Sun) This is the Kaua'i branch of the Portland-based fashion boutique with boho flavor. It offers dresses and gowns of varying elegance, the best of which are under the India Ella label and are made from upcycled Indian saris. It has a rack of cute, Kaua'i-made bikinis and lovely sea-glass jewelry too.

Vicky's Fabrics
ARTS & CRAFTS

(☑808-822-1746; www.vickysfabrics.com; 4-1326 Kuhio Hwy; ◎9am-5pm Mon-Sat) Established in the early 1980s by Vicky Masuoka, this simple storefront stocks a wide selection of Hawaiian, Japanese and batik-print fabrics for quilters and crafters. Vicky's daughter Maile Bloxom now runs the shop on a daily basis, but original seamstress Vicky is still very involved with the business. Also worth perusing are their handmade Hawaiian quilts and bags.

Island Hemp & Cotton
CLOTHING

(☑808-821-0225; www.facebook.com/IslandHemp CottonCo; 4-1373 Kuhio Hwy; ◎9:30am-6pm Mon-Sat, 10am-5pm Sun) Firmly and proudly entrenched in the hippie fashion niche, it offers bags, wallets, hats and all manner of flowing garments made from hemp or organic cotton, including a small collection of very cool, and quite pricey, Johnny Was pieces. Though it has a Kuhio Hwy address, the entrance is on Huluili St.

Calabash
FASHION & ACCESSORIES

(☑808-482-1856; www.calabashcollection.com; 4-1351 Kuhio Hwy; ◎9am-5pm Mon-Sat) A quirky yet upscale gallery of wearable wood, and lots of it. Yes, here are wooden belts, caps with flexible wooden bills, and lots of wooden jewelry including all-wood watches. Most of the gear is made from Hawaiian favorite, koa wood.

Earth & Sea Gallery
GIFTS & SOUVENIRS

(☑808-821-2831; 4504 Kukui St; ◎10am-8:30pm) A simple but nourishing handicrafts gallery offering wooden bowls, handblown glass, hand-bound journals, sarongs, crystals and more. Even the earnest, inspirational quotes carved into wood resonate without irony here. That in itself is a miracle. Set in the wonderful Dragon building.

Bamboo Works
GIFTS & SOUVENIRS

(☑808-821-8688; www.bambooworks.com; 4-1396 Kuhio Hwy; ◎10am-6pm Mon-Sat, 11am-4pm Sun) A gallery of all things bamboo – furniture, lanterns, picture frames and room dividers, and even sunglasses frames, bowls, cutting boards, and, wait for it, surfboards! Heck, they even have socks made out of bamboo.

Kauai Store
GIFTS & SOUVENIRS

(☑808-631-6706; www.thekauaistore.com; 4-1191 Kuhio Hwy; ◎10am-6pm Mon-Sat) Forgot to buy gifts for the people you claim to love? Drop into this one-stop souvenir shop for Kaua'i-made chocolate, body creams, candles and soaps. There is red sea salt from Hanapepe, and mango-chili sauce from Kauai Juice Co. It also stocks clothing, ceramics, macadamia nuts and much more.

Hee Fat General Store CHILDREN'S CLOTHING
(☑808-823-6169; 4-1354 Kuhio Hwy; ☉10am-6pm) The best goods at this gift and clothing shop are in the kids' section. Think cute T-shirts and onesies featuring critters that live beneath the sea. Oh, and it has fish ashtrays too. It sells popular shave ice around the corner.

Deja Vu Surf CLOTHING
(☑808-822-4401; www.dejavusurf.com; 4-1419 Kuhio Hwy; ☉9:30am-6pm) A vast air-conditioned emporium of beach and beach-ish gear featuring name brands including Billabong, Da Kine, O'Neill and Volcom. It has a small kids' section, a range of sun-glasses, and the most recent GoPros and Skullcandy headphones as well.

❶ Information

First Hawaiian Bank (☑808-822-4966; www.fhb.com; 4-1366 Kuhio Hwy; ☉8:30am-4pm Mon-Thu, to 6pm Fri) Has a 24-hour ATM.

Kapa'a Post Office (☑808-822-0093; www.usps.com; 4-1101 Kuhio Hwy; ☉9am-4pm Mon-Fri, to 1pm Sat)

Samuel Mahelona Memorial Hospital
(☑808-822-4961; www.smmh.hhsc.org; 4800 Kawaihau Rd) Basic 24-hour emergency care. Serious cases are transferred to Lihu'e's Wilcox Memorial Hospital (p272).

❶ Getting There & Away

Kapa'a is 8 miles north of Lihu'e airport. To avoid the paralyzing crawl to and from Wailua, take the Kapa'a Bypass road.

Linking Lihu'e to Hanalei, Kaua'i Bus (p279) runs north and south through Kapa'a approximately hourly from 6am to 10pm on weekdays (limited weekend service).

Old Town Kapa'a is walkable. To get to nearby beaches and some outlying sights, rent a bike from Kapa'a Beach Shop (p125) or Coconut Coasters (p126).

Family firm **Rent A Car Kauai** (☑808-822-9272; www.rentacarkauai.com; 4-1101 Kuhio Hwy) has great customer service, and is a good choice for renting economy-sized cars and larger 4WD SUVs. Most vehicles are older models that have racked up a lot of miles. Five-day-minimum rental required; free pickups and drop-offs at Lihu'e Airport.

Anahola
POP 2200

Most travelers don't even stop in sleepy Anahola, a Hawaiian fishing and farming village with rootsy charm and a stunning coastline. Pineapple and sugar plantations once thrived here, but today the area is mainly residential, with subdivisions of Hawaiian homestead lots. The few who spend the night will find rural seclusion among longtime locals.

Grouped together at the side of Kuhio Hwy, just south of mile marker 14, Anahola's diminutive commercial center includes a post office and a convenience store with a fantastic deli.

◎ Sights

★**'Aliomanu Beach** BEACH
(🏖) Secluded 'Aliomanu Beach is a spot frequented primarily by locals, who pole- and throw-net fish and gather *limu* (edible seaweed). It's a mile-long stretch of beach, with gritty golden sand, a few rocks in the shallows and crystalline water. Windswept and rugged in winter, it's serene all summer, and a spectacular stretch of virgin beach all year long.

You can get to the beach's pretty northern end by turning onto the second 'Aliomanu Rd, just past mile marker 15 on the Kuhio Hwy. Turn left onto Kalalea View Dr, then drive around 0.5 miles and hang your first right.

Hole in the Mountain LANDMARK
Ever since a landslide altered this once-obvious landmark, the *puka* (hole) in Pu'u Konanae has been a mere sliver. From slightly north of mile marker 15 on Hwy 56, look back at the mountain, down to the right of the tallest pinnacle: on sunny days, light shines through a slit in the rock face.

Legend says that the original hole was created when a warrior threw his spear through the mountain, causing the water stored within to gush forth as waterfalls.

Anahola Beach Park BEACH
(🏖🏖) Despite having no sign from the highway, this locals' beach is an easy getaway. Backed by pines and palms, it's blessed with excellent swimming thanks to a wide, sandy bay with a sheltered cove at the south end. At the beach's choppy northern end is the surf break Unreals (p132).

Because this county park sits on Hawaiian Home Lands, you'll probably share the beach with Hawaiian families, especially

HAWAIIAN HEALING HANDS

In the late 1970s, Angeline Kaihalanaopuna Hopkins Locey moved home to Hawaii after years of living in California. Back in her native land, Angeline, who is three-quarters Native Hawaiian and grew up on O'ahu, experienced a cultural homecoming as well as a geographic one. She embraced Hawaiian healing, studied with *lomilomi kumu* (traditional Hawaiian massage teacher) Margret Machado on the Big Island, and in the mid-1980s established a homestead in Anahola, where she began to share her gift of therapeutic touch with the community. Over the years 'Auntie Angeline' became a local icon, and today her son Michael and granddaughter Malia carry on her legacy.

Angeline's Mu'olaulani (☎ 808-822-3235; www.angelineslomikauai.com; Kamalomalo'o Pl; massage treatments $175; ◷ 9am-2pm Mon-Fri, by appointment only) is an authentic introduction to Hawaiian healing practices and remains untouristy and frequented by locals. Don't expect plush towels, glossy marble floors or an endless menu of face and nail pampering. A trip to Angeline's is more like visiting a friend's bungalow, with an outdoor shower, wooden-plank deck, massage tables separated by curtains, and simple sarongs for covering up. Treatments include a steam, a sea-salt-clay scrub and a Hawaiian *oli* (chant).

As an expression of *ho'okipa* (hospitality), the Loceys invite guests to stay and sip a drink on the patio after the treatment. The facilities (including showers and sauna) are unisex, but the staff is glad to provide same-sex facilities upon request. Advance reservations are a must; last appointment at noon.

on weekends. Remember, it's their beach: respect the locals. There are two ways to get here: for the south end, turn off Kuhio Hwy onto Kukuihale Rd at mile marker 13, drive a mile down and then turn onto the dirt beach road. For the north end, take 'Aliomanu Rd at mile marker 14 and park in the sandy lot.

🏃 Activities

Unreals   SURFING

On the Eastside, Unreals breaks at Anahola Bay. It's a consistent right point that can work well on an easterly wind swell, when *kona* (leeward) winds are offshore.

🛏 Sleeping

Kaleialoha   RENTAL HOUSE $$

(☎ 888-311-5252; www.kauaialoha.com; 4934 'Aliomanu Rd; d $175-300; 🛜) Set on the north end of the Anahola Beach area, these four romantic wooden houses are sprinkled in a lovely quiet neighborhood fronting the beach. Some have a kitchenette or full kitchen, but there's no telephone. Ask about weekly discounts.

Aliomanu Palms   RENTAL HOUSE $$$

(☎ 808-245-8841; www.kauaivacationrentals. com; 4880 'Aliomanu Rd; from $350; 🛜) A gorgeous sea-foam-green beach cottage, and a larger three-bedroom house on one property fronting the beach. Both are for rent. Interiors are grandmother chic, but the setting is magic.

🍴 Eating

★ Whaler's General Store   DELI $

(☎ 808-822-5818; 4-4350 Kuhio Hwy; poke by the pound $7-15; ◷ 6am-9:30pm) At first it looks like your basic minimart, but hidden among the cold drinks, snacks, flip-flops and sunblock is a damn good deli with sushi and a range of *poke* by the pound. Flavors include ahi, octopus, shrimp and kimchi, and *pipa kaula* – a raw marinated peppery beef. Grab yours to go and *grind* (eat) on the beach.

Anahola Farmers Market   MARKET $

(Hokualele Rd; meals around $10; ◷ 10am-2pm Sun; 🍴) Not so much a traditional farmers market, but a worthy stop for fantastic handicrafts and drums, sterling-silver jewelry, fresh-cut fruit, cold coconuts and tasty wild boar, *huli-huli* (rotisserie-grilled) chicken and sautéed shrimp plate lunches, not to mention fresh-baked mango bread. There's a warm and welcoming vibe here.

Duane's Ono Char-Burger   FAST FOOD $

(☎ 808-822-9181; 4-4350 Kuhio Hwy; burgers $5-9; ◷ 10am-6pm Mon-Sat, 11am-6pm Sun; 🍴) If you're a fan of In-N-Out and Dairy Queen, you'll go nuts over this drive-in. Try the 'old fashioned' (cheddar, onions and sprouts) or the 'local girl' (Swiss cheese, pineapple and teriyaki sauce). Burgers come slathered in mayo, just FYI. Add a side order of crispy onion rings and a milkshake.

▼ Drinking & Nightlife

Kalalea Juice Hale   JUICE BAR
(4390 Pu'u Hale; drinks $5-9; ⊙8am-5pm Tue-Fri,
9am-5pm Sat & Sun; 🚻🐾) 🍴 Across from the
post office, this juice shack has cold coconuts,
raw *noni* juice (a Polynesian elixir), acai
bowls, green juice, *liliko'i* (passion fruit)
lemonade, and a range of smoothies. Ask
about the 'Popsicle of the Day,' usually a tasty
concoction incorporating local produce
like coconut, pineapple and honey. Many
ingredients are organic.

ℹ Information

Anahola Post Office (☑808-822-4710; www.
usps.com; 4-4350 Kuhio Hwy; ⊙10am-1:30pm
& 2-3:30pm Mon-Fri, 9:30-11:30am Sat)

ℹ Getting There & Away

You're either on the bus from Lihu'e to Hanalei,
which stops in the town center, or you're driving
the glorious Kuhio Hwy.

Ko'olau Road

Ko'olau Road is a peaceful, scenic drive
through rich green pastures dotted with
white cattle egrets and bright wildflowers.
It makes a nice diversion and it's the way
to less-visited beaches. Note there are
no public facilities at these more remote
beaches.

★**Moloa'a Beach**   BEACH
This classically curved bay appeared in the
pilot for *Gilligan's Island*. There's a shallow
protected swimming area good for families
at the north end; to the south, the waters
are rougher but there's more sand. When the
surf's up stay dry, stroll the beach, and enjoy
the comingling of aquamarine shallows and
deep blues beyond, and birds flitting about
the estuary.

Monk seals can surface on this beach. If
you see one, give them space to relax. To
get here, follow Ko'olau Rd and turn onto
Moloa'a Rd, which ends about 0.75 miles
down at a few beach houses and a little
parking area.

Larsen's Beach   BEACH
This long, loamy, golden-sand beach, named
after L David Larsen (former manager of the
Kilauea Sugar Company), is stunning, raw
and all-natural, with a scrubby backdrop
offering afternoon shade. However, although
the aquamarine waters may look inviting,
beware of a vicious current that runs along
the beach and out through a channel in the
reef. Better to stroll along the waterline and
watch the old locals collecting seaweed and
tako (octopus) from the tide pools.

To get here, turn onto Ko'olau Rd from
whichever end (ie where it intersects either
Kuhio Hwy or Moloa'a Rd); go just over a
mile then turn toward the ocean on a dirt
road (it should be signposted) and take
the immediate left. It's about a mile to the
parking area and then a five-minute walk
downhill to the beach.

Moloa'a Sunrise Juice Bar   CAFE $
(☑808-822-1441; 6011 Ko'olau Rd; items $3-11;
⊙7:30am-5pm Mon-Sat, 8am-4pm Sun; 🚻🐾) A
roadside shack that sells fresh tropical fruit
and tasty smoothies, healthful multigrain-
bread sandwiches, fish tacos, garden salads
and addictive chocolate-chip and macadamia-
nut cookies. Satisfying if not sensational, it's
still an affordable and convenient stop.

ℹ Getting There & Away

Ko'olau Rd connects with the Kuhio Hwy about
0.5 miles north of mile marker 16 and again just
south of mile marker 20.

Kaua'i Bus does not serve the beaches here.
To explore the region properly, you'll need your
own wheels.

AT A GLANCE

POPULATION
5839

LARGEST TOWN
Kilauea

**BEST
EQUINE ADVENTURE**
Silver Falls Ranch
(p147)

**BEST
FARMSTAY COTTAGE**
North Country Farms
(p148)

**BEST BEACH
FOR FAMILIES**
'Anini Beach Park
(p154)

WHEN TO GO
Jan–Mar
The peak season for
whale-watching.

Apr–Oct
Calmer seas and
the best time to sea
kayak the Na Pali
Coast.

May–Sep
Serene seas and the
least rain – a fine
time for families to
visit. Hiking trails
are also in good
condition.

Kalalau Beach (p138)
TEC PETAJA/LONELY PLANET ©

Hanalei & the North Shore

E ven on an island famous for extreme beauty, Kauaʻi's North Shore is something special. Here in the oldest part of Hawaii's main islands, erosion has had five million years to sculpt an extraordinary landscape. Always looming on the horizon, the sumptuous, pleated, razor-edge cliffs of the Na Pali Coast encapsulate the very essence of a Polynesian paradise, all the more tantalizing for being unreachable by road. Instead, the only close-up views come from hiking the epic Kalalau Trail, kayaking or joining a boat cruise, or from a helicopter.

Three very different small communities line the North Shore highway: relaxed, residential Kilauea; the landscaped enclave of Princeville; and the funky surfers' haven that is Hanalei. The further you go, the more spectacular the scenery, and the gentler the pace of life. Note that since 2018, to drive to the very end of the road you have to reserve parking in advance.

HIKING ON THE NORTH SHORE

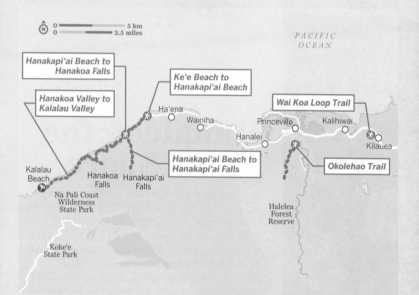

0 — 5 km
0 — 2.5 miles

PACIFIC
OCEAN

Hanakapi'ai Beach to
Hanakoa Falls

Ke'e Beach to
Hanakapi'ai Beach

Wai Koa Loop Trail

Hanakoa Valley to
Kalalau Valley

Ha'ena

Wainiha

Princeville

Kalihiwai

Kilauea

Hanalei

Hanakapi'ai Beach to
Hanakapi'ai Falls

Okolehao Trail

Kalalau
Beach

Hanakoa
Falls

Hanakapi'ai
Falls

Na Pali Coast
Wilderness
State Park

Halelea
Forest
Reserve

Koke'e
State Park

KALALAU TRAIL

START KE'E BEACH

END KE'E BEACH

LENGTH 22 MILES (ROUND-TRIP),
TWO DAYS

Hawaii's most spectacular hiking route, the world-class Kalalau Trail inches along the oceanfront edge of the Na Pali cliffs for 11 miles, from Ke'e Beach to Kalalau Valley. It only returns to sea level once en route, 2 miles along at Hanakapi'ai Beach, from where a separate 2-mile trail climbs to towering Hanakapi'ai Falls. The 8-mile round-trip trek to the falls is the longest possible day hike, and typically takes six to eight hours.

Although trailfinding is not difficult, the Kalalau Trail is a seriously challenging hike. Wear the appropriate gear – including footwear suitable for stream crossings – and bring all the food and water you need, or purify fresh water drawn en route. Don't wade streams deeper than knee-high, don't swim at Hanakapi'ai Beach and take extra care after rain.

To continue beyond Hanakapi'ai Beach, which is only advisable for hardy, experienced hikers with no fear of heights, you must obtain **camping permits** in advance. A maximum of five nights' camping is allowed, shared between Hanakoa Valley 4 miles further along – where you can only stop for one night in each direction – and Kalalau Valley at the far end. Permits, available 90 days in advance and often sold out, cost $20 per person per night ($15 for Hawaii residents); for full details, see www.dlnr. hawaii.gov/dsp/hiking/kauai/kalalau-trail.

In addition, **parking permits** for Ha'ena State Park must also be reserved in advance. For a day hike you'll likely need two slots, 6:30am to 12:30pm and 12:30pm to 5:30pm, and you may find one or both are sold out. Most hikers therefore arrive via the North Shore Shuttle instead, which makes its final departure for Hanalei or Princeville at 5pm daily. There's no overnight parking here.

The rain-lashed, impossibly lush North Shore of Kaua'i feels like a corner of Eden that bobbed away to the Pacific. This tropical dreamscape is ripe for exploration – lace up those boots!

☆ Ke'e Beach to Hanakapi'ai Beach

The Kalalau Trail begins with a steep uphill ascent from its **Ke'e Beach** trailhead. For the first half-mile much of the path is cobbled, but it's still quite a climb. Fortunately, it's also beautiful, with lush tropical vegetation and superb views. A mile along, at the highest point on this stretch – 400ft above the ocean – vast panoramas open up ahead, looking westward along the coast. The trail then winds through successive hanging valleys, crossing trickling cascades at each inland curve before veering back out to the next headland.

It takes most hikers approaching two hours to complete the 2-mile trek to **Hanakapi'ai Beach**. As the trail drops back down to the sea, you have to cross broad Hanakapi'ai Stream; a helpful rope is often strung between the banks. The white-sand beach at the river mouth is constantly re-configured by the waves and may take the form of a sandbar, cut off beyond a small lagoon. Be warned, though: numerous hikers have drowned here, and it's never safe for swimming.

☆ Hanakapi'ai Beach to Hanakapi'ai Falls

The 4-mile round-trip hike from Ke'e to Hanakapi'ai and back takes up to four hours. You can double that, to create an unforgettable 8-mile all-day hike by adding on the spur trail that branches inland from Hanakapi'ai Beach to the waterfall at the back of the valley. Alternatively, the falls can simply be a side attraction on your way to Kalalau. This narrow valley is prone to flash flooding, so only hike in fair weather.

The falls trail runs up the valley for two miles, parallel to **Hanakapi'ai Stream.** This was once a densely populated agricultural area, and you may spot traces of long-abandoned taro fields and coffee groves. At times the pathway follows a raised ledge, at others it crosses the stream itself. Water

shoes can be a great help, both for wading through the water and then, as the canyon squeezes between mossy walls on the rocky upper part of the trail, for clambering over slippery boulders. Where rocks are covered with slick algae, it's worse than walking on ice.

Eventually you come to spectacular **Hanakapi'ai Falls**, where water tumbles 300ft into a wide pool that's placid enough for swimming. Directly beneath the falls, the torrent forces you back from the rock face – a warning from nature, as falling rocks are common. The setting is superb but seldom sunny, thanks to the massive cliff ahead of you and the soaring walls behind.

☆ Hanakapi'ai Beach to Hanakoa Falls

Hiking along the Kalalau Trail beyond Hanakapi'ai Beach is only allowed if you have camping permits. Setting off means you've got 9 miles left, and you're committed to the entire 22-mile round-trip.

The trail switchbacks steeply out of Hanakapi'ai, climbing 840ft in just over a mile, and doesn't return to the ocean until Kalalau. Once again it's magnificently verdant, penetrating deep into unspoiled hanging valleys and returning to high, exposed viewpoints at the headlands. The overlook that provides your first sight of **Hanakoa Valley** also offers the first long-range prospect of the full majesty of the Na Pali Coast's pleated, cathedral-like cliffs, stretching all the way to Honopu Valley in the distance.

At Hanakoa too, 4 miles on from Hanakapi'ai, you have to cross the main valley stream, this time twice. If you've already detoured to see Hanakapi'ai Falls, you'll probably be ready to pitch your tent for the night. This valley too, though, holds a waterfall: **Hanakoa Falls**, thundering a colossal 2000ft down the cliffs. A rough trail climbs a third of a mile through the forest to the pool at the base, where swimming is forbidden.

☆ Hanakoa Valley to Kalalau Valley

Over its final 5-mile stretch, beyond Hanakoa, the trail becomes drier and more exposed, and the lapping of the blue Pacific far below taunts that much more. With less vegetation to bind the hillsides together, the path is often just a narrow ledge scraped into a denuded slope of crumbling red gravel, and you may be glad of hiking poles to spare your quivering legs.

Toward the end, the trail leads across the front of **Kalalau Valley**, where you'll feel dwarfed beneath 1000ft lava-rock cliffs, then proceeds to the campsites on idyllic Kalalau Beach, at the valley's western end. Kalalau no longer has a permanent population, and it's not the hippie hangout it used to be either, but it remains something very close to an earthly Paradise.

In summer only, very strong swimmers can swim another half-mile along the coast to reach Honopu Beach; wear fins, because there's a strong current against you when you try to swim back.

When you're finally ready to leave Kalalau, simply retrace your steps for the 11 miles back to Ke'e. If you time it right and the weather works out, you might just end your journey with a magical sunset.

OKOLEHAO TRAIL

START 0.5 MILES ALONG OHIKI RD

END LOOKOUT ABOVE HANALEI

LENGTH 2.5-MILE (ROUND-TRIP), HALF-DAY

This 2.5-mile round-trip climbs a steep forest ridge for tremendous views over Hanalei's taro fields, the start of the Na Pali Coast and, on clear days, east to Kilauea Lighthouse. The demanding and often muddy ascent – bring plenty of water – is rewarded with successive sweeping panoramas. Expert hikers continue beyond the official end toward even higher peaks, but that's a dangerous all-day expedition. The trail is named for a Hawaiian moonshine liquor, distilled from the roots of *ti* plants.

Coming from Hanalei, turn right along Ohiki Rd immediately before Hanalei Bridge, staying on the west side of the river. Follow the road alongside the taro fields for roughly half a mile, until you spot a parking area on the left. A little footbridge that leads into the woods on the other side of the road marks the start of the trail.

VENTU PHOTO/SHUTTERSTOCK ©

Kauapea (Secret) Beach (p145)

The first half-mile is a real quad burner that runs along a deeply rutted red-dirt path and zigzags up the ridge, picking its way between tangled tree roots. Especially after rain, and even though plastic webbing has been embedded into the mud in tricky places, conditions are liable to be very slippery – and that's just a foretaste of what's to come.

After around 20 literally breath-taking minutes, you come to a small clearing that's dominated by a mighty utility-company pole. The green fields of the **Hanalei National Wildlife Refuge** lie at your feet, with the town of Hanalei on the far side and the rich curve of Hanalei Bay beyond. The views don't change much after this point, so if you've only time for a short hike you could turn back here.

From the clearing, the trail doubles back on itself and becomes, if anything, even narrower and steeper. Climbing through a mixed forest of wild guava, silk oak, eucalyptus and koa trees, it offers photo opportunities galore before ending another half-hour along. The final stretch is almost vertical, so there's usually a knotted rope in place to help you haul yourself up. At the top you'll find a lookout, equipped with a bench, 1200ft above the slow shuffle of Hanalei. Settle in and enjoy your picnic – you did remember to bring one, didn't you? – while you watch the lines roll toward Pine Trees, Middles and Waikoko beaches.

A clearly visible footpath continues along the ridge from the official end of the trail, dwindling ever narrower as it grows more and more perilous. We strongly advise against attempting to reach the twin manta-wing peaks in the distance, which tower another 1000ft higher.

Hanakapi'ai Stream (p137)

ALEXANDER HOWARD/LONELY PLANET ©

WAI KOA LOOP TRAIL

START ANAINA HOU COMMUNITY PARK
END ANAINA HOU COMMUNITY PARK
LENGTH 3 MILES (LOOP), 1½ HOURS

Setting off from the roadside **Anaina Hou Community Park** (p145; also home to Kauai Mini Golf), this generally flat loop trail meanders through the greater Namahana Plantation, which is the largest mahogany plantation in the US. As well as rows of towering hardwood trees, laid out with geometric precision, it passes fruit orchards and heads out into meadows that survey gorgeous mountain vistas. An easy 3--mile hike that takes perhaps 90 minutes, it's largely in shade, but be sure to bring bug spray and sunscreen.

Unfortunately, the most scenic part of the trail is currently closed to visitors, and likely to remain so for the foreseeable future. It centered on the Stone Dam, which was constructed in 1880 to channel water to the plantations of Kilauea. Resembling a natural waterfall, and set amid ravishing gardens, the dam was all but destroyed by the floods of 2018, and the cost of rebuilding appears to be prohibitive. Check the park website for current conditions.

You can hike for free – and it's terrific terrain for a trail run too – but as the trail is on private property you must first sign a waiver, in the park visitor center alongside the mini-golf.

ROAD TRIP >
KUHIO HIGHWAY

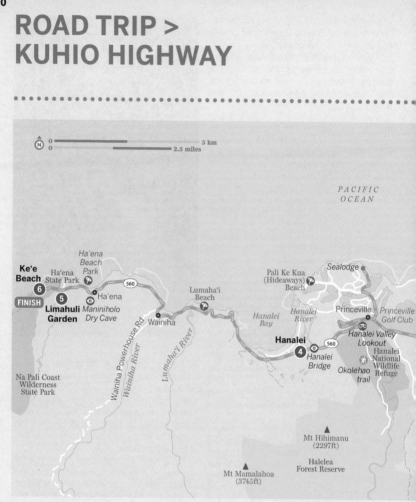

En route to gorgeous Ke'e Beach at road's end, Kuhio Hwy runs along the North Shore for 15 wondrous miles. Some of the sublime roadside beaches offer idyllic swimming in turquoise seas, others are only safe for luscious strolling. Amid the dreamy scenery beyond laidback Hanalei, as you cross one single-lane bridge after another, time itself seems to slow down.

❶ Kilauea Point National Wildlife Refuge

Start your drive at **Kilauea Point National Wildlife Refuge** (p143), where the plentiful birdlife, swirling sea and historic lighthouse can't be missed. Look west to see gorgeous Kauapea (Secret) Beach beckoning.

The Drive > Head south along Kilauea Rd to Kilauea town.

Start Kilauea Point National Wildlife Refuge

End Ke'e Beach

Length Four hours; 17.5 miles

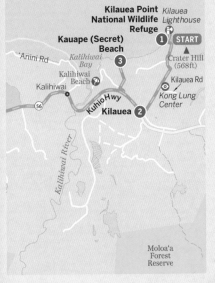

❷ Kilauea

Drive through Kilauea town, pausing to browse in the plantation-era **Kong Lung Center** (p151), and check out the cemetery and stained glass at **Christ Memorial Episcopal Church** (p145).

The Drive > Follow Kuhio Hwy northwest and turn right at the first intersection, Kalihiwai Rd, then turn right again and drive to the end of the beach access road.

❸ Kauapea (Secret) Beach

Pick your way carefully down the trail to stunning, albeit not-so-secret, Kauapea (Secret)

Beach. If it's summer, take a breath and go for a swim; otherwise, simply stroll the endless sands.

The Drive > Hike back up to your car, return to Kuhio Hwy and head west.

❹ Hanalei

Just 3 miles past the Princeville Center, stop at the **Hanalei Valley Lookout** (p155) to look across the checkerboard fields of the **Hanalei National Wildlife Refuge** (p163) toward the mountains beyond. Now follow Kuhio Hwy as it sweeps down to cross the Hanalei River and continue into Hanalei itself.

The Drive > Continue west of Hanalei, curving around Hanalei Bay as you set off along the chain of one-lane bridges that punctuate the 7-mile drive to Limahuli Garden.

❺ Limahuli Garden

Allow a few moments to feel the golden sands of look-but-don't-swim **Lumaha'i Beach** (p175) beneath your feet, 2 miles beyond Hanalei. Then continue to ravishing **Limahuli Garden** (p176), arrayed at the foot of the Na Pali cliffs. To visit, you must book a time slot in advance. You may spot whales out at sea from its velvety slopes in winter.

The Drive > You can only park at Limahuli Garden while you're visiting, so get back in your car and drive the quarter-mile to Ha'ena State Park.

❻ Ke'e Beach

Shortly after Limahuli Garden, attendants in a roadside kiosk will check you've made the necessary parking reservation for **Ha'ena State Park** (p178). From the parking lot just beyond, a verdant boardwalk winds to the superb **Ke'e Beach** (p178), where you can swim in a lovely, lifeguard-supervised lagoon and enjoy sunset views along the Na Pali Coast. You may even have time for a short hike on the **Kalalau Trail** (p136).

Hanalei & the North Shore Highlights

1 Kalalau Trail (p136)
Hiking these 11 cliff-hugging miles along the Na Pali Coast, the most popular overnight trek in all Hawaii, and for good reason.

2 Limahuli Garden (p176)
Exploring Kaua'i's unique native flora, overlooked by the mighty Na Pali cliffs at the edge of a pristine wilderness.

3 Hanalei Bay (p162)
Strolling 2 miles of golden sand washed with frothy surf may feel like heaven, but it's just Hanalei.

4 Kilauea Point (p143)
Drinking in panoramic views of the North Shore – and its soaring seabirds – from the doorstep of its century-old lighthouse.

5 Ke'e Beach (p178)
Driving to the end of the road to take in a superlative sunset from a postcard-perfect beach is an island rite of passage.

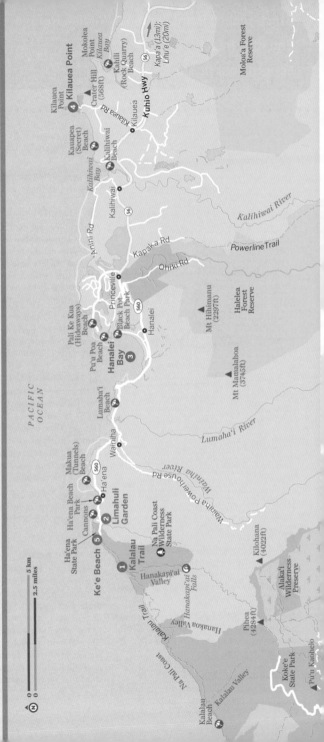

History

The North Shore in general, and Hanalei Valley in particular, rank among the most fertile agricultural lands in all Hawaii, and are thought to have been chosen as home by some of Kaua'i's first Polynesian settlers. Considering *kalo* (taro) to be their direct ancestor and 'staff of life,' these early arrivals carried seedlings on their trans-Pacific voyages of colonization, and planted extensive *lo'i* (taro patches) in the flatlands beside the Hanalei River. They also grew large amounts of *mai'a* (bananas), *'ulu* (breadfruit), *'uala* (sweet potatoes) and *niu* (coconuts). Residents would greet visiting royalty with the ancient custom of *ho'okupu* (gift giving), bringing offerings such as fruits, vegetables, fish and pigs.

Following the arrival of Captain Cook, other agricultural ventures took hold, including the cultivation of tobacco, coffee, rice, sugarcane, cotton and fruits like pineapples, tamarinds, oranges and peaches. The plantation era brought Japanese, Chinese, Filipino and Portuguese immigrants to labor in the fields, and thus shaped Kaua'i's present-day multiethnic population.

Though Hanalei has always carried a reputation of strong aloha, as recently as the 1970s the social temperature and lawlessness hereabouts had echoes of the 'Wild West.' With an influx of mainland hippies seeking a tropical utopia, and international surfers pining for an endless summer, growing pains were unavoidable.

Since the mid-20th century – and thanks in part to Hollywood's cameras – Hanalei and the North Shore have gained celebrity status, and real-estate prices have soared way beyond the reach of local pockets.

❶ Getting There & Away

The North Shore is easy to reach either by public transport, or under your own steam. As always on Kaua'i, a rental car, best picked up at the airport, gives the most flexibility. Taxis are expensive and hard to wrangle.

Kaua'i Bus (p279) Public bus service connecting Hanalei, Princeville and Kilauea with the rest of the island.

North Shore Shuttle (☑888-409-2702; https://kauainsshuttle.com; single ride/day pass/week/month $5/10/20/40) Shuttle service running from Hanalei and Princeville to Ha'ena State Park, at the end of Kuhio Hwy.

Kilauea

☑ 808 / POP 2800

Stretching north from the highway to Kaua'i's northernmost point, Kilauea is still recognizable as the 19th-century sugar plantation town it used to be. These days, though, it's more of a residential community, home to a generally harmonious mix of longtime locals and more recent, New Age-tinged arrivals from California. Visitors who race through risk missing a wildlife refuge surrounding a century-old lighthouse, sustainable farms, peaceful accommodations and one of the island's very best beaches.

◉ Sights

★**Kilauea Point**
National Wildlife Refuge WILDLIFE RESERVE
(☑808-828-1413; www.fws.gov/kilaueapoint; Kilauea Rd; adult/child under 16yr $10/free; ⊙10am-4pm Tue-Sat, closed federal holidays) ⚑ The gloriously scenic wildlife refuge that marks the northernmost tip of the major Hawaiian islands protects both nesting seabirds on the coastal cliffs and marine mammals in the waters offshore. Visitors can only access a small area, where Kilauea Point holds a photogenic lighthouse, but the views are exhilarating and terrific informative panels explain the species on show.

To your right as you follow the three-minute trail from the entrance station to the lighthouse, the steep slopes of neighboring Crater Hill are usually a-flutter with darting white shapes. Thanks to predator-proof fencing, it's a safe habitat for red-footed boobies. Laysan albatrosses, by contrast, prefer the flatter clifftops to the west, while you're also likely to see Pacific golden plovers, red-tailed and white-tailed tropic birds and the nene, the threatened species of Hawaiian goose. Helpful docents lend out free binoculars. Out to sea, whales breach in winter only, but spinner dolphins can be glimpsed year-round.

Built in 1913, the 52ft **Kilauea Lighthouse** was decommissioned in 1976, though it was shut down during WWII to help the island avoid the attention of Japanese bombers. Free tours to the top are offered on Wednesday and Saturday, hourly between 10:30am and 2:30pm. Numbers are limited, so sign up as soon as you arrive.

To reach the refuge, turn oceanward off the highway at Kilauea's gas station, then turn left onto Kilauea Rd and follow signs for 2 miles.

North Shore

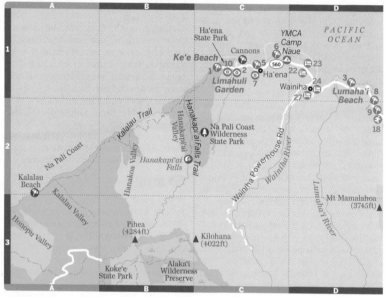

North Shore

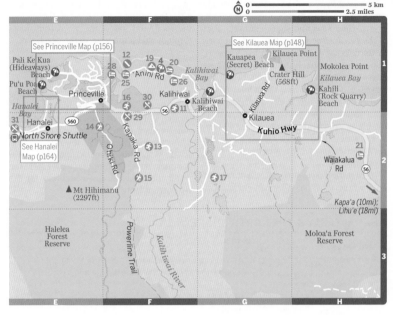

Anaina Hou Community Park PARK
(☑808-828-2118; http://anainahou.org; 5-2723 Kuhio Hwy; ☺8am-dusk; ⓟ⛟) Set up by the late founder of E-Trade as a gift to the people of Kaua'i, this community park is home to a mini-golf course, a cafe and an excellent children's playground, and hosts a weekly farmers market. It's also the starting point for the popular Wai Koa Loop Trail (p139), offering a gentle 3-mile hike into the lush backcountry.

Christ Memorial Episcopal Church CHURCH
(www.christmemorialkauai.org; 2509 Kolo Rd; ☺services 9am Sun) This historic stone church and cemetery date from 1924. Sunday services are held in its humble chapel, glowing with stained glass, while mossy tombstones spread beneath the palms to all sides.

Na 'Aina Kai Botanical Gardens & Sculpture Park GARDENS
(☑808-828-0525; http://naainakai.org; 4101 Wailapa Rd; tours $35-85; ☺tours 9am, 9:30am & 1pm Tue-Thu, 9am & 9:30am Fri) While undeniably pretty in parts – how could it not be, in this clifftops-to-ocean setting? – this private garden holds disappointingly few Hawaiian species and offers little sense of Kaua'i's culture and traditions.

Tours focus more on the couple who laid it all out, and peppered the lawns with banal 'lifesize' sculptures, than on the actual plants. Check schedules online; reservations required.

To get here, turn right onto Wailapa Rd, between Miles 21 and 22 on the Kuhio Hwy, and look for signs.

⛱ Beaches

As Kilauea spreads across a plateau that's perched well above the ocean, it takes a bit of effort to reach its beaches. Rest assured that effort will be rewarded. Car break-ins are common, so don't leave valuables in your vehicle.

★Kauapea (Secret) Beach BEACH
(Kauapea Rd) Far from being 'secret,' must-see Kauapea Beach is renowned as one of the most breathtaking beaches on Kaua'i. You won't see it signposted, though, and can only reach it via a steep 10-minute hike. Down below the cliffs, its powdery golden sands stretch for over a mile towards Kilauea Point, wrapping around two rock reefs. Thanks to a massive shore break and strong currents that sweep its full length, however, swimming is only safe on the calmest summer days.

For most visitors, it's the sheer spectacle that's the thing, with a sandy ocean floor, crystal-clear seas and superb sunsets. Part of the beach's 'secret' reputation dates back to its days as an (illegal) nudist hangout, but you're less likely to see nudity these days. Expert local surfers do brave the waves, especially during the winter swells that make swimming even more hazardous than usual. If the swells are even a little bit big or rough, don't venture into knee-deep water, and don't clamber on the rocky outcrops, which are notorious for drownings.

Turn *makai* (seaward) onto Kalihiwai Rd half a mile north of Kilauea's gas station,

then take a right on the first dirt road, just after the initial bend. Park at the end of the road, and follow the steep trail down through wild plum trees to the beach.

Kahili (Rock Quarry) Beach   BEACH

Scenic, rugged Kahili Beach nestles between the cliffs at the point where Kilauea Stream meets the ocean. Only its western section is readily accessible, though determined hikers can also reach the rougher eastern portion. There's no protective barrier reef at the river mouth, so it's a popular surfing spot. On calm summer days, swimmers can enter the water further west, but watch out for the rip current from the stream.

HANALEI BAY & THE NORTH SHORE IN...

Two Days

Start by getting your bearings with sweeping views from Kaua'i's northernmost spot. **Kilauea Point and Lighthouse** doubles as a National Wildlife Refuge and sanctuary for Hawaiian seabirds.

Browse Kilauea's many intriguing stores, concentrating on the historic **Kong Lung Center** (p151), and enjoy fresh *poke* at the casual **Kilauea Fish Market** (p150).

Cruise the ribbon road west beyond Hanalei, crossing a succession of the North Shore's signature one-way bridges. In Ha'ena, hit **Makua (Tunnels) Beach** (p176), where reef-snorkeling and swimming opportunities abound in summer.

Cap off your day with sunset at road's-end **Ke'e Beach** (p178) – you'll need a parking permit, booked in advance – then double back to Hanalei for a divine wine-splashed dinner at **Bar Acuda** (p172).

On day two get your blood pumping with the steep, short climb up **Okolehao Trail** (p163), then grab a coffee and pastry in town at **Hanalei Bread Company** (p170) before renting a kayak or SUP and paddling up the **Hanalei River**.

Decompress as the sunlight fades with a beach walk on idyllic **Lumaha'i Beach** (p175) or splashing in the shallows at **Hanalei Pavilion Beach Park** (p163). After dark, belly up to the bar at **Tahiti Nui** (p173). Ideally it's Wednesday, luau night; if not, just enjoy (surprisingly good) dinner and (many) drinks.

Four Days

Rise on day three, make like a local and have coffee at **Kilauea Bakery** (p150), and then take a long walk along the sand at **Kauapea (Secret) Beach** (p145). If it's summertime, go for a swim.

In the afternoon go for a horseback ride on **Princeville Ranch Stables** (p157), before settling down to a gourmet feast at the alfresco tables of **Kaua'i Ono** (p160).

The next morning, start with a kombucha or cold-pressed juice at **Kauai Juice Co** (p150), drink in the view from **Hanalei Valley Lookout** (p155), then head on up the road to magical **Limahuli Garden** (p176).

On the way back, glorious **Ha'ena Beach Park** (p177) is worth some quiet time. Unless, of course, you have a surf lesson booked in Hanalei. They say all it takes is one wave and you're hooked.

Wind down by walking the Hanalei strip, ducking into fun clothing boutiques and art galleries, and pausing for shave ice at **Wishing Well** (p170), before landing at the **Hanalei Dolphin** (p172) for an exquisite sushi dinner.

Then it's straight back to **Tahiti Nui** (p173), because this is Hanalei and that's where the mellifluous Hawaiian tunes draw a kinetic crowd (especially on weekends).

The dirt road down to Kahili Beach branches left half a mile along Wailapa Rd from the point where it cuts north from Kuhio Hwy (between mile markers 21 and 22). Starting at a bright-yellow water valve, it's a rough half-mile drive to the rather magical grove of trees backing the ocean; if you don't have 4WD, it's generally best to walk.

🏃 Activities

Kilauea does hold some options for activity-oriented travelers, but the main focus of North Shore action is Hanalei Bay, just 8 miles west.

North Shore Charters
SNORKELING
(☑ 808-828-1379; http://kauainorthshorecharters. com; 4270-G Kilauea Rd; per person $170) The booking office and check-in point for half-day sightseeing tours aboard a 32ft, 18-passenger catamaran. Operating all year round, the tours set off along the spectacular Na Pali Coast from 'Anini Beach, visiting pristine bays to snorkel and swim, and entering sea caves when conditions permit.

Silver Falls Ranch
HORSEBACK RIDING
(☑ 808-828-6718; www.silverfallsranch.com; 2888 Kamo'okoa Rd, off Kahililholo Road; rides $104-144; ⊙ daily scheduled tours, by reservation; ⊕) Guided horseback rides into the island's lush northern interior. At 90 minutes, the Hawaiian Discovery Ride is the shortest option, while the three-hour Tropical Trail Adventure includes a picnic and the chance to swim in one of Kalihiwai Valley's waterfalls. Private rides also available.

Kaua'i Mini Golf & Botanical Gardens
GOLF
(☑ 808-828-2118; http://anainahou.org; 5-2723 Kuhio Hwy; adult/child 4-12yr/child under 4yr $18.50/15/free; ⊙ 9am-6pm, last entry 5pm; ⊕) Winding through areas planted to evoke Native Hawaiian, Polynesian, plantation-era and East Asian heritage, this hugely enjoyable mini-golf course doubles as a botanical garden. Each fun, tricksy hole offers close-up views of exquisite flora.

Garden Island Chocolate
FOOD
(☑ 808-634-6812; www.gardenislandchocolate. com; 5-2719 Kuhio Hwy; adult/child 4-12yr/child 3yr & under $89/29/free; ⊙ 9:30am-12:30pm Mon, Wed & Fri; ⊕) A cacao farm that produces fine gourmet chocolate, right here on the North Shore. Three-hour tours of the farm start from the Chocolate Factory alongside, three mornings a week, and include an

KALIHIWAI VALLEY

Sandwiched between Kilauea and 'Anini, Kalihiwai ('Water's Edge' in Hawaiian) is a hidden treasure that's easy to miss. Assuming you can find it, **Kalihiwai Beach** is ideal for sunbathing, sandcastle building and, swells permitting, swimming, though bodyboarding and surfing below the cliff on the eastern shore are more common activities.

Kalihiwai Rd originally looped down from the highway to run alongside Kalihiwai Beach, but the old Kalihiwai Bridge was washed out by a 1957 tsunami and never rebuilt. Now there are two Kalihiwai Rds, one on each side of the river. To reach the beach, take the easternmost Kalihiwai Rd, half a mile northwest of Kilauea's gas station.

extensive tasting of over 20 different types of chocolate – dark, light, spiced, truffled and creamed among them.

Metamorphose Yoga Studio
YOGA
(☑ 808-828-6292; http://metamorphoseyoga. com; Kilauea Plantation Center, 4720 Kilauea Rd; drop-in class $25, 5-class pass $90) The bright, cheery environs of our favorite yoga studio on Kaua'i reflect its owner, locally beloved teacher Carolyn Dumeyer. Most classes are in the flowing Vinyasa style, though restorative classes are offered too. If you've never dangled from a wall, this is the place to try it!

Anahata Spa & Sanctuary
SPA
(☑ 808-652-3698; www.tajjure.net; 4356 Kahili Makai St; ⊙ by appointment only) A healing center set up by hypnotherapist, cranial sacral worker and sound healer Taj Juré, where massage treatments are also available. She also offers in-house residential retreats (from $145 per night).

Pineapple Yoga
YOGA
(☑ 808-652-9009; www.pineappleyoga.com; 2518 Kolo Rd; drop-in class/weekly pass $20/90; ⊙ usually 7:30-9:30am Mon-Sat) Based in the parish house of Christ Memorial Church, Pineapple offers classes in Mysore-style Ashtanga yoga, which links the breath with 'moving meditation' to create heat throughout the body and sweat (lots of sweat) that detoxifies muscles and organs.

Kilauea

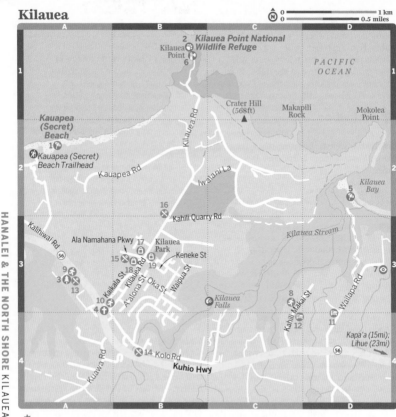

✨ Festivals & Events

Fall Festival CARNIVAL
(https://kauaifestivals.com; Kauai Christian Academy, 4000 Kilauea Rd; ⏰ late Oct; 🅿️) **FREE**
The Kauai Christian Academy's annual fundraiser features local food and art vendors, a silent auction, live music, carnival games, a corn maze and pony and hay rides.

🛏️ Sleeping

Sleepy Kilauea holds a handful of B&Bs. What they lack in ocean views, they make up for with peaceful rural settings.

Green Acres Cottages INN $
(☎️866-484-6347, 808-828-0478; www.greenacres cottages.com; 5-0421c Kuhio Hwy; d $75-90; 🅿️🛜) Set in a fruit orchard well back from the highway, these three 'cottages' are private, separate rooms attached behind the owner's house. Cheerily furnished and equipped with kitchenettes, they're great value – especially the largest, Nautical Nights. Spend your mornings picking bananas and avocados or cracking macadamia nuts, and evenings winding down in a communal hot tub. Beach toys provided gratis.

North Country Farms COTTAGE $$
(☎️808-828-1513; www.northcountryfarms.com; 4387 Kahili Makai Rd; d $170) 🌿 Run by organic farmers, this cabin-like farmstay cottage comes with a basket of breakfast goodies, and you're free to harvest fruit and veggies. A 500-sq-ft studio on stilts, it has a full kitchen and a hammock on the lanai (veranda). The compact Garden Studio with a kitchenette sleeps four. Cleaning fee is $95. There's a three-night minimum.

Fehring Family Farm FARMSTAY $$
(☎️808-346-0364; www.fehringfamilyfarm.com; 4320 Wailapa Rd; cottage $245; 🛜) A 500-sq-ft wooden cottage on a working, 7.6-acre organic farm. There's a vaulted ceiling in the living room, a queen bed in the bedroom,

Kilauea

and a hot tub and hammock in the garden to help you unwind. Cleaning fee of $110 is required regardless of the length of stay.

✕ Eating

Targeted more at residents than tourists, Kilauea's restaurants tend to prioritize affordability over fine dining, but there are some really nice places around, and the local supermarkets have excellent deli sections.

Kilauea Market & Cafe SUPERMARKET **$**
(☏808-828-1282; www.kilaueamarket.com; 2555 Ala Namahana Pkwy; mains $12.50-18; ☉6am-10pm) The centerpiece of Kilauea's latest shopping development, this gleaming store is part high-end supermarket, stocking imported groceries from Europe in particular, and part deli-cafe. Pick up good-value *poke* (cubed raw fish mixed with *shōyu*, sesame oil, salt, chili pepper, *'inamona* or other condiments) bowls or order pizzas, burgers and plate lunches to eat in the bright dining area.

Kilauea Farmers Market MARKET **$**
(☏808-828-2118; http://anainahou.org; Anaina Hou Community Park, 5-2723 Kuhio Hwy; ☉9am-1pm Sat; ☏⚲) ⚑ Kilauea's busiest weekly market, beside the highway, attracts farmers and food trucks from all over the island.

Stop and shop for fresh goat cheese and sourdough bread, poi (steamed, mashed taro) bagels, fresh pasta and Kaua'i-grown organic fruits and veggies. There's often live music, while the park's playground is good for distracting kids.

Sushigirl SUSHI **$**
(☏808-320-8646; www.sushigirlkauai.com; Kong Lung Center, 2484 Keneke St; mains $12-18; ☉11am-7pm Mon-Sat, noon-4pm Sun) A former food truck now relocated in a trailer in the Kong Lung mall, Sushigirl delivers generous maki (hand) rolls, sushi burritos, and mixed *poke* bowls with ahi (yellowfin tuna) and *ono* (white-fleshed wahoo) drizzled with *ponzu* (Japanese citrus) sauce. Charging extra for mayo and avocado seems a little cheap, though, and there's minimal seating alongside.

Trilogy CAFE **$**
(www.trilogycoffeekauai.com; Kilauea Plantation Center, 4270 Kilauea Rd; snacks $4-12; ☉7:30am-5pm Mon-Sat, 8am-2pm Sun) Along with serving excellent coffee and snacks, this smart little cafe has set about introducing Kaua'i to all sorts of newfangled concoctions – try the mushroom milk and beetroot latte. All seating is outdoors.

Fehring Family Farm ICE CREAM **$**
(www.fehringfamilyfarm.com; 5-2719 Kuhio Hwy;
snacks $8-9; ⊙10am-5pm) An offshoot of the
nearby Fehring Family Farm (p148), this
roadside stand at Anaina Hou Community
Park sells delicious fruit smoothies, juices,
frosties, popsicles, piled-high acai bowls
and whatever fresh-grown fruit is available,
often including the farm's sweet signature
sugarloaf pineapple.

Healthy Hut Market & Cafe HEALTH FOOD **$**
(☑808-828-6626; www.healthyhutkauai.com;
4480 Ho'okui Rd; ⊙7:30am-9pm; ☑) ⭕ This
cheerfully crowded and chaotic store
serves all the gluten-free, dairy-free and all-
natural groceries, funky superfoods, snacks
and supplies you're likely to need, sourced
whenever possible on Kaua'i. Thumbs up for
the juice and smoothie bar, open until 7pm
daily, that serves organic coffee and espresso
drinks.

Anaina Hou Cafe CAFE **$**
(☑808-828-2118; http://anainahou.org; Anaina
Hou Community Park, 5-2723 Kuhio Hwy; espresso
drinks $2-7, snacks $3-10; ⊙9am-6pm) In a
garden setting adjoining the visitor center
for Anaina Hou park, this friendly little cafe
doubles as the ticket office for the mini-golf.
It serves good organic coffee, juices, beer and
wine, plus a simple menu of bagels, waffles,
hot dogs and acai bowls. There's usually a
Mexican food truck across the yard as well.

Kilauea Sunshine Market MARKET **$**
(Kilauea Community Agricultural Center, 4000
Kilauea Rd; ⊙3:30-5pm Thu; ☑) ⭕ This
modest, county-run market has a friendly
hippie vibe. A dozen or so local, mostly
organic farmers show up to sell mangoes,
papaya, cucumbers, tomatoes, salad greens,
fresh coconuts and more.

★**Kilauea Bakery &**
Pau Hana Pizza BAKERY **$$**
(☑808-828-2020; www.kilaueabakery.com; Kong
Lung Center, 2484 Keneke St; snacks & soups
from $5, pizzas $12-33; ⊙6am-9pm, pizza from
10:30am) ⭕ Calling itself 'the original social
network,' this lively bakery-cafe is Kilauea's
all-day comfort food and social hub. Order
from the amazing array of sweet and savory
breads, pastries and buns – try a breadfruit
bagel topped with breadfruit hummus – and
then sit outside. Pick of the pizza menu is
the 'Billie Holliday,' with smoked *ono* and
Gorgonzola.

Kilauea Fish Market SEAFOOD **$$**
(☑808-828-6244; Kilauea Plantation Center, 4270
Kilauea Rd; mains $10-21; ⊙11am-8pm Mon-Sat)
Come to this seafood-lovers' dream to pick
up a piled-high *poke* bowl or rice plate
topped with seared fresh catch. Despite the
name, it also serves all sorts of barbecue
meat plate lunches. Only water and green
tea are available, but you can pick up beer or
wine at the neighboring supermarket before
taking a seat at the picnic tables outside.

★**Bistro** HAWAIIAN **$$$**
(☑808-828-0480; www.thebistrohawaii.com;
Kong Lung Center, 2484 Keneke St; mains lunch
$12.50-25, dinner $24-36; ⊙noon-9pm Mon-Sat,
3-9pm Sun) This plantation cottage makes
a romantic venue to enjoy excellent food.
Lunch ranges through burgers, salads and
sandwiches, while dinner options include
sharing plates like lamb lollipops and *poke*
nachos, and mains like grilled or blackened
fish. Our favorite? Fish rockets (seared ahi
wrapped in lumpia dough, served with
wasabi aioli). There's live Hawaiian music
on Thursday and Saturday nights.

🍷 Drinking & Nightlife

★**Kauai Juice Co** JUICE BAR
(☑808-631-5529; www.kauaijuiceco.com; 4270
Kilauea Rd; ⊙8am-5pm Mon-Sat, 9am-3pm Sun)
A link in a healthy, happy chain that reaches
across the island, Kauai Juice Co offers 14
cold-pressed juice combinations, along with
hand-pressed nut milks, protein shakes,
coconut manna butter to spread on toast or
stir into coffee, and its own kombucha.

Palate WINE BAR
(☑808-212-1974; www.palatewinebar.net; Kong
Lung Center, 2474 Keneke St; ⊙5-10pm) A good-
eating, great-drinking wine bar with a one-
man open kitchen (mains $16 to $32) that
produces creative flatbreads (including one
with macnut pesto sauce), salads, cheese and
charcuterie plates, one or two substantial
entrées per day and some scrumptious
desserts. It offers free wine tastings from
5pm to 6pm on Sundays.

🛍 Shopping

Whether you're looking for groceries or
gifts, Kilauea is a surprisingly busy shopping
destination. Three separate malls cluster
at the intersection of Kilauea (Lighthouse)
Rd and Keneke St, half a mile north of the
highway.

Kong Lung Center MALL

(www.konglungkauai.com; 2484 Keneke St) This small shopping-and-dining complex is based around the site where Kilauea's original general store was opened by a Chinese immigrant in 1902.

★ Kong Lung Trading ARTS, CLOTHING

(☑ 808-828-1822; www.konglung.com; Kong Lung Center, 2484 Keneke St; ◎10am-6pm Mon-Sat, from 11am Sun) Attractively laid out in a beautifully restored stone building that dates from 1877, this Asian-inspired art and clothing boutique sells a wide array of artful tchotchkes (trinkets), silken clothing and aloha wear.

There's also a sizeable kids' section, filled with clothing, books and toys.

Banana Patch Studio GIFTS & SOUVENIRS

(☑ 808-828-6522; www.bananapatchstudio.com; Kong Lung Center, 2484 Keneke St; ◎9am-5pm Mon-Sat, to 4pm Sun) This Kilauea outpost of the Hanapepe original is an artist-owned gallery selling colorful, appealing ceramic tiles and dishware, almost all designed by the owner and painted by her Hanapepe artisan crew. The lei kitties and hula bunnies are best sellers, and those wooden postcards are pretty cool. Ninety per cent of the stock is Hawaiian made.

Coconut Style CLOTHING

(☑ 808-828-6899; www.coconutstyle.com; Kong Lung Center, 2484 Keneke St; ◎10am-5:30pm Mon-Sat, from 10:30am Sun) A real and refreshing blast of color, Coconut Style traffics in all things aloha, handmade and hand-painted. Shirts and robes are typically priced around $120, sarongs at $40, and you'll also find gorgeous duvet covers from $750.

Island Soap & Candle Works GIFTS & SOUVENIRS

(☑ 808-828-1955; www.islandsoap.com; 2555 Ala Namahana Pkwy; ◎9am-8pm) ✎ The pick of several such shops on Kaua'i, in enlarged new premises but still making its soap in-house. Botanical lotions, body butters, bath oils and creamy shampoos and conditioners to make the folks back home envious. The company is notable for its commitment to solar power, forest-friendly packaging and sustainably harvested palm oil.

Ahuimanu MALL

(www.ahuimanu.com; 2555 Ala Namahana Pkwy) Kilauea's latest shopping mall, significantly further upscale than its neighbors and focused on the Kilauea Market, finally opened in 2019. At press time only a handful of tenants had moved in; watch this space.

Shared Blessings Thrift Shop VINTAGE

(www.christmemorialkauai.org; 2509 Kolo Rd; ◎2-5pm Tue, Thu & Fri, 9:30am-12:30pm Wed, 9:30am-3pm Sat, closed Sun & Mon) This church-run thrift shop, set in the 1925 Parish Hall across from the chapel, benefits its food pantry and sells everything from espresso makers and juicers to used clothes, linens and hats.

It has a huge stock of secondhand books priced at $1 each – handy on an island with so few bookstores – and it evens sells surfboards.

Palate Market WINE

(☑ 808-212-1974; www.palatewinebar.net/market; Kong Lung Center, 2474 Keneke St; ◎10:30am-10:30pm Mon-Sat, from noon Sun) A well-curated liquor store adjacent to the eponymous wine bar. It offers small-batch spirits and good deals on great wines.

Hunter Gatherer HOMEWARES

(☑ 808-828-1388; www.huntergathererhawaii.com; Kilauea Plantation Center, 4270 Kilauea Rd; ◎10am-6pm Mon-Sat, to 2pm Sun) Gift shop and gallery with a strong New Age influence, stocking an eclectic blend of clothing, books, art, bath and beauty products, and home furnishings, most with little connection to Hawaii.

Oskar's Boutique CLOTHING

(☑ 808-828-6858; www.oskarsboutique.com; Kilauea Plantation Center, 4270b Kilauea Rd; ◎10:30am-6pm Mon-Fri, from noon Sat; ⊕) ✎ Island-inspired casual and beachwear for men, women and children. The blouses, beach bags and jewelry are especially good. Check the sales rack out front for deals.

ⓘ Getting There & Away

Kilauea is 24 miles north of Lihu'e Airport, via Kuhio Hwy. Kaua'i Bus (p279) stops by the Shell Garage at the main highway intersection, and also detours briefly north to the Kong Lung Center. To explore in any depth, though, a car is essential.

North Shore Cab (☑ 808-639-7829; www.northshorecab.com) is a Kilauea-based company that offers island tours and a shuttle service for Kalalau Trail hikers, as well as standard cab rides.

HANALEI & THE NORTH SHORE KILAUEA

LAZY DAYS IN NORTH SHORE & HANALEI BAY

The North Shore of Kaua'i bears an uncanny resemblance to the kind of tropical screensaver you might put on your office computer during the dead of winter. A place this beautiful deserves a little extra time; here's how we like to spend it.

BEACH

The smooth, buttery scallop of **Hanalei Bay** (Map p164) cradles what's simply one of the world's great beaches. World-class surfing is the norm, but you want to relax, right? Well, the surf culture that surrounds Hanalei devotes its energies to chill times, seaside picnics and plenty of mellow ukelele riffs. Enjoy that sunset.

DINING

When you get tired of swimming and hiking, and swimming some more and hey, let's take another walk, there are few more enjoyable ways to recharge your batteries than to venture down a North Shore foodie rabbit hole. From fresh *poke* (cubed raw fish mixed with *shōyu*, sesame oil, salt, chili pepper, *'inamona* or other condiments) to burgers by the beach, sushi to ramen, and shave ice to vegan pasta, there's a flavor for every palate.

HIKING

The earthly Eden that is Kaua'i's North Shore begs to be explored on foot. Straight up, we have to admit the full **Na Pali Coast** (p179) hike requires at least two days to complete. A long trek may not be the laziest way to spend your time, but it does provide a way to totally disconnect from the outside world – and in any case, there are any number of shorter, more casual options afoot (pun intended).

STEVE MINKLER/SHUTTERSTOCK ©

1. Hanalei Bay (p162) ;
2. Waterfall, Na Pali Coast (p179)

'Anini

A beloved beach destination for locals who spend entire weekends here camping, fishing, diving or just 'beaching' it.

⊙ Sights

'Anini Beach Park BEACH
('Anini Rd; ⊞) Winding along the seashore, fringed by overhanging trees, long 'Anini Beach is a narrow strip of sand that at several points dwindles to the slenderest of sandy slivers. Protected by one of the longest and widest fringing reefs in all Hawaii, extending up to 1600ft offshore, it's hugely popular with families. The shallow waters are ideal for gentle swimming; just keep away from the channel at the western end. There's great snorkeling here too, especially toward the beach's eastern end, where it abuts a gorgeous lava cliff. Be wary at low tide, when the shallows bottom out and you may have to dodge exposed coral and sea urchins.

Exposed to strong winds, this is also one of Kaua'i's finest spots for windsurfing and kiteboarding. There's a good campground here, but no food or drink is available.

🏃 Activities

★ Freedive Kauai DIVING
(☑808-212-7043; www.freedivekauai.com; Basic Freediver $150, Freediver $375, Advanced Freediver $695) Kaua'i's only freediving school offers progressively advanced PADI certification courses off 'Anini Beach or Koloa Landing, commencing with the half-day Freediver. Within three days, even novices learn to plummet to 66ft (20m) on a single breath.

Co-owner Michelle Marsh has competed for the USA in the World Championships.

Windsurf Kaua'i WINDSURFING
(☑808-828-6838; www.windsurfkauai.com; 'Anini Beach Park; 2hr lessons $125; ⊙10am & 1pm Mon-Fri, by appointment only) Celeste Harvel can teach you what it's like to glide on water; she guarantees you'll be sailing in your first lesson. Refresher courses and advanced lessons also available.

🛏 Sleeping

**'Anini Beach
Park Campground** CAMPGROUND $
(www.kauai.gov/Camping/Anini-Beach-Park; 'Anini Rd; adult/Hawaii resident/child under 18yr $3/free/free; ⊙open 24hr, closed 10am Tues-noon Wed) At the only North Shore county campground to remain open at press time, you set up your tent on well-shaded lawns just back from the beach, with restrooms, picnic tables and freshwater showers alongside. There are no stores, food trucks or restaurants nearby. Obtain permits via the Hanalei Neighborhood Center (p169).

★ Anini Lani Kai RENTAL HOUSE $$$
(☑808-651-3085; www.vrbo.com/77508; 3976 'Anini Rd; house per night $329) This tin-roof plantation cottage stands on an acre of land right beside luscious 'Anini Beach. It looks and feels like 19th-century Hawaii, with swaying coconut palms in the garden and an outdoor shower. Book well ahead. Seven-night minimum stay, cleaning fee $175.

Plumeria RENTAL HOUSE $$$
(☑808-828-0811; www.surfsideprop.com; 3585 'Anini Rd; 3-bedroom house per night/week $375/2500; 🛜) This chic and comfortable house has an enviable location only a short walk from the beach. Expect modest luxury, Hawaii-style, with a polished wood interior, sweeping views, and indoor and outdoor showers. Add to this amicable caretakers and beach and snorkel gear, kayaks and bicycles to borrow. Cleaning fee $175.

Nakea RENTAL HOUSE $$$
(☑808-245-8841; www.kauaivacationrentals.com; 4343 'Anini Rd; 2-bedroom house from $429; 🛜) An all-wood, two-bedroom, two-bathroom home that sleeps six, with ocean views from a luscious lanai, walking distance to the sand. For groups, it's an affordable beachfront choice. One caveat: it holds one queen bed and four twin mattresses.

ⓘ Getting There & Away

The bus doesn't make it down to 'Anini, so you'll need your own transport. To reach it, stay on Kuhio Hwy across Kalihiwai Bridge, turn right just up the hill onto (the second) Kalihiwai Rd, then bear left onto 'Anini Rd soon afterward.

Princeville

POP 2400

While Princeville enjoys a spectacular clifftop setting, it doesn't feel at all like a town. Instead it's a landscaped real-estate development that's as carefully controlled and protected as any film set. Comprising high-end resorts and manicured golf courses, plus a mix of cookie-cutter residences, vacation rentals and even some working-class condo complexes, what Princeville lacks in personality it makes up for in convenience.

History

Princeville traces its roots to Robert Wyllie, a Scottish doctor who became foreign minister to King Kamehameha IV. In 1853 Wyllie acquired land for a sugar plantation in Hanalei. When the king and his wife, Queen Emma, came to visit in 1860, Wyllie dubbed his plantation Princeville in honor of their two-year-old son, Prince Albert, who died only two years later. The plantation later became a cattle ranch, which was ultimately sold for redevelopment in 1969.

◉ Sights

Hanalei Valley Lookout　　　VIEWPOINT
Immediately west of the Princeville Center, a roadside overlook offers a superb panoramic view over verdant Hanalei Valley, with Hihimanu Mountain towering beyond. The valley floor is a checkerboard of flooded taro fields, known as *lo'i kalo* in Hawaiian. Most are usually lurid green, bursting with growing plants; those where young taro has yet to poke above water level remain muddy brown. The area is protected as the Hanalei National Wildlife Refuge (p163).

Hanalei Plantation Road Lookout　　　VIEWPOINT
This spectacular overlook commands views over not only the Hanalei River and its valley, but also the bay and its beaches. To reach it, simply follow Hanalei Plantation Rd, which starts a quarter-mile west of the Princeville Center, to the clearing where it ends, just under a mile along. This spot also holds the Nourish (p159) farm stand.

A trail leads straight ahead, through the site of the former Hanalei Plantation Resort and down to Pu'u Poa Beach. The resort itself, which became a Club Med before closing in the mid-1980s, was linked to the beach by a tramway. It's a haunting spot, where the lawns are still mown regularly but the buildings have been reduced to moss-covered mounds of rubble. There are persistent reports that the site will be redeveloped to hold a luxury hotel in the near future.

🏖 Beaches

★ Pali Ke Kua (Hideaways) Beach　　　BEACH
Hideaways Beach, also known as Pali Ke Kua, is a cove notched beneath the Princeville cliffs, with a short strand of golden sand and turquoise shallows. It's an ideal snorkel and swim spot – when it's calm – with a teeming reef just off the beach. There's only very limited parking at the trailhead above, however, and the descent is steep, with the initial stairway swiftly becoming a precipitous muddy slope. When no parking spots are available, use the valet parking at Princeville Resort instead. There's another trail from the Pali Ke Kua condos, but that's exclusively for guests.

SeaLodge Beach　　　BEACH
(Kamehameha Rd) Accessed via a steep 10-minute hike from the eponymous condos, exquisite SeaLodge Beach – officially Kaweonui Beach – is a short stretch of coarse-grained golden sand that's quiet enough to be a haunt of Hawaiian monk seals and green sea turtles. Safe in summer only, the snorkeling is excellent.

The trail down from SeaLodge starts beside seven parking spots reserved for hikers. It's a slippery scramble through thick woods; head left at the electricity substation halfway down. If the waves are pounding the oceanfront rocks when you reach sea level, go no further. Otherwise head right to find a little waterfall, or left around the headland to the beach itself.

Pu'u Poa Beach　　　BEACH
Lovely little Pu'u Poa Beach stands immediately below the Princeville Resort, on the edge of Hanalei Bay. It's a great spot for family swimming and snorkeling. The waves beyond the reef are the domain of expert surfers only. Resort guests inevitably dominate the beach – they can simply ride the elevator down. To get here otherwise, use the resort's valet parking, or hike from the end of Hanalei Plantation Rd.

Princeville

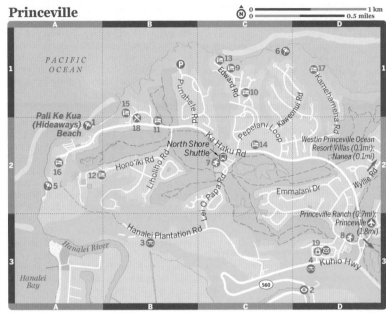

Princeville

🏃 Activities

⭐ Island Sails Kaua'i   BOATING

(📞 808-212-6053; www.islandsailskauai.com; Pu'u Poa Beach; 90min cruises adult/child from $119/99; ☺ Apr-Sep, by reservation only) Whether you fancy snorkeling in the morning, cruising in the afternoon or catching a sunset, this is your chance to ride in a traditional Polynesian sailing canoe. The red-painted *Ku'upa'aloa,* which carries up to six passengers, pulls right up onto the beach in front of the Princeville Resort.

⭐ Princeville Ranch Stables   HORSEBACK RIDING

(📞808-826-7669; http://princevilleranch.com; Kuhio Hwy at Kapaka Rd; lessons from $100, tours $129-189; ☺Mon-Sat, by appointment only; 👶) A beautiful expedition suited to beginners and experienced riders, the 3½-hour trip to Kalihiwai Falls includes picnicking and a swim. Other possibilities include a cattle drive or zipline experience. Find the stables east of Princeville on Kuhio Hwy. Wear jeans and bring sunblock and insect repellent. Maximum weight limits and the minimum age for riders (eight to 10 years) vary.

Halele'a Spa   SPA

(📞 808-826-2405; www.princevilleresorthawaii. com; Princeville Resort, 5520 Ka Haku Rd; treatments from $150; ☺10am-4pm, by appointment only) This 11,000-sq-ft palatial escape – which translates as 'house of joy' – incorporates native Hawaiian woods and natural fibers. Massages, based on traditional Hawaiian medicine and available in couples and VIP rooms – utilize botanical and ocean resources, such as taro, clay and seaweed. Treatments include complimentary fitness center access.

Princeville Ranch Adventures   ADVENTURE

(📞 808-826-7669; http://princevilleranch.com; Kuhio Hwy at Kapaka Rd; hiking and/or kayaking from $129, ziplining from $139, ATV tour from $169; ☺ by reservation only; 👶) This family-oriented enterprise is designed to bring out your adventurous side, whether you sign up for a waterfall hike, a zipline ride, or a kayak tour to a secluded swimming hole. Age requirements vary. Reservations required.

Blue Hawaiian Helicopters   SCENIC FLIGHTS

(📞 808-871-8844, 800-745-2583; www.blue hawaiian.com; Princeville Airport, 5-3541 Kuhio Hwy; 45min tours $309) For anyone staying on the North Shore, it makes sense to take a scenic helicopter tour from Princeville Airport rather than Lihu'e. Flights from Princeville can also focus a little more exclusively on Kaua'i's finest scenery, in that they loop over the Na Pali Coast and Waimea Canyon without also covering the East or South coasts.

Makai Golf Club   GOLF

(📞 808-826-1912; www.makaigolf.com; 4080 Lei O Papa Rd; standard green fee incl cart rental $299, resort guests $239, 9-hole Woods Course $69; sunset cart tour for 2 $69) The 18-hole Makai Course, designed by Robert Trent Jones Jr, meanders through the heart of Princeville and is championship rated. Check online for current rates; guests at most Princeville hotels can get discounts. Certain holes have superb ocean views best admired on sunset cart tours. The separate nine-hole Woods Course charges a flat green fee.

Tennis at the Makai Club   TENNIS

(📞 808-826-1912; www.makaigolf.com; 4080 Lei O Papa Rd; 90min court rental per person $20, minimum $40) Gorgeous outdoor hard courts host lessons – offered daily by the club pro – and pickup games, though you can book out courts for private play too. Call up to a week in advance for reservations. Racket rental available.

Prince Albert Park   PLAYGROUND

(4304 Emmalani Dr; ☺ dawn-dusk; 👶) A gorgeous stretch of green with jungle gyms and a backstop for baseball, if your kids need a place to ramble and romp off beach.

Hot Yoga Princeville   YOGA

(📞 808-826-4040; www.hotyogaprinceville.com; Princeville Center, 5-4280 Kuhio Hwy; drop-in classes $25, 5-class pass $85) In Bikram style, a skilled team of yogis leads classes for any and all willing to practice in a room heated to 95–100°F (35–38°C). Mat ($1) and towel ($2) rentals available. Find current class schedules online.

Mana Yoga   YOGA

(📞 808-652-3823; www.manayoga.com; 3812 Ahonui Pl; classes $30, 4-class pass $80; ☺8:30-10am Wed) Michaelle Edwards has devised her own version of yoga, targeted at straightening even the most unruly of spines. Combining massage and yoga, it aims to heal with natural poses.

Powerline Trail   HIKING

(Kepaka Rd) Constructed so electricity pylons could connect Wailua with Princeville, the

QUEEN'S BATH

A natural tide pool on the Princeville shoreline, formed by a sharp lava-rock shelf, Queen's Bath may look beautiful, but it's the deadliest spot on Kaua'i. Dozens of people have drowned here. In winter especially, it's notorious for powerful waves that pull visitors out to sea. Most are swept off as they walk along the ledge to access the pool. We recommend staying away.

13-mile Powerline Trail penetrates parts of Kaua'i that visitors seldom see. Once a broad dirt road, it's now so overgrown that only its initial 2-mile stretch can be recommended. A round-trip hike of 4 miles leads past a towering waterfall to some great viewpoints looking westward over Hanalei Valley.

To join the trail, turn south off the highway at Princeville Ranch, and follow Kepaka Rd for just under 2 miles. Look for the Na Ala Hele trailhead sign just beyond a water tank, where the road turns to red dirt. If you're up for a serious bushwacking expedition, and can arrange for a pick up at the far end, the full 13-mile hike to Wailua's Keahou Arboretum will take at least six hours.

⭐ Festivals & Events

Princeville Night Market   FOOD & DRINK
(www.princevillecenter.com; Princeville Center, 5-4280 Kuhio Hwy; ⊙4-8pm 2nd Sun of month) Tented stalls set up in and around the Princeville Center sell everything from locally roasted coffee to stationery, and from handicrafts to original art. All the mall's restaurants are open, food trucks come from around the island and there's live music too.

🛏 Sleeping

Princeville holds a small cluster of resorts, along with myriad vacation rentals. Its planned country-club atmosphere may not suit everyone, but its central location on the North Shore is certainly convenient, and larger groups or extended families have a better chance of finding sizeable properties to share.

Nihilani   CONDO **$$**
(✏800-325-5701; www.parrishkauai.com; 4919 Pepelani Loop; 3-bedroom townhouse from $225; P☀🛜🏊) Set on a loop road in the heart

of Princeville, this manicured complex of individually owned condos is not cliffside, nor does it have sea views, but it evokes the architecture of Hawaii's plantation era. Townhouses show off louvered awnings and shutters, while an up-to-date pool area and outdoor BBQ grills make it ideal for family vacations. Cleaning fee $200.

Pali Ke Kua   CONDO **$$**
(✏808-826-9394; www.palikekua.com; 5300 Ka Haku Rd; 1-/2-bedroom condo from $228/283; ☀🛜🏊) Perched atop the cliffs, just short of the Princeville Resort, Pali Ke Kua offers an easy trail down to its namesake beach, also known as Hideaways. Some units have both ocean and mountain views. Units vary in size and are individually listed with rental agencies as well as on the collective website; compare quotes online. Additional fees charged for cleaning.

Sealodge   CONDO **$$**
(✏800-585-6101; www.hestara.com; 3700 Kamehameha Rd; 1-/2-bedroom condo from $130/150; ☀🛜🏊) Basking in 180-degree views of the deep blue Pacific from their gorgeous cliffside location, these wind-weathered, wooden-shingled condos make a dramatic spectacle. Some units are in better shape than others and not all interiors are wonderful, so ask local rental agencies for up-to-date pictures before you book online. Cleaning fee $95 to $115.

Princeville Vacations   ACCOMMODATIONS SERVICES **$$**
(✏800-800-3637, 808-828-6530; www.princeville-vacations.com) A decent selection of midrange choices for condos and vacation homes, including properties in all the major condo resorts.

Emmalani Court   CONDO **$$**
(✏800-325-5701, 808-826-0002; www.parrish kauai.com; 5250 Ka Haku Rd; 1-/2-bedroom condo from $165/225; ☀🏊) These whitewashed villas are in a quieter part of the Princeville development, adjacent to the Makai Golf Club. They're roomy and well kept, and some afford ocean views. There's a small, tiled outdoor swimming pool. Five-night minimum stay; cleaning fee from $175.

Westin Princeville Ocean Resort Villas   RESORT **$$$**
(✏866-837-4254, 808-827-8700; www.westin princeville.com; 3838 Wyllie Rd; studio/1-bedroom condo from $375/455; ☀@🛜🏊) This spacious,

luxurious clifftop resort is the one Princeville property that sets out to rival the Princeville Resort itself. Each condo-like 'villa' boasts a full kitchen and washer-dryer, while studio units have kitchenettes; all share a multi-level, kid-friendly pool complex. The views are expansive, and between November and March even a casual gaze over the ocean may reveal a whale.

Cliffs   CONDO $$$
(☑ 808-826-6219; www.cliffsatprinceville.com; 3811 Edward Rd; 1-bedroom condo from $345) This large condo development, perched on the grassy Princeville cliffs, is comprised of three-story wooden turquoise-brushed buildings with slanted roofs that enjoy spectacular views. Units have hardwood floors, granite counter tops, two baths and custom wood furnishings. Paying a little extra gets you one with a master bedroom plus sleeping loft.

Holly's Kauai Condo   CONDO $$$
(☑ 480-831-0061; www.hollyskauaicondo.com; Ali'i Kai, 3830 Edward Rd; 2-bedroom condo $260; ❋ ☎) Perched cliffside with nothing but water between you and Alaska, this 1200-sq-ft, two-bedroom, two-bathroom unit in the Ali'i Kai development, complete with bamboo furnishings and top-of-the-line kitchen, is a great deal. Guaranteed whale sightings – pretty much from your bed – in winter. Three-night minimum stay; cleaning fee $165. Book far in advance.

Kauai
Vacation Rentals   ACCOMMODATIONS SERVICES $$$
(☑ 808-245-8841; www.kauaivacationrentals. com) A wide range of condo rentals on the North Shore, including properties in several Princeville resorts.

Parrish
Collection Kaua'i   ACCOMMODATIONS SERVICES $$$
(☑ 808-826-0002, 800-325-5701; www.parrish kauai.com; Princeville Center, 5-4280 Kuhio Hwy) An upscale collection of vacation rental options, including several around Princeville.

Hanalei Bay Resort   RESORT $$$
(☑ 877-344-0688, 808-826-6522; www.hanalei bayresort.com; 5380 Hono'iki Rd; r from $279; ☎) Location is the name of the game for this timeshare property, poised just above lovely Pu'u Poa Beach and effectively sharing it with the Princeville Resort. Suites can be steeply priced, but units vary drastically in quality and not all have the same amenities. Check details and photos before you book.

Princeville Resort   RESORT $$$
(☑ 833-623-2111, 808-826-9644; www.princeville resorthawaii.com; 5520 Ka Haku Rd; d from $463; ❋ ☎ ☎) Tumbling down the hillside to luscious Pu'u Poa Beach, with breathtaking views across Hanalei Bay, the 250-room Princeville Resort was in a state of flux at press time. New owners took over the former St Regis in 2018, but promised renovations have yet to materialize. Staffing and maintenance levels have declined, and the main restaurant remains closed.

Check the latest situation online. Drop in for a cocktail in the Princeville Bar (p160), but for the moment, the room rates – and additional resort fees – are too high for what you get.

Ali'i Kai   RESORT $$$
(☑ 808-445-1116; www.aliikairesort.com; 3830 Edward Rd; condos per night from $360) With their Polynesian motifs, the two-bedroom condos in this clifftop development evoke mid-century Hawaii. All are individually owned, but they can be rented via the resort itself or, in some cases, other agents. There's a pool and outdoor BBQs, but this place is more about the soul than the amenities.

✖ Eating

Apart from a couple of hotel dining rooms, Princeville's restaurants are largely concentrated in the humdrum Princeville Center mall. Hanalei and Kilauea hold more interesting choices.

Nourish   HEALTH FOOD $
(☑ 808-346-2254; www.nourishhanalei.com; 5225 Hanalei Plantation Rd; items $9-14; ⊘ 11am-3pm Tue-Fri) ✔ Set on a little-known Princeville back road, this little farm stand overlooks an amazing Hanalei panorama taking in beach, town, river and valley. It serves a simple but healthy lunchtime menu of homegrown salads, fruit bowls and smoothies.

North Shore
General Store & Cafe   AMERICAN $
(☑ 808-826-1122; www.pizzakauai.com; Princeville Center, 5-4280 Kuhio Hwy; burritos & burgers $6-8, pizzas $12-26; ⊘ 8am-7:30pm) Congratulations, you may have found the best gas station mini-mart in the US of A, at the entrance to the Princeville Center. As well as serving up bagel sandwiches, legendary breakfast burritos, grass-fed Princeville beef burgers

and coffee, it offers daily specials like an $8 *poke* bowl and sells locally made hot sauce.

Lappert's Hawaii   ICE CREAM $

(☑ 808-826-7393; www.lappertshawaii.com; Princeville Center, 5-4280 Kuhio Hwy; ☺10am-9pm; 🖈) The comforting smell of waffle cones beckons, as do scoops of sweet island flavors such as Kaua'i pie (Kona coffee ice cream with coconut flakes and macadamia nuts).

Foodland   SUPERMARKET $

(☑ 808-826-9880; www.foodland.com; Princeville Center, 5-4280 Kuhio Hwy; ☺6am-11pm) The North Shore's largest and best-value supermarket has an abundance of fruits and vegetables, freshly prepared sushi and some damn good *poke*, wine, and beer.

The Spot   CAFE $

(☑808-320-7605; www.thespotkauai.com; Princeville Center, 5-4280 Kuhio Hwy; items $8-13; ☺7am-2pm) Sharing its large deck with a vigorous population of scavenging birds, this caffeine filling station dishes up acai bowls, eggs Benedict bowls, breakfast sandwiches and thick smoothies along with its coffee, and offers prime people-watching too. Expect long lines in the morning.

Sandwich Isle   DELI $

(☑808-827-8272; Princeville Center, 5-4280 Kuhio Hwy; sandwiches $11-14; ☺7-10am & 11am-3:30pm Mon-Fri, 11am-2:45pm Sat & Sun) A little deli window in one corner of the Princeville Center, with a few dedicated tables out on the deck. It does an 'Italian Job' sub with salami, mortadella, pepperoni, pickled peppers and provolone; a 'Philly' with roast beef, Muenster cheese and horseradish aioli; and a 'New Yorker,' pairing pastrami with aged white cheddar.

Lotus Garden   THAI $

(☑808-826-9999; Princeville Center, 5-4280 Kuhio Hwy; mains $10-20; ☺10am-9pm) A Thai and Chinese takeout joint offering Thai-curry mahimahi, honey-orange, steamed bok choy with tofu, and all the curries, noodles and Chinese stir-fries you might desire. There are a couple tables outside.

PV Eats   AMERICAN $$

(☑808-826-1695; www.pveatskauai.com; 5-3900 Kuhio Hwy; mains $16-28; ☺8am-10pm Mon-Sat, food served 11am-9pm) Part high-end supermarket, part wine bar, and part deli/restaurant, PV Eats occupies the former clubhouse of the now-private Prince golf course, 2 miles east of Princeville proper.

Good burgers cost $16, local steaks and pan-seared fresh catch are good value, the bright dining area has lush views, and you can sample some great wines by the glass.

Hideaways Pizza Pub   PIZZA $$

(☑ 808-378-4187; www.hideawayspizzapub.com; 5300 Ka Haku Rd; mains $16-35, pizzas $13-33; ☺5-10pm) You'll only find Hideaways if you go looking for it, hard; it's tucked away on the Pali Ke Kua property, 2 miles off the highway. Once here, choose between an 'old school' pizza like pepperoni, or a 'new school' one such as the Greek, with cucumber sauce and feta cheese. It also serves pastas, ginger-crusted ahi and pepper-pork tenderloin.

★ Kaua'i Ono   HAWAIIAN $$$

(☑ 808-634-3244; www.kauaiono.com; Princeville Ranch, 4520 Kapaka St; 5-course dinner $70; ☺6:30pm Tue & Wed) 🍷 For something different and delicious – *'ono* being Hawaiian for delicious – join the twice-weekly crowd for this outdoor feast at Princeville Ranch. From a fancy trailer, chef Justin Smith delivers a five-course menu of fresh produce from Kaua'i farms – the likes of *kalua* pork with mashed breadfruit – to communal tables beneath a huge awning. Check schedule and reserve online; BYOB.

Nanea   HAWAIIAN $$$

(☑800-827-8808; www.westinprinceville.com; Westin Princeville Ocean Resort Villas, 3838 Wylie Rd; mains lunch $17-19, dinner $35-46; ☺7-10:30am, 11am-2:30pm & 6-9pm Mon-Sat, 8:30am-12:30pm & 6-9pm Sun) 🍷 Despite Nanea's attractive resort location facing the Westin's pool, its fusion-style cuisine is not quite special enough to merit going far out of your way. Lunch is the better value, with fish tacos or *loco moco* (dish of rice, fried egg and hamburger patty topped with gravy or other condiments) at under $20; dinner mains, using fresh island ingredients, cost double.

🍸 Drinking & Nightlife

★ Princeville Bar   LOUNGE

(☑808-826-9644; www.princevilleresorthawaii.com; Princeville Resort, 5520 Ka Haku Rd; ☺3-10pm) Beckoning beyond the lobby of the Princeville Resort, this formal but welcoming lounge commands one of the finest views in all Hawaii, westward across Hanalei Bay toward the Na Pali cliffs. It's the perfect venue for a sunset cocktail, whether out on the lanai or in the cool comfort behind its tinted windows.

Tiki Iniki Bar & Restaurant BAR

(☑ 808-431-4242; www.tikiiniki.com; Princeville Center, 5-4280 Kuhio Hwy; ⊘ 11:30am-midnight; 🐟) Complete with thatched roof and trappings from Kaua'i's long-gone Coco Palms Resort, rocker Todd Rundgren's tiki bar, created with wife Michele, is the kind of tourist trap more suited to sipping cocktails like mai tais or the 'Hanalei Sling' than eating, but there's a menu of burgers, wraps, seafood and pasta (mains lunch $13 to $22, dinner $18 to $36). There's also live music at weekends.

🛍 Shopping

Magic Dragon TOYS

(☑ 808-826-9144; Princeville Center, 5-4280 Kuhio Hwy; ⊘ 9am-6pm) Stuffed toys and kites, board games and playing cards, remote-control choppers and matchbox-style cars – put it all together and you have one of Princeville's most distinctive shops.

It also has a nice arts supply corner where you can stock up on oils, water-colors and acrylics, sketchbooks and paintbrushes.

Princeville Wine Market WINE

(☑ 808-826-0040; www.princevillewinemarket.com; Princeville Center, 5-4280 Kuhio Hwy; ⊘ 10am-8pm) Well-curated new- and old-world wines, infused vodkas and high-end spirits of all kinds, plus a small array of hams, cheeses and chocolate.

Walking In Paradise SHOES

(☑ 808-827-8100; www.facebook.com/walkingin paradisekauai; Princeville Center, 5-4280 Kuhio Hwy; ⊘ 9am-6pm) If you, your partner or your children need sandals for beachcombing, running or hiking shoes, or something a bit more versatile for day or night, the selection here is surprisingly good. It also stocks hats, handbags and socks (including those weird gloves for your feet).

Fish Eye PHOTOGRAPHY

(☑ 808-631-9645; www.fisheyekauai.com; Princeville Center, 5-4280 Kuhio Hwy; ⊘ 9am-6pm) The standout items at this all-purpose gallery, which also sells paintings on driftwood and little koa-wood knick-knacks, are the dramatic photos of Kaua'i's glorious scenery, including some amazing underwater shots.

Beauty Bar Kauai COSMETICS

(☑ 808-826-6264; www.beautybarkauai.com; Princeville Center, 5-4280 Kuhio Hwy; ⊘ 10am-6pm Sun-Thu, to 8pm Fri & Sat) A proper cosmetics bar with abundant makeup, perfumes and scrubs, and makeup artists on call. Local labels in stock include Ili, which makes a popular coffee body scrub, and Leahlani, which does face scrubs and a perfumed beauty balm. It even sells its own brand of sea-salt hair spray.

Azure Island Clothing CLOTHING

(☑ 808-826-4433; Princeville Center, 5-4280 Kuhio Hwy; ⊘ 10am-6:30pm) The widest-ranging clothes store in the Princeville Center, albeit conservative by the standards of Hanalei. As well as aloha wear for men and women, it sells dresses, golf shirts and jewelry.

Island Soap & Candle Works GIFTS & SOUVENIRS

(☑ 808-827-8111; www.islandsoap.com; Princeville Center, 5-4280 Kuhio Hwy; ⊘ 10am-6pm) Belonging to a small Kaua'i chain, this sweet-smelling little mall store makes and sells handmade soaps and candles, body lotions and more.

Princeville Center MALL

(☑ 808-826-9497; www.princevillecenter.com; 5-4280 Kuhio Hwy) If you're staying in Princeville, you're pretty sure to end up prowling this assortment of island and lifestyle shops at least once per day. Focused around the Foodland supermarket and Chevron gas station, it also holds several low-key restaurants.

There's live local entertainment nightly (6pm to 8pm) in its central court, with hula on Wednesdays.

ℹ️ Information

MONEY

Bank of Hawaii (☑ 808-826-6551; www.boh.com; Princeville Center, 5-4280 Kuhio Hwy; ⊘ 8:30am-4pm Mon-Thu, to 6pm Fri)

First Hawaiian Bank (☑ 808-826-1560; www.fhb.com; Princeville Center, 5-4280 Kuhio Hwy; ⊘ 8:30am-4pm Mon-Thu, to 6pm Fri)

POST

Princeville Mail Service Center (☑ 808-826-7331; Princeville Center, 5-4280 Kuhio Hwy; per 20min $5; ⊘ 9am-5pm Mon-Fri)

Princeville Post Office (☑ 808-828-1721; www.usps.com; Princeville Center, 5-4280 Kuhio Hwy; ⊘ 10:30am-2:30pm Mon-Fri, to noon Sat)

ⓘ Getting There & Away

Princeville spreads northward across the clifftops from the main Kuhio Hwy. The Kaua'i Bus (p279) between Lihu'e and Hanalei stops at the Princeville Center mall hourly on weekdays, less frequently on weekends. The resort's one arterial road, Ka Haku Rd, runs through the middle, with a paved recreational path alongside that's great for walking, running or bicycle cruising.

North Shore Shuttle (☑ 888-409-2702; https://kauainsshuttle.com; Lei O Papa Rd; single ride/day pass/week/month $5/10/20/40) This shuttle service makes seven daily runs from Princeville's Makai Golf Club, where there's a dedicated parking lot, to Ha'ena State Park, for Ke'e Beach and the Kalalau Trail. The first bus is at 7:15am; the last return service leaves Ha'ena at 5pm.

Call ahead for details of overnight parking for campers hiking the Kalalau Trail.

ⓘ Getting Around

The **Chevron gas station** (Princeville Center, 5-4280 Kuhio Hwy; ☉ usually 6am-10pm Mon-Sat, to 9pm Sun) is the last place to gas up before the end of the North Shore road.

Hanalei

POP 500

Precious few towns can boast the majestic natural beauty and barefoot soul of Hanalei. The bay is the thing, of course, home to a half-dozen legendary surf breaks. Even if you haven't come for the waves, the beach will demand your attention with its wide sweep of cream-colored sand and magnificent jade mountain views.

And so too will the pint-sized town, languidly stretching along the highway around a half-mile from the beach. In its attractive historic buildings, you can shop for vintage treasures, chic beach gear and stunning art, dine on seafood or snack on sushi, or duck into a world-class dive bar. Sure, Hanalei has its fair share of adults with Peter Pan syndrome, and you'll see as many perma-tanned men in their 60s waxing their surfboards as you will gilded youth. Which begs the query: why grow up at all when you can grow old in Hanalei?

◉ Sights

Wai'oli Mission House　　HISTORIC BUILDING
(http://grovefarm.org; 5-5373 Kuhio Hwy; $10; ☉ guided tours 9am-3pm Tue, Thu & Sat) Home to missionaries from 1837 onward, this historic two-story dwelling lies hidden from the highway at the far end of a footpath that leads behind Wai'oli Hui'ia church. Set in lush gardens, surrounded by a white picket fence and furnished in authentic period style, it offers guided tours to walk-in visitors (no reservations).

Wai'oli Hui'ia Church　　CHURCH
(☑ 808-826-6253; www.hanaleichurch.org; 5-5393 Kuhio Hwy; ☉ 10am-2pm Mon & Wed-Fri, 9:30am-noon Sun, service 10am Sun) The green clapboard Wai'oli Hui'ia church stands on a huge manicured lawn just west of central Hanalei, against a beautiful mountain backdrop. It was originally built by Hanalei's first missionaries, William and Mary Alexander, who arrived here in 1834 in a double-hulled canoe. The current version, with its graceful stained-glass windows and curving pews, dates from 1912.

Hanalei Bridge　　LANDMARK
This attractive one-lane bridge is the only crossing over the Hanalei River, east of town. When it's closed due to flooding or construction, there's no way in or out of Hanalei.

🏖 Beaches

A perfect crescent of golden sand lines the 2-mile stretch of beautiful **Hanalei Bay** that runs west from the mouth of the Hanalei River. It's divided into four named sections, though as you enjoy a beachfront walk you can't tell where one ends and the next begins. Each offers different conditions for swimming and surfing, so don't assume it's safe to enter the ocean wherever you choose along the continuous strip.

★ Black Pot Beach Park (Hanalei Pier)　　BEACH
The short easternmost stretch of Hanalei Bay, alongside the river mouth, usually offers the calmest surf among the wild North Shore swells, and is popular with novice surfers. It's also known as Hanalei Pier for its unmistakable landmark jetty, perfect for a sunset stroll. In summer, swimming, snorkeling and SUP are decent – though the river itself can carry bacteria. Kayakers launch from a boat ramp on the river.

Although the beach has reopened after a year-long closure following the 2018 floods, its camping facilities remained closed at the time of writing.

HANALEI NATIONAL WILDLIFE REFUGE

Among the largest rivers in the state, the Hanalei River winds through a fertile valley that has been a major agricultural resource ever since the first *kanaka maoli* (Native Hawaiians) planted taro here. Many taro patches became rice paddies in the 19th century to feed the Chinese laborers on the sugar plantations, and four rice mills were operating in the valley by the 1930s. Although taro production has greatly declined elsewhere in Hawai, here in Hanalei it dominates once more.

The Hanalei National Wildlife Refuge, which occupies 917 acres of the valley floor, was established in 1972 to protect five endangered native waterbirds: *ae'o* (Hawaiian stilt; slender with black back, white chest and long pink legs), *'alae kea* (Hawaiian coot; slate gray with white forehead), *'alae 'ula* (Hawaiian moorhen; dark gray with black head and distinctive red-and-yellow bill); *koloa maoli* (Hawaiian duck; mottled brown with orange legs and feet); and nene (native Hawaiian goose; black head and striped neck), which is no longer officially considered to be endangered. A further 45 bird species are regular visitors.

The refuge is closed to the public, but the Hanalei Valley Lookout (p155) in Princeville offers a distant overview, and you can enter it on foot by joining the Ho'opulapula Haraguchi Taro Farm Tour (p168). It's also possible to drive into the refuge by turning left onto Ohiki Rd, immediately after the Hanalei Bridge, but parking is only permitted at the trailhead for the Okolehao Trail (p163).

Hanalei Pavilion Beach Park   BEACH

Pretty much at the center of Hanalei Bay, this scenic beach park commands a white-sand crescent just made for walking or jogging. Waters are typically not as calm as beside the pier, but swimming and paddling are usually possible in summer. Facilities include restrooms and outdoor showers. There's only a small parking lot, but street-parking spaces are often available.

Wai'oli (Pine Trees) Beach Park   BEACH

Offering respite from the sun, this park is equipped with restrooms, outdoor showers, beach volleyball courts and picnic tables. Winter brings big swells, and locals dominate the surf spot that's known as Pine Trees in honor of the waterfront ironwoods. There's a more challenging shore break here than anywhere else on Hanalei Bay, and swimming is dangerous, except during summer calms.

Waikoko Beach   BEACH

Protected by a reef on the western bend of Hanalei Bay, sandy-bottomed roadside Waikoko Beach – literally 'blood water' – offers shallower and calmer waters than the middle of the bay. It's thus the safest for family swimming, but sadly it has no facilities. Local surfers call the break here Waikokos; watch them at work to spot where it is.

Middles Beach   BEACH

West of Hanalei in Waipa, not far beyond Waikoko Beach at mile marker 4 on the *makai* side of the road, is a small, scrubby parking area. Walk along the beach or look out to the ocean to see three surf breaks; from left to right, **Waikokos**, **Middles** and **Chicken Wings**. This little beach is informally known as Middles, after the break.

🏃 Activities

As well as being the summer launching point for cruises west along the Na Pali Coast, Hanalei Bay stands at the mouth of the Hanalei River. Less crowded than the Eastside's Wailua River, it offers roughly 6 miles of tranquil scenery, ideal for kayaking or stand up paddle surfing.

Okolehao Trail   HIKING

(Ohiki Rd) For a dramatic overview of the taro fields of Hanalei Valley, and the crescent bay beyond, climb the grueling but rewarding Okolehao Trail. Ascending a sharp wooded ridge, it reaches successive forest clearings where views open up east to Kilauea Lighthouse and west to the Na Pali Coast. Carry lots of water and expect plenty of mud. Most hikers turn back after 1.25 miles, but informal and very precarious pathways lead higher up toward inaccessible peaks.

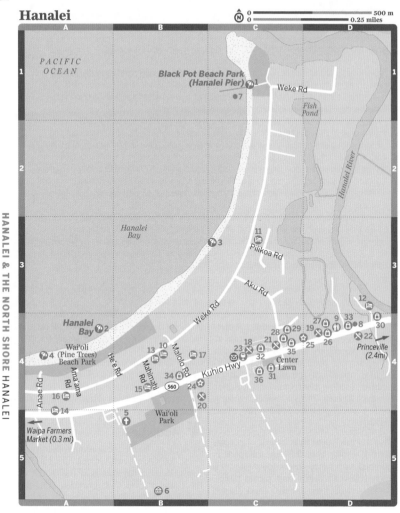

Waipa Foundation VOLUNTEERING

(📞808-826-9969; www.waipafoundation.org; 5-5785 Kuhio Hwy) This nonprofit organization owns and manages an entire traditional Hawaiian *ahupua'a*, a fundamental land division extending from peak to shore.

Volunteer opportunities include sessions on the fourth Saturday of each month, when visitors join hands-on community activities such as clearing invasive plants from waterways, or working in the taro fields. Sign up in advance and they'll prepare lunch for you.

Black Coral YOGA

(📞808-320-0755; www.blackcoralhanalei.com; Hanalei Center, 5-5161 Kuhio Hwy; drop-in class $24) This central yoga and wellness studio, upstairs in the Hanalei Center above Bar Acuda (p172), typically offers seven or eight classes per day, always including at least one Vinyasa session. Travelers can pay $58 to join three classes, or $70 for a week.

Kayaking & SUP

Kayak Kaua'i KAYAKING

(📞808-826-9844, 888-596-3852; www.kayak kauai.com; Na Pali 1-day tour late April-early Oct

Hanalei

$250; Na Pali camping trips May-Sep, from $368, Blue Lagoon Tour adult/child 5-12yr $105/95, kayak rental per day with delivery $45-55) Based on the Wailua River on the Eastside, this outfitter offers one-day tours along the full length of the Na Pali shore; multiday paddling trips with camping at Kalalau or Miloli'i; and Blue Lagoon paddling and snorkeling day trips around Hanalei. It will also rent and deliver camping and paddling gear island-wide.

Pedal 'n Paddle   ADVENTURE SPORTS
(☑ 808-826-9069;   http://pedalnpaddle.com; Ching Young Village, 5-5190 Kuhio Hwy; ⊗ 9am-6pm) This full-service rental shop, conveniently located in the heart of Hanalei, offers good daily and weekly rates for renting snorkel sets, boogie boards, SUP sets, kayaks, bicycles and almost all the camping gear you could need for trekking the Na Pali Coast.

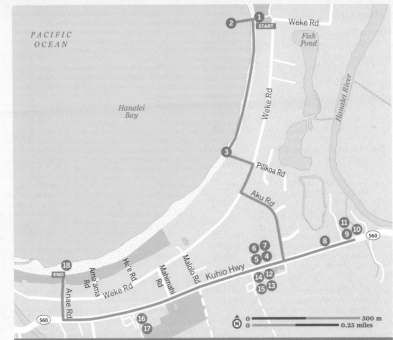

Town Walk
Hanalei Stroll

START BLACK POT BEACH
END WAIʻOLI (PINE TREES) BEACH PARK
LENGTH 2.3 MILES (ONE WAY), TWO HOURS

Start at ① **Black Pot Beach** (p162), where ② **Hanalei Pier** (p162) stretches out to sea and the mocha-tinted Hanelei River empties into the bay. Once you've admired the view from the pier, slip off your shoes and walk a half-mile to ③ **Hanalei Pavilion Beach Park** (p163), absorbing the beauty of Hanalei Bay. If the waves are large, you'll see surfers charging the point break way offshore; if seas are calm, have a swim before heading south on Weke Rd.

Turn left on Aku Rd to reach ④ **Ching Young Village**. Test your uke skills at ⑤ **Hanalei Strings** (p173), then browse the galleries and shops along Kuhio Hwy, heading back toward the river. If you're into Asian art and design, hit the wonderful ⑥ **On the Road to Hanalei** (p173). Stock up on sweets at ⑦ **Chocolat Hanalei** (p174), then shuffle on to ⑧ **Barn 808**

(p174) for stylish fashion. At the final shopping center before the bridge, step into ⑨ **Haleleʻa Gallery** (p174) and ⑩ **I Heart Hanalei** (p174) for art, clothing and jewelry that are quirky and beautiful. Then pop into the fish market behind ⑪ **Hanalei Dolphin** (p172) to buy hand rolls or a *poke* bowl for a picnic. The highway doesn't always have a sidewalk; be mindful of traffic.

After lunch, cross the street and return toward ⑫ **Hanalei Center** (p174), visiting the museum-like ⑬ **Havaiki** (p173) before hunting for vintage gems at ⑭ **Yellowfish Trading Company** (p173). Stop for a coffee and some people-watching at ⑮ **Hanalei Bread Company** (p170), then step west to historic ⑯ **Waiʻoli Huiʻia Church** (p162). Follow the footpath behind to the secluded ⑰ **Mission House** (p162), ring the bell behind the chimney, and your guide will appear. Afterward, cross the street, hang a right on Anae Rd, lose your shoes and enjoy the rest of the afternoon relaxing at ⑱ **Pine Trees Beach** (p163).

Kauai Island Experience
WATERSPORTS

(☎808-346-3094; www.kauaiexperience.com; 4489 Aku Rd; 1½hr group/private surfing lesson $80/160, surfboard rental per day $20; 🐾) Waterman Mike Rodger's team will teach you to surf, SUP, snorkel, fish, paddle a traditional Hawaiian canoe and more.

Kayak Hanalei
WATERSPORTS

(☎808-826-1881; http://kayakhanalei.com; 5-5070a Kuhio Hwy; rental per day surfboard $23, kayak set $35-75, SUP set $40, 2hr surfing or SUP lessons $85-130, kayak tours adult/child 5-12yr $109/99; ⊕8am-4:30pm) The only Hanalei-based outfit offering kayak rentals and local tours, this long-established, family-run outfitter also rents SUP sets and surfboards. Tours, available weekdays only, start on the river and head to Princeville and back. Beginners surfing and SUP lessons can be booked daily except Sunday.

Diving

Kauai Down Under Dive Team
DIVING

(☎808-742-9534, 877-538-7442; http://kauai downunderscuba.com; 2 tanks $236; ⊕Mon-Fri, Jun-Sep only) Based on the South Shore, this outfitter offers shore dives to explore the Tunnels reef – for experienced, certified divers only – during the calmer summer months. Generally, you'll be able to dive the lava tubes both outside and inside the barrier reef that's just south of Ha'ena Beach Park (p177).

Fathom Five Divers
DIVING

(☎800-972-3078, 808-742-6991; http://fathom five.com; dives $110-155; ⊕Mon-Fri May-Sep only) Koloa's PADI-certified Fathom Five outfit gears up for small-group North Shore dives at the reef off Makua (Tunnels) Beach in summer only. Although they offer one-tank dives for non-certified divers, they strongly recommend Tunnels for the more experienced. Ask about their (cheaper) night dives, if you dare.

Surfing

Titus Kinimaka's
Hawaiian School of Surfing
SURFING

(☎808-652-1116; www.hawaiianschoolofsurfing. com; 5-5088 Kuhio Hwy; 90min lessons $75, extreme tow-in classes $250, board rental per hr/day/week $10/40/75; ⊕by appointment only) To arrange a surf lesson in Hanalei Bay with one of the team set up by legendary pro big-wave surfer Titus Kinimaka, drop in at the Quiksilver store or contact them in advance. No more than three students per instructor.

Bonus: they'll let you use the boards for a couple of hours after the lesson.

Hawaiian
Surfing Adventures
WATERSPORTS

(☎808-482-0749; www.hawaiiansurfing adventures.com; 5-5134 Kuhio Hwy; 90min group surfing lesson $75, SUP lesson $65, surfboard/SUP rental per day from $20/40; ⊕store 9am-3pm, last lesson starts 2pm) Surfing lessons for novices include 30 minutes on land and one hour in the water. SUP lessons could even get you doing yoga poses atop your board.

Hanalei Surf Company
SURFING

(☎808-826-9000; www.hanaleisurf.com; Hanalei Center, 5-5161 Kuhio Hwy; rental per day snorkel set with fins $6, surfboard $20-25; ⊕8am-9pm) This busy central store is ideal for watersports rentals and can also arrange coaching geared toward advanced surfers. In-house coach Russell Lewis has worked with many of Kaua'i's best-known pro surfers.

Kauai Surfboard Rentals
SURFING

(☎808-855-0957; www.kauaisurfboardrentals. com; 5-5088 Kuhio Hwy; surfboard/SUP rental per day from $40, incl delivery; ⊕9am-7pm) Based at the Quiksilver store in Hanalei, this rental outfit will deliver surfboards or SUPs to all the main resort areas on the island.

👉 Tours

⭐ Na Pali Kayak
KAYAKING

(☎808-826-6900; www.napalikayak.com; 5075 Kuhio Hwy; tours per person $225 plus tax & state park fees) Kayaking the full length of the extraordinary Na Pali Coast is one of the greatest outdoor adventures the world has to offer. This Hanalei operator offers full-day guided trips, in which participants share two-person kayaks, between April and October. If you're uncertain about the physical challenges involved, talk it through with them in advance.

Tours put in around 6:30am at Ha'ena Beach Park; dip into sea caves and waterfalls en route; pause for a picnic on otherwise inaccessible Miloli'i Beach; and return by van from Polihale Beach Park in the evening. It's also possible to arrange trips with overnight camping at Kalalau Valley and/or Miloli'i, or to take a shorter, five-hour day trip from Polihale.

The shop rents out kayaks and camping gear too, allowing you to paddle in the Hanalei River on your own, or, if you can prove your credentials, on the Na Pali Coast.

Ho'opulapula

Haraguchi Taro Farm Tour   FOOD & DRINK

(☑808-651-3399; www.haraguchiricemill.org; 5-5070a Kuhio Hwy; tours incl snack adult/child 5-12yr $70/50; ☺9:45am Wed, by reservation only) ✎ Learn about cultivating taro on Kaua'i at this sixth-generation family-run nonprofit farm. Three-hour farmer-guided tours take you out into the *lo'i kalo*, offering a small glimpse of the otherwise inaccessible Hanalei National Wildlife Refuge and demonstrating the processes involved in preparing the crop.

Na Pali Coast Hanalei   BOATING

(☑808-826-6114; www.napalitours.com; 4489 Aku Rd; 4hr tours $239) This 32ft catamaran – the smallest and nimblest on the North Shore, also known as the UFO, or 'Unidentified Fishing Object' – sets off twice daily from Hanalei on four-hour Na Pali Coast tours. In theory tours keep going year-round, but they're best in summer when calmer seas enable passengers to enter sea caves and snorkel in pristine lagoons.

Na Pali Explorer   BOATING

(☑808-338-9999; www.napaliexplorer.com; 4½hr tour from Hanalei $149, 6hr tour from Kikiaola $189; 👪) Rigid-hull inflatable rafts, being hard-bottomed, give a smoother ride than all-inflatable Zodiacs. The summer-only 4½-hour Na Pali tours from

Hanalei are in a 48ft raft, carrying up to 36 passengers, with a restroom and a canopy for shade. They also offer six-hour tours from Kikiaola Harbor on the West Coast, potentially including beach landings, in a 24ft, 14-passenger raft.

Na Pali Catamaran   BOATING

(☑866-255-6853, 808-826-6853; www.napali catamaran.com; Ching Young Village, 5-5190 Kuhio Hwy; 4hr tours $250) This exceptional outfit offers morning and afternoon Na Pali cruises from Hanalei between March and October. Its 35ft power catamaran is smaller and less majestic than a sailing cat but much less exposed than a Zodiac, and doesn't feel crowded. When conditions are right, it can venture into sea caves. Minimum age five years. Check for online or phone discounts.

Captain Sundown   BOATING

(☑808-826-5585; https://captainsundown.com; 3hr tours $151, 6hr $259) During the summer season – generally, late April until early October – this sailing catamaran offers six-hour snorkeling adventures along the Na Pali Coast, plus three-hour sunset cruises. While too large to enter sea caves, it ensures a relatively smooth ride, and the trampoline nets upfront are a joy. Captain Bob has plenty of stories. No children under seven years of age.

⭐ Festivals & Events

Music & Mango Festival   MUSIC, FOOD

(☑808-826-9969; www.waipafoundation.org; 5-5788 Kuhio Hwy; adult/child $10/1; ☺mid-Aug; 👪) ✎ This celebration of locally harvested food and live music takes place on a summer Sunday at the farmlands of the nonprofit Waipa Foundation, a mile west of central Hanalei.

⭐ Kalo Festival   FOOD, CULTURAL

(http://waipafoundation.org; 5-5785 Kuhio Hwy; adult/child $5/1; ☺Dec; 👪) ✎ Every December, Halulu Fish Pond hosts a Sunday of demonstrations of growing taro and pounding poi, along with traditional Hawaiian games for kids, local food vendors and live music. The Waipa Foundation helps to preserve and reflect a traditional Hawaiian community that extended from the mountaintop to the ocean, and this is a fun way to support and explore it.

THE 2018 HANALEI FLOOD

Between April 14 and April 15, 2018, Hanalei set one of the least desirable records imaginable. Within 24 hours, it was deluged by an astonishing 49.69in of rain – considerably more than has ever been recorded anywhere in the United States. Floodwaters up to 8ft deep inundated almost every building in town, while multiple landslides along Kuhio Hwy rendered Hanalei inaccessible by road for weeks afterwards, and the road to the west remained closed for over a year.

Hanalei itself has more or less returned to normal, though several businesses have closed down altogether. For visitors, the most obvious legacy of the flooding has been the introduction of the permit system for drivers heading to the end of the North Shore road.

> ### SACRED SHARKS
> ....
> Being attacked by a *mano* (shark) can certainly be deadly; precautions like not swimming in murky waters, especially after rain, will help you avoid them. Statistically speaking, though, you're more likely to die from a bee sting than a shark attack, and you should be more concerned about contracting leptospirosis or giardiasis in those infamous muddy waters than becoming a lunchtime snack.
>
> Rather than letting any hardwired phobia of large predators get you down, try considering the *mano* from another perspective: as sacred. For many Hawaiian families, the *mano* is their *'aumakua* (guardian spirit). *'Aumakua* are family ancestors whose *'uhane* (spirit form) lives on in the body of an animal, watching over members of their living *'ohana* (family). Revered for their ocean skill, *mano* were also considered the *'aumakua* of navigators. Even today, *mano 'aumakua* are said to guide lost fishermen home, or toward areas of plentiful fish to make for a bountiful sojourn.

🛏 Sleeping

Hanalei

Neighborhood Center   ACCOMMODATIONS SERVICES
(☑ 808-826-5153; www.kauai.gov; 5-5358 Kuhio Hwy; ⊙ 10am-1pm & 2-5pm Mon-Fri) The place to pick up permits for county campgrounds. The closest currently open is at 'Anini Beach Park (p154).

Rainbow House &
Garden Cottage   COTTAGE **$$**
(☑ 808-346-4371; www.kayakkauai.com; 5278 Malolo Pl; Rainbow House/Garden Cottage $405/205; 🛜) In this two-story property just off Hanalei's main drag, the well-appointed three-bedroom unit upstairs, Rainbow House itself, enjoys great views, while the downstairs cottage is more of a rustic surf habitat with terra cotta floors, a tiny kitchen with a two-burner stovetop and a BBQ grill out by the hammock on the patio.

Hale Reed Hanalei   RENTAL HOUSE **$$**
(☑ 415-662-1086; www.hanalei-vacation.com; 4441 Pilikoa St; rental per week $1550-2750; 🛜) A short walk from the white sands of Hanalei Bay, Hale Reed's location is key. The house can either be rented in its entirety or in two separate sections, with a two-bedroom garden unit downstairs and an airier three-bedroom upstairs section complete with loft and wraparound lanai. Boards and beach gear come with the territory. Cleaning fee $175 to $300.

Hanalei Inn   INN **$$**
(☑ 877-769-5484, 808-826-9333; www.hanaleiinn.net; 5-5468 Kuhio Hwy; r $159-169; ❄🛜) This ramshackle garden inn, half a mile west of central Hanalei, holds four basic studios. Each has a kitchenette or kitchen, private lanai and retro Hawaiiana furniture. There's no maid service and management presence is minimal, but you have to pay for your entire stay a month before you arrive, with no refunds or credit for cancellations.

⭐ **Hanalei Dolphin Cottages**   COTTAGE **$$$**
(☑ 877-465-2824; www.hanaleidolphincottages.com; 5-5016 Kuhio Hwy; 2-bedroom cottages $329; 🅿🛜) Tucked behind the namesake Dolphin restaurant at the eastern end of Hanalei, these four cottages are similarly styled, with bamboo furniture, full kitchen, BBQ grill, private outdoor (and indoor) showers, front-of-house bedrooms and airy quasi-lounge areas facing the river. Launch a canoe, kayak or SUP board right from your backyard on the Hanalei River. Cleaning fee $130.

⭐ **Hanalei Surfboard House**   INN **$$$**
(☑ 808-651-1039; www.hanaleisurfboardhouse.com; 5459 Weke Rd; ste $350; ❄🛜) Built with recycled and salvaged materials, this stylish surfers' haven is one minute's walk from the beach. Each of the two suites – 'Elvis' and 'Cowgirl' – features unique vintage Hawaiiana decor and has a kitchenette, while they share a backyard lanai with a BBQ grill. Cleaning fee $95. Seven-night minimum required. Adults only.

Camp Magic   RENTAL HOUSE **$$$**
(☑ 855-447-3685; www.hawaiilife.com; 5325 Weke Rd; Camp Magic 1/2 $600/850) Two stand-alone homes on one property a block from the beach. Offering three and four bedrooms respectively, the per-night price doesn't seem quite so high split among a group. Camp Magic 2 (sleeping up to eight people) is the nicer option with blond-wood floors in the living room, a screened lanai with distant waterfall views and a billiard table.

Camp Magic 1 is slightly smaller but also has vaulted ceilings and a hot tub, along with a game room. It has three bedrooms and sleeps six. Both come stocked with beach toys and require three-night minimums and a cleaning fee.

Hanalei Hideaway   RENTAL HOUSE $$$

(☑ 808-245-8841; www.kauaivacationrentals.com; 5319 Weke Rd; house $375-450) A simple two-bedroom, one-bathroom bungalow standing on stilts across the street from the beach, at what for these parts counts as an affordable price. It sleeps up to four people and offers solid value.

✖ Eating

With most of its restaurants targeted at day-trippers, Hanalei is more a place to grab a quick filling meal than to linger over a romantic dinner. Nowhere has a sea view, either. It does hold some fine-dining options, though, as well as food trucks and roadside stands offering excellent cheap alternatives.

★ Wishing Well Shave Ice   ICE CREAM $

(☑ 808-639-7828; www.wishingwellshaveice. com; 5-5080 Kuhio Hwy; shave ice from $5; ⊙ 9:30am-5pm) It's worth paying a few dollars extra at Hanalei's finest shave-ice stand for its organic rather than its regular syrups; the liliko'i (passion fruit) and mango flavors in particular are out of this world. It also serves acai bowls and cold-pressed coffee, and has some well-shaded picnic tables.

Hanalei Bread Company   BAKERY $

(☑ 808-826-6717; Hanalei Center, 5-5183 Kuhio Hwy; mains $9-14; ⊙ 7am-5pm) Great coffee and breakfast specials – like bacon and onion pizzas with soft eggs cracked on top – draw morning crowds to this organic bakery and cafe in the heart of Hanalei; expect to wait in line. And eat those fresh-baked pastries and breads quick – they wilt fast in the humidity.

Waipa Farmers Market   MARKET $

(☑ 808-826-9969; www.waipafoundation.org; 5-5788 Kuhio Hwy; ⊙ 2-4pm Tue; 🖉 🖶) 🖋 Spreading across a lush roadside field a mile west of central Hanalei against a wonderful mountain backdrop, this small but ample weekly market features prepared foods from local chefs and artisans, fresh produce including breadfruit, tropical fruit and leafy greens, and island handicrafts.

Hanalei Taro & Juice Co   HAWAIIAN $

(☑ 808-651-3399; www.hanaleitaro.com; 5-5070a Kuhio Hwy; dishes $5-15; ⊙ 10am-3pm; 🖉) 🖋 Find this roadside trailer near Hanalei's eastern end for a taste of poi – the traditional Hawaiian staple, prepared on the family's nearby taro farm – or other typical luau foods like kalua pig. Almost everything comes taro flavored, from tropical smoothies to hummus, burgers or rice cakes. They also serve wraps, sandwiches and sizeable plate lunches.

Chicken in a Barrel   BARBECUE $

(☑ 808-826-1999; www.chickeninabarrel.com; Ching Young Village, 5-5190 Kuhio Hwy; meals $9-20; ⊙ 11am-8:30pm Mon-Sat, to 7pm Sun; 🖶) Hanalei's outpost of this small BBQ chain occupies center stage – literally, its tables are on a little bandstand – in Ching Young Village. Cooking up chicken in a custom-made 50-gallon barrel drum smoker, it also serves burgers, ribs, pulled pork and hoagie sandwiches with chili-cheese fries.

Harvest Market   MARKET $

(☑ 808-826-0089; www.harvestmarkethanalei. com; Hanalei Center, 5-5161 Kuhio Hwy; ⊙ 9am-7pm Mon-Sat, to 6pm Sun; 🖉) 🖋 Pick up organic and all-natural snacks and groceries at this local favorite food store. The salad bar and smoothie station (both open until 3pm) and weighable bulk foods section (dried fruit, nuts and such) can help you put together a beach picnic, but take care as prices can sneak up on you.

Trucking Delicious   FOOD TRUCK $

(☑ 808-482-4101; www.truckingdeliciouskauai. com; 5100 Kuhio Hwy; mains $10-18; ⊙ 11:30am-4pm Tue-Sat) Amid a cluster of permanently parked food trucks, this one serves a tempting array of local-style plate lunches. The precise menu changes weekly, with ahi poke, kalua pork, miso chicken and macnut-crusted mahimahi among regular favorites, and dragonfruit lemonade to cool you down.

Pink's Creamery   ICE CREAM $

(☑ 808-212-9749; www.pinkscreamerykauai.com; 4489d Aku Rd; items $4-9; ⊙ 11am-9pm; 🅿 🖉) This side-street ice cream shop scoops tropical flavors like banana-macnut brittle, mango and a surreal haupia (coconut pudding). It also whips up liliko'i and lychee sorbet, tropical fruit popsicles, date shakes and tasty grilled-cheese sandwiches on island-style sweet bread with Muenster cheese, kalua pig and pineapple.

Hanalei Farmers Market MARKET $
(☑808-826-1011; www.halehalawai.org; 5299 Kuhio Hwy; ☺9:30am-noon Sat; ⚓🖶) 🖊 One of Kauai's most popular farmers markets takes place on the sports fields adjoining the community center, Hale Halawai 'Ohana 'O Hanalei. Locals line up before the market opens, then literally run to their favorite farmers' booths. North Shore artisans sell crafts, jewelry and tropical soaps, perfect for gifts or souvenirs.

Village Snack Shop & Bakery BREAKFAST $
(☑808-826-6841; Ching Young Village, 5-5190 Kuhio Hwy; mains $4-13; ☺6:30am-3pm Mon-Sat, to 2pm Sun; 🖶) This basic mom-and-pop storefront, tucked in the back of the Ching Young mall, is perfect for filling up on macnut pancakes before you hike the Na Pali Coast. Show up later in the day for heaped plate lunches and chocolate *haupia* pie.

Pat's Taqueria TACOS $
(Ching Young Village, 5-5190 Kuhio Hwy; items $5-10; ☺noon-3pm; 🖶) Much-loved local food truck permanently parked beside the Big Save supermarket that serves crisped-up tacos and larger burritos at good-value prices. Fillings include *kalua* pig, carne asada, and fresh mahimahi, all with beans and rice on the side. Kids' portions available. Cash only.

Fresh Bite SANDWICHES $
(☑808-652-0744; www.freshbitekauai.com; 5100 Kuhio Hwy; mains $10-16; ☺11am-4pm Mon & Thu-Sat, to 3pm Sun) 🖊 Drawing on local, organic produce wherever possible, this 'farm-to-beach' food truck serves steak, chicken or veggie sandwiches, along with salad-based wraps or bowls.

Jo Jo's Shave Ice ICE CREAM $
(☑808-378-4612; Ching Young Village, 5-5190 Kuhio Hwy; shave ice from $5) There's always a line at this shave-ice stand, where you choose up to four of 30 flavors of sweet syrupy goodness – the menu includes coconut, *liliko'i,* and piña colada – to be drizzled over silky ice shavings. Profits benefit local youth.

Big Save SUPERMARKET $
(☑808-826-6652; www.timessupermarkets.com; Ching Young Village, 5-5172 Kuhio Hwy; ☺6am-10pm) For supply runs or immediate snacks, Hanalei's only supermarket offers good produce at decent prices, along with an enticing selection of fresh fish and 'The Kitchen,' a deli offering $8 *poke* bowls.

★Ama NOODLES $$
(☑808-826-9452; www.amahanalei.com; Hanalei Center, 5-5161 Kuhio Hwy; mains $19; ☺5-9pm) This no-reservations offshoot of neighboring Bar Acuda enjoys Hanalei's finest outdoor setting, facing mountains cascading with waterfalls. Treating Japanese-style ramen noodles as fine dining and topping them with seared ahi, chicken or pork, it makes its succulent broth using pork belly, but also offers a vegetarian version. Sides include spicy, deep-fried Brussels sprouts, while dessert is homemade donuts.

Wear bug spray to deter critters in the foot-level vegetation.

Hanalei Poke SEAFOOD $$
(☑808-855-5574; Ching Young Village, 5-5172 Kuhio Hwy; bowls $15-19; ☺11:30am-5pm) Drop by this small white truck alongside Big Save supermarket for mouthwatering *poke* bowls, topped with various combinations of wasabi, sesame, avocado, mango and watermelon, and available in different degrees of spiciness. A few shady tables stand nearby – as does the Aloha Juice Bar (p173). Just saying.

Hanalei Gourmet CAFE, DELI $$
(☑808-826-2524; www.hanaleigourmet.com; Hanalei Center, 5-5161 Kuhio Hwy; mains lunch $11-16, dinner $19-33; ☺10am-10:30pm) Harking back to Hanalei's hippie heyday and soundtracked by the Grateful Dead, this former schoolroom offers substantial lunchtime sandwiches plus good (if unadventurous) dinner entrées ranging from crab cakes or chicken to pasta or fresh fish. In the evening it's very much a bar, noisy and cheery rather than romantic, and it stays open later than anywhere else around.

Hanalei Bay Pizzeria PIZZA $$
(☑808-827-8000; www.hanaleibaypizzeria.com; Ching Young Village, 5-5190 Kuhio Hwy; pizzas $12-31; ☺11:30am-8:30pm Mon-Sat) Tasty pizzas in this funky Ching Young dive feature a terrific crust made with Hawaiian honey and organic extra virgin olive oil (there's a gluten-free version too). Sausages and *kalua* pig are housemade, there are four sauces to choose from (red, pesto, garlic butter and pineapple BBQ), and it doesn't skimp on the mozzarella.

HOMAGE TO KALO

Hawaiian cosmology relates that Papa (earth mother) and Wakea (sky father) gave birth to Haloa, a stillborn brother to man. Haloa was planted in the earth and from his body came the *kalo* plant, known as taro in English, a staple crop for Oceanic cultures and the major food source in pre-contact Hawaii.

Kalo is still considered sacred, hailed as the 'staff of life' and imbued with tradition and spiritual significance. Hanalei is home to the largest taro-producing farm in the state, Ho'opulapula Haraguchi (p168), growing the purple, starchy potato-like plant in *lo'i kalo* (wet taro fields). Rich in nutrients, *kalo* is usually boiled and pounded into poi, an earthy, sticky paste that serves as a basic starch.

Families enjoy poi in different ways. Some prefer it fresh, while others prefer sour poi, or *'awa'awa* (bitter) poi, possibly derived from the method in which poi used to be served – it might sit in a bowl on the table for a considerable period.

Traditional households show respect for taro: when the bowl of poi is on the table, one is expected to refrain from arguing or speaking in anger. That's because any bad energy is *'ino* (evil) – and can spoil the poi.

Tropical Taco
TACOS $$

(☑ 808-827-8226; www.tropicaltaco.com; 5-5088 Kuhio Hwy; mains $15-17; ⊙8am-8pm Mon-Fri, 11am-5pm Sat & Sun) OK, so the tacos here may not be authentic to Mexico, but they're authentic to Kaua'i. Originally a food truck and now housed in an open-fronted pavilion, Tropical Taco offers burritos, tostadas and tacos in thick handmade flour tortillas, piled with local produce like grass-fed ground beef, grilled fish or island veggies. Servings are large and will satisfy.

NorthSide Grill
PUB FOOD $$

(☑ 808-826-9701; www.northsidegrillhanalei.com; Ching Young Village, 5-5190 Kuhio Hwy; mains $16-32; ⊙11:30am-8:30pm) While the menu covers most bases competently, from burgers to pasta and ribs to fresh fish, and there's a decent dinner-only sushi bar, the mountain views across the highway are the biggest appeal of this upstairs dining room.

Kalypso
PUB FOOD $$

(☑ 808-826-9700; www.kalypsokauai.com; 5-5156 Kuhio Hwy; mains $11-19; ⊙11am-9pm Mon-Fri, from 8am Sat & Sun) A breezy, open-sided sports bar that's a popular all-day hangout. The Hawaiian-themed pub grub includes fish tacos, *poke pupu* (snacks), *huli-huli* chicken, blackened fish entrées and taro burgers.

Bar Acuda
MEDITERRANEAN $$$

(☑ 808-826-7081; www.restaurantbaracuda.com; Hanalei Center, 5-5161 Kuhio Hwy; shared plates $15-25; ⊙5:30-10pm, kitchen closes 9:30pm) Reserve well in advance to dine and drink in this smart 'tapas and wine' restaurant, which is Hanalei's most chef-driven spot. It typically takes four or five of its sharing plates, including selections like fresh Hawaiian fish, Spanish meatballs and French lentils, to provide a satisfying dinner for two. The excellent wine list features both new- and old-world vintners.

Postcards Cafe
SEAFOOD $$$

(☑ 808-826-1191; www.postcardscafe.com; 5-5075 Kuhio Hwy; mains $28-42; ⊙5:30-9pm; 🖊) 🍃 This charming clapboard cottage, marked by a rusted anchor out front, specializes in seafood dishes with world-fusion flavors like wasabi-crusted ahi or fennel-crusted lobster tail. There's no meat on the menu, but vegetarian and vegan alternatives are available.

Hanalei Dolphin
SEAFOOD $$$

(☑ 808-826-6113; www.hanaleidolphin.com; 5-5016 Kuhio Hwy; mains lunch $12-16, dinner $26-42; ⊙restaurant 11:30am-9pm, market 10am-7pm) Arrive early at this lovely riverside setting in Hanalei's eastern end for lunch or a sunset dinner, with fresh fish served cooked or as sushi, and steak and chicken options too. The *poke* and raw fish in their adjoining fish market is the best deal, but there's nowhere to eat it on-site. This restaurant does not take reservations.

🍷 Drinking & Nightlife

Like most of Kaua'i, Hanalei is not a nightlife destination. Most restaurants have bars that buzz at happy hour then mellow as the night builds. The one real exception is the lively, much-loved Tahiti Nui.

★**Tahiti Nui**   BAR
(☎808-826-6277; http://thenui.com; 5-5134
Kuhio Hwy; ⊙11am-10pm Sun-Wed, to 1am Thu-
Sat) The legendary Nui (rendered famous by
its cameo role in *The Descendants*) is a tiki
dive bar with heart and history, and a rather
tasty dinner menu. Usually crowded from
mid-afternoon onward, it gets rollicking
nightly with live Hawaiian music from
6:30pm until 8:30pm. It's especially busy
on weekends, when it's the only place open
past 10pm.

Aloha Juice Bar   JUICE BAR
(☎808-639-2826; Ching Young Village, 5-5190
Kuhio Hwy; drinks & bowls from $7; ⊙10am-4pm)
In a red shack at the west end of Ching
Young Village, this irresistible juice stand is
renowned for its thick fruit smoothies and
fresh veggie juices; look for cut-price offers
on surplus fruit. It also has acai bowls (of
course), pineapple whip, chocolate-dipped
bananas, cracked coconuts and fresh and
dried local fruits.

★ Entertainment

★**Tahiti Nui Luau**   LUAU
(☎808-826-6277; http://thenui.com; 5-5134
Kuhio Hwy; adult/senior/teen/under-13 $80/67/
47/37; ⊙5pm Wed) While not as slick as the
resort equivalents elsewhere on Kaua'i, the
North Shore's one weekly luau is everything
a Hawaiian luau should be. Housed in
a separate dining room adjoining the
much-loved Tahiti Nui bar, it has the feel
of a genuine family party, with homespun
entertainment followed by small-scale but
authentic hula displays and fire dancing.

The food is much better too, comple-
menting succulent roasted *kalua* pork with
marinated fish, salads and garlic bread, and
the mai tais can't be faulted.

**Hawaiian Slack
Key Guitar Concerts**   LIVE MUSIC
(☎808-826-1469; www.hawaiianslackkeyguitar.
com; Hanalei Community Center, Malolo Rd;
adult/13-19yr/6-12yr $25/20/10; ⊙4pm Fri, 3pm
Sun) Veteran local musicians Doug and
Sandy McMaster perform Hawaiian-style
slack key guitar and ukulele year-round in
a refreshingly relaxed informal atmosphere.

🔒 Shopping

Hanalei's stores and boutiques sell
everything from tourist kitsch to beach chic

to evocative art. The biggest concentrations
are in the old-guard Ching Young Village
and the more upscale Hanalei Center
across the highway, but more galleries and
one-of-a-kind stores are strung all along the
main drag.

★**Yellowfish Trading Company**   VINTAGE
(☎808-826-1227; www.yellowfishtradingcompany.
com; Hanalei Center, 5-5161 Kuhio Hwy; ⊙10am-
8pm) This irresistibly upbeat gallery offers
a mix of true vintage and vintage-inspired
art, handicrafts, books and much more.
It's the vintage stuff that's the true gold,
with mid-century glassware; 1950s-era
Hawaiian guidebooks, lamps and guitars; a
wigglesome troupe of dashboard hula girls;
and a well-priced crop of antique aloha
shirts. It's the Hawaii *Mad Men* episode in
treasure-chest form.

★**Havaiki**   ART
(☎808-826-7606; www.havaikiart.com; Hanalei
Center, 5-5161 Kuhio Hwy; ⊙10am-6pm) Tucked
at the back of the Hanalei Center and
flagged by fascinating outdoor displays, this
wonderful shop sells superb handcrafted
Polynesian and Oceanic artifacts, including
exquisite Niihau shell leis priced up to
$50,000. Stock ranges from evocative Asmat
shields and ornately carved oars from
the Marquesas to pieces crafted around
crocodile and even human skulls.

On The Road To Hanalei   CLOTHING, GIFTS
(☎808-826-7360; Ching Young Village, 5-5190
Kuhio Hwy; ⊙10am-7pm Mon-Sat, to 6pm Sun)
Vibrant batik-print dresses and *pareus*
(Tahitian sarongs), handcrafted silver jewelry
and Japanese cracked-glaze tableware are
just a few of the treasures inside this rustic
wooden-floored shop, which unquestionably
ranks among the best Hanalei has to offer.

★**Hanalei Strings**   MUSICAL INSTRUMENTS
(☎808-826-9633; www.hanaleistrings.com; Ching
Young Village, 5-5190 Kuhio Hwy; ⊙10am-8pm)
This long-established, always welcoming
shop channels two passions: music and
knitting. Alongside a wide range of guitars
and ukuleles from concert size to tenor and
beyond, it sticks George Formby songbooks
and the like, while the knitting supply flip
side features hand-dyed yarns.

Beginner ukulele lessons costing $25 are
offered on Tuesday and Thursday from 6pm
to 7pm.

Hanalei Center
MALL

(5-5161 Kuhio Hwy) Hanalei's former school house, built in 1926, moved to this site in 1989. Now complemented by a cluster of buildings that similarly evoke Hawaii's plantation era, it forms the centerpiece of an attractive mall of shops, cafes and restaurants.

Hanalei Surf Company
OUTDOOR EQUIPMENT

(✉808-826-9000; www.hanaleisurf.com; Hanalei Center, 5-5161 Kuhio Hwy; ☺8am-9pm) Surf is the name of the game in this store, which stocks all the gear any surfer girl or beach boy might need for riding waves, including boards, along with good-value water shoes and equipment rental. Its Backdoor store is across the street.

Backdoor
CLOTHING, OUTDOOR EQUIPMENT

(✉808-826-1900; www.facebook.com/hsc backdoor; Ching Young Village, 5-5190 Kuhio Hwy; ☺8am-9pm) The coolest clothing shop in Ching Young Village offers board shorts, bikinis and rashies for all ages, sundresses, surf and skate boards, sunglasses and a nice stock of Vans too.

Chocolat Hanalei
CHOCOLATE

(✉808-826-4470; www.chocolathanalei.com; Ching Young Village, 5-5190 Kuhio Hwy; ☺noon-6pm) The aroma alone is enough to lure you into this compact chocolatier linked with a farm in nearby Wainiha Valley and filled with treats. Specialty confections include surfboard-shaped caramels, dark chocolate turtles and macadamia nuts covered in white chocolate and cardamom.

I Heart Hanalei
CLOTHING

(✉808-826-5560; www.ihearthanalei.com; 5-5016 Kuhio Hwy; ☺10am-9pm) This beachy clothing boutique has more stock than most. Peruse racks of stylish bikinis, beach cover-ups, sun hats, shorts and yoga wear from labels like Flynn Skye, Acacia, August and One Teaspoon.

There's a small collection of men's denim and board shorts too.

Root
CLOTHING

(✉808-826-2575; www.facebook.com/theroot hawaii; 4489 Aku Rd; ☺10am-6pm Mon-Sat, from noon Sun) Among Hanalei's more fashionable boutiques devoted entirely to women's clothing, the Root offers much more than just beachy threads, including dresses, denim, skirts, blouses and plenty else besides.

Pualani
CLOTHING

(✉808-923-3403; www.pualanihawaii.com; 5-5412 Kuhio Hwy; ☺10am-6pm) This small, stand-alone boutique across from Hanalei school west of the center offers cute bikinis and hip beachwear for women, designed by surfer Iwalani Isbell.

Halele'a Gallery
ART

(✉808-826-0001; www.haleleagallery.com; 5-5016 Kuhio Hwy; ☺10am-9pm) In front of the Dolphin (p172) restaurant, this high-end gallery showcases plentiful original artworks by local artists along with jewelry made using Black Pearl Tahitian pearls.

Barn 808
CLOTHING

(✉808-320-3555; www.thebarn808.com; 5080 Kuhio Hwy; ☺10am-6pm) This rustic yet stylish wood-floored boutique deals in Nick Fouget hats, one-of-a-kind sport coats, jeans, and all sorts of linen clothing, drapery and tie-dyes. It also sells leather bracelets, wallets, beach bags, dreamcatchers and aroma-therapy votives.

Bikini Hanalei
CLOTHING

(✉808-826-1314; 5-5084 Kuhio Hwy; ☺10am-6pm) Associated with Pualani further west, this bright and cheerful bikini shop is a cut above most of its neighbors, selling bikinis of all brands as well as throws, ball caps, beach bags, dresses and flip-flops.

Sand People
GIFTS & SOUVENIRS

(✉808-826-1008; www.sandpeople.com; Hanalei Center, 5-5161 Kuhio Hwy; ☺9:30am-8pm Mon-Sat, from 10am Sun) The original outlet of what's become a Hawaii-wide chain, this cheery shop is bursting with reproduction sign-age, gift books, beauty products, tableware and linens, plus a small, collection of women's wear from labels like Hard Tail and Johnny Was.

Water Sports Swap Meet
SURFBOARDS

(www.hanaleisurf.com/swap-meet-1; Hanalei Center, 5-5161 Kuhio Hwy; ☺9am-1pm 1st Sat of month) Like the name suggests, this is an old-fashioned swap meet devoted to (used) surfboards and related equipment. Everything's laid out on the lawn in front of the former schoolhouse. If you plan to stay for a while, it's a good place to pick up a board you can unload on your way out of town.

Tropical Tantrum
CLOTHING

(✉808-826-6944;www.tropicaltantrum.com;Hanalei Center, 5-5161 Kuhio Hwy; ☺10am-6pm) A mind-blowing array of all-but-psychedelic sarongs and beachwear flows through this dazzling boutique and out onto the veranda of the old schoolhouse.

Hula Beach Boutique CLOTHING
(☑808-826-4741; Hanalei Center, 5-5161 Kuhio Hwy; ☺10am-6pm; 🐾) The sarongs are lovely, and there are dresses, clutches, handbags and aloha shirts for men too, but the toys, cute beach outfits and aloha shirts for kids are the real draw. Check the sale rack out front for bargains.

Kokonut Kids CHILDREN'S CLOTHING
(☑808-826-0353; www.kokonutkids.com; Ching Young Village, 5-5190 Kuhio Hwy; ☺10am-6pm; 🐾) A super-cute kids shop with rash guards, T-shirts, beach hats and aloha wear for groms, along with cuddly stuffed toys and cute horseshoe-shaped pillows for the flight home.

Bikini Room CLOTHING
(☑808-826-9711; www.thebikiniroom.com; 4489 Aku Rd; ☺10am-5pm) Whether you need a wrap, a lovely ball cap with paintings of mountains, flowers or waves, or a new bikini, there's plenty to sort through in this tiny shop that somehow squeezes in a massive amount of stock.

Crystals and Gems Gallery NEW AGE
(☑808-826-9304; www.crystals-gems.com; 4489 Aku Rd; ☺9am-7pm) The whiff of Nag Champa, the jingle of cut-crystal wind chimes, the glint of blue agate pyramids, phallic wedges of smoky quartz, crystal skulls, earrings and bracelets, cutesy crafts and some Buddha sculpture too.

ⓘ Information

Hanalei has no bank, but there are ATMs at the Hanalei Liquor Store and Big Save supermarket.
Hanalei Post Office (☑808-826-1034; www.usps.com; 5-5226 Kuhio Hwy; ☺10am-4pm Mon-Fri, to noon Sat) On the *makai* (seaward) side of the road, just west of Big Save supermarket.

ⓘ Getting There & Away

There's only one road into and out of Hanalei. During heavy rains common in winter, the Hanalei Bridge sometimes closes due to flooding; anyone on the 'wrong' side is stuck until it reopens. Parking in town can be a headache and absent-minded pedestrians even more so.

Everything in Hanalei is walkable, and a bicycle makes things even easier.

The North Shore Shuttle (p143) links Waipa, a half-mile west of Hanalei, with Ha'ena State Park, for access to Ke'e Beach and the Kalalau Trail.

ⓘ Getting Around

Pedal 'n Paddle (☑808-826-9069; http://pedalnpaddle.com; Ching Young Village, 5-5105 Kuhio Hwy; ☺9am-6pm) rents cruisers (per day/week $15/60) and hybrid road bikes ($20/80), all including helmets and locks.

Wainiha
POP 300

Located between Hanalei and Ha'ena, this little neighborhood is steeped in history. The sheer-walled recesses of Wainiha Valley are famous for being the last refuge of Hawaii's legendary 'little people,' on the basis of an 1820 census in which 65 locals described themselves as *menehune*. Today the valley remains a holdout for Hawaiians, though vacation rentals have also popped up. There can be an unwelcoming vibe; if the locals stare you down, don't take it personally.

◉ Sights

★**Lumaha'i Beach** BEACH
Countless Kaua'i locals consider Lumaha'i their favorite beach on an island blessed with dozens of beauties. It's utterly cinematic, with thick loamy sand backed by lush mountains and lava rock outcrops to either end. In the 1958 movie *South Pacific,* this was where Mitzi Gaynor wanted to 'wash that man' right out of her hair.

Stretching just over a mile from one lava-rock tabletop to the other, Lumaha'i may be beautiful, but it's renowned as one of the most dangerous beaches on Kaua'i. Even if the turquoise shallows and deep-blue depths appear inviting, the inlet lacks barrier reefs and breaks, so swimming is risky. Too many visitors have drowned in its rough rip currents and powerful waves. Stay dry instead and take a stroll, which still requires being water savvy. This is also the North Shore's best spot for beach running.

Of the two ways onto Lumaha'i Beach, the first and more scenic involves a steep three-minute hike. The trail slopes down to the left from the end of the retaining wall of a parking area beside the Kuhio Hwy, 0.75 miles west of mile marker 4. On the beach, the rocky ledges are popular for sunbathing and photo ops, but beware: bystanders have been washed away by high surf and rogue waves.

You can also access Lumaha'i at sea level at its western end, just before the road crosses the Lumaha'i River Bridge. The beach at this point is lined with ironwood trees.

🛏 Sleeping

★ **Kauai Paradise House** RENTAL HOUSE $$$
(📞844-261-0464, 808-346-5155; www.hawaiian
beachrentals.com/Hawaii/Kauai/Wainiha/
KauaiParadise3BRHome.htm; 6608 Kuhio Hwy;
3-bedroom house $560; 🛜) Directly across the
street from Wainiha's now-defunct General
Store, this tortoise-green house looks straight
out over the river mouth sandbar, with killer
ocean views. It has three bedrooms – including
twin master suites – and it's equipped with a
gleaming new-model kitchen, beach toys and
a grill. Cleaning fee $260.

★ **River Estate** RENTAL HOUSE $$$
(📞808-826-5118, 808-635-2929; www.riverestate.
com; 5-6691 Kuhio Hwy; Guesthouse/Riverhouse
from $275/300; ❄🛜) This lovely property, set in
jungle-like grounds beside the Wainiha River,
holds two luxurious vacation rentals, each
perfect for honeymooners or a family. The
airy, two-bedroom Guesthouse has a wrap-
around lanai, while the three-bedroom River-
house, perched on 30ft stilts, has Brazilian
hardwood floors and a screened-in lanai (for
mosquito-free BBQs) with hot tub. Weekly
rates available. Cleaning fee from $250.

ℹ Getting There & Away

Wainiha is a mere blip along the Kuhio Hwy,
separated from Hanalei by a series of one-lane
bridges. You'll be best suited with a rental car,
but North Shore Shuttle (p143) passes through
and connects with the Kaua'i Bus (p279) in
Hanalei. The bike ride from Hanalei is gorgeous
and not too hilly, though there are blind curves,
so don't ride at night.

Ha'ena

POP 450

Remote, resplendent and idyllic, the village
of Ha'ena marks where the ribbon road
ends amid lava rock pinnacles, lush forest
and postcard-perfect beaches. In the wet
season the cliffs are positively weeping
with waterfalls. It's also long been the
site of controversy, as many of its luxury
homes were built atop *iwi kupuna* (ancient
Hawaiian burial grounds).

◉ Sights

★ **Limahuli Garden** GARDENS
(📞808-826-1053; http://ntbg.org/gardens/
limahuli; 5-8291 Kuhio Hwy; self-guided adult/
student/child under 18yr $20/10/free, 2½hr
guided tours adult/student & child 10-17yr $40/20;
⊙9:30am-4pm Tue-Sat, guided tours 10am Tue-
Fri; 🅿♿) 🌿 Perhaps the most beautiful
spot on an island of unsurpassed beauty,
this magnificent garden is a must-see
stop on any North Shore itinerary. Besides
cherishing species unique to this region of
Kaua'i – some to this very valley – it also
displays plants brought to Hawaii from
elsewhere. While guided and self-guided
tours follow a 0.75-mile trail through its
landscaped front portion, the preserve's
985 acres extend back into the sheer-walled
depths of the valley, where its serious
conservation work takes place.

This wonderful place forms part of the
National Tropical Botanical Garden, which
also runs two gardens in Po'ipu. To give
it the time it deserves, come as early as
possible, before the day's full heat sets in.
Allow 1½ hours to walk the trail, enjoying
spectacular close-up views of Makana Peak
(popularly known as Bali Hai). In winter,
it's common to see whales breaching
offshore.

The garden's driveway climbs inland just
before the stream that marks the boundary
of Ha'ena State Park (p178). Although you
don't need a permit to drive here, you have
to reserve in advance for a specific time,
and you're only allowed to park here during
your actual visit.

Makua (Tunnels) Beach BEACH
Yet another too-good-to-be-true North
Shore beach. Named for the underwater
caverns and lava tubes that pepper the
near-shore reef, Tunnels ranks among
Kaua'i's finest snorkel spots in summer.
It's also the North Shore's most popular
dive site, suitable for shore dives. In winter,
however, the swell picks up and the surf
can be heavy.

In the shoulder season, the snorkeling
can still be decent, but always check with
lifeguards before heading into the water.
Beware especially of a current flowing west
toward the open ocean.

Access to Makua Beach is notoriously
difficult. Two short dirt roads link it with
the highway, but parking is very limited, and
you may attract hostility. Most beachgoers
park at Ha'ena State Park (p178), then walk
a half-mile along the sandy foreshore.

Ha'ena Beach Park   BEACH

At this beautiful county-run beach, just under a mile before the end of the road, the sea is usually smooth and safe for swimming in summer. Ask lifeguards about conditions before going in, though, especially between October and May, when it's rendered dangerous by an endlessly pounding shore break that creates a strong undertow. Camping facilities remained closed at press time following the 2018 flooding, but the beach has restrooms and showers, and there are usually a couple of food trucks parked alongside.

Maniniholo Dry Cave   CAVE

Flat-bottomed Maniniholo Dry Cave, across from Ha'ena Beach Park, is deep, broad and fun to explore, though the further you penetrate, the lower the ceiling and the darker your surrounds. A constant seep of water from the walls keeps the interior dank. As you inch toward the rear wall, remember that you are standing below a massive monolith of Jurassic proportions.

🏃 Activities

Hanalei Day Spa   SPA

(☑808-826-6621; www.hanaleidayspa.com; Hanalei Colony Resort, 5-7130 Kuhio Hwy; massage 50/80min $110/140; ⊙9am-6pm Tue-Sat) If you're tired or need to revitalize, this friendly (if modest) spa offers competitively priced massages, including *lomilomi* (traditional Hawaiian massage), and body treatments like an Ayurvedic body wrap.

🛏 Sleeping & Eating

YMCA Camp Naue   CAMPGROUND $

(☑808-826-6419; http://ymcaofkauai.org/camp naue.html; Kuhio Hwy; tent sites per person aged 3 or over $20) In a superb location just a short walk from Tunnels, there's tent camping around a wide, flat, soft lawn that reaches right to the beach. Old green plantation shacks on the same site serve as bunkhouses, but they're usually rented in their entirety to local youth or church groups.

Hale Ho'o Maha   B&B $$

(☑800-851-0291, 808-826-7083; http://halemaha. com; 7083 Alamihi Rd; r incl breakfast $245; @ 🕱) The word 'communal' was made for this quirky four-room home, but don't let that turn you off. You'll share everything with your hosts, including a hot tub, high-end kitchen, guest-use computer, elevator and even a pet macaw. Suites feature quilted bedspreads and private lanai. It's on the North Shore Shuttle route.

★ Hanalei Colony Resort   HOTEL $$$

(☑808-826-6235, 800-628-3004; www.hcr.com; 5-7130 Kuhio Hwy; 2-bedroom ste from $324; P 🕱 🖾) 🍽 It's hard to imagine a more knockout location for the only resort west of Princeville. Located right beside an exquisite beach and bay, this is as secluded and peaceful as it gets. Nicely furnished suites, all with kitchens and lanai, and many with huge ocean views, occupy an arc of two-story waterfront buildings. The resort is served by the North Shore Shuttle.

DRIVING WITH ALOHA

As you follow the breathtaking and impossibly beautiful drive to the 'end of the road' on the North Shore, try to resist the impulse to pull over for that must-have photograph. Accidents occur when drivers stop suddenly, in a place with no shoulder, or on a blind curve, to grab the perfect shot.

If you're heading all the way to Ke'e Beach (p178) – and you have the necessary parking permit (p179) – take it slowly and enjoy crossing the seven one-lane bridges en route, the first of which is in Hanalei.

At each bridge, do as the locals do:

➡ When the bridge is empty and you reach it first, you can go.

➡ If fewer than five cars are already crossing as you approach, simply follow them. If you're the sixth car and others are waiting to cross from the far side, yield.

➡ When you see cars approaching from the opposite direction, yield to the entire queue of approaching cars for at least five cars, if not all.

➡ Give the *shaka* sign ('hang loose' hand gesture, with index, middle and ring fingers downturned) to thank any drivers who yield from the opposite direction.

Hale Oli   RENTAL HOUSE $$$

(☑ 808-631-5771; www.jeanandabbott.com/
properties/hale-oli; 7097 Alimihi Rd; 2-bedroom
house per night/week from $300/2250; 🕾)
Propped on stilts, this place boasts nothing
but greenery between its front lanai and
Ha'ena's jutting mountains. Inside it's
Hawaiian-meets-Zen decor, queen-sized beds
in each bedroom and a full-sized kitchen.

On the back lanai, you'll find a spacious
hot tub and a sliver of an ocean view. There's
a $250 cleaning fee.

Opakapaka   SEAFOOD $$

(☑ 808-378-4425; www.opakapakagrillandbar.
com; Hanalei Colony Resort, 5-7132 Kuhio Hwy;
mains $15-36; ⊘ 11am-9pm; ℗) The only
restaurant west of Hanalei is so close to the
beach that ocean breezes waft through the
windows. Its well-judged menu includes
everything from fresh catch to burgers to
pasta – appetizers like fish tacos or the *poke*
bowl are enough for a decent lunch – and
there's a lively bar. Linger a while; as our
waitress advised, 'you've got all day.'

🛍 Shopping

Na Pali Art Gallery &
Coffee House   ARTS & CRAFTS

(☑ 808-826-1844; www.napaligallery.com; Hanalei
Colony Resort, 5-7132 Kuhio Hwy; ⊘ 7am-6pm Mon-
Sat, to 1pm Sun; 🕾) At this small gallery, you
can peruse a quality array of local artists'
paintings, woodwork, sculptures, ceramics,
jewelry and collectibles. It's also the perfect
spot to pick up an early morning coffee as
you head for the Kalalau Trail.

ℹ Getting There & Away

Ha'ena is linked to Hanalei along Kuhio Hwy via
several one-lane bridges. If a bridge floods, you'll
be cut off. The North Shore Shuttle (p143) stops
at the Hanalei Colony Resort, en route to and
from the end of the highway.

Ha'ena State Park

As it nears its end, overshadowed by the
looming Na Pali cliffs, Kuhio Hwy fords a
flowing stream beyond wonderful Limahuli
Garden to enter Ha'ena State Park, burning
with allure, mystique and beauty.

◎ Sights

★ **Ke'e Beach**   BEACH

Long renowned as one of the North Shore's
most glorious beaches, lovely Ke'e Beach,
beside the Kalalau trailhead at the end of
Kuhio Hwy, has been given a new lease of
life by recent parking restrictions. There's
usually safe swimming in the reef-enclosed
area at its western end, hard against the Na
Pali cliffs. Always follow lifeguards' advice,
however; Ke'e's looks can be deceptive,
and vicious currents can suck swimmers
through the reef and out to sea.

BACKYARD GRAVEYARDS

Ancient burial sites lie underneath countless homes and hotels throughout Hawaii.
Construction workers often dig up *iwi* (bones) and *moepu* (funeral objects), while locals
swear by eerie stories of equipment malfunctioning until bones are properly reinterred and
prayers given.

Desecration of *iwi* is illegal and a major affront to Native Hawaiians. Thanks to the Native
American Graves Protection and Repatriation Act, passed by Congress in 1990, burial
councils on each island oversee the treatment of remains and the preservation of burial
sites.

One of Kaua'i's best-known cases involved Naue Point in Ha'ena, the site of some
30 confirmed *iwi*. Starting in 2002 and lasting close to nine years, the case went through
numerous phases of court hearings, public demonstrations and burial-treatment proposals
and ended with the state allowing the landowner to build.

What might potentially happen? Could a landowner lose the right to build? Probably not.
It's more likely for the state to approve a burial-treatment proposal to remove the *iwi* and
reinter them off-site, an outcome that Native Hawaiians find woefully inadequate. In any
case, many hotels and condos have been constructed on land with *iwi* now sitting in storage
or remaining underground. What happens to those restless spirits?

At Po'ipu's Grand Hyatt Resort, the director of Hawaiian and community affairs performs
blessings somewhere on resort grounds at least once a month to quell any 'spiritual
disturbance.'

Walk eastward along the sands, fringed by trees that seem to perch on spiders' legs since erosion exposed their roots, and you'll soon start getting sensational views back along the Na Pali cliffs.

Ke'e is no longer notorious for over-crowding now that the only access is via a scenic quarter-mile boardwalk from the road's-end parking lot, for which permits have to be booked well in advance. The North Shore Shuttle stops there, and waits to pick up passengers until 5pm daily.

Ancient lava-rock platforms on the slopes immediately west of Ke'e are said to be where the art of hula was first developed. They're not currently accessible to visitors, so these days Ke'e serves instead as a place for a refreshing dip for hikers fresh from the Kalalau Trail.

Wet Caves   CAVE

Two wet caves lie within Ha'ena State Park. Carved by the endless pounding of the ocean, the massive cavern of Waikapala'e Wet Cave is as enchanting as it is spooky. It's a short walk from the parking lot, across the highway, while Waikanaloa Wet Cave is on the south side, further along.

ℹ Getting There & Away

To park at Ha'ena State Park, you must have a permit (www.gohaena.com). Available for three distinct slots each day – 6:30am to 12:30pm, 12:30pm to 5:30pm and 4:30pm to sunset – they're sold online up to a month in advance and often sell out. If you're planning a day hike, you'll likely need more than one permit.

The park is also the end point for the North Shore Shuttle (p143). Buses back to Princeville or Hanalei operate to no fixed schedule, simply waiting at Ha'ena until they fill up, but the last bus out leaves at 5pm.

Overnight parking is forbidden at Ha'ena, so if you plan to camp on the Kalalau Trail, either come by shuttle or contact YMCA Camp Naue (p177), which at times offers parking for $5 per night.

Na Pali Coast Wilderness State Park

Pristine and hauntingly beautiful, this 16-mile-long stretch of soaring green-clad cliffs, white-sand beaches, turquoise coves and gushing waterfalls is Kaua'i's most magnificent natural spectacle. Each of the five major valleys – Kalalau, Honopu, Awa'awapuhi, Nu'alolo and Miloli'i – is more stunning than the last. No road could negotiate such stark wilderness, and even the legendary Kalalau Trail (p136) is ultimately defeated by sheer buttresses of rock. While fit trekkers can at least hike as far as Kalalau Valley, it's also possible to experience the coastline by kayak, raft or catamaran.

🏃 Activities

Kaua'i Nature Tours   TOURS

(☑ 888-233-8365, 808-742-8305; www.kauai naturetours.com; 10hr tours adult/child 7-12yr $185/165; ☺ by reservation only) Geologist Chuck Blay's company guides an excellent 8-mile (round-trip) hike to Hanakapi'ai Falls. All-day tours depart by shuttle van from Po'ipu Beach Park on the South Shore.

ℹ Information

Hawaii State Parks (http://camping.ehawaii. gov) Camping permits for Na Pali Coast State Wilderness Park are available up to 90 days in advance. Make reservations as soon as possible, or you may miss out altogether.

ℹ Getting There & Away

Since the flooding of 2018, you can no longer park alongside Ke'e Beach. Instead you have to park at nearby Ha'ena State Park, for which you have to book at least one timed parking slot well in advance. Most hikers arrive instead on the North Shore Shuttle (p143), for which, naturally, you do not need a parking permit.

Cliff divers, Po'ipu (p192)
DAVE FIMBRES PHOTOGRAPHY/GETTY IMAGES ©

Po'ipu & the South Shore

P o'ipu is, for good reason, the epicenter of South Shore tourism. Among the sunniest spots on Kaua'i, it receives significantly less rain than the North Shore. Yes, it's slightly less green, but it's still spectacularly beautiful. Besides amazing sun-kissed beaches, it holds top-end resorts and quality condos, plus many of the island's best restaurants.

While most vacations center on the beaches and ocean activities like surfing, diving, snorkeling and paddleboarding, the South Shore boasts world-renowned botanical gardens showcasing superb collections of endemic species. Immediately east, the lithified sand-dune cliffs and pounding surf of the Maha'ulepu Coast make for an unforgettable hike.

Away from the resorts, the historic towns of Koloa and Kalaheo bear witness to the sugar plantation era, their clapboard centers now offering friendly art galleries, intimate restaurants and fascinating perspectives on the past.

INCLUDES

HIKING & CYCLING ON THE SOUTH SHORE

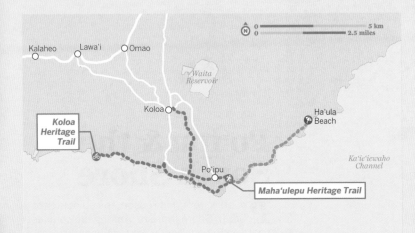

WALKING TOUR: MAHAʻULEPU HERITAGE TRAIL

START SEAVIEW TERRACE

END HAʻULA BEACH

LENGTH 7 MILES (ROUND-TRIP); THREE TO FIVE HOURS

Among the very finest coastal trails on Kauaʻi, this sumptuous hike takes you along the shoreline east of Poʻipu, passing lithified sand dunes, a jaw-dropping sinkhole filled with prehistoric fossils and madly crashing waves, to reach a succession of all-but-empty beaches. You could easily spend all day playing here, or simply enjoy a morning walk to take in the full glory of the south coast.

Start with a light breakfast of pastries and espresso at the Grand Hyatt's **Seaview Terrace** (p203) – you're sure to love the view. Then set off down from the lobby, skirting the resort's amazing array of swimming pools and waterfalls to reach the thick sands of **Shipwreck Beach** (p195).

Head eastward, clambering up onto **Makawehi Point** to join the **Mahaʻulepu Heritage Trail** (🚶). Continue past ironwood and kiawe trees on the high-looming cliffs over a geologic formation known as the Paʻa Dunes, which was laid down some 8000 years ago. For the next half-mile or so, several alternative pathways head in the same general direction, so if you find the edge of the bluff precarious, simply follow a parallel route inland.

As you climb toward the **Poʻipu Bay Golf Course** (p196) you'll see pinnacles of limestone and sandstone, and pass lava-rock tide pools. High walls of black boulders looming over the trail and stretching down to the ocean mark the temple site known as Heiau Hoʻouluiʻa, where ancient Hawaiians made offerings for success in fishing.

From here, the marked trail has been forced to run on the golf course itself for a few hundred yards by coastal erosion; keep

Although they're less well known than the trails elsewhere on Kaua'i, the South Shore holds some superb walking routes. Best of all are the breathtaking coastal vistas along the Maha'ulepu Heritage Trail.

an eye out for nene geese and flying golf balls. Then, plunging back into the clifftop grasslands, it regains its original route near Panahoa Point, a hard-rock collection of dunes that formed over 300,000 years.

Rounding the corner, you pass the paddocks of CJM Stables and a short spur trail climbs inland to fascinating **Makauwahi Cave** (p192), where volunteer scientists offer daily guided tours to explain its rich fossil record. Across narrow Waiopili Stream, sandy **Maha'ulepu Beach** (p196) stretches ahead, interrupted by a single solitary dwelling. There's pretty good snorkeling here, and it's a great picnic spot too. You might encounter Hawaiian monk seals beached after a good meal, and keep your eyes on the horizon in winter to spot spouting humpback whales.

Beyond Maha'ulepu Beach, either plod through thick sand around the next headland or follow the dirt road direct to **Kawailoa Bay** (p196), which houses another virgin beach. From there, the trail climbs along jagged cliffs, past spouting blowholes, to a grassy headland adorned with a memorial **labyrinth** (Momilani Kai, Maha'ulepu Heritage Trail).

The next little bay along is rather scrappy, scattered with flotsam, but press on another half-mile and you'll be rewarded by reaching the lost beach at **Ha'ula** (p196) at trail's end.

CYCLING TOUR: KOLOA HERITAGE TRAIL

START SPOUTING HORN PARK

END KOLOA

LENGTH 10 MILES (ONE WAY); FIVE TO SEVEN HOURS

This unexpected trail leads past some of the most notable historic sites along the south coast. You can follow it by bicycle or on foot. Begin at **Spouting Horn Park** (p193) at the west end of Po'ipu, where it's possible to stand mesmerized for hours, waiting for the biggest spout ever to blast from the shore-level blowhole.

From there, head east along Lawa'i Rd to **Prince Kuhio Park** (p193), and then turn sharp right onto Po'ipu Beach Rd just before you reach the roundabout at the Shops at Kukui'ula mall. That will lead you back down to the mouth of Waikomo Stream, where you'll pass **Koloa Landing** (p197). Once Kaua'i's largest seaport and a major whaling center, this is now a favorite spot for snorkeling.

Continue along the coast past the Sheraton to the awesome gardens known as the **Moir Pa'u a Laka** (p193), which lie within the Kiahuna Plantation condo complex. Head for the beach here to reach the black-lava outline of the **Kihahouna Heiau**, an ancient temple that was devastated by Hurricane 'Iniki in 1992. You can still see the *hala lihilihi'ula* trees that marked the perimeter.

Walkers can stick to the coast to get to **Po'ipu Beach Park** (p193), a great spot to stop for a swim; cyclists have to detour inland along Po'ipu Rd. From here, get on Ho'owili Rd to Pe'e Rd, dropping down a small track if you're on foot, to reach **Shipwreck Beach** (p195), which marks the start of the Maha'ulepu coastal hiking trail.

If you're ready for a break, make your way into the opulent **Grand Hyatt** (p200) for lunch, then emerge onto Po'ipu Rd on its inland side, and go west. Now head inland on Hapa Rd. With its lava-rock walls, this route has been used since 1200 CE, and more recently had a train line running parallel; these days it's closed to cars, but serves as a community access route.

Things get a little more lush as you approach the former plantation village of Old Koloa Town (p187). Allow a couple of hours to visit the sights, shops and galleries of what's now a lively arts colony. Start by visiting the **Koloa Jodo Mission**, a still-active Buddhist temple, then head west into the downtown core to check out the Sugar Monument, historic buildings and old churches. The open-air Koloa History Center holds good exhibits on local heritage. Finish with a little treat at Koloa Mill Ice Cream and Coffee.

ROAD TRIP > SOUTH SHORE DRIVING TOUR

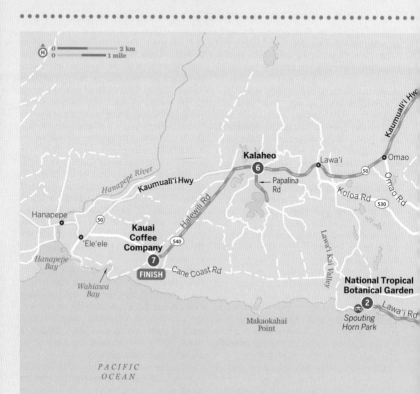

Get to know the South Shore on this fun tour of the scenic, horticultural, historic – and prehistoric – highlights of Po'ipu and its surrounds. Swim from magnificent beaches, admire the power of the Pacific, learn about coffee, sugar and tortoises, and explore colorful tropical gardens.

❶ Po'ipu Breakfast

Kick off your day at the Shops at Kukui'ula mall in Po'ipu, enjoying breakfast and maybe shopping for a picnic lunch at **Living Foods Gourmet Market & Cafe** (p201).

The Drive > Head westward along the coast, make a quick stop at Spouting Horn Park, then park at the National Tropical Botanical Garden.

Start Living Foods Gourmet Market
End Kaua'i Coffee Company
Length Five to seven hours; 30.7 miles

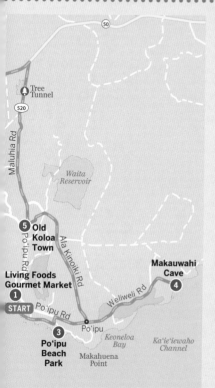

children, this is the ideal spot for ocean play; otherwise walk west along the seashore to encounter larger waves.

The Drive > Follow Po'ipu Rd east until it becomes a dirt road, then continue a further 2.2 miles to Makauwahi Cave.

❹ Makauwahi Cave

Burrowing into the base of a sinkhole, mind-boggling **Makauwahi Cave** (p192) has, as volunteer guides explain, yielded fossils of Kaua'i's long-lost original flora and fauna. You'll even see giant tortoises, and spectacular Maha'ulepu Beach is a short walk away.

The Drive > Head back to the Kukui'ula roundabout along Po'ipu Rd, then turn inland and drive 1.5 miles north to Old Koloa Town.

❺ Old Koloa Town

Spots worth seeing in Koloa include its historic downtown, a Buddhist temple, the remains of Hawaii's first sugar mill and several cool art galleries. If you're not carrying a picnic, grab a seafood lunch from **Koloa Fish Market** (p189).

The Drive > Head north up Maluhia Rd, and drive through the splendid Tree Tunnel. At Kaumuali'i Hwy, 3.3 miles along, head west to Kalaheo.

❻ Kalaheo

Stop in locally loved **Kalaheo Café & Coffee Co** (p207), then head toward the sea from the main intersection, just up the road, to reach supercool **Kukuiolono Park** (p205). Besides one of the cheapest golf courses this side of San Francisco, it holds an interesting Hawaiian Rock Garden. Break out that picnic lunch while you enjoy the sweeping vistas.

The Drive > Take HI-540/Halewili Rd 6 miles to Kauai Coffee Company.

❼ Kauai Coffee Company

The last of each day's free guided walking tours of the grounds of the **Kauai Coffee Company** (p217) sets off at 4pm. You'll learn all about coffee cultivation and the roasting process, and you get to sample a truly out-of-this-world chocolate and mac-nut brew.

❷ National Tropical Botanical Garden

Whether you plan to see one or both parts of the **National Tropical Botanical Garden** (p192), allow at least a couple of hours – and reserve ahead. Five walking trails in McBryde Garden can be explored on a self-guided visit, while Allerton Garden can only be seen on 2½-hour guided tours.

The Drive > Drive back to Po'ipu, turning right onto Po'ipu Rd at the roundabout.

❸ Po'ipu Beach Park

The sandy beaches of central Po'ipu are best accessed by parking across from **Po'ipu Beach Park** (p193). If you're traveling with

Po'ipu & the South Shore Highlights

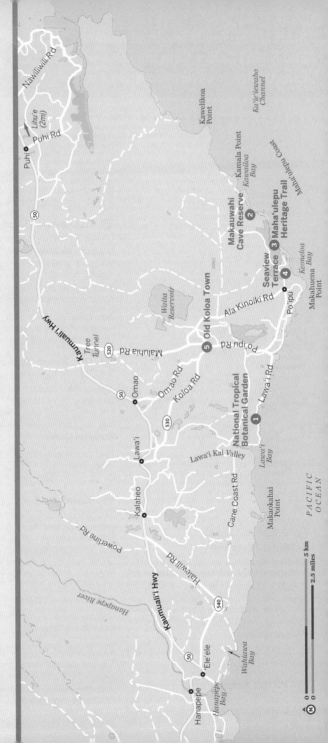

1 National Tropical Botanical Garden (p192)
Exploring two beautiful gardens in luscious Lawa'i Valley, sanctuaries for stunning native flora.

2 Makauwahi Cave Reserve (p192) Scrambling into a cavern filled with intriguing fossils – and encountering giant tortoises.

3 Maha'ulepu Heritage Trail (p182) Hiking a wonderful coastal path to reach a succession of breathtaking isolated beaches, far from Po'ipu's crowds.

4 Seaview Terrace (p203)
Marveling at the views from the bar/lounge at the Grand Hyatt Kauai Resort, which transcends the neighboring cookie-cutter condos.

5 Old Koloa Town (p187)
Stepping back in time in Hawaii's first sugar plantation town, which changed forever the way of life across the Hawaiian islands.

ℹ️ Getting There & Away

Most reach the South Shore by rental car. You can also get here with Kaua'i Bus (p279) or **South Shore Cab** (☎808-742-1525).

ℹ️ Getting Around

You can easily get around the Po'ipu area on foot or by cycling. To get further afield, you'll want a rental car.

KOLOA

☎808 / POP 2600

The district of Koloa centers on a historic sugar plantation town where the cottages now hold shops, restaurants and galleries. Known today as Old Koloa Town, it was founded in 1835 by New England missionaries turned sugar entrepreneurs.

Placards throughout the town, especially in the block west of the Waikomo Stream that holds the Koloa History Center, tell the story of Koloa and the rise of sugar. To explore in greater depth, visit the Sugar Monument, church and Jodo Mission.

Coming from Lihu'e, follow Maluhia Rd (Hwy 520), which leads through the enchanting Tree Tunnel, a mile-long canopy of towering swamp mahogany trees. Pineapple baron Walter McBryde planted it as a community project in 1911, using trees left over after landscaping his estate.

History

When William Hooper, an enterprising 24-year-old Bostonian, arrived on Kaua'i in 1835, he took advantage of two historical circumstances: Polynesians' introduction of sugarcane to the islands and Chinese immigrants' knowledge of refinery. With financial backing from Honolulu businesspeople, he leased land in Koloa from the king and paid a stipend to release commoners from their traditional work obligations. He then hired the Hawaiians as wage laborers and Koloa became Hawaii's first plantation town. Visitation led to the establishment of the first hotel in Kaua'i, the Koloa Hotel, which you can still see today.

The town withered following the decline of Big Sugar, but like the rest of Kaua'i has made a successful transition to tourism while retaining its historic facade.

⊙ Sights

Koloa History Center   MUSEUM

(www.oldkoloa.com; Koloa Rd) `FREE` This small open-air museum traces local history through photos and historic artifacts such as old barber chairs, kerosene dispensers, plows, yolks, saws and sewing machines. In effect, the museum extends through the whole town, as many buildings hold placards recounting their history.

Koloa Jodo Mission   TEMPLE

(☎808-742-6735; www.koloajodo.com; 3480 Waikomo Rd) Serving the local Japanese community for more than a century, this sect of Buddhism practices a form of chanting meditation. The original temple, on the left, dates from 1910, while the larger temple on the right hosts services, classes and other events to no fixed schedule – everyone welcome. For a guided tour, call ahead.

Sugar Monument (Old Mill)   HISTORIC SITE

(Koloa Rd) Hawaii's sugar industry, once the largest element in the islands' economy, started with the construction of the first mill in Koloa in 1835. This memorial marks the site. Little survives besides a foundation, an old stone chimney and a bronze sculpture depicting the ethnically diverse laborers of the plantation era.

St Raphael's Catholic Church   CHURCH

(☎808-742-1955; www.st-raphael-kauai.org; 3011 Hapa Rd) Kaua'i's first Catholic church was constructed in 1854 using lava rock and coral mortar to build walls 3ft thick. It was plastered over when enlarged in 1936, giving it a more familiar whitewashed look, but the original style remains visible in the rectory alongside.

🏃 Activities

⭐ **Fathom Five Divers**   DIVING

(☎800-972-3078, 808-742-6991; http://fathomfive.com; 3450 Po'ipu Rd; shore dives from $80, boat dives from $145) Kaua'i's best dive outfit offers a full range of options, from Ni'ihau boat dives to certification courses and enticing night dives. Newbies can expect reassuring hand-holding during introductory shore dives. Groups max out at six people, and mixing skill levels is avoided. The full-service shop rents scuba and snorkel gear. Book well in advance.

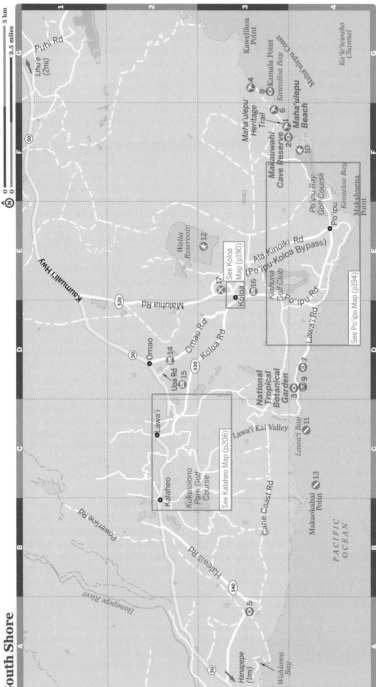

South Shore

South Shore

Boss Frog's WATERSPORTS
(☑ 808-742-2025; www.bossfrog.com; 3414 Po'ipu Rd; ⊗ 8am-5pm) This outfit rents well-used snorkel gear pretty cheaply, which you can return to its Maui or Big Island shops. Rental bodyboards, surfboards, SUPs, beach chairs and umbrellas are also available.

Snorkel Bob's WATERSPORTS
(☑ 808-742-2206; www.snorkelbob.com; 3236 Po'ipu Rd; ⊗ 8am-5pm) The king of snorkel gear rents and sells enough styles and sizes to assure a good fit, as well as wetsuits, flotation devices and bodyboards. You can return gear to any location on Kaua'i, O'ahu, Maui or the Big Island.

☞ Tours

Koloa Zipline ADVENTURE
(☑ 808-742-2734; www.koloazipline.com; 3477a Weliweli Rd; $149; ⊗ by reservation only) Take the plunge and zip upside down while enjoying superlative views. Kaua'i's longest zipline tour – measured in feet, not minutes – is the only one to allow tandem zipping and superman flights. The eight lines take you zooming around the hills near Waita Reservoir. Book well in advance or check for last-minute openings.

Kauai Z Tourz BOATING
(☑ 808-742-7422; http://kauaiztours.com; 3417e Po'ipu Rd; tours adult/child 5-12yr from $102.50/87.50) 'Z' is for Zodiac, the boat that whisks you on a snorkeling tour of South Shore sites including reefs off Spouting Horn, Prince Kuhio Park and Allerton Gardens. Cheaper snorkeling tours don't use boats, entering the water from the beach instead, while winter boat trips go dolphin- and whale-watching, without snorkeling.

Koloa Bass Fishing FISHING
(☑ 808-742-2734; www.koloabassfishing.com; Waita Reservoir; per person $150) Take a four-hour flat-bottomed boat cruise on the Waita Reservoir in search of largemouth bass, tilapia, peacock bass and more.

★彡 Festivals & Events

★ **Koloa Plantation Days** CULTURAL
(☑ 808-652-3217; www.koloaplantationdays.com;) The South Shore's biggest annual celebration spans 10 days from mid- to late July, with family-friendly attractions (many free) including a parade, *paniolo* (Hawaiian cowboy) rodeo, traditional Hawaiian games, Polynesian dancing, a craft fair, film nights, live music, guided walks and hikes, a beach party and plenty of 'talk story' about the old days.

✖ Eating

Good-value restaurants and cafes congregate in the town center, though none attempt to match the fine-dining restaurants of the resort areas. There are some creative food trucks nearby.

★ **Koloa Fish Market** SEAFOOD $
(☑ 808-742-6199; 3390 Po'ipu Rd; $10-16; ⊗ 10am-5pm Mon-Fri, to 4pm Sat) Line up with in-the-know locals at this spacious fish store-cum-takeout. It serves outstanding *poke* in all flavors (spicy kimchi is the hands-down winner), Japanese-style *bentō* (boxed meals), sushi rolls, seaweed salads and plate lunches grilled to order. Thick-sliced, seared ahi (yellowfin tuna) and rich slabs of homemade *haupia* (coconut) and sweet-potato pie can prove addictive.

PO'IPU & THE SOUTH SHORE KOLOA

Koloa

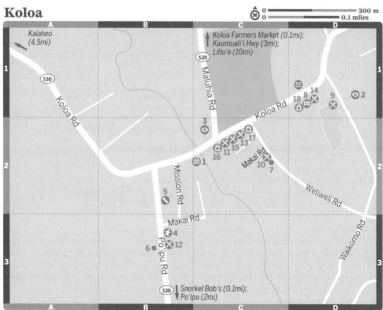

Koloa

◉ Sights
1 Koloa History Center	C2
2 Koloa Jodo Mission	D1
3 Sugar Monument (Old Mill)	C2

◎ Activities, Courses & Tours
4 Boss Frog's	B3
5 Fathom Five Divers	B2
6 Kauai Z Tourz	B3
7 Koloa Zipline	C2

⊜ Sleeping
8 Po'ipu Connection Realty	D1

⊗ Eating
9 Big Save	D1

10 Chalupa's	C2
11 Garden Island Grille	C2
12 Koloa Fish Market	B3
13 Koloa Mill Ice Cream & Coffee	C2
14 La Spezia	D1
15 Pizzetta	C2
Sueoka Snack Shop	(see 16)
Sueoka Store	(see 16)

◎ Drinking & Nightlife
Aloha Roastery	(see 1)

⊜ Shopping
16 Christian Riso Fine Art	C2
17 Island Soap & Candle Works	C2
18 The Wine Shop	D1

★ **Garden Island Grille** AMERICAN $
(☏808-639-8044; www.gardenislandgrille.com; 5404 Koloa Rd; $12-27; ☉11:30am-8pm, closed Wed; ☎) Super-friendly casual restaurant in a plantation-era structure where there's live Hawaiian music in the central garden courtyard (6pm to 8pm). The simple pub menu includes burgers and tasty fish or shrimp tacos as well as more substantial mains like seared ahi, and the atmosphere's so welcoming that many diners settle in at the bar after eating.

Koloa Farmers Market MARKET $
(www.kauai.gov/SunshineMarkets; Koloa Ball Park, Maluhia Rd; ☉noon-1:30pm Mon; ☎) ✎ Vendors sell mostly flowers and produce, including island fruit – drink the milk from a whole coconut. Bring small bills and change, and show up on time, as competition is fierce once the whistle blows.

Koloa Mill Ice Cream & Coffee CAFE $
(☏808-742-6544; www.koloamill.com; 5424 Koloa Rd; items from $3; ☉7am-9pm) Homemade cotton candy, Kaua'i coffee, pastries, and

nothing but the best Maui-made Roselani Tropics ice cream, served with a smile. If you can't pick a flavor, try the macadamia nut or 'Pauwela Sunrise,' which contains pineapple chunks.

Chalupa's MEXICAN $
(☑ 808-634-4016; www.chalupaskauai.net; 3477 Weliweli Rd; $9-14; ☺ 10am-7pm Mon-Sat) Among the best of several food trucks in central Koloa, Chalupa's – owned by a chef from Veracruz – serves takeout plates of fish tacos and shrimp (garlic, Cajun or spicy *diabla*) to enjoy at picnic tables alongside. Neighboring Craving Thai is pretty good too.

Sueoka Snack Shop AMERICAN $
(☑ 808-742-1112; www.sueokastore.com; 5392 Koloa Rd; items $3-9; ☺ 9am-5pm) This little yellow takeout window adjoining Sueoka's grocery store, is the smart place to order that picnic lunch, be it teriyaki burgers, fish and chips or mixed plates. It's as inexpensive a meal as you'll find on Kaua'i. For better or worse, all food tastes home-cooked. Cash only.

Big Save SUPERMARKET $
(☑ 808-742-1614; www.timessupermarkets.com; 5516 Koloa Rd; ☺ 6am-11pm) Fill the kitchen of your vacation rental at one of the best branches of this Hawaiian chain, which stocks plenty of local produce; the ahi *poke* is great value.

Sueoka Store SUPERMARKET $
(☑ 808-742-1611; www.sueokastore.com; 5392 Koloa Rd; ☺ 6:30am-8:30pm Mon-Sat, from 7:30am Sun) This small local grocery store on the town's main drag holds its own by stocking the basics, plus prepackaged Japanese snacks and Kaua'i-made Taro Ko chips.

Pizzetta ITALIAN $$
(☑ 808-742-8881; www.pizzettakauai.com; 5408 Koloa Rd; mains $13-21, pizzas $18-30; ☺ 11am-9pm) More than the pasta bowls it's the baked pizzas, with toppings such as *kalua* (pit cooked) pork, Hawaiian BBQ chicken or spinach with goat's cheese, that draw diners to this casual spot. If the interior seems noisy, grab a patio table out back.

La Spezia ITALIAN $$
(☑ 808-742-8824; www.laspeziakauai.com; 5492 Koloa Rd; mains breakfast $10-14, dinner $15-25; ☺ 8-11:30am & 5-10pm Tue-Sat, 8am-1pm & 5-10pm Sun) Aiming for an Italian ambience rather than a Hawaiian feel, this place crafts flatbreads, crunchy crostini and housemade

sausage and pasta, and also holds a wine bar. Surprisingly, it doubles as a creative breakfast spot – come for stuffed French toast and Bloody Marys at Sunday brunch. Reservations for parties of six or more only.

🍷 Drinking & Nightlife

Aloha Roastery COFFEE
(☑ 808-651-4514; www.aloharoastery.com; 5356 Koloa Rd; ☺ 7am-5pm Mon-Sat; 🛜) The California-style 'third wave of coffee' vibe might be incongruous in funky Koloa, but there's no disputing this little cafe serves the best coffee for miles around (and no, they don't use Kaua'i coffee). Step out from the minimal interior to drink your brew (and eat a fine pastry) beneath the monkeypod tree in the courtyard.

🛍 Shopping

Island Soap & Candle Works GIFTS & SOUVENIRS
(☑ 888-528-7627, 808-742-1945; www.kauaisoap.com; 5428 Koloa Rd; ☺ 9am-9pm) 🌿 The aromas wafting from this shop are enough to turn your head. Wander in to sample all-natural Hawaii botanical bath and body products, including lip balms, soaps, lotions and tropically scented candles. Some are made on-site at the back of the store.

The Wine Shop WINE
(☑ 808-742-7305; www.thewineshopkauai.com; 5470 Koloa Rd; ☺ 10am-7pm Mon-Sat, 11am-6pm Sun) In addition to their selection of international wines, cold beers and gourmet foods, this shop sells local products including Kaua'i-made mead in flavors like ginger spice.

Christian Riso Fine Art ART
(☑ 808-742-2555; www.facebook.com/christianrisofineart; 5400 Koloa Rd; ☺ 9am-8:30pm) This cute gallery stocks lots of prints, watercolors and sculptures by local artists, as well as a fine collection of original oils, including works by the owner.

ℹ Information

First Hawaiian Bank (☑ 808-742-1642; www.fhb.com; 3506 Waikomo Rd; ☺ 8:30am-4pm Mon-Thu, to 6pm Fri) Has a 24-hour ATM.

Koloa Post Office (☑ 808-742-1319; www.usps.com; 5485 Koloa Rd; ☺ 9am-4pm Mon-Fri, to 11am Sat) Serves both Koloa and Po'ipu.

ℹ Getting There & Away

Kaua'i Bus (p279) stops in Koloa en route between Po'ipu and Kalaheo, where you can pick up onward connections to Lihu'e or the west side.

PO'IPU & THE SOUTH SHORE KOLOA

PO'IPU

☑808 / POP 1070

Despite its name – which misleadingly translates as 'completely overcast' – the number-one destination on the South Shore is dependably sunnier and drier than the North Shore. Po'ipu is not so much a town as a pleasant resort area where no building stands taller than a palm tree. It holds a scattering of larger hotels and condos galore, plus two open-air malls filled with shops and restaurants.

The biggest attraction is the beaches, which range from sheltered golden sands where the calm waters are ideal for families with young children, to magnificently wild strands that rival Kaua'i's most dramatic scenery. The swimming, snorkeling, diving and surfing here are nothing short of fantastic, and there's also some tremendous coastal hiking.

And don't miss Po'ipu's legendary sunsets, as reflected in the dizzy smiles of swooning tourists, lost in wonder as they lean against each other on the sand.

◉ Sights

★ **National Tropical Botanical Garden**   GARDENS
(NTBG; ☑808-742-2623; www.ntbg.org; 4425 Lawa'i Rd; McBryde Garden adult/child 6-12yr $30/15, guided tours $45-100; ☉visitor center 8:30am-5pm, tours by reservation only) 🖉 Two superb gardens in lush Lawa'i Valley, run by the National Tropical Botanical Garden, are open to visitors. Allerton Garden, spreading back from a ravishing beach, once belonged to Hawaii's Queen Emma. From 1938 onwards, it was landscaped by Chicago transplant Robert Allerton, who besides extensive planting added 'garden rooms' featuring pools, sculptures and gazebos. Gorgeous McBryde Garden, further inland, showcases palms, flowering and spice trees, orchids and rare endemic species, plus a pretty stream and waterfall.

Both gardens are accessible by shuttle bus only from the same visitor center up on Lawa'i Rd west of Poi'pu. For budget travelers, the best value is a self-guided visit to McBryde Garden, which allows you to wander in the vast grounds for as long as you choose. Five interpretative trails here, covering such themes as the plants brought by Kaua'i's original Polynesian settlers, are lined with information panels. Hourly

shuttle buses leave from the visitor center on the half-hour, and pick up from McBryde Garden on the hour.

Guided tours include the standard 2½-hour tour of Allerton Garden (adult/child aged 6 to 12 years $60/30), and the three-hour Sunset tour ($100/50), which peeks inside Allerton's home; the 2½-hour Wailele tour ($45/22.50), which leads to a waterfall in McBryde Garden; and the 2½-hour 'Behind the Scenes' tour ($60/30), which covers both gardens and focuses especially on their conservation and horticultural activities. Current schedules are posted online; reserve well in advance.

Chartered by the US Congress, the National Tropical Botanical Garden is a nonprofit organization whose research, conservation and education is aimed at the preservation and survival of tropical plants. As well as Allerton and McBryde gardens, where the NTBG began, it also owns the magnificent Limahuli Garden, near Ha'ena on Kaua'i's North Shore; the Kahanu Garden on Maui; the Awini and Ka'upulehu preserves on the Big Island; and the Kampong Garden on Florida's Biscayne Bay.

★ **Makauwahi Cave Reserve**   CAVE
(☑808-631-3409; www.cavereserve.org; donations welcomed; ☉10am-4pm or by appointment) This amazing natural site is also a paleontological treasure house. Seen from above, it's a deep, circular sinkhole, possibly formed by the collapse of an oceanfront blowhole. Scramble through the 3ft-high crawlspace at its base to reach a 'lost world' where a sand-floored cave holds what's arguably the richest fossil record in the Hawaiian Islands. Excavations since 1996 have provided evidence of the widespread extinction of native plants and animals since Hawaii was first settled by humans.

Volunteers are on hand daily in the cave itself to explain the full story, while a walking trail follows the rim of the sinkhole up above. The reserve is also being extensively replanted with native species, and an enclave has even been populated with giant tortoises. Their sharp beaks are thought to mimic the grazing action of the flightless birds that once lived here.

Reach the reserve either by hiking along the Maha'ulepu Heritage Trail (p182), or driving along the dirt road beyond the Grand Hyatt, following signs for a total of 2.2 miles.

Kaneiʻolouma   ARCHAEOLOGICAL SITE
(www.kaneiolouma.org; Poʻipu Rd at Hoʻowili Rd; ☉ sunrise-sunset) The site of a precontact Hawaiian village just inland from Poʻipu Beach was set aside by the county in 2010. You can't enter the complex, which is being restored by community volunteers. During the 14th century, it held a heiau (temple) dedicated to Kāne, the god of fresh water, as well as homes, fishponds and taro patches. A viewing area stands beside a stone platform that was used for astronomical observations, where four carved *kiʻi* (tiki images) have been re-erected.

Spouting Horn Park   VIEWPOINT
The surf jets through like a mini-geyser through these two blowholes in the lava-rock reef. The spurts are typically less than 30ft and last only seconds, but can reach twice that height during big surf. This is a major stop on coach tours, so the path from the parking lot is lined with tacky souvenir stands. To get here, follow Lawaʻi Rd west along the coast from the Kukuiʻula roundabout for just under 2 miles.

Kukuiʻula Small Boat Harbor   HARBOR
(Lawaʻi Rd) With its pavilion and camp tables, Poʻipu's small commercial harbor is not a bad place for a picnic. Walk the jetty, check out the scuba boats and even sunbathe on the small roadside beach.

Prince Kuhio Park   PARK
(Lawaʻi Rd) Dedicated to the memory of Prince Jonah Kuhio (1871–1922), the Territory of Hawaii's first delegate to the US Congress, this landscaped park holds little to see but lava foundations. They mark the ruins of an ancient Hawaiian heiau and fishpond.

Moir Paʻu a Laka   GARDENS
(☏ 808-742-6411; www.outrigger.com; Kiahuna Plantation, 2253 Poʻipu Rd; ☉ sunrise-sunset) **FREE** On the grounds of Outrigger's Kiahuna Plantation complex, this diverting, if modest, cactus and exotic flower garden established in the 1930s boasts winding paths, a koi pond and colorful shocks of orchids. It is now home to a restaurant, the Plantation Gardens (p202).

🏊 Beaches

Poʻipu has two very different beach areas. The in-town beaches, which front resorts and condos, are popular and crowded, while the wilder beaches along the Mahaʻulepu

Coast to the east remain majestically unspoiled.

Poʻipu Beach Park   BEACH
(🏖) There are no monster waves or idyllic solitude at the South Shore's most popular beach, but it's a go-to spot with something for everyone. Patrolled by resident *honu* (sea turtles) in the shallows, the beach is protected by a rocky reef that attracts fish of all kinds. It spills into two separate bays connected by the reef offshore and bisected by a sandbar. Add lifeguards, picnic tables, toilets and outdoor showers, and you have one safe, family-friendly beach.

There's parking across from the beach, at the end of Hoʻowili Rd. A grassy lawn links to Brennecke's Beach just east, and there are three surf breaks nearby.

Poʻipu Beach   BEACH
This long swath of prime sand west of Poʻipu Beach Park is open to all, even if it does stretch right in front of the hotel and condo complexes from which it gets its alternative nicknames, Sheraton Beach and Kiahuna Beach. The water is often too rough for kids, although an offshore reef tames the waves enough for strong ocean swimmers and snorkelers. To get here, drive to the end of Hoʻonani Rd. Experienced surfers and bodyboarders can attempt the breaks near the Sheraton, but those waters are famous for sneaker sets (rogue waves that appear from nowhere), and the rocky coast makes it difficult to get offshore and back.

Brennecke's Beach   BEACH
With a sandbar bottom and a notch of sand and sea wedged between two lava-rock outcrops, this little beach flanks the eastern edge of Poʻipu Beach Park. Check with lifeguards there before venturing out. No surfboards are allowed near shore, so bodyboarders rule, bobbing in the water, waiting for the next set at any time of day or year. Tourists sit on the roadside stone wall, gawking at the action.

Baby Beach   BEACH
(🏖) Introduce tots to the ocean at this beach, where the water is barely thigh high. The sandy shore runs behind the beach homes on Hoʻona Rd west of Koloa Landing. Access is easy – look for the sign marking the path – but parking is limited (don't block driveways). There's another Baby Beach in Kapaʻa on the Eastside.

Poʻipu

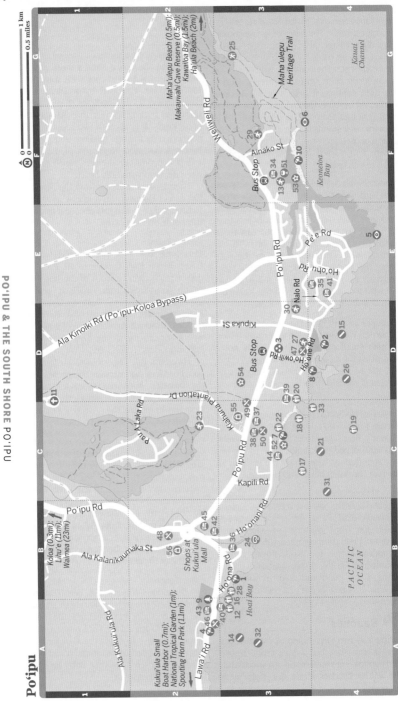

Po'ipu

Lawa'i (Beach House) Beach BEACH
For such a tiny beach, this snorkeling and surfing spot gets lots of attention. Just west of the landmark Beach House (p202), it's not particularly scenic or sandy. But during calm surf, this is rich snorkel territory, especially for novices. Expect a crowd of vacationers from nearby condos. There are restrooms, outdoor showers and a few public parking spaces across the street.

Shipwreck Beach BEACH
Unless you're an expert surfer, bodyboarder or bodysurfer, keep your feet dry at 'Shipwrecks,' the half-mile crescent of light gold sand that skirts Keoneloa Bay in front of the Grand Hyatt. Row after row of waves crash close to shore, giving Shipwrecks a rugged, untamed feel, so it's best to simply enjoy an invigorating walk. This is the starting point for the hike along the magnificent Maha'ulepu Coast.

Rocky **Makahuena Point** to the west, covered with condos, is the southernmost tip of Kaua'i. Makawehi Point (p182), the gigantic lithified sand dune that looms immediately east, is famous as a site for daredevil cliff-jumpers, many of whom have been seriously injured or even killed.

Maha'ulepu Coast Beaches

The windswept Maha'ulepu Coast, accessible via either a wonderful hiking trail or a couple of miles of dirt-road driving, resembles no other on Kaua'i. Home to lithified sand-dune cliffs, pounding surf, secluded coves and three outstanding and often deserted beaches, it's also where you'll find the extraordinary Makauwahi Cave. Swimming can be dangerous even in summer, so use your best judgment.

★ **Maha'ulepu Beach**   BEACH

(Gillin's Beach) This secluded sandy beach feels as though it's sitting on the reef, so it's no surprise that there's excellent snorkeling. To get here, hike the Maha'ulepu Heritage Trail (p182) or drive the dirt road that starts shortly beyond the Grand Hyatt, first for 1.6 miles to the junction where gates both left and ahead force you to turn right, and then for another 0.8 miles to the parking area, from which a trail leads to the beach.

This final stretch of road is open 7:30am to 6pm daily, to 7pm in summer.

Kawailoa Bay   BEACH

Kawailoa Bay has sand dunes at one end and cliffs at the other. Reliable breezes mean it's a popular spot for windsurfing and kitesurfing as well as fishing. Ironwood trees shade an impromptu beachfront picnic area. Coming from Maha'ulepu Beach, continue along the Maha'ulepu Heritage Trail on foot or simply follow the inland dirt road by car.

Ha'ula Beach   BEACH

At the far eastern end of the Maha'ulepu Heritage Trail (p182), Ha'ula is an isolated bay and pocket beach nestled into the shoreline. You'll feel like Robinson Crusoe here, especially if you're swinging in a hammock made from a fishing net. The beach is a 15-minute walk beyond Kawailoa Bay along the coast, past a rugged headland.

🏃 Activities

Anara Spa   SPA

(☑ 808-742-1234; www.anaraspa.com; Grand Hyatt Kauai Resort & Spa, 1571 Po'ipu Rd; treatments from $180 for 50min; ⊙ by appointment only) Excellent spa treatments, many inspired by Hawaiian healing arts, are given in private garden-view rooms. Paying a little extra for an individual garden hut, amid tropical foliage and waterfalls, gives access to a serene post-treatment relaxation area. Use of lap pool, sauna, steam room and fitness center is included with a minimum spend; don't miss the outdoor lava-rock showers.

Po'ipu Bay Golf Course   GOLF

(☑ 800-858-6300, 808-742-8711; www.poipu baygolf.com; 2250 Ainako St; green fees incl cart rental $184-219, club rental $65) Known for its magnificent views of mountains and sea, this 18-hole, par-72 course designed by Robert Trent Jones Jr hosted the PGA Grand Slam for the 13 years up to 2006. It sports 85 bunkers, five water hazards and unpredictable winds. Rates drop in the afternoons. Club and shoe rentals available.

Skyline Eco-Adventures   ZIPLINE

(☑ 800-425-9374; www.zipline.com/kauai; Shops at Kukui'ula, 2829 Ala Kalanikaumaka St; zipline $100-140; ⊙ 7am-9pm) Choose either five or eight zips with this chain operation. Check-in is at their Po'ipu HQ, while the canopy platform is outside Oma'o. Reservations required.

Outfitters Kauai   BICYCLE RENTAL

(☑ 888-742-9887, 808-742-9667; www.outfitters kauai.com; 2827a Po'ipu Rd; bicycle rental per day $25-50; ⊙ 9am-4:30pm) Perhaps because of the lack of bike lanes, cyclists are scarce in Po'ipu. However, you can rent bikes here, including road, mountain and hybrid models. Rates include helmet and lock. Phone reservations recommended.

Spa at Koa Kea   SPA

(☑ 808-742-4277; www.koakea.com; Koa Kea Hotel & Resort, 2251 Po'ipu Rd; ⊙ by appointment only) This boutique spa offers massage styles including Hawaiian *lomilomi* and *pohaku* (hot stone), as well as body scrubs and treatments using island-sourced ingredients such as *kukui* (candlenut) and coconut oils, Kaua'i coffee and red clay. As well as its five treatment rooms (including one for couples), it has tented oceanfront beds. Book ahead.

Kiahuna Golf Club   GOLF

(☑ 808-742-9595; www.kiahunagolf.com; 2545 Kiahuna Plantation Dr; 18 holes $99, 9 holes $65, rental clubs $32-52) A relatively inexpensive and forgiving 18-hole, par-70 course designed by Robert Trent Jones Jr, interestingly incorporating some archaeological ruins. The scenery is excellent thanks to some ocean views, although the course is often windy. Rental clubs available.

CJM Country Stables   HORSEBACK RIDING

(☏808-742-6096; www.cjmstables.com; off Po'ipu Rd; 2hr group rides $110-150, private rides from $210; ⏰rides usually 9:30am & 2pm Mon-Sat, 1pm Wed & Fri; ⛟) The Maha'ulepu Coast is a perfect landscape to see on horseback. CJM offers two gentle guided tours of the purely nose-to-tail walking variety suitable for the whole family. More-experienced riders may opt for a private ride. Do like the cowboys do and wear long pants.

Poipu Kai Tennis Club   TENNIS

(☏808-742-8706; www.poipukai.org/tennis.html; 1775 Po'ipu Rd; per person per day $20, racket rental $5; ⏰8am-noon & 2-6pm) Rent one of six hard courts or two artificial grass courts with ocean views at this resort racquet club. It has tennis clinics and round-robin tourneys. You can either make a reservation or just show up.

Diving

The Po'ipu coast holds many of Kaua'i's finest dive sites, including Sheraton Caverns, General Store, and shallower Nukumoi Point. Dive boats and catamaran cruises typically depart from Kukui'ula Small Boat Harbor (p193).

★ Seaport Divers   DIVING

(☏808-742-9303; www.seasportdivers.com; Po'ipu Plaza, 2827 Po'ipu Rd; shore/boat dives incl equipment rental from $142/182; ⏰8am-6pm) This leading outfit schedules dives from shore or by boat, including twice-daily South Shore boat trips and three-tank dives to less frequently visited sites. Any group with noncertified divers includes an additional instructor for no additional fee. Book in advance.

Kauai Down Under   DIVING

(☏808-742-7442; www.kauaidownunderscuba.com; Sheraton Kaua'i Resort, 2440 Ho'onani Rd; boat dives incl equipment rental from $195; ⏰by reservation only) This operator offers introductory noncertified one-tank dives, two-tank scooter dives and night dives for the truly adventurous. With one instructor per four guests, personal attention is guaranteed. It also offers the academic portion of the certification online, pre-arrival, if you want to maximize your on-island playtime. Make sure you reserve ahead.

Sheraton Caverns   DIVING

Located 400yd offshore from the Sheraton, this uberpopular boat dive takes you to partial lava tubes, overhangs and archways. It's sea turtle heaven.

Koloa Landing   SNORKELING, DIVING

Koloa Landing, at the mouth of Waikomo Stream, was once Hawaii's third-busiest whaling port, surpassed only by Honolulu and Lahaina, Maui; 19th-century farmers also shipped sugar, oranges and sweet potatoes from here. Today only a small boat ramp remains, but it's the best shore-diving site on the South Shore, with underwater tunnels and a sizable population of eels.

Beach House   DIVING

In the waters fronting the Beach House, this intermediate and advanced boat dive takes you down 35 to 75ft. The highlight is an arch where a school of blue-striped grunts live. Also expect turtles and tang.

Brennecke's Ledge   DIVING

This drift dive is best for experienced divers. You'll be rewarded with a ledge that drops to an overhang and tons of fish. The current moves fast, so you need to be comfortable in the water.

Ice Box   DIVING

A good spot for intermediate divers, with dives to ledges around 60ft to 90ft. You might just see soldier fish, white-tip reef sharks and turtles.

Nukumoi Point   DIVING

Relatively shallow at 30ft to 60ft, this popular diving spot is a habitat for green sea turtles.

General Store   DIVING

Better suited to intermediate and advanced divers because of the current, this spot has it all: black coral, butterfly fish, conch, plenty of chances of spotting dolphins and even the remains of a sunken freighter.

Turtle Bluffs   DIVING

Located west of General Store dive site, this is a good spot to find turtles, snappers and the occasional reef shark.

Three Fingers   DIVING

A good site for beginners, with little current and shallow dives 25ft to 75ft, this boat dive site outside the harbor features three lava fingers (yep, that's where it gets its name), plus schools of blue-striped grunts and surgeon fish.

SOUTH SHORE SNORKELING HOT SPOTS

Take the plunge at these top-rated South Shore snorkeling areas, all of which offer handy beach access.

Koloa Landing (p197) Po'ipu's best shore-diving site is also great for advanced snorkelers. Expect to see large schools of fish, eels and the usual turtles. Avoid the sandy middle ground.

Lawa'i (Beach House) Beach (p195) If you don't mind the crowds, you'll find good coral, lots of reef fish and sea turtles, all within a depth of 3ft to 12ft. Restrooms and outdoor showers onshore.

Maha'ulepu Beach (p196) Though its seclusion means it's often overlooked – and it's only safe when both wind and water are calm – this nearshore reef is arguably the best of the lot.

Po'ipu Beach Park (p193) Ranging from 3ft to 12ft, this shallow protected bay is great for families, but experts will enjoy it too. Head left as you enter for the best snorkeling. Facilities include lifeguards, outdoor showers and restrooms.

Prince Kuhio Park (p193) Ocean waters across the street from this grassy park range 3ft to 21ft deep, and appeal to beginners and advanced snorkelers alike. The shoreline is rocky, but the bay is protected.

Surfing & Stand-up Paddleboarding (SUP)

Po'ipu's mix of safe beginners' spots, killer breaks and year-round waves make it a popular spot for surfing lessons and rentals.

★ **Kaua'i Surf School** SURFING, SUP
(☑ 808-651-6032; www.kauaisurfschool.com; Kiahuna Plantation Resort, 2400 Po'ipu Rd; 2hr group/private surfing lessons $75/250, SUP lessons $100; ☺ by reservation only; 🖝) With 90 minutes of teaching, 30 minutes of free practice and only four students per instructor, you get your money's worth. Ages four and up are welcome in group lessons as long as they can swim; alternatively, book a special one-hour private lesson for kids. Ask about surf clinics, surf camps, private coaches and SUP lessons.

Hoku Water Sports SURFING, SUP
(☑ 808-639-9333; www.hokuwatersports.com; Koa Kea Hotel & Resort, 2251 Po'ipu Rd; 2hr group/private surfing lessons $80/250, 80min SUP lessons $90, outrigger canoe tours $55; ☺ by reservation only) Group surfing lessons include just one hour with an instructor and an hour of free surfing. For a unique experience, surf the waves as part of the crew of a Hawaiian outrigger canoe.

Kauai Stand-up Paddle & Surf SURFING, SUP
(☑ 808-652-9979; www.kauaisurfandsup.com; 2hr group/private surfing lessons $75/120, 2hr SUP lessons $85, surfing & SUP tours $120-150; 🖝)

This locally owned, small-group outfitter runs kids' surf camps in summer, offers family discounts and brings over 30 years of experience. It's also the only operator providing custom SUP tours island-wide.

Nukumoi Surf Shop WATERSPORTS
(☑ 808-742-8019; www.nukumoi.com; 2100 Ho'one Rd; snorkel set/bodyboard/surfboard/SUP rental per day from $8/8/25/60; ☺ 7:45am-sunset) Visit this shop right across from Po'ipu Beach Park for surfboard, snorkel and SUP rentals. Check your gear carefully before heading out. Great local surf beta.

Po'ipu Surf SURFING
(☑ 808-742-8797; www.poipusurf.com; Shops at Kukui'ula, 2829 Ala Kalanikaumaka St; snorkel set/bodyboard/surfboard/SUP rental per day $6/6/20/40; ☺ 9am-8:30pm) This surf and skate shop rents beginner and performance surfboards and SUP sets at competitive rates. Weekly discounts available.

PK's SURFING
Good wave with an easy takeoff outside the Prince Kuhiuo Condos, suited to intermediate riders who at least know how to make it to the lineup.

Cowshead SURFING
At its best when the waves are at 4ft to 10ft, this long right-hander is nice and hollow.

Centers SURFING
A bit fickle, this break is not quite as reliable as others here. Split-peak on a reef.

Donovans
SURFING

(Learners; 📷) Nearly all of the area's surf lessons happen here, so it's the place to come if you're just getting going. Rolls all the way into the sand – less worry about rocks.

First Break
SURFING

At a couple of hundred yards out, this one's quite a paddle. Look for 8ft to 12ft for solid right rides; it doesn't break when it's small.

Waiohai
SURFING

Always breaking by the Marriott. Two to 8ft is good, making it decent for pretty good beginner riders.

Acid Drop
SURFING

A reef break better suited to experts, this South Shore surfing break has both lefts and rights, and is best ridden at 6ft to 10ft.

🧭 Tours

Outfitters Kauai
KAYAKING

(📞808-742-9667; www.outfitterskauai.com; 2827a Po'ipu Rd; kayak tours $109-249, zipline $50-189; ⏰7am-5pm) Drop in at the Po'ipu office to hear about kayaking and ziplining tours. Kayak on the Na Pali Coast or Wailua River, or opt for jungle ziplines. Tandem, open-cockpit kayaks or sit-on-top, self-bailing kayaks with pedal rudders make it easy for novices, but if you get seasick, think twice.

Captain Andy's
Sailing Adventures
BOATING

(📞808-335-6833; www.napali.com; Kukui'ula Small Boat Harbor; 2hr tours adult/child 2-12yr $95/75; ⏰departs 4pm or 5pm Thu) Captain Andy usually sails to the Na Pali Coast from Port Allen (p217), but once a week his 55ft catamaran offers scenic sunset cruises down the Maha'ulepu Coast from Kukui'ula, including appetizers, cocktails and live music. Cross your fingers to spot whales between December and April. Book at least three days ahead.

Travel Hawaii
TOURS

(📞808-742-7015; Po'ipu Shopping Village, 2360 Kiahuna Plantation Dr; ⏰9am-9pm) This friendly tourist information kiosk, run by Diamond Resorts, can book tours, give you local advice and get you out on adventures large and small.

🎆 Festivals & Events

Prince Kuhio Celebration
CULTURAL

(📞808-240-6369; Prince Kuhio Park, Lawa'i Rd) South Shore enthusiastically participates in this statewide two-week celebration in early to mid-March. Events typically include hula performances and slack key guitar music, a rodeo, canoe racing, 'talk story' time, Hawaiian cultural presentations on *kapa* (bark cloth), lei and poi making, and much more.

🛏 Sleeping

While Po'ipu holds abundant lodging options – almost exclusively upscale – most are condos and vacation rentals, with just a handful of full-service resorts. Individual condo owners tend to offer better rates, while booking via a rental agency can help connect you with the right property and assist with any problems during your stay.

★ Parrish
Collection Kaua'i
ACCOMMODATIONS SERVICES

(📞800-325-5701, 808-742-2000; www.parrish kauai.com; 3176 Po'ipu Rd) Renting condos and vacation homes in Po'ipu and along the North Shore and Westside, this excellent agency has professional, friendly. Browse their listings for a fine selection of ocean-view properties along the Po'ipu shoreline.

Po'ipu
Connection Realty
ACCOMMODATIONS SERVICES

(📞800-742-2260, 808-742 2233; www.poipu connection.com; 5488 Koloa Rd) Condo rentals – especially at Prince Kuhio Resort – at decent rates, with personalized service.

Prince Kuhio Resort
CONDO $

(📞888-747-2988; www.prince-kuhio.com; 5061 Lawa'iRd; studio/1-/2-bedroom condo from $90/150 /179; 🛏🏊) This 72-unit complex has an enviable location across from Lawa'i Beach. Condos vary in quality and amenities, but all have full kitchens and lanai (veranda), and most face across the road to the ocean. The pool is no slouch, and the grounds are well kept.

Last-minute rentals can be great value. Cleaning fee is $95 to $180.

Kuhio Shores
CONDO $$

(www.kuhioshores.net; 5050 Lawa'i Rd; 1-/2-bedroom condos from $199/275; ❄🏊) Set on a grassy outcrop that juts into the sea opposite Prince Kuhio Park, this aging but perennially popular oceanfront complex claims the most stunning vistas in Po'ipu. Each privately owned condo spills out on to a patio or lanai. Amenities vary.

Book well ahead. The cleaning fee starts at $95.

Waikomo Stream Villas
CONDO **$$**

(☎ 800-325-5701; www.parrishkauai.com; 2721 Po'ipu Rd; 1-/2-bedroom condos from $125/165; P 🛜 ⚊) Near the Kukui'ula roundabout and a half-mile from the beach, this can be a steal. The 60 condos vary, and not all have views, but many are very smart, and they're all huge, with kitchens, washer-dryers and lanais. There's a good pool, and the split-level two-bedroom units soar. Cleaning fee from $150.

Kaua'i Cove
COTTAGE **$$**

(☎ 808-651-0279; www.kauaicove.com; 2672 Pu'uholo Rd; $149-229; @ 🛜) In a low-key neighborhood near Koloa Landing, this studio cottage blends modern amenities with a tropical bungalow feel. Its efficient layout allows for a bamboo canopy bed, vaulted ceilings and a full kitchenette. Add tasteful decor, lustrous hardwood floors and parking on your doorstep. Cleaning fee $75.

The same owners also offer Po'ipu Kai rentals; see website for details.

Nihi Kai Villas
CONDOS **$$**

(☎ 808-325-5701; www.parrishkauai.com; 1870 Ho'one Rd; 2-bedroom condo from $225, 3 bedroom from $390; P 🛜 ⚊) Get a top-floor room in this large condo complex for a better chance for a view down to the ocean. You'll also get vaulted ceilings and hardwood beams that provide a welcome nod to the islands. Brennecke's Beach (p193) is just a 100yd up the coastal road. The pool also has good views out to sea.

Hideaway Cove Poipu Beach
CONDO **$$**

(☎ 808-635-8785; www.hideawaycove.com; 2307 Nalo Rd; studio/1-/2-bedroom condos from $240/255/375; ✳ 🛜) A five-minute walk east of Brennecke's Beach, these impeccable, professionally managed units are a cut above their peers. Condos have the feel of private homes, with private lanais, hardwood flooring, art and antiques, and Jacuzzi tubs. Cleaning fees from $165 per stay.

Po'ipu Bed & Breakfast Inn
B&B **$$**

(☎ 808-639-0947; www.poipubedandbreakfast inn.com; 2720 Ho'onani Rd; r incl breakfast from $165.50) This original plantation house just east of Waikomo Stream has a few cozy rooms, plus slightly outdated condos out back. The rooms are just decent, with tropical comforters and the feel of staying in your Aunt Mary's house. Nonetheless, it's friendly and definitely one of the cheaper buys in this area.

⭐ Grand Hyatt Kauai Resort & Spa
RESORT **$$$**

(☎ 808-742-1234; www.grandhyattkauai.com; 1571 Po'ipu Rd; r/ste $688/2209; P ✳ 🛜 ⚊) 🏊 Sprawling through tropical gardens down to the Pacific, this quintessential Hawaiian resort is all glamor. Beyond its soaring atrium lie wonderful lounges and restaurants, a huge spa and a magnificent pool complex, cascading into a salt-water lagoon. Nearly all its 600 luxurious, high-ceilinged rooms have ocean views and gorgeous baths. The nearest beach, however, is beautiful but unsuitable for swimming. There's plenty of free parking for visitors.

Koa Kea Hotel & Resort
HOTEL **$$$**

(☎ 877-276-0768; www.koakea.com; 2251 Po'ipu Rd; r from $433; P ✳ 🛜 ⚊) This romantic boutique resort occupies a unique niche in Po'ipu. A decidedly adult property, it's a bold exploration of design instead of the Hawaiiana leitmotif of other local hotels. With 121 rooms, it's intimate and inwardly focused. The U-shaped ground plan opens onto the beach, leaving many rooms facing each other across the central pool.

Kiahuna Plantation Resort Kaua'i by Outrigger
CONDO **$$$**

(☎ 808-742-6411, 866-956-4262; http://outrigger kiahunaplantationcondo.com; 2253 Po'ipu Rd; 1-/2-bedroom condo from $289/432; P 🛜 ⚊) This wonderfully underappreciated resort harks back to the golden age of Kaua'i tourism. Surrounding massive central lawns with the feel of an oceanfront park, the comfy units have fully equipped kitchens and large lanais, but vary in quality. Guests can use the nearby Poipu Beach Athletic Club fitness center and pool.

Sheraton Kaua'i Resort
RESORT **$$$**

(☎ 888-627-8113, 808-742-1661; www.sheraton kauai.com; 2440 Ho'onani Rd; r from $319; P ✳ 🛜 ⚊ 🏊) The Sheraton enjoys an undeniable advantage, occupying a prime stretch of sandy, swimmable, sunset-perfect beach, with a pool and luau gardens right by the ocean. Its open-air design highlights its setting, but only half the rooms have sea views; those in the Garden Wing are set well back on the inland side of the road.

Kiahuna Plantation & Beach Bungalows
CONDO **$$$**

(☎ 877-367-1912; www.castleresorts.com; 2253 Po'ipu Rd; 1-/2-bedroom condo from $279/459; ⚊) While the Castle Resorts half of Kiahuna

Plantation is set back from the central gardens, its rooms are a little more consistent and share the property's overall old-school feel. All feature huge lanais. Guests have access to the Poipu Beach Athletic Club fitness center and pool across the road.

🍴 Eating

Some Po'ipu restaurants, especially in the big resort hotels, exploit ocean views as an excuse to charge inflated prices for average food. The Shops at Kukui'ula mall holds some great options, though, while budget travelers can find cheaper alternatives in and around the Kukui'ula Market grocery store nearby, or up the road in Koloa.

Da Crack   MEXICAN $
(☎808-742-9505; www.dacrackkauai.com; 2827 Po'ipu Rd; $10.50-15; ⏰11am-8pm Mon-Sat, to 3pm Sun; 🚗) A guilty pleasure, this taco shop is just a hole in the wall of the Kukui'ula Market grocery store, with no tables nearby. Lines form daily to get hold of its tacos, burritos and rice-and-beans bowls overstuffed with batter-fried fish, carnitas (braised pork), shredded chicken or chipotle shrimp.

Little Fish Coffee   CAFE $
(☎808-742-2113; www.littlefishcoffee.com; 2294 Po'ipu Rd; $8-12; ⏰6:30am-3pm) Standing alone in lush green lawns peppered with well-shaded tables on the *mauka* (inland) side of the highway, this little shack makes a great place to kick start the day. Early-morning java fiends wait in line for espresso coffee drinks and fruit-laden acai bowls; later on there's a good menu of smoothies, bagels, salads and sandwiches. One warning: there's no restroom.

Kukui'ula Market   SUPERMARKET $
(☎808-742-1601; 2827 Po'ipu Rd; ⏰8am-8:30pm Mon-Fri, to 6:30pm Sat & Sun) This old-style grocery store has much more local flavor than its big-mall rivals; stock up your condo kitchen here to sample some genuine Kauaian foods. On top of that, it's home to the superb Makai Sushi and the fabulous Anake's Juice Bar (p203), which share a spacious seating area at the rear.

Papalani Gelato   ICE CREAM $
(☎808-742-2663; www.papalanigelato.com; Po'ipu Shopping Village, 2360 Kiahuna Plantation Dr; scoop $4.75; ⏰11am-9:30pm; 🚗) All the deliciously sweet treats at this self-styled Shake Shack are made on-site. You can't go wrong with classic pistachio, but for local flavor, get a scoop of macadamia-nut butter or coconut gelato, or guava, *liliko'i* (passion fruit) or lychee sorbet.

Kaua'i Culinary Market   MARKET $
(☎855-742-9545; www.theshopsatkukuiula.com; Shops at Kukui'ula, 2829 Ala Kalanikaumaka St; ⏰3:30-6pm Wed; 🚗) 🌿 An upscale take on the traditional weekly market, featuring a couple dozen local farmers and food vendors, along with live music, cooking demonstrations, and *pau hana* (happy hour) drinks in an outdoor beer and wine garden adjoining Merriman's (p202).

Living Foods
Gourmet Market & Cafe   SUPERMARKET $
(☎808-742-2323; http://shoplivingfoods.com; Shops at Kukui'ula, 2829 Ala Kalanikaumaka St; mains $10-18; ⏰7am-9pm; 🚗) 🌿 High-priced even by island standards, the often-organic, gluten-free and/or all-natural products sold here include cheeses, meats and imported wines, along with assorted local produce and artisanal foodstuffs such as Kaua'i-made juices, nuts, honey, and cookies. The cafe sells *poke* bowls, wood-fired pizzas and more.

Bubba's Burgers   BURGERS $
(www.bubbaburger.com; Shops at Kukui'ula, 2829 Ala Kalanikaumaka St; $4-12; ⏰10:30am-9pm) As its sign makes clear – 'Health Food Sucks' – Bubba's knows where it stands. Burgers are delightfully greasy, with crispy fries and grass-fed Kaua'i beef; the teriyaki burger is the pick of the menu.

The mall location maintains the beach burger shack feel of this local chain's other outlets.

Puka Dog   FAST FOOD $
(☎808-742-6044; www.pukadog.com; Po'ipu Shopping Village, 2360 Kiahuna Plantation Dr; hot dogs $8.50; ⏰10am-8pm; 🚗) More popular with tourists than with locals, these specialty hot dogs come with a toasty Hawaiian sweet bread bun, a choice of Polish sausage or veggie dog, a 'secret' sauce and tropical fruit relish (mango and pineapple, yum).

⭐ Makai Sushi   SUSHI $$
(☎808-639-7219; www.makaisushi.com; Kukui'ula Market, 2827 Po'ipu Rd; $14.50-18; ⏰11am-7pm Mon-Fri, 11am-5pm Sat & Sun) This grocery-store sushi counter keeps its menu simple with just six choices. Its *poke* bowls are wonderful, but then so are the sushi rolls. There are indoor picnic tables here, or you could always take your food to the beach.

PO'IPU & THE SOUTH SHORE PO'IPU

★Kiawe Roots   BARBECUE $$

(☑808-631-3622; www.eatatkiawe.com; Shops at Kukui'ula, 2829 Ala Kalanikaumaka St; mains $12-19; ⏰11am-9pm, from 5pm Mon & Tues) Exceptionally good value by local standards, this popular barbecue restaurant occupies an attractive upstairs dining room adorned with carved doors from Guadalajara. Whether you go for pork, wasabi pea-crusted fish, or *tinono* (the Filipino take on barbecue), it's all delicious. Unusually, you wait in line to place your order, before being shown to a table and receiving full restaurant service.

The Dolphin Poipu   HAWAIIAN $$

(☑808-742-1414; www.hanaleidolphin.com; Shops at Kukui'ula, 2829 Ala Kalanikaumaka St; sushi $18-28, mains $21-31; ⏰11:30am-3:30pm & 5:30-9:30pm) The South Shore offshoot of Hanalei's famous Dolphin (p172) has a less scenic location and does little to stand out from the Po'ipu crowd, but still makes a solid option. On the standard menu, seafood dishes are complemented by unadventurous meat and vegetarian choices, but there are plenty of more-inventive sushi and sashimi dishes.

Brennecke's Beach Broiler   AMERICAN $$

(☑808-742-7588; www.brenneckes.com; 2100 Ho'one Rd; deli sandwiches $7-12, restaurant mains lunch $16-25, dinner $21-45; ⏰deli 7am-7pm, restaurant 11am-10pm, bar 10am-close) Part sports bar, part restaurant, this local institution across from Po'ipu Beach Park (p193) claims to have served up a million mai tais, along with endless plates of ribs, steak, fresh fish, pasta, burgers and tacos for three decades.

The downstairs deli offers the only breakfast burrito or club sandwich within range of your beach towel.

Eating House 1849   HAWAIIAN $$$

(☑808-742-5000; www.eatinghouse1849.com; Shops at Kukui'ula, 2829 Ala Kalanikaumaka St; $20-50; ⏰5-9:30pm) In his Kaua'i showcase, legendary restaurateur Roy Yamaguchi offers an island-appropriate menu of 'plantation cuisine,' with six appetizers and six mains. Signature dishes like blackened ahi with soba noodles, or honey-mustard short ribs, are pitch perfect, while cheaper alternatives include a Reuben sandwich and a flavorful *poke*.

On the mall's upper level, the open-air dining room enjoys distant ocean views.

Beach House Restaurant   HAWAII REGIONAL $$$

(☑808-742-1424; www.the-beach-house.com; 5022 Lawa'i Rd; mains lunch $13-23, dinner $34-49; ⏰11am-9pm; 🍴) 🌿 A sublime oceanfront location makes Kaua'i's favorite special-occasion restaurant perfect for a romantic sunset dinner; book well in advance. Reinvigorated following a takeover by top chef Peter Merriman, its Hawaiian-fusion cuisine is beautifully prepared and presented. Lunchtime sees sandwiches, salads and daily specials; fancier dinner mains include the likes of wasabi-buttered fresh catch and coconut lobster curry.

Merriman's Fish House   HAWAII REGIONAL $$$

(☑808-742-8385; www.merrimanshawaii.com; Shops at Kukui'ula, 2829 Ala Kalanikaumaka St; Gourmet Pizza mains $10-18, Fish House mains $26-59; ⏰Gourmet Pizza 11am-9pm, Fish House 5:30-9pm) 🌿 Celebrated chef Peter Merriman runs two very different but equally good restaurants in the same plantation-style building. Upstairs the Fish House offers fine dining with long-range views, concentrating on fusion preparations of local seafood; its tasting menu costs $75 per person. Downstairs is the self-explanatory, family-friendly Gourmet Pizza & Burgers (happy hour 3:30pm to 5:30pm daily).

Plantation Gardens
Restaurant & Bar   HAWAIIAN $$$

(☑808-742-2121; http://pgrestaurant.com; Kiahuna Plantation, 2253 Po'ipu Rd; mains $19-39; ⏰5-9pm Wed-Mon) Spreading through a historic plantation house open to the ocean breezes amid tropical gardens lit by tiki-torches, this charming restaurant probably won't give you the best food of your trip, but in this lovely setting it might be your nicest evening anyway. The menu meanders from Asian-influenced seafood like marinated *monchong* to all-American pork chops and burgers.

Keoki's Paradise   HAWAII REGIONAL $$$

(☑808-742-7534; www.keokisparadise.com; Po'ipu Shopping Village, 2360 Kiahuna Plantation Dr; bar mains $14-18.50, restaurant mains $26-51; ⏰restaurant 4:45-9:15pm, bar 11am-10:30pm) Natural woods, tiki torches and water features combine to form a warm jungle lodge atmosphere. The higher-priced, dinner-only dining room offers grilled meats and seafood, while the all-day Bamboo Bar is all about tropical *pupu* (snacks) and pub grub. Throw in a great selection of draft beers and nightly live music, and Keoki's is a winner.

Red Salt
FUSION $$$

(📞808-828-8888; www.koakea.com; Koa Kea Hotel & Resort, 2251 Po'ipu Rd; mains $37-55, tasting menu $79 per person; ⊘restaurant 6:30-11am & 5-9pm, lounge 5-10:30pm) At this minimalist modern dining room, looking across the gardens to the ocean from the resort lobby, fusion dishes such as pan-seared *opah* (moonfish) with king crab and a sake-spiked coconut broth elevate the culinary game. Seafood appetizers, sushi and strong cocktails are also served in the svelte lounge. Complimentary valet parking.

Rum Fire
FUSION $$$

(📞808-742-4786; www.rumfirekauai.com; Sheraton Kaua'i Resort, 2440 Ho'onani Rd; $28-49; ⊘5:30-9:30pm Tue-Sat) Serving a mix of fusion-flavored seafood and continental cuisine at the western tip of the Sheraton (p200), the sleek Rum Fire is one of the more elegant beachfront spots on the South Shore. The large open dining room provides 180-degree views of the Pacific, while its cool blue-and-green lighting oozes cosmo-chic with little left over for island romance.

🍷 Drinking & Nightlife

Po'ipu offers the most energetic nightlife on the South Shore – but even that is severely lacking. For the liveliest atmosphere, head to the restaurants in the malls or to the biggest resorts.

★ Seaview Terrace
LOUNGE

(📞808-240-6456; http://kauai.hyatt.com; Grand Hyatt Kauai Resort & Spa, 1571 Po'ipu Rd; ⊘5:30-11am & 1-10:30pm) Don't miss Po'ipu's most memorable ocean view at the *makai* (seaward) end of the Hyatt's vast open atrium. In early evening, a torch-lighting ceremony announces sunset, and there's live Hawaiian music and hula dancing until 9:30pm (no reservations). Drinks are at premium prices, but it's still great value. In the morning, this stepped terrace is a (Starbucks) espresso cafe.

★ Anake's Juice Bar
JUICE BAR

(📞808-742-1601; www.facebook.com/anakesjuice bar; Kukui'ula Market, 2827 Po'ipu Rd; ⊘8am-4pm Mon-Fri, to 3pm Sat & Sun) The island's most creative juice bar is tucked at the back of the Kukui'ula Market grocery store. As well as great-value, piled-high acai bowls, you can pick from a mouthwatering array of fruit and/or veggie smoothies and juices, or opt for homemade kombucha or fruit-infused coconut water. There's indoor seating.

ISLAND INSIGHTS

Here's a Po'ipu secret: if you want a front-row sunset table at the iconic Beach House Restaurant but haven't reserved in time, don't worry; there's more than one way to fillet that fish. The bar-lounge has the same great view, serves the dinner menu – and you can just walk in at 5pm!

Bangkok Happy Bowl
LOUNGE

(📞808-742-9888; http://aspenthai.net/kauai-thai-food; Po'ipu Shopping Village, 2360 Kiahuna Plantation Dr; ⊘11am-9:30pm Mon, Wed & Sun, to midnight Tue, Thu & Sat, to 10pm Fri) The sushi and Thai food at this open-air Po'ipu Shopping Village eatery are passable (mains $15 to $17). This is also one of the few places hereabouts with a lively bar-lounge scene. There's live music most nights, and karaoke Thursdays are popular with locals and visitors.

☆ Entertainment

'Auli'i Luau
LUAU

(📞808-634-1499; http://auliiluau.com; Sheraton Kaua'i Resort, 2440 Ho'onani Rd; adult/teen/child 3-12yr from $119/81/57; ⊘6pm Mon & Thu Mar-Sep, 5:30pm Mon & Thu Oct-Feb) The Sheraton's luau trades above all on its superb oceanfront setting, right alongside Po'ipu Beach (p193) and timed to coincide with sunset. Otherwise, both the Polynesian revue and the dinner buffet are pretty standard. Beware: the joker emcee demands audience participation. When it rains, the luau takes place in a hotel ballroom instead – not fun.

Po'ipu Beach Athletic Club
LIVE MUSIC

(📞808-742-2111; www.poipuclub.com; 2290 Po'ipu Rd) This athletic club and pool doubles as the best concert venue on the South Shore. Salt-N-Pepa, UB40 and other superfun acts have played its open-air stage.

Grand Hyatt Kauai Luau
LUAU

(📞808-240-6456; www.hyatt.com; Grand Hyatt Kauai Resort & Spa, 1571 Po'ipu Rd; adult/teen/child from $135/108/69; ⊘5:30-8pm Thu & Sun) Despite the sterling work of its singers and dancers who make a musical journey through Polynesia, the Grand Hyatt's luau is a little lackluster, set on underlit lawns well back from the sea. Though the food may be run-of-the-mill, the bottomless beverages can't be faulted.

PO'IPU ON A BUDGET

McBryde Garden (p192) The self-guided hike here (half the price of touring adjoining Allerton Garden) lets you stroll at your own pace amid palms, orchids and rare native species.

Maha'ulepu Heritage Trail (p182) Hike Kaua'i's last accessible undeveloped coastline to see striking limestone cliffs unlike anything elsewhere in Hawaii.

Shoreline snorkeling If you don't want to pay for a boat cruise, simply wade out from the beach, and explore Po'ipu's eye-catching marine life from just beyond the shore.

Beach House Restaurant lawn (p202) If you can't afford dinner at this fine-dining icon, park yourself on the adjacent grassy knoll and enjoy the free show: blazing sunsets, lithe local surfers and an unobstructed horizon.

Kukuiolono Golf Course (p205) This neighborhood nine-hole course is welcoming, unpretentious – and costs $10.

Shopping

Malie Organics Boutique   BEAUTY, GIFTS
(✆808-339-3055; www.malie.com; Shops at Kukui'ula, 2829 Ala Kalanikaumaka St; ⊙10am-9pm) *Kukui* nuts, mangoes, coconuts and vanilla are just a few of the plant 'essences' utilized by this homegrown bath-and body-products company. It stocks Kaua'i's high-end resorts with its sprays, soaps, body creams and candles, but this is its only on-island retail outlet.

Shops at Kukui'ula   MALL
(✆808-742-9545; www.theshopsatkukuiula.com; 2829 Ala Kalanikaumaka St; ⊙10am-9pm) A cluster of plantation-style wooden buildings, this upscale shopping mall is conveniently located at the Po'ipu roundabout. As well as a dozen generally high-end restaurants and food outlets, it holds a handful of galleries, some big-name clothing boutiques – check out the classy aloha wear at Tori Richard – and a beach-rentals outlet, Po'ipu Surf (p198). There's a Longs Drugs store alongside.

National Tropical Botanical Garden Gift Shop   BOOKS, GIFTS
(✆808-742-2623; www.ntbg.org; 4425 Lawa'i Rd; ⊙8:30am-5pm) The visitor center for Allerton and McBryde gardens stocks an excellent array of books (especially nature and Hawaiiana titles), as well as quality nature-themed gifts and souvenirs.

Po'ipu Shopping Village   MALL
(✆808-742-2831; www.poipushoppingvillage.com; 2360 Kiahuna Plantation Dr; ⊙most shops 9am-9pm Mon-Sat, 10am-7pm Sun) This veteran small-scale mall holds affordable, vacation-centric shops including Honolua Surf Co for surf-style fashions; Whalers General Store for groceries and the like; and By the Sea for a huge range of 'rubbah slippahs' (flip-flops).

There are a half-dozen restaurants and takeouts here too.

ℹ Information

Clinic at Po'ipu (✆808-742-0999; http://kauai.hhsc.org; Shops at Kukui'ula, 2829 Ala Kalanikaumaka; ⊙8am-5pm Mon-Fri) Smart medical clinic, offering immediate urgent care, without an appointment, for vacation health problems ranging from rashes and injuries to colds and headaches.

Poipu Beach Resort Association (www.poipubeach.org) Go online for visitor information about Po'ipu and the South Shore, including beaches, activities, accommodations, dining, shopping and events.

ℹ Getting There & Away

Finding your way around is easy. Po'ipu and Lawa'i Rds, the two main routes, head east and west respectively from the roundabout at the Shops at Kukui'ula. It's possible to walk beside the roads, but Po'ipu is more suburbia than surf town, and to get anywhere apart from the beach you'll want a car, scooter or bike.

The Kaua'i Bus (p279) runs through Koloa into Po'ipu, stopping along Po'ipu Rd at the turnoff to Po'ipu Beach Park and also by the Hyatt. You can use it to get here from other towns, but it's little help getting around the resort area.

KALAHEO

📞 808 / POP 5100

Pass through on the highway and Kalaheo seems little more than a one-stoplight cluster of simple diners. Along the back roads, though, this neighborly town offers rolling green hills, calm serenity and peaceful accommodations away from the tourist trail.

Attractions are few up here, away from the coast. The shrines at the Lawa'i International Center are otherworldly, and you can play golf super cheap at Kukuiolono Park, but Kalaheo serves essentially as a bedroom community for the South Shore. If you plan to hike at Waimea Canyon and Koke'e state parks, while still enjoying easy access to Po'ipu and the beaches, its central location is ideal.

◉ Sights

Lawa'i International Center　　HISTORIC SITE

(📞808-639-4300; www.lawaicenter.org; 3381 Wawae Rd, Lawa'i; admission by donation; ⊙tours depart 10am, noon & 2pm, 2nd & last Sun of the month) **FREE** Open for occasional tours, this sublimely peaceful site once held a Hawaiian heiau. In 1904, however, Japanese immigrants placed 88 miniature Shingon Buddhist shrines along a steep hillside path here, symbolizing the pilgrimage shrines of Shikoku, Japan. Since the 1980s, the shrines have been beautifully restored, and a wonderful wooden temple added, the Hall of Compassion. Leisurely tours include a trail walk that amounts to a mini-pilgrimage. All welcome.

Kukuiolono Park　　PARK

(854 Pu'u Rd; ⊙6:30am-6:30pm) You're only likely to visit this little park if you're staying in Kalaheo. It's worth a quick stop to stroll through its fascinating **Hawaiian Rock Garden**, displaying rocks brought from nearby sites that were significant to pre-contact Hawaiians. The park also holds the inexpensive nine-hole Kukuiolono golf course.

🏃 Activities

Kukuiolono Golf Course　　GOLF

(📞808-332-9151; www.facebook.com/kukuiolono; Kukuiolono Park, 854 Pu'u Rd; green fees $10; ⊙dawn-dusk) This cut-price public golf course may only have nine holes, but they come with spectacular ocean and valley views, and zero attitude. It was built in 1927 by Walter McBryde (of McBryde Garden fame), who clearly loved golf: he's buried by the eighth hole. The driving range and cart and club rentals are as cheap as the green fees.

Kalaheo Yoga　　YOGA

(📞808-378-8533; www.kalaheoyoga.com; 4427 Papalina Rd; per class $22, 3-/5-class pass $60/95) A bright, harmonious yoga space one block from the highway that teaches a few classes daily, including gentle, restorative and vinyasa flow. Preregister online.

🛏 Sleeping

Boulay Inn　　APARTMENT $

(📞808-742-1120; www.boulayinn.com; 4175 'Oma'o Rd; 1-bedroom apt $90; 🖥) This airy apartment in quiet residential 'Oma'o sits atop a garage, but has its own wraparound lanai, full kitchen, high ceilings, washer-dryer and free beach gear. Fresh flowers and a breakfast basket welcome your arrival. Three-night minimum stay; cleaning fee $75.

Kalaheo Inn　　INN $

(📞808-332-6023; www.kalaheoinn.com; 4444 Papalina Rd; r $83, 1-/2-/3-bedroom ste $93/127/159; 🖥) Dependable, low-key and quiet – though thin-walled – this motel-like property is hidden away south of the highway in central Kalaheo behind a steak restaurant belonging to the same owners. Its kitchenette studios may suit budget travelers, but, although its simply furnished one- and two-bedroom suites are decent, you can do better.

Sea Kauai　　APARTMENT $

(📞808-332-9744; www.seakauai.com; 3913 Ulu Ali'i St; d $95; 🖥) A comfortable one-bedroom ground-floor suite with a full kitchen, separate living and dining areas, beds for four (one king and two twins), plus Japanese *shōji* (rice-paper sliding doors) and sunset ocean views. Free beach gear to borrow. There is a three-night minimum stay and cleaning fee $75.

★ Kaua'i Banyan Inn　　INN $$

(📞888-786-3855; www.kauaibanyan.com; 3528b Mana Hema Pl, Lawa'i; ste $175-240; 🖥) This chic inn perches on a lush Lawa'i hillside. Each of its four impeccable suites features polished hardwood floors, a kitchenette or full kitchen, a private lanai and quality furnishings, and they share a washer/dryer. The only upstairs suite, Ali'i, has the best views, up to the mountain and down to the ocean. Breakfast food provided, cleaning fee $45.

Kalaheo

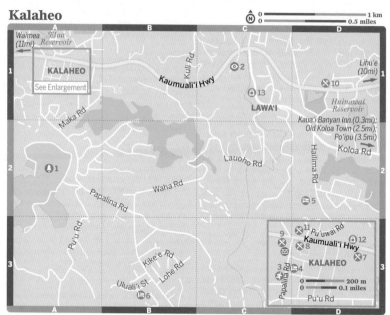

Kalaheo

◉ Sights
1 Kukuiolono Park	A2
2 Lawa'i International Center	C1

✪ Activities, Courses & Tours
3 Kalaheo Yoga	C3
Kukuiolono Golf Course	(see 1)

🛏 Sleeping
4 Kalaheo Inn	D3
5 Marjorie's Kaua'i Inn	D2
6 Sea Kauai	B3

✪ Eating
Fresh Shave	(see 13)
7 Kalaheo Café & Coffee Co	D3
8 Kalaheo Farmers Market	D3
9 Kauai Kookie Bakery & Cafe	C3
Kickshaws	(see 13)
10 Monkeypod Jam	D1
11 The Right Slice	D3

⛍ Shopping
12 Aloha XCHNG	D3
Collection at the Cafe	(see 7)
13 Warehouse 3540	C1

Marjorie's Kaua'i Inn   B&B $$

(☎ 808-332-8838; www.marjorieskauaiinn.com; 3307d Hailima St, Lawa'i; r $245-295; 🖥 🐾) After a long day's adventures, relax at this class-act B&B with a 50ft saltwater lap pool and great views over Lawa'i Valley. The three rooms are tastefully furnished (one has a hot tub), and each comes with a kitchenette and private lanai. A phenomenal breakfast is served on the upper deck.

✗ Eating

Kalaheo's restaurants are concentrated near the central crossroads.

★ Fresh Shave   DESSERTS $

(☎ 808-631-2222; www.thefreshshave.com; Warehouse 3540, 3540 Koloa Rd, Lawa'i; shave ice from $6; ⊙ 11am-5pm Mon-Sat; 🖉 🚲) 🍃 Out of a shiny vintage Aristocrat trailer comes the best shave ice on the island, made using fresh, organic ingredients such as apple bananas and coffee. Just for good measure, each menu item is named for a style of mustache!

Kickshaws   FOOD TRUCK $

(☎ 808-651-6750; www.kickshaws808.com; Warehouse 3540, 3540 Koloa Rd, Lawa'i; mains $11-15; ⊙ 11am-3pm Wed-Fri; 🖉) This gourmet food truck serves lunch three times weekly at Warehouse 3540. The changing menu features self-taught chef Seth Peterson's rich, upscale take on classics like pulled pork, fried chicken or 'colossal cauliflower' sandwiches, and tuna melts. Look out for Kickshaws at large elsewhere on Kaua'i, including Sunday evenings at the Princeville's Sunday Night Market.

Monkeypod Jam CAFE $
(☏ 808-378-4208; www.monkeypodjam.com; 2-3687 Kaumuali'i Hwy; snacks $2-7; ⊘ 7am-4pm Mon-Sat) ✐ As well as serving pastries, coffee, sandwiches and salads, this smart little roadside cafe doubles, irresistibly, as a 'Jam Tasting Room.' They buy fruit from local growers, and turn it into succulent jams and curds that you can sample and buy. A word of caution: there's no restroom.

The Right Slice PIES $
(☏ 808-212-5798; www.rightslice.com; 2-2459 Kaumuali'i Hwy; $2.50-30; ⊘ 8:30am-7pm Mon-Fri, 10am-6pm Sat, 10am-4pm Sun) This busy lime-green bakery sells takeout pies both sweet and savory, ranging from *liliko'i* cheesecake to chicken chili pot pie. You can buy anything from a tiny '*menehune*' slice to a whole pie, and they'll even pack it up and ship it to the mainland.

Kauai Kookie Bakery & Cafe CAFE $
(☏ 808-631-6851; www.kauaikookie.com; 2-2436 Kaumuali'i Hwy; mains $6-14; ⊘ 6am-8pm Mon-Fri, 6:30am-8pm Sat, 6:30am-5pm Sun) This down-home diner at Kalaheo's central crossroads caters to a largely local clientele. Along with simple but filling breakfasts, it serves Asian and island-style plate lunches including *loco moco*, plus sandwiches, *bentō* and saimin. For an even larger selection of its famous cookies, visit the factory store (p225) in Hanapepe.

Kalaheo Farmers Market MARKET $
(www.kauai.gov; Kalaheo Neighborhood Center, 4480 Papalina Rd; ⊘ 3-5pm Tue) ✐ At this straightforward, small-town produce market – one of the countywide Sunshine Markets – no shopping is allowed before the whistle blows. It had temporarily relocated to Kalawai Park (at 2541 Paniolo Dr) at the time of research.

★**Kalaheo Café & Coffee Co** CAFE $$
(☏ 808-332-5858; www.kalaheo.com; 2-2560 Kaumuali'i Hwy; mains breakfast & lunch $7-15, dinner $16-35; ⊘ 6:30am-2:30pm Mon-Sat, to 2pm Sun, 5-8:30pm Tue-Thu, to 9pm Fri & Sat) Adored by locals and visitors alike, this always-busy cafe has a spacious dining room and brews strong coffee. Order egg scrambles with grilled cornbread for breakfast or a deli sandwich (*kalua* pork with guava BBQ sauce – yum) and a salad of local greens for lunch. Weightier dinner plates include hoisin-glazed fresh catch and salt-rubbed ribs.

🛍 Shopping

★**Warehouse 3540** ARTS & CRAFTS
(www.warehouse3540.com; 3540 Koloa Rd, Lawa'i; ⊘ stores 10am-4pm Mon-Sat, market Fri 10am-2pm) A welcome boost to the island shopping scene, a world away from the big-name chains of the resorts, this converted warehouse hosts a half-dozen quirky, crafty little stores, including that of acclaimed Kaua'i fashion designer machinemachine (www.machinemachineapparel.com); Lily Koi, for boho jewelry; and Ocean Paper, selling watercolors and stationery. High-quality food trucks outside include Fresh Shave and Kickshaws.

Collection at the Cafe ARTS, GIFTS
(☏ 808-332-5858; 2-2560 Kaumuali'i Hwy; ⊘ 9am-3pm) An airy walk-through gallery alongside the Kalaheo Café, displaying ever-changing works by local artists including oil paintings, watercolors and prints, hand-crafted shell jewelry and more.

Aloha XCHNG SPORTS & OUTDOORS
(☏ 808-332-5900; www.thealohaexchange.com; 2-2535 Kaumualii Hwy; ⊘ 10am-6pm Mon-Sat, 11am-4pm Sun) This small-time Kalaheo outdoors shop stocks local branded clothing, along with a limited supply of surfboards and camping gear. Service tends to be inattentive.

ℹ Information

Kalaheo Post Office (☏ 808-332-5800; www.usps.com; 4489 Papalina Rd; ⊘ 9am-3:30pm Mon-Fri, to 11:30am Sat)

ℹ Getting There & Away

Kaua'i Bus (p279), which stops at the main intersection in town, offers connections with Lihu'e, Po'ipu and Waimea. A rental car gives much greater flexibility.

PO'IPU & THE SOUTH SHORE KALAHEO

AT A GLANCE

POPULATION
11,463

STARWATCH SPOT
Kaumakani Park
(p224)

**BEST
LOCAL BOOKSHOP**
Talk Story Bookstore
(p224)

**BEST
REMOTE BEACH**
Polihale State Park
(p235)

BEST SHOPPING
Blü Umi (p225)

WHEN TO GO
Year-round
Kaua'i's western
leeward side is
generally drier than
the island's eastern
windward side.

Jan–Mar
Tours leave from
Port Allen for whale-
watching trips
to see migrating
humpbacks.

June–Sep
The driest and best
time for hiking in the
Koke'e State Park.

Waimea Canyon State Park (p233)
MNSTUDIO/SHUTTERSTOCK ©

Waimea Canyon & the Westside

Four million years ago, a colossal earthquake almost split Kaua'i in two. The resultant chasm has yawned wider ever since, forming the Waimea Canyon. A scenic spectacle unlike any in Hawaii – astonishing for such a small island – it ranges from raw red-earth cliffs to striated peaks, and plummeting waterfalls to verdant forest. And beyond it, up on the roof of Kaua'i, remote Koke'e State Park is just as extraordinary, commanding wondrous views over the Na Pali Coast, and holding magnificent wilderness trails.

Not surprisingly, the Westside feels a world apart from the rest of Kaua'i. While it lacks plush resorts and fancy restaurants, it compensates with natural splendor and a palpable sense of Hawaiian tradition. Hanapepe evokes the plantation era while Waimea itself is redolent with history, and there's a good chance you'll hear spoken Hawaiian, spot a real-life *paniolo* (cowboy) and see shoreline fishers throwing their nets.

HIKING IN WESTERN KAUA'I

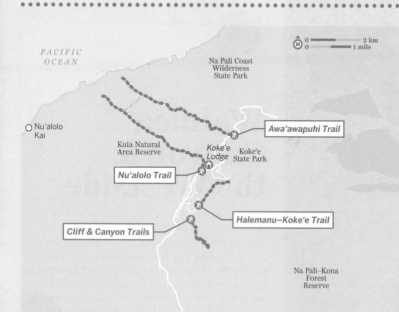

AWA'AWAPUHI & NU'ALOLO TRAILS

START KOKE'E LODGE

END KOKE'E LODGE

LENGTH 10 MILES (LOOP); EIGHT TO 10 HOURS

This stupendous full-day loop leads to two remote clifftop lookouts high above the Na Pali Coast. A wilderness route that involves substantial elevation changes and slippery terrain, with no facilities en route, it's most suitable for experienced hikers, and not recommended for under-12s.

Start from **Koke'e Lodge** (p242) – ideally before it opens, unless you fancy a pancake breakfast first. You can get a jump on your day by staying at Koke'e State Park Cabins or YWCA Camp Sloggett.

The hike begins by descending the **Nu'alolo Trail** (p240); as the steeper of the day's two major trails, it's best to go down this one and up the other. The trailhead is a few hundred feet downhill from the lodge. The early stretches are swampy, so you'll soon find out whether your fancy hiking boots really are waterproof. As you descend through thick rainforest, only occasional long-range views open up across to parallel ridges and out to the island of Ni'ihau. Eventually, though, after 3.75 miles, you emerge onto a narrow ledge that leads to **Lolo Vista Point** (p239), where you're greeted by astonishing Na Pali views.

Retrace your steps for 0.75 miles – which entails clambering up via slick muddy footholds – to join the **Nu'alolo Cliffs Trail** at a conspicuous intersection. Long renowned as terrifying, this reopened in 2017 after much-needed repairs; now it's merely scary. After 2.1 miles of winding through dense woods and head-high grass,

Home to both Waimea Canyon – the 'Grand Canyon of the Pacific' – and the forests and swamps of Koke'e State Park, atop the Na Pali Coast, Kaua'i's Westside boasts some phenomenal hiking trails.

and inching above a fearsome bare-earth abyss, it meets the **Awa'awapuhi Trail.** (p240)

Head oceanwards for 0.3 miles to reach the magnificent **Awa'awapuhi Lookout** (p238), a stark headland perched 2500ft above a sinuous valley, which in legend was carved by a slithering eel (*puhi*, in Hawaiian).

To return to Koke'e Rd, double back on the Awa'awapuhi Trail and climb for 3.1 miles. The Awa'awapuhi trailhead is 1.7 miles up the road from Koke'e Lodge, so you'll have to walk back down the highway, thumb a ride, or, if you're hiking in a group, leave a car there too.

CLIFF, CANYON & HALEMANU–KOKE'E TRAILS

START CLIFF & CANYON TRAILS TRAILHEAD

END YWCA CAMP SLOGGETT

LENGTH 4.6 MILES (ONE WAY); FIVE TO SIX HOURS

Combining several top-notch trails in Koke'e State Park, this day-long adventure will bring you closer to a towering waterfall, amazing views and plenty of feathered friends.

Start your journey early, when the birds are out and the trails still empty. If you aren't a true crack-of-dawner, stop at the **Koke'e Museum** (p239) before the hike. It has good trail descriptions, plus interesting exhibits on local flora, fauna and natural history.

From there, drive or walk to the **Cliff & Canyon Trails trailhead** (p240). Right from the start you'll get remarkable views of Waimea Canyon. The **Cliff Trail** itself is just 0.1 miles, just enough to get your heart started before you begin your descent into the canyon. Rounding the ridge, you'll hit the **Canyon Trail** – not to be confused with the entirely distinct **Waimea Canyon Trail** (p235), lower downstream. With over

1700ft of up-and-down elevation change as it dips into the upper reaches of the canyon, this one's a knee-buster. If you have problems with your joints, or it's wet, bring hiking poles or a stout stick to support you down the steeper sections.

Every step of the descent, the views are truly awesome. You're sure to spot soaring seabirds, and you might see some wild game or feral goats. Once the trail has bottomed out and climbed up the other side of the canyon, things get a little more lush and tropical.

Soon, though, you emerge on the long, exposed promontory you may already have seen from the **Pu'u Hinahina Lookout** (p234), a panoply of reds, browns and naked earth. As you pick your way along the narrow path, it's all about the grand views, sheltering Hawaiian sky and the chance to spot a perfect rainbow encircling the canyon like a warm Technicolor hug.

A half-mile or so from here, the trail doubles back on itself to reach a lookout over the valley that is nothing short of heavenly. Follow signs to **Waipo'o Falls**, but don't expect to see the actual falls; instead, you'll find a pool with some small cascades running into it. At this point, you're right at the top of the falls, but it's too dangerous to venture any lower. Stop here for lunch, enjoying the lyrical breeze and sound of falling water.

Well rested, follow the trail up to the canyon rim at **Kumuwela Lookout** (p240). From here, you backtrack most of the way. If you're tired, head directly back to the car, though otherwise it's worth taking a brief detour on the **Black Pipe Trail** (p241), which adds just another 0.5 miles to the route back to the road. Look carefully for native hibiscus and *iliau* (a plant endemic to Kaua'i's Westside).

For the second, much less demanding half of your day hike, head a few hundred feet north along the road, to the start of the **Halemanu–Koke'e Trail** (p241). This is one of the better birding trails in the park, thanks to the presence of endemic koa and ohia trees. As you hike, there's a chance you may glimpse an *apapane* or *'i'iwi* (Hawaiian honeycreepers), as well as the occasional feral chicken (no, you don't need to feed them) or lost seabird. If you're lucky enough to spot a nene (native Hawaiian goose, Hawaii's state bird), be sure not to disturb its nest. You'll also see a lot of banana *poka* plants here. These draping vines have pretty pink flowers, but are one of the most invasive species in the park. If you want to help get rid of non-native plants, consider volunteering for a day with the **Koke'e Resource Conservation Program** (p240).

The trail is pretty passable, even for families with youngsters, and ends near **YWCA Camp Sloggett** (p242). To return to your starting point, you can either hike back on the same trail, bum a ride, or hoof it along the road (an easier walk, though traffic can be burdensome). Real adventurers should consider a night at Camp Sloggett. It's as rough as you get – bring your own bedding – but waking in the morning to the sound of songbirds in this small corner of Eden is a delightful experience you won't forget.

For all these hikes, remember to bring plenty of food and water. The trails get downright nasty in rain, though the Canyon Trail is among the better options. For protection from the sun, slather on sunscreen and wear a good hat. You might also want to bring along binoculars and a bird guide.

Road to Waimea Canyon State Park (p233)

Na Pali Coast (p179)

Awa'awapuhi Trail (p211)

ROAD TRIP >
WAIMEA CANYON DRIVE

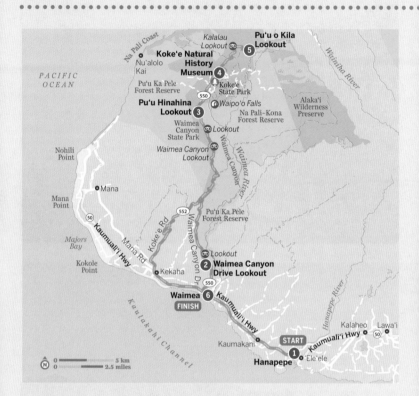

Perhaps the most iconic drive in all Hawaii, the long slow climb up Waimea Canyon takes you from the coastal flats along the rim of a magnificent mile-wide abyss, past towering, tumbling waterfalls. Eventually you come to the mysterious rainforest at the very summit of the island, and stupendous views out across the cliffs of the Na Pali Coast.

Start Hanapepe

End Waimea

Length Five to seven hours; 45 miles

❶ Hanapepe

Start your day in the funked-out arts village of **Hanapepe** (p220), with breakfast at Bobbie's or Little Fish Coffee. When you've had your fill of granola or *loco moco*, hop in the car and head westwards on the Kaumuali'i Hwy to the foot of Waimea Canyon Dr (also known as Hwy 550).

The Drive > You'll start your ascent from the coast by following the ever-winding Waimea Canyon Dr as it sweeps in sumptuous curves high above the Waimea River, climbing toward the lookouts higher up.

❷ Waimea Canyon Drive Lookout

At Mile 4.5, get out of the car to check out the unexpectedly Martian-looking waterfalls that burrow through the roadside red dirt at the first **Waimea Canyon Drive Lookout** (p234).

Now skedaddle up to the second, impossibly gorgeous **lookout** (p234) at Mile 5.5. This one offers a little bit of hiking and rock scrambling that's fun for the whole family.

The Drive > Not far up from here, Waimea Canyon Dr merges with Koke'e Rd, on which you'll continue northward to enter Waimea Canyon State Park.

❸ Pu'u Hinahina Lookout

The true majesty of Waimea Canyon comes into clearer focus at the **Waimea Canyon Lookout** (p234), near Mile 10. By now you're already 3400ft above sea level, and the yawning chasm displays a staggering palette of reds, browns and greens.

You'll soon start glimpsing the 800ft Waipo'o Falls, cascading down the far canyon wall, but for a breathtaking full-on view pull in at the **Pu'u Ka Pele Lookout** (p234), shortly before mile marker 13.

A mile further on, from the **Pu'u Hinahina Lookout** (p234), you can spot daredevil hikers on the clifftop Canyon Trail, which leads to the falls, and also access a separate viewpoint facing the island of Ni'ihau.

The Drive > Head on upward from the Pu'u Hinahina Lookout, and within a mile you'll reach Koke'e State Park.

❹ Koke'e Natural History Museum

As you enter Koke'e State Park, the landscape switches in an instant from rusted red to rainforest green. The park centers on a lush meadow, cradled in a roadside hollow at Mile 15.

Stop off to check out the historical and scientific displays at the **Koke'e Natural History Museum** (p239), and get up-to-the-minute advice on hiking trails. **Koke'e Lodge** (p242) alongside sells simple meals and supplies.

The Drive > Koke'e Rd finally comes to an end 4 miles up from the museum, at a couple of superlative lookouts.

❺ Pu'u o Kila Lookout

Up on the very roof of Kaua'i, at Mile 18, the **Kalalau Lookout** (p239) perches atop all-but-vertical green-clad cliffs. Kalalau Valley far below, the largest of the Na Pali Coast valleys, is only accessible on foot, along the legendary shoreline **Kalalau Trail** (www.dlnr.hawaii.gov/dsp/hiking/kauai/kalalau-trail).

Another mile along, the equally gorgeous **Pu'u o Kila Lookout** (p239) marks the start of the **Pihea Trail** (p240), an adventurous route where even the briefest hike brings rich rewards.

The Drive > Set off back down Koke'e Rd, allowing at least 45 minutes for the 19-mile descent to Waimea.

❻ Waimea

When you're in Waimea, stroll through the historic plantation-era downtown, head along the beach at sunset to Captain Cook's original landing site, drive inland to admire the ancient Menehune Ditch, or pick up some amazing seafood at Ishihara Market.

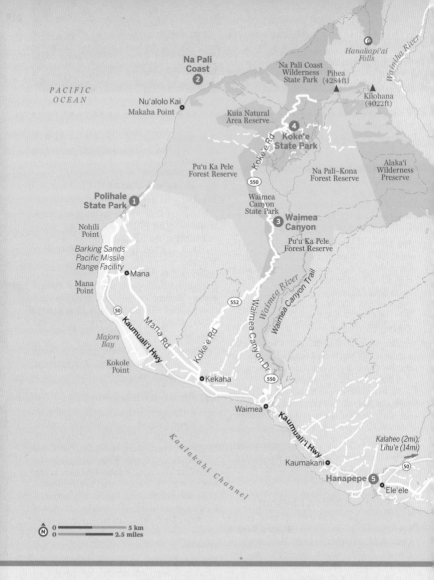

Waimea Canyon & the Westside Highlights

1 **Polihale State Park**
(p235) Pondering eternity at
the edge of the world, which
ancient Hawaiians saw as the
jumping-off point for souls
departing for the underworld.

2 **Na Pali Coast** (p217)
Taking a boat tour to zip into
sea caves, bounce over waves
and snorkel remote reefs – aah!

3 **Waimea Canyon** (p233)
Driving the jaw-dropping
canyon rim above a yawning
multicolored chasm that's
bursting with rainbows and
waterfalls.

4 **Koke'e State Park**
(p238) Swooning over views
into pristine valleys from
roadside lookouts, then lacing

up your hiking boots and
hitting the trails.

5 **Hanapepe** (p220) Feeling
groovy every Friday, when
Hanapepe's main street fills
with local artists and food
vendors for Art Night.

❶ Getting There & Away

Kaua'i Bus (p279) runs via Hanapepe and Waimea to the end of the road beyond Kekaha, but not up to Waimea Canyon.

To explore the area, you're way better off with a rental car, but bear in mind that some rental agencies forbid users to drive the dirt road to Polihale or the back roads inland.

PORT ALLEN & AROUND

Kaua'i's most important port until it was supplanted by Lihu'e a century ago, Port Allen remains an industrialized harbor. For visitors, though, it's more significant as the base for most of the island's Na Pali Coast tours, which leave from the jetty and have their offices along Wai'alo Rd, which leads down to it from the highway.

Although the little town of 'Ele'ele guards the approach to Port Allen, the small Port Allen Airport stands across the bay from the harbor, close to Salt Pond Beach (p221), and is accessed via Hanapepe.

◉ Sights

Kauai Coffee Company   FARM
(Map p188; ☎800-545-8605, 808-335-0813; http://kauaicoffee.com; 870 Halewili Rd; ⊙9am-5:30pm Jun-Aug, to 5pm Sep-May, guided walking tours 10am, noon, 2pm & 4pm) 🖉 **FREE** With more than four million trees planted on former sugar fields, Hawaii's largest coffee estate produces around 60% of the state's entire crop. In the company store, visitors can glimpse the roasting process, inspect historical photos and sample estate-grown coffees (which don't enjoy a particularly high reputation among connoisseurs). Follow a short walking trail to see trees and machinery close-up, or join a free guided tour to learn more.

You can also dive further into the brewing process on the hour-long Coffee on the Brain tour ($20; 8:30am Tuesday, Thursday & Sunday), or take a two-hour tram tour through the estate (adult/child $60/40; 9am Monday to Friday).

The farm is signposted off Kaumuali'i Hwy, 1.6 miles along Hwy 540 east of Port Allen, and 2.5 miles southwest of Kalaheo.

Glass Beach   BEACH
(Port Allen) While certainly not a swimming beach, this little cove lures visitors to pick through the well-worn debris along the shoreline. The glass hasn't come far; it's washed out to sea from an old dump nearby, shaped and rounded by the way, then returned as colorful 'pebbles' here. Whether there's anything interesting or attractive the day you come is pure luck.

To get here, simply turn left on Aka'ula St just before Port Allen wharf.

McBryde Sugar Company Cemetery   CEMETERY
(Glass Beach, Port Allen) **FREE** Recently unearthed following decades of neglect, this cemetery above Glass Beach has an impressive view. Worker camps encircled this area during the 19th-century sugar boom, and many laborers died in the tough conditions. The ornate Chinese and Japanese headstones are especially beautiful.

☞ Tours

Several companies offer similar Na Pali Coast snorkeling, sunset and dinner tours. In summer, you'd do better to take a Na Pali cruise from Hanalei or another North Shore beach; Port Allen comes into its own in winter, with whale-watching tours hugely popular. Motion sickness is especially common on Zodiac rafts, which offer little respite from the waves and sun. The journey may be less rough departing from the small boat harbor at Kikiaola, north of Waimea, instead.

★**Captain Andy's Sailing Adventures**   BOATING
(☎808-335-6833; www.napali.com; Port Allen Marina Center, 4353 Wai'alo Rd; tours adult/child 2-12yr from $149/129; 👶) High-end sailing experiences aboard the 65ft *Southern Star* catamaran, and a rugged, adrenaline-addled Zodiac tour of the sea caves and secluded beaches of the Na Pali Coast. Six-hour raft trips include a beach landing at Nu'alolo Kai (weather permitting, April to October only), along with snorkeling and easy hiking.

Blue Dolphin Charters   BOATING
(☎808-335-5553; www.bluedolphinkauai.com; Port Allen Marina Center, 4353 Wai'alo Rd; tours adult/teen/child 5-11yr from $130/120/105) This outfit offers catamaran tours including a 7½-hour Na Pali and Ni'ihau snorkel trip and a four-hour sunset dinner cruise; it also runs excursions on Zodiac rafts with hydrophones for listening to whales in winter and sport fishing charters. Uniquely, it'll take you on a one-tank dive – even if it's your first time scuba diving.

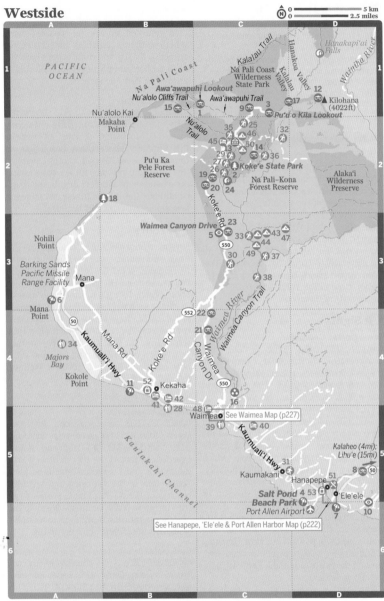

Westside

Kaua'i Sea Tours — BOATING
(☎ 800-733-7997, 808-335-5309; www.kauaisea
tours.com; Port Allen Marina Center, 4353 Wai'alo
Rd; tours adult/child 5-12yr from $125/95) Take a
seat on the 60ft catamaran *Lucky Lady* for
a snorkel or sunset dinner cruise, or clamber
aboard a rigid-hull inflatable raft for a
more adventurous Na Pali trip. In summer,
6½-hour raft tours add a beach landing
and walking tour at Nu'alolo Kai (weather
permitting, April to November), along with
sea cave and waterfall explorations.

Westside

Holo Holo Charters BOATING
(☎800-848-6130, 808-335-0815; www.holoholo charters.com; Port Allen Marina Center, 4353 Wai'alo Rd; tours adult/child 5-12yr from $139/119) Na Pali snorkeling tours and sunset sails on a 50ft sailing catamaran or rigid-hull inflatable raft. The 3½-hour sunset power-cat tour includes substantial appetizers and cocktails, while the marathon seven-hour Ni'ihau and Na Pali snorkeling combo offers continental breakfast and buffet lunch.

Catamaran Kahanu BOATING
(☎808-645-6176; www.catamarankahanu.com; Port Allen Marina Center, 4353 Wai'alo Rd; tours adult/teen/child 5-12yr from $75/69/55) This small-group catamaran affords a personal experience, whether you take a Na Pali snorkel trip, a sunset dinner or winter whale-watching cruise. The super-friendly captain and crew talk story about Hawaiian culture and marine traditions along the way.

✕ Eating

Pueo Fish Market SEAFOOD $
(☎808-320-7940; www.facebook.com/pueofish market; 2-118 Kaumuali'i Hwy; mains $5-14; ⊗5am-9pm Mon-Thu, 5am-11pm Fri, 7am-11pm Sat) Modeled on similar 'fish markets' elsewhere on Kaua'i, here with more of a fast-food slant, this barnlike roadside building is good for a quick meal. Besides good-value *poke* bowls, it offers fish specials and plate lunches, while burgers start at $5. Take your purchase to the beach, or look for the inconspicuous lanai (veranda) with distant ocean views.

WAIMEA CANYON & THE WESTSIDE PORT ALLEN & AROUND

🍸 Drinking & Nightlife

Kauai Island Brewery & Grill BREWERY
(📞 808-335-0006; www.kauaiislandbrewing.com; 4350 Wai'alo Rd; ⏰ 11am-9pm) This excellent brewpub stands just up from the jetty at Port Allen. Sample its hoppy, high-alcohol IPAs, the lauded Pakala Porter, light *liliko'i*-infused ale, or its signature Wai'ale'ale Ale (for anyone from Kaua'i that's a *really* funny joke). Drinks and decent pub grub (mains $14 to $18) are discounted during happy hour (3:30pm to 5:30pm daily).

Port Allen Sunset Grill & Bar BAR
(📞 808-335-3188; Port Allen Marina Center, 4353 Wai'alo Rd; ⏰ 11am-9:30pm) Thanks to its ocean-view patio, this laid-back harborfront bar is a great place to hang out before or after a boat tour – especially for a sunset cocktail or two. Popular food picks (mains $14 to $21) include a macnut-crusted calamari steak.

Aloha Ke Kai Espresso & Juice CAFE
(📞 808-335-6090; www.alohakekai.com; Port Allen Marina Center, 4353 Wai'alo Rd; ⏰ 6am-4pm) Tucked into an alleyway in the middle of the mall, and attached to a beachwear store, this little cafe makes a handy stop-off to grab a coffee or acai bowl before an early-morning cruise. It should still be open, serving paninis and smoothies, when you get back.

🛍️ Shopping

Kauai Chocolate Company FOOD
(📞 808-335-0448; Port Allen Marina Center, 4341 Wai'alo Rd; ⏰ 10am-6pm Mon-Sat, noon-3pm Sun) Sample fudge and truffles with creamy ganaches, mousses and delicate creams of papaya, *liliko'i*, coconut, guava, Kaua'i coffee or sugarcane. The foil-wrapped *'opihi* (limpet) is the biggest seller, followed by handmade chocolate bars chock full of macnuts.

Original Red Dirt Shirt CLOTHING
(📞 800-717-3478; www.dirtshirt.com; 4350 Wai'alo Rd; ⏰ 8am-9pm) Bearing punny slogans like 'Older than Dirt' and 'Life's Short, Play Dirty,' these shamefully touristy T-shirts can be handy for hikers, since Kaua'i's dirt longs to destroy your clothing and dye your shoes permanently red. The store has a new sideline in blue shirts, designed to evoke water.

'Ele'ele Shopping Center MALL
(Kaumuali'i Hwy) This humdrum commercial plaza, alongside Kaumuali'i Hwy at the intersection where Wai'alo Rd heads down to the harbor, is home to a Big Save supermarket, Longs Drugs and a post office.

Port Allen Marina Center MALL
(Wai'alo Rd) Stretching beside the road just before the harbor, this mall is filled with tour boat and activity operators.

ℹ️ Information

'Ele'ele Post Office (📞 808-335-5338; www.usps.com; 4485 Wai'alo Rd; ⏰ 9am-noon & 1-4pm Mon-Fri, 10am-noon Sat)

ℹ️ Getting There & Away

Port Allen is roughly 30 minutes' drive (20 miles) west of Lihu'e. Kaua'i Bus (p279) stops at the Marina Center, which is convenient for boat tours, and also at the Kauai Coffee Company.

HANAPEPE

📞 808 / POP 2650

Although sleepy, endearing little Hanapepe was not itself a plantation town, it had its heyday during Hawaii's sugar-plantation era. Nestled in a wide, red-earth valley, hemmed in by craggy cliffs and accessed by a sinuous riverside road, it was more of a farming community, and taro, a touch of cane and other crops are still grown hereabouts. In the last few decades, however, an influx of young entrepreneurs have turned Kaua'i's 'biggest little town' into what's arguably the island's hippest, most creative place. Quirk is cool, and the surf culture that's dominant elsewhere is much less prevalent. To see Hanapepe at its very best, time your visit for Friday's Art Night.

History

Hanapepe was built by entrepreneurial immigrants, largely from Asia. They were responsible for its architectural style of false fronts and porches, just as in the Old West. Many laborers who disliked working conditions on the sugar plantations, or had simply retired, came here to start small farms or businesses. So too did labor union organizers, who were forbidden to live in the plantation camps. A pitched battle between Filipino strikers and police in 1924, remembered as the Hanapepe Massacre, left 20 dead.

Kaua'i's commercial center until Lihu'e took over in the 1930s, Hanapepe then morphed into a military R&R town. After a postwar period of decline, artists began settling in and the town reinvented itself once more.

THE HANAPEPE MASSACRE

On September 9, 1924, Hanapepe was the scene of a dramatic but surprisingly little-known moment in Hawaiian history.

At the time, sugar workers throughout Hawaii were on strike, demanding a decent minimum wage, an eight-hour workday, and equal pay for men and women. Filipino workers had their own particular grievances. The last group of laborers to arrive in Hawaii, they were generally given the worst housing and lowest-paying jobs. More than half were not even considered residents.

On Kaua'i, 575 Filipino workers joined the strike and set up their headquarters in Hanapepe. After six weeks of little progress, the frustrated strikers seized two Filipinos who had not joined the strike and held them in a schoolhouse. Kaua'i deputy sheriff William Crowell arrived with 40 troops, including many trained sharpshooters, whom he positioned on a nearby hill. Crowell went in with three deputies and demanded that the strikers turn over their captives. After they did, a crowd followed Crowell from the schoolhouse, waving their cane knives in the air.

It's not clear what happened next – whether Crowell and his men were attacked, or whether the sharpshooters opened fire prematurely – but in the ensuring melee, 16 strikers were gunned down and four deputies stabbed to death. Crowell was injured, but survived. There was little public outcry and the Hanapepe Massacre disappeared into the history books. No one even knows where the strikers are buried.

Hanapepe also has a proud cinematic history: it doubled as the Australian outback in the TV miniseries *The Thorn Birds* (1983), the Filipino Olongapo City in the movie *Flight of the Intruder* (1991) and as a model for the Hawaiian town in Disney's animated *Lilo and Stitch* (2002).

◉ Sights

★ Salt Pond Beach Park   BEACH

(🏊) One of Kaua'i's safest and loveliest-looking beaches, a favorite with local families, Salt Ponds owes its off-putting name to the separate saltwater flats alongside. The beach itself is superb, a gentle crescent where swimming is sheltered by a reef that juts to either side. Stronger swimmers and snorkelers can venture through the narrow keyhole in the reef to explore the rugged coastline to the west. As ever, check conditions with the lifeguards before you set off.

Important in traditional culture, the actual salt ponds are reserved for use by Native Hawaiians only. During one month each year, in summer, they're drained and harvested for reddish-pink sodium crystals. You can't buy it anywhere, though; Hawaiian culture does not permit the sale of salt.

To get here, turn *makai* (seaward) off the highway onto Lele Rd, immediately west of Hanapepe. Facilities include outdoor showers, restrooms, picnic shelters with BBQ grills and camping. There's usually a Mexican food truck parked alongside, too.

If you ever wonder what locals get up to at a genuine Hawaiian beach party, ask the restroom attendant to explain the 'No Rubber Balloons in Restroom' sign.

Swinging Bridge   LANDMARK

First erected to span the Hanapepe River in 1911 and rebuilt after the 1992 hurricane, this wood-and-cable suspension footbridge is just three planks wide. A thrill for children especially, it swings and sways and moans with every tread – or even just in the wind.

Hanapepe Valley Lookout   VIEWPOINT

As you approach Hanapepe from the east, shortly after Mile 14, this roadside lookout offers a view deep into Hanapepe Valley, where the red-clay cliffs are topped by wild green sugarcane. First-time visitors often imagine they're seeing Waimea Canyon, but this is more of a teaser for the dramatic vistas further on.

🎆 Festivals & Events

★ Art Night   ART, FOOD

(www.hanapepe.org; ⊘ 5-9pm Fri) Hanapepe comes to life every Friday night, offering an extended peek into its art world to one and all. Stores and galleries stay open late, and Hanapepe Rd, through the historic core, is transformed by musicians and street vendors. Visitors and locals stroll, browse and snack streetside on everything from barbecue to hot, sugary donuts.

Hanapepe, 'Ele'ele & Port Allen Harbor

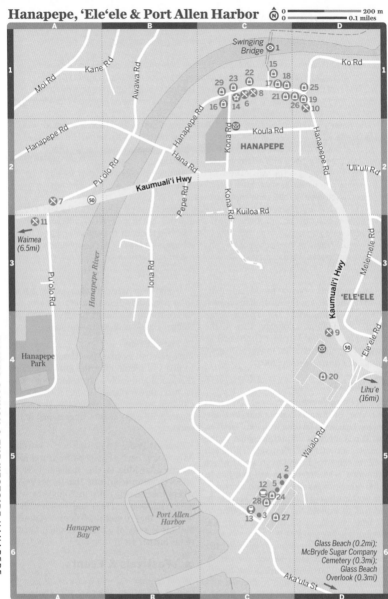

Kaua'i Chocolate & Coffee Festival FOOD & DRINK

(☏808-223-6040; www.kauaichocolateandcoffee festival.com; Hanapepe Rd; ⏱mid-Oct) Over a Friday evening and Saturday daytime, this caffeine fest sees Hanapepe Park filled with stalls and food trucks, and features tastings, demonstrations, live entertainment and farm tours.

Hanapepe, 'Ele'ele & Port Allen Harbor

✕ Eating

To find Hanapepe's best and most characterful restaurants, leave the main highway and cruise through the old center along Hanapepe Rd.

★ Taro Ko Chips Factory   HAWAIIAN $
(☑ 808-335-5586; 3940 Hanapepe Rd; per small bag $5; ☉ 8am-5pm) This tumbledown shack looks like it's been closed for decades, but find your way in through the side door for a quintessential Kaua'i experience. Somewhere inside, someone – often the farmer who grew the crop in question – is tending a deep wok filled with slivers of *kalo* (taro), sweet potato or breadfruit, seasoned with garlic salt and slathered with oil. Unforgettable!

★ Midnight Bear Breads   BAKERY $
(☑ 808-335-2893; www.midnightbearbreads.com; 3830 Hanapepe Rd; sandwiches $9-13; ☉ 6:30am-5pm Mon & Wed, 9am-5pm Thu, to 9pm Fri, to 3pm Sat) 🍞 Hands-down Kaua'i's best bakery, this small organic cafe offers everything from delicate pastries and cinnamon rolls to sourdough loaves and baguettes, and fresh-made sandwiches. Pick up a picnic en route to Waimea Canyon or drop by for a daily special like a grilled sandwich with macnut pesto and cheese.

Look for their stall at farmers markets elsewhere on the island.

Little Fish Coffee   CAFE $
(☑ 808-335-5000; www.littlefishcoffee.com; 3900 Hanapepe Rd; items $3-12; ☉ 7am-3pm; 🐾) The menu at this cute coffee shop lures customers with espresso drinks, fruit smoothies, granola bowls, homemade soups, garden salads, and bagel and panini sandwiches. Sit inside amid retro artwork and music, or in the shared, shaded courtyard out back.

Lappert's Hawaii   ICE CREAM $
(☑ 808-335-6121; www.lappertshawaii.com; 1-3555 Kaumuali'i Hwy; scoops from $5; ☉ 11:30am-5pm) Hawaii's famed ice cream chain started operations right here in 1983. Lappert's is way too big for Hanapepe-based production now, but this quaint little roadside shop is still scooping sumptuous tropical flavors such as 'Kauai Pie' (Kona coffee ice cream, chocolate fudge, macadamia nuts, coconut flakes and vanilla-cake crunch).

Hanapepe Farmers Market   MARKET $
(Hanapepe Town Park; ☉ 3-5pm Thu) 🍎 One of the county-wide Sunshine Markets. Small-scale farmers truck in the goods themselves, and locals keen to score the best produce line up before the whistle blows.

Bobbie's   HAWAIIAN $
(☑ 808-334-5152; 3824 Hanapepe Rd; meals $10-15; ☉ 10am-3pm Mon-Wed, 10am-2:30pm & 5-8pm Thu, 10am-2:30pm & 5-8:30pm Fri, 10am-2:30pm

WAIMEA CANYON & THE WESTSIDE HANAPEPE

STARGAZING

Because of minimal light pollution, Kaua'i's Westside is ideal for contemplating the night sky. **Kaua'i Education Association for Science & Astronomy** (KEASA; 808-332-7827; www.keasa.org; Kaumakani Park, Mile 18, Kaumuali'i Hwy) holds regular free 'Starwatches' in Kaumakani Park, usually on the Saturday of a new moon. From sunset onwards, educators share both gear and insights with visitors. Bring a light jacket, lawn chair, insect repellent and small flashlight, preferably covered with red cellophane.

And prepare to have your mind blown. Space: it goes on forever.

Sat) In a small storefront, this humble lunch counter makes huge plate lunches like *loco moco* and chicken *katsu* (deep-fried fillets), plus BBQ chicken and ribs a couple of nights a week. It's not good-for-you food, but it certainly tastes darn good.

Wong's Restaurant & Omoide Bakery CHINESE $
(808-335-5066; www.wongsomoide.com; 1-3543 Kaumuali'i Hwy; mains $7-16; 9:30am-9pm Tue-Sun) Part Chinese restaurant, part local bakery, this Hanapepe fixture serves up favorites from saimin (local-style noodle soup) with pork to a whole roasted duck. The best reason to stop by is the *liliko'i* chiffon pie.

★**Japanese Grandma** JAPANESE $$
(808-855-5016; www.japanesegrandma.com; 3871 Hanapepe Rd; items $9-22; 11am-3pm & 5:30-9pm) With its local take on Japanese cuisine, this smart little restaurant has earned a sky-high, island-wide reputation. The sushi is impeccable, but there's a whole lot more on the menu too, including *poke* and *bentō* bowls bursting with fresh ahi (yellowfin tuna), and *futomaki-rito*, a combination of sushi and burrito filled with shrimp or eel.

☆ Entertainment

Hanapepe may come alive every Friday for Art Night (p221), but it has no nightlife to speak of.

Storybook Theatre of Hawaii THEATER
(808-335-0712; www.storybook.org; 3814 Hanapepe Rd; 90min walking tour $12; tours depart 9:30am Tue & Thu;) The Storybook Theatre tours Hawaii with puppets who 'talk story' (chat). Schedules vary, but drop in on Art Night, when it sometimes hosts kids' activities. Book ahead to join a historical walking tour of Hanapepe (no puppets, sorry!), ending with a herbal tea in the garden.

🔒 Shopping

Hanapepe is rivaled only by Hanalei as the most enjoyable shopping destination on Kaua'i. Thanks to the substantial number of artists and craftworkers who have made their homes here, its shops and galleries – the distinction between the two is often blurred – are filled with intriguing artworks, gifts, and souvenirs.

★**Kauai Fine Arts** ART
(808-652-3274; www.kauaifinearts.us; 3751 Hanapepe Rd; 9:30am-4:30pm Mon-Thu, to 9pm Fri, 11am-4pm Sat & Sun) This rather wonderful antique art store specializes in maps and prints from the age of European Pacific exploration. Genuine lithographs by John Webber, the artist who sailed with Captain Cook, sell for thousands of dollars, but you can peruse antique and newer tiki carvings, prints of old Pan Am ads, old-world maps, vintage botanical prints and even fossilized shark teeth.

Talk Story Bookstore BOOKS
(808-335-6469; www.talkstorybookstore.com; 3785 Hanapepe Rd; 10am-5pm Sat-Thu, to 9pm Fri) The USA's westernmost bookstore is, even more crucially, the only genuine bookstore on Kaua'i. As such, it's a godsend, cramming over 100,000 (largely secondhand) books onto its shelves, along with vintage Hawaiian sheet music and vinyl records. Look for new books by local authors up front.

Aloha Spice Company GIFTS & SOUVENIRS
(808-335-5960; www.alohaspice.com; 3857 Hanapepe Rd; 10am-4:30pm Mon-Thu, to 9pm Fri, to 4pm Sat, 11am-3pm Sun) You can smell the savory, smoky goodness as soon as you step inside. In addition to local spices, this place also sells sauces and jams, lotions and oils,

nuts and chocolate, and gifts ranging from books and carved-wood figures to tea towels.

Blü Umi CLOTHING
(☑808-634-0101; www.facebook.com/bluumi hawaii; 3871 Hanapepe Rd; ⊙10am-5pm Sat-Thur, to 9pm Fri) Sharing its premises with the Japanese Grandma restaurant – some items are discounted for diners – this fancy little store has a slicker vibe than its Hanapepe neighbors. Along with tasteful women's clothing, it sells jewelry and gorgeous retro graphic prints by O'ahu artist Nick Kuchar.

JJ Ohana GIFTS & SOUVENIRS
(☑808-335-0366; www.jjohana.com; 3805b Hana-pepe Rd; ⊙8am-5pm Sat-Thur, to 9pm Fri) There can't be many places where you can find both $2.50 comfort food and a $7000 necklace. This family-run spot offers daily food specials (such as chili and rice) plus high-quality crafts like koa wood bowls, coral and abalone-shell jewelry, and Ni'ihau shell lei. Look for the Lilo and Stitch cut-out outside.

Banana Patch Studio ARTS & CRAFTS
(☑808-335-5944; www.bananapatchstudio.com; 3865 Hanapepe Rd; ⊙10am-4:30pm Mon-Thu, to 9pm Fri, to 4pm Sat, 11am-3pm Sun) Usually packed with shoppers, this large studio-cum-store creates functional, vividly colorful crafts for the home rather than fine art – koi watercolors, wooden tiki bar signs, pottery with tropical flowers, souvenir ceramic tiles and coasters.

Bright Side Gallery ARTS & CRAFTS
(☑808-634-8671; www.thebrightsidegallery.com; 3890 Hanapepe Rd; ⊙11am-4pm Mon-Fri, plus 6-9pm Fri) Representing both island and US mainland artists, this fun, whimsical space never takes itself too seriously. Surf themes show up in many of the oils, acrylics and giclées, though it's the wood carvings that really steal the show.

Island Art Gallery ART
(☑808-335-0591; www.islandartkauai.com; 3876 Hanapepe Rd; ⊙10:30am-5pm Mon-Sat, to 9pm Fri) Contemporary Hawaiian art including reverse acrylic paintings and giclée prints on wood and metal that are luminous blends of color, along with a few baubles, bracelets and foodstuffs.

Jacqueline on Kaua'i CLOTHING
(☑808-335-5797; www.facebook.com/jaqueline onkauai; 3837 Hanapepe Rd; custom shirts $60-200; ⊙9am-6pm Mon-Thu, Sat & Sun, to 9pm Fri) Friendly Jacqueline makes bespoke aloha shirts while you wait (usually one to two hours), including children's sizes, with coconut buttons no less. You choose the fabric and she does the rest. Place an order at the start of Art Night (p221) and you're good to go by the end.

Lu.La CLOTHING
(☑808-855-0215; www.hanapepe.org/lula; 3900 Hanapepe Rd; ⊙10:30am-5pm Mon-Sat, to 9pm Fri) Run by the owners of the neighboring Island Art Gallery, this appealing gallery specializes in island-styled women's cloth-ing, including Becky J Wold's original marbled silk scarves and sarongs.

Salty Wahine FOOD
(☑808-378-4089; http://saltywahine.com; 1-3529 Kaumuali'i Hwy; ⊙9am-5pm) This roadside shop is a smorgasbord of salt and spice blends, with island flavors from herbs to fruit. 'Black Lava' and kiawe (Hawaiian mesquite) sea salt, coconut-infused cane sugar and li hing mui (dried plum) margarita salt are bestsellers. The salt used doesn't come from Kaua'i, incidentally.

You can find their products cheaper in island grocery stores.

Amy-Lauren's Gallery ART
(☑808-634-8660; www.amylaurensgallery.com; 4545 Kona Rd; ⊙11am-5pm Mon-Thu, to 9pm Fri, noon-5pm Sat) Here's a chance to buy (or at least gaze upon) an original instead of a giclée print. This boutique gallery beckons browsers with vibrantly colored oil paintings, photography, and mixed media.

Kauai Kookie Company FOOD
(☑808-335-5003; www.kauaikookie.com; 1-3529 Kaumuali'i Hwy; ⊙8am-5pm Mon-Fri, from 10am Sat & Sun) Some say it's more novelty than delicious, but Kauai Kookie has a devoted local following. Classic tastes sold at the factory shop include Kona coffee and chocolate chip–macadamia nut.

❶ Information

American Savings Bank (☑808-335-3118; www.asbhawaii.com; 4548 Kona Rd; ⊙8am-5pm Mon-Thu, to 6pm Fri) Has a 24-hour ATM.

WAIMEA CANYON & THE WESTSIDE HANAPEPE

Bank of Hawaii (☑ 808-335-5021; www.boh.com; 3764 Hanapepe Rd; ☺ 8:30am-4pm Mon-Thu, to 6pm Fri) Has a 24-hour ATM.

Hanapepe Post Office (☑ 808-335-5433; www.usps.com; 3817 Kona Rd; ☺ 9am-1:30pm & 2-4pm Mon-Fri)

🛈 Getting There & Away

As you drive into Hanapepe, coming from points east, turn *mauka* (inland) off Kaumuali'i Hwy to reach Hanapepe Rd, the main drag. Kaua'i Bus (p279) stops where Kaumuali'i Hwy meets Kona Rd.

WAIMEA

☑ 808 / POP 1855

Kaua'i's Waimea may be less well known than the other Waimeas in Hawaii – O'ahu's legendary surf spot, and the Big Island's upscale cowboy town – but it's every bit as intriguing. The original landing spot of Captain Cook remains the jumping-off point for visiting spectacular Waimea Canyon and Koke'e state parks.

Waimea means 'reddish-brown water,' referring to the river that washes rich red earth from the namesake canyon to color the ocean a deep brown. Sugar plantations brought the town prosperity, and the skeleton of the long-defunct old mill still stands amid the tech centers that house defense contractors working at the nearby Pacific Missile Range, along with an even more controversial presence: multinational chemical companies that develop genetically modified seeds for worldwide crop cultivation.

While many itineraries skip the town, there's enough history here, plus a decent beach for walking, to make Waimea a fun afternoon adventure.

⊙ Sights

Russian Fort Elizabeth
State Historical Park   HISTORIC SITE
(www.fortelizabeth.org; off Kaumuali'i Hwy; ☺ dawn-dusk) **FREE** A Russian fort in Hawaii? Yes, really. Constructed in 1817 above the southern bank of the mouth of Waimea River on the site of an ancient heiau (temple), the octagonal Fort Elizabeth was named after the Empress of Russia. Only its impressive outer walls, some 20ft high, are still standing. It once harbored a Russian Orthodox chapel and a cannon.

Follow the trail 100 yards beyond the fort to reach a pretty riverfront beach. While not suitable for swimming, it makes for a pleasant afternoon stroll.

Menehune Ditch   ARCHAEOLOGICAL SITE
(Kikiaola; Menehune Rd) Little is now visible of Hawaii's most remarkable example of pre-contact cut-and-dressed stonework, supposedly constructed within a single night by the *menehune*, or 'little people.' A seven-mile aqueduct that channeled water from the Waimea River to ancient agricultural sites, it was described by Captain Vancouver in 1793 as standing 24ft tall, with its top serving as a pathway into Waimea Canyon. Only a short masonry wall survives; the rest is said to remain intact beneath the modern road.

To get here, follow Menehune Rd inland from Kaumuali'i Hwy for almost 1.5 miles to a footbridge across the Waimea River, and look for the interpretive signboard opposite.

West Kaua'i
Technology & Visitor Center   MUSEUM
(☑ 808-338-1332; www.westkauaivisitorcenter.org; 9565 Kaumuali'i Hwy; ☺ 10am-4pm Mon, Tue, Thu & Fri) **FREE** Waimea's friendly visitor center holds modest but interesting exhibits on Hawaiian culture, Captain Cook, sugar plantations and the US military. Its gift shop sells local artisan crafts, including rare Ni'ihau shell lei.

Waimea State Recreational Pier   BEACH
(www.hawaiistateparks.org; La'au Rd) Flecked with microscopic green crystals called olivine, this wide, dark-tinged beach stretches between two scenic rock outcroppings and is bisected by the eponymous fishing pier. It's especially beautiful at sunset. Facilities include restrooms, picnic areas and drinking water.

Waimea Hawaiian Church   CHURCH
(4491 Halepule Rd; ☺ services 9am Sun) Sunday's Hawaiian-language mass at this simple low-slung church makes an interesting way to connect with local culture. Waimea's first Christian missionaries arrived in 1820. This church is a century-old replica of one built by Reverend George Rowell in 1865, after a bitter theological dispute had obliged him to leave the nearby United Church of Christ.

Waimea

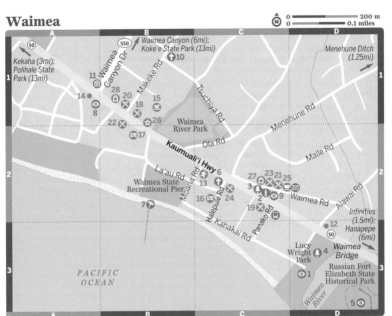

N 0 ———————— 200 m
   0 ———————— 0.1 miles

Waimea

Captain Cook Monument MONUMENT
(Hofgaard Park, cnr Waimea Rd & Kaumuali'i Hwy)
A statue of Captain James Cook stands on
Waimea's central green space. When his
ships *Resolution* and *Discovery* sailed into
Waimea Bay in January 1778, Cook changed
the course of world history.

This likeness is a replica of an original by
Sir John Tweed in his home town of Whitby,
northern England.

THE COMING OF CAPTAIN COOK

English navigator Captain James Cook was on his third voyage of Pacific exploration when he chanced upon Kaua'i in 1778. Cook was sailing north, hoping to discover the fabled Northwest Passage back to the Atlantic, but the Hawaiian islands had such obvious strategic importance that he decided to investigate and reprovision his ships, the *Resolution* and the *Discovery*.

When local canoeists came on board, Cook reported that 'I never saw Indians so much astonished at entering a ship before.' He in turn was astonished to find they shared the same Polynesian culture he had encountered thousands of miles south. After Cook went ashore at the rivermouth on January 20, where he was greeted by several hundred prostrated islanders, a brisk trade arose. Hawaiians obtained iron – which, surprisingly, they seemed to have seen before – in return for food and supplies.

The English ships struggled to remain at anchor in Kaua'i's winter surf. Within three days they were washed across to Ni'ihau, and they soon departed for points north. Cook returned to Hawaii the next year and met his death on the Big Island. Waimea was soon to see more European ships; the first fur traders arrived in 1786, and sandalwood merchants followed five years later.

Until Cook's visit, Hawaiians had lived in a natural world inseparable from the spiritual realm, while Cook embodied a culture in which God ruled heaven and men walked the earth. In some ways those two worldviews continue to collide to this day.

Lucy Wright Park   PARK

It's a telling reflection of how locals feel about Captain Cook that the beach where he first landed is named not for Cook but for Waimea's first Native Hawaiian teacher. This small riverfront park holds picnic tables, restrooms and outdoor showers.

Camping is permitted on the flat grassy area, but it's not a very appealing spot.

Waimea Town Center   ARCHITECTURE

Waimea's plantation-era core offers some interesting architecture. Take a short stroll to admire the neoclassical First Hawaiian Bank (p231; 1929), the art-deco Waimea Theater (p231; 1938) and the historic, restored Waimea United Church of Christ with its distinctive covering of coral.

Waimea United Church of Christ   CHURCH

(☑808-338-9962; www.waimeachurch.org; 4080 Makeke Rd; ☺Sun service 10am) What's now the Waimea United Church of Christ was originally erected in 1847 by Reverend George Rowell. Protestant missionaries had lived in Waimea for over 20 years by then, but the previous church on this site had collapsed. Rowell built its replacement using limestone and ohia wood from Koke'e, and clad it in crushed coral brought up by Native Hawaiian divers. Destroyed by Hurricane 'Iniki, it was faithfully reconstructed in the 1990s.

Hofgaard Park   PARK

This small grassy park at Waimea's main intersection holds a statue of Captain Cook. Display panels explain local history.

Waimea Sugar Mill   FACTORY

(9630 Kaumuali'i Hwy) **FREE** The evocative skeleton of this 19th-century sugar mill still looms over Waimea. Pumping out sugar from the Westside, it fueled Kaua'i's economy until 1945. Successive waves of immigrants from Germany, England, China, Norway and beyond toiled here. A good spot for a picnic, it makes an evocative backdrop to the Menehune Products Fair (p231).

Captain Cook Landing Site   LANDMARK

(Lucy Wright Park) The precise spot where Captain Cook first set foot on Hawaiian soil being unknown, a large boulder near the mouth of Waimea River was arbitrarily chosen to hold a commemorative plaque. That plaque was stolen several years ago, presumably by locals reluctant to celebrate Cook's impact, so there's nothing to see.

🏃 Activities

Waimea Rivermouth   SURFING

This river break takes you both right and left; southern swells work best. Expect it to be crowded. And since it's a river break, expect the water to be dirty.

Waimea Swimming Pool   SWIMMING
(☑ 808-338-1271; www.kauai.gov; 9678 Haiki Rd; ⊙ 7:30am-9:30pm Tue-Fri, 10am-11pm Sat, noon-4:30pm Sun) A county-run public pool tucked away behind the Waimea Theater.

Tours

Taking a Na Pali Coast cruise from Kikiaola Small Boat Harbor, north of Waimea, should spare exposure to the rougher seas you may encounter if you sail from Port Allen.

Na Pali Riders   BOATING
(☑ 808-742-6331; www.napaliriders.com; 9600 Kaumuali'i Hwy; 4hr tour adult/child 5-12yr $149/129) Get a first-hand peek at sea caves (weather permitting) on Captain Chris Turner's Zodiac raft tour. Warning: it's a high-speed, no-shade, bumpy ride that's not for the faint of heart. Morning and afternoon departures available. Cash discounts.

Na Pali Explorer   BOATING
(☑ 808-338-9999; www.napaliexplorer.com; 9814 Kaumuali'i Hwy; standard tour adult/child $149/129, beach landing $187/175) This Westside shop does it right, with small raft tours. You can choose whether to beach and hike to an ancient village, or go for the rip-roaring experience aboard a rigid-hull inflatable that at least has a canopy.

Liko Kaua'i Cruises   BOATING
(☑ 808-338-0333; www.liko-kauai.com; 4516 Alawai Rd; 5hr cruise adult/child 4-12yr $149/109) This outfit sails to the Na Pali Coast in a 49ft power catamaran with shade canopy and forward-facing padded seats. Snorkel gear provided. In summer, tours go all the way

to Ke'e Beach. Liko himself is a Kaua'i-born-and-raised Hawaiian whose ancestors hailed from Ni'ihau.

Festivals & Events

★ **Waimea Town Celebration**   CULTURAL
(www.waimeatowncelebration.com; ⊙ mid-Feb; ⛶) 🆓 Spread over two weekends and the week between, the fun includes a *paniolo* rodeo; hula perfor-mances; storytelling; canoe, SUP and surf-skiing races; food vendors; film screenings; carnival games; an arts-and-crafts fair; and lei-making and ukulele-playing contests.

Sleeping

Coco's Kaua'i   B&B $
(☑ 808-639-1109, 808-338-0722; www.cocoskauai.com; btwn Miles 21 & 22, Kaumuali'i Hwy, Makaweli; r $139; 🐾) Glorious rural accommodations in the large guest room of a private home, kitchenette-equipped and facing across a huge meadow with fruit trees. Breakfast is optional, at $20 for two, and features eggs from their own chickens. Sit out on the patio in the evening; once the sun goes down, the night sky is a revelation for city-dwellers.

Waimea Inn   INN $
(☑ 808-652-6852; www.westkauailodging.com; 4469 Halepule Rd; r from $129, cottage $249; 🐾) This central inn feels like a much-loved family summer house that has welcomed many generations. Suites feature claw-foot tubs and other vintage-style furnishings, while the king-bedded Taro Room is ADA-compliant with a roll-in shower. They also rent out a quaint two-bedroom cottage nearby.

RUSSIAN FORT ELIZABETH

So how did the Russians end up with a fort (p226) on Kaua'i? At the start of the 19th century, the Russian American Company in Sitka, Alaska, sought to open trade with Hawaii and secure food for its settlements. They sent several ships, one of which was wrecked in Waimea in 1815. Another, led by the wily Georg Anton Schäffer, was sent to recover the cargo and set up a permanent trading post. Schäffer signed an agreement with King Kaumuali'i of Kaua'i granting the Russians certain trading rights.

After failing to win assistance from King Kamehameha on the Big Island, Schäffer tried to persuade the already rebellious Kaumuali'i to turn against Kamehameha under Russian protection.

Construction of three forts followed, two in Hanalei and one commanding the river in Waimea. Fort Elizabeth was the largest, equipped with cannon, barracks, a trading house, gardens, homes for 30 families and a Russian Orthodox chapel. The fort was not yet complete, however, when allegiances shifted decisively against the high-handed Schäffer. Acting on Kamehameha's request, Kaumuali'i expelled the entire Russian contingent, and Fort Elizabeth was taken over by the kingdom of Hawaii.

WAIMEA CANYON & THE WESTSIDE WAIMEA

West Inn

INN $$

(☎808-338-1107; www.thewestinn.com; 9690 Kaumauli'i Hwy; r from $198; ❄❄) Across from Waimea Theater, this has the look of a budget motel, but its spacious rooms are better than you might expect, with high ceilings, quality mattresses, granite countertops, microwaves and mini-refrigerators. More expensive suites have full kitchens. The decor is bright but uninspiring, though, and rates are comparatively high.

★Waimea Plantation Cottages

INN $$$

(☎800-716-6199, 808-338-1625; www.waimea plantation.com; 9400 Kaumauli'i Hwy; 1-bedroom $261-286, 2-bedroom $321-351, 3-bedroom $381-411; ❄❄❄) If you're planning to stay in Waimea, this is the prime spot. These rebuilt plantation cottages from the 1930s and 1940s once housed sugarcane laborers. The 57 tin-roofed, clapboard, pastel-painted sweethearts with wide porches and rattan seating are scattered over a wide lawn, studded with golden bamboo, swaying coconut groves and banyans.

Larger cottages are close enough to catch ocean views and breezes. The golden-sand beach here is great for walking, less so for swimming. Oceanside yoga classes, massages and spa services available.

✖ Eating

While Waimea may not have any fancy restaurants – that's not the Westside way – you can certainly sample pretty much any local cuisine here, including items at Ishihara's you may never have seen anywhere else.

★Ishihara Market

SUPERMARKET, DELI $

(☎808-338-1751; 9894 Kaumauli'i Hwy; ⊙6am-7:30pm Mon-Thu, to 8pm Fri & Sat, to 7pm Sun) The eye-popping deli counter at this famed Japanese supermarket is guaranteed to revive even the most jaded palate. With local favorites like kimchi sea snails, you're free to try before you buy. Daily specials usually include spicy ahi *poke* and smoked marlin, while marinated ready-to-barbecue meat and fish are always available.

Porky's

BARBECUE $

(☎808-631-3071; www.porkyskauai.com; 9899 Waimea Rd; mains $11; ⊙11am-4pm Mon-Fri, to 3pm Sat) Promising 'aloha in a bun,' this much-loved little town-center diner keeps things simple. Everyone's here for the juicy pulled pork, served on rice, in a grilled-cheese sandwich or in the signature bun.

Chicken in a Barrel

BARBECUE $

(☎808-320-8397; www.chickeninabarrel.com; Waimea Plantation Cottages, 9400 Kaumauli'i Hwy; meals $11-18; ⊙8am-9pm; ❄) This roomy and rather lovely wood-built bar/restaurant has been through various incarnations over the years, including stints as a fine-dining haven and then a microbrewery. It now makes a classy venue for this popular local chain, which sells tacos and burritos as well as its trademark barbecue chicken.

G's Juicebar

HEALTH FOOD $

(☎808-639-8785; 9691 Kaumauli'i Hwy; snacks from $8; ⊙9am-4:30pm Mon-Fri, 9am-3pm Sat; ❄) Your quest for Kaua'i's top acai bowl might reach the finish line right here. A Marley Bowl comes with hemp seed, kale and bee pollen, and the Avatar with rice milk, blueberries and shaved coconut. Fresh tropical fruit smoothies and yerba maté tea will quench your thirst.

Super Duper Two

ICE CREAM $

(☎808-338-1590; 9889 Waimea Rd; snacks from $3; ⊙noon-9pm Sun-Thu, to 10pm Fri & Sat) This place lives up to its moniker. Stop in for tropically flavored shakes, sundaes, or old-fashioned scoops of Maui-made Roselani ice cream in crispy handmade waffle cones.

Gina's Anykine Grinds Cafe

DINER $

(☎808-338-1731; http://ginasanykinegrindscafehi. com; 9691 Kaumauli'i Hwy; mains $5-10; ⊙7am-2:30pm Tue-Thu, 7am-1pm & 6-8pm Fri, 8am-1pm Sat) 'Friendly, filling, and reasonably priced' sums up this local institution, formerly known as Yumi's, where you can get a plate lunch with chicken *katsu* or teriyaki beef, or special saimin. Be sure to order a slice of coconut pie or the pumpkin crunch for dessert.

Jo-Jo's Anuenue
Shave Ice & Treats

DESSERTS $

(www.facebook.com/jojos.anuenue; 9899 Waimea Rd; snacks from $3; ⊙10am-5:30pm; ❄) This shack delivers icy flavor: all syrups are homemade without additives and won't knock you out with sweetness. The superstar is the *halo halo* (Filipino-style mixed fruit).

Island Taco

MEXICAN $

(☎808-338-9895; www.islandfishtaco.com; 9643 Kaumauli'i Hwy; mains $6-14; ⊙11am-5pm) Tortillas at this island fusion taqueria are stuffed with wasabi-coated or Cajun-dusted seared ahi, fresh cabbage and rice. Wet burritos and taco salads round out the menu. It's a local chain, but still feels pretty boutique in its approach.

Shrimp Station   SEAFOOD $
(☑808-338-1242; www.theshrimpstation.net; 9652 Kaumuali'i Hwy; mains $8-13; ☺11am-5pm; 🚻) Craving shrimp? Whether sautéed scampi-style, coconut- or beer-battered, in taco form or ground up into a 'shrimp burger,' crustaceans are what this roadside chow hut is all about. Look for the flamingo-pink sign out front.

Wrangler's Steakhouse   STEAK $$
(☑808-338-1218; www.wranglerssteakhousehi. com; 9852 Kaumuali'i Hwy; mains lunch $10-17, dinner $18-35; ☺11am-8:30pm Mon-Thu, 11am-9pm Fri, 5-9pm Sat; 🚻) Yes, it's touristy, but this Western-style saloon dishes up plantation lunches in authentic *kaukau* (food) tins full of shrimp and vegetable tempura, teriyaki steak, rice and kimchi. Sizzling dinner steaks are decent – the seafood and soup-and-salad bar less so. Opt for atmospheric seating on the front lanai or back porch, and save room for peach cobbler.

🍷 Drinking & Nightlife

Aloha-n-Paradise   COFFEE
(☑808-338-1522; www.aloha-n-paradise.com; 9905 Waimea Rd; ☺7am-noon Mon-Sat; 📶) Watch Waimea's world go by from the spacious front porch of this ramshackle plantation-era building facing the town park. Inside, a large gallery-lounge has island art on the walls and comfy sofas; the espresso bar, tucked in the back, sells coffee, muffins and a $5 cereal bar. The wi-fi remains on when the cafe is closed.

☆ Entertainment

Waimea Theater   CINEMA
(☑808-338-0282; www.waimeatheater.com; 9691 Kaumuali'i Hwy; adult/child 5-10yr $9/7) This art-deco movie theater is the place for a rainy day or for an early-evening reprieve from sun and sea. Kaua'i is a little behind with new releases and schedules are erratic, but there are only two functioning cinemas on the island (the other is in Lihu'e), so no one's complaining.

🛍 Shopping

Kaua'i Granola   FOOD
(☑808-338-0121; 9633 Kaumuali'i Hwy; ☺10am-5pm Mon-Sat) Drop by this island bakery on your way up to Waimea Canyon, for snacks like trail mix, macadamia-nut cookies or chocolate-dipped coconut macaroons; their signature tropically flavored granola is sold across the island.

Aunty Lilikoi
Passion Fruit Products   FOOD, GIFTS
(☑866-545-4564, 808-338-1296; www.auntylilikoi. com; 9875 Waimea Rd; ☺10am-6pm) Find something for almost any occasion: award-winning passion fruit–wasabi mustard, passion fruit syrup, or massage oil, all made with at least a kiss of, you guessed it, *liliko'i*.

Menehune Products Fair   ARTS & CRAFTS
(9630 Kaumuali'i Hwy; ☺11am-3pm Tue-Sat) Browse crafts stalls, sample BBQ chicken or just talk story at this home-spun fair alongside the old sugar mill. Some days there won't be many vendors, but it's a fun stop and a chance to see craftspeople at work.

❶ Information

First Hawaiian Bank (☑808-338-1611; www. fhb.com; 4525 Panako Rd; ☺8:30am-4pm Mon-Thu, to 6pm Fri) Has a 24-hour ATM.

Kauai Veterans Memorial Hospital (☑808-338-9431; http://kauai.hhsc.org; 4643 Waimea Canyon Dr) With 24-hour emergency services.

Waimea Public Library (☑808-338-6848; 9750 Kaumuali'i Hwy; ☺noon-8pm Mon & Wed, 9am-5pm Tue & Thu, 10am-5pm Fri; 📶) Free wi-fi; online computer terminals available with temporary nonresident library card ($10).

❶ Getting There & Away

Waimea is easily reached by rental car and served by Kaua'i Bus (p279). There's no public transportation up to the state parks, however.

KEKAHA
☑808 / POP 3600

The former working-class sugar town of Kekaha is now home to many military families. There's no town center here and no services to speak of, but Kekaha Beach Park offers one of the most beautiful sunsets on the island. If you're looking for a scenic beach near the base of Waimea Canyon, staying here is an option.

◉ Sights & Activities

Kekaha Beach Park   BEACH
The Westside is renowned for its unrelenting sun and vast beaches. At the west end of Kekaha town, this long stretch of sand is best for beachcombing and catching sunsets. It lacks reef protection so check with a lifeguard whether it's OK to swim before you jump in. The currents are extremely dangerous in high surf, but under

WAIMEA CANYON & THE WESTSIDE KEKAHA

NU'ALOLO KAI: A LAST PARADISE?

On the remote, rugged Na Pali Coast and accessible only from the sea, Nu'alolo Kai is perhaps the ultimate end-of-the-earth location. Its beach is trapped between two soaring cliffs, framing an empty ocean that goes on for thousands of miles. The site is blessed by a fringing reef that is teeming with fish and shellfish.

Nu'alolo Kai was once linked by a precarious cliffside path to Nu'alolo 'Aina, a terraced valley whose fertile soil was planted with taro and whose walls held burial caves. This isolated paradise was inhabited by about 100 people for 600 years, until 1919. They lived in thatched pole houses, commuting between reef and fields, completely self-sufficient. Men did most of the fishing, while women and children harvested seaweed and shellfish. They weren't entirely cut off from the rest of the island, however. A trail, long since washed away, led here from Koke'e, while their beach was the safest stop for Hawaiians canoeing between Hanalei and Waimea.

All that survives today are the stone foundations of various structures. To help preserve Nu'alolo Kai, just three companies have landing rights: Kaua'i Sea Tours (p218) and Captain Andy's Sailing Adventures (p217) provide guided tours of the archaeological site, while Waimea-based Na Pali Explorer (p229) only lands on the beach. Weather usually restricts boat landings to between mid-April and late October only.

the right conditions it's good for surfing and bodyboarding. Facilities include outdoor showers, restrooms and picnic tables.

Barking Sands Beach   BEACH
Between Kekaha Beach Park and Polihale State Park, the Westside's biggest beach stretches for around 15 miles. Much of it is taken up by the US Navy's **Barking Sands Pacific Missile Range Facility**, which is closed to the public.

Davidson Point   SURFING
This exposed reef break works all year-round. It gets going with offshore winds from the northeast, and it's best suited for strong intermediate and advanced riders. Be careful of rips.

Major's Bay   SURFING
Steep point break with a nearby beach break that offers mostly rights. Make sure you don't intrude on the military base.

🛏 Sleeping

Although Kekaha is way off the tourist track, it has dozens of beautiful homes and condos – many with ocean views – available for short- and long-term rentals. They tend to be much cheaper here, largely because there are no restaurants or shops hereabouts.

Kekaha Oceanside   ACCOMMODATIONS SERVICES $
(☎808-337-1149, 800-351-4609; www.kekaha oceansidekauai.com; rental homes from $140) This fine collection of vacation rental homes and

cottages in and around Kekaha ranges from simple backstreet residences to gorgeously renovated beachfront properties.

Hale Makai   RENTAL HOUSE $$
(☎760-492-7583; www.vrbo.com/135835; 4635 Palila Loop; 2-bedroom house from $210; ❀🖤) Children are welcome at this house a short walk from the beach. Polished wooden floors, a full kitchen, two en-suite bedrooms, a screened-in lanai and a private hot tub are among welcome amenities. Minimum four-night stay. Cleaning and reservation fees $150.

Hale La   RENTAL HOUSE $$$
(☎808-652-6852; www.kekahakauaisunset.com; 8240a Elepaio Rd; 5-bedroom house $595; ❀🖤) Rented in its entirety, this green-painted oceanfront house offers three suites with cherrywood and bamboo furnishings, and two with private lanai and ocean views. Watch whales off the beach in winter. Three-night minimum stay. Cleaning fee $395.

🛍 Shopping

Kekaha Farmers Market   MARKET
(www.kauai.gov; Kekaha Neighborhood Center, 8130 Elepaio Rd; ⊙9-10am Sat) A handful of local farmers and flower growers gather just off Kaumuali'i Hwy every Saturday morning.

ⓘ Getting There & Away

Just east of Kekaha, near Kikiaola Small Boat Harbor, Kekaha Rd branches away from the coastal Kaumuali'i Hwy to run parallel and a few blocks inland. It holds little more than a post office and a couple of tiny stores, but it's the route followed by the Kaua'i Bus (p279).

WAIMEA CANYON STATE PARK

Of all Kaua'i's wonders, none can touch Waimea Canyon for grandeur. Few would expect the island to hold such a gargantuan abyss of lava rock; popularly known as 'the Grand Canyon of the Pacific,' it's 10 miles long and over 3500ft deep. Waimea River flows through it, fed by tributaries that flush reddish-brown waters from the mountaintop plateau that cradles the Alaka'i Swamp.

Waimea Canyon was created when Kaua'i's original shield volcano, Wai'ale'ale, slumped along an ancient fault line. The horizontal striations along its walls represent successive volcanic eruptions. The red colors indicate where water has seeped through the rocks, draining mineral rust from the iron ore inside.

On a clear day, driving the one road up the canyon's western flank is phenomenal. Don't be disappointed by rain; that's what makes the waterfalls gush. Sunny days following rain are ideal for prime views, though slick mud makes hiking challenging.

◉ Sights

★ **Waimea Canyon Drive**   NATURAL FEATURE
(Hwy 550) This magnificent scenic drive traces the entire length of Waimea Canyon's western rim and continues into Koke'e State Park, climbing 19 miles from the coast to Pu'u o Kila Lookout. Starting from Waimea's visitor center as Waimea Canyon Dr, it meets Koke'e Rd after 8 miles, and takes its name. Scenic lookouts along the way offer superb views – plus restrooms and the occasional food truck – and several have short hiking trails too, but there are no gas stations.

Come first thing in the morning and you can beat the crowds by driving straight to the far end of the road, then visiting the lookouts in reverse order as you descend.

WAIMEA CANYON & THE WESTSIDE IN...

Two Days

Make it your first priority to drive up Rte 550. Stop at the stunning lookouts into Waimea Canyon (p233) en route, and keep going all the way to Pu'u o Kila in Koke'e State Park (p238), at the top. Drop in at Koke'e Natural History Museum (p239), where you can also plan a hike for day three.

Head back down to plantation-era Hanapepe (p220), for lunch at Japanese Grandma (p224). Then stroll the main street for souvenirs, objets d'art and a few shots of the 'Old West.' Ideally you'll coincide with Friday Art Night (p221).

The morning of day two brings the chance to see the stupendous Na Pali cliffs from a very different angle – out at sea, from a raft trip (p217). Now explore Waimea (p226). Where else can you visit a Russian fort, Captain Cook's statue and an ancient Hawaiian aqueduct, all in an hour? There's not a great deal to see at any one stop, but you'll feel like you're wandering through a historical tag sale.

Stop by the West Kaua'i Technology & Visitor Center (p226) to pick up the self-guided walking tour, Touring Waimea.

Five Days

On day three, head back up to Koke'e (p238) for a hike. Choose one long trail, or a couple of short ones, and spend the whole day exploring the extraordinary landscape. If you're in good shape, loop around the Nu'alolo and Awa'awapuhi trails (p210).

Day four provides some well-deserved reflection time. Contemplate eternity beneath the cliffs at Polihale Beach (p235). No answers? Have some deli eats from Wailea's ultra-local Ishihara Market (p230).

Later on, dine at Wrangler's Steakhouse (p231); after a few days of Westside adventures, you deserve a thick steak, not to mention a saloon. Then head to Kekaha Beach Park (p231) for an unforgettable sunset. This is as good as the ol' yellow orb gets on the Westside, with great views to the satellite isles of Ni'ihau and Lehua.

If the kids need a break from the action, spend day five at mellow, family-style Salt Pond Beach Park (p221), replete with lifeguards and facilities. Be sure to pack a snorkel and, if you're really ambitious, the requisites for a BBQ picnic.

Consider a sunset trip to Glass Beach (p217), with drinks to follow at the Kauai Island Brewery & Grill (p220).

Waimea Canyon Lookout   VIEWPOINT
(Mile 10.3, Hwy 550) This breathtaking vista, at an elevation of 3400ft, stands at the intersection of several almighty raw red cracks in the earth. The views here are very different in the morning, when it's usually very misty, from the glowing russet tones of the late afternoon. Koai'e Canyon, clearly visible splitting away east of Waimea Canyon, is accessible to backcountry hikers.

Pu'u Hinahina Lookout   VIEWPOINT
(just before Mile 14, Hwy 550) The main viewpoint at this large lookout (elevation 3640ft) faces down the deep gorge carved by Waiahulu Stream as it races to join Waimea Canyon. Look straight ahead to spot hikers on the Canyon Trail (p235) heading along the exposed red-rock promontory across the gulf.

A separate, signposted overlook faces in the opposite direction, over the Pacific toward the island of Ni'ihau, on the horizon 17 miles southwest. It's best seen in the morning; by sunset, it's lost in the haze.

Waimea Canyon Drive Lookout 1   LOOKOUT
(Mile 4.5, Waimea Canyon Dr) FREE The first lookout as you climb Waimea Canyon Dr offers a good introductory view to the canyon, stretching to the east. Cross the road (carefully) to check out a little red-earth waterfall route cascading down the other side.

Waimea Canyon Drive Lookout 2   LOOKOUT
(Mile 5.5, Waimea Canyon Dr) Walk east from this roadside lookout for amazing views of the verdant canyon below.

Pu'u Ka Pele Lookout   VIEWPOINT
(just before Mile 13, Hwy 550) This canyon-edge lookout, across from a picnic area equipped with restrooms and drinking water, is a superb vantage point from which to admire the 800ft Waipo'o Falls, tumbling down the far side of the canyon.

You may already have seen the falls from a couple of small unmarked lookouts a little lower down the highway, before Mile 12.

🏃 Activities

Hiking
Several rugged trails, suitable for experienced hikers only, lead deep into Waimea Canyon. Shared with pig hunters – so be careful, and wear brightly colored clothing – they're busiest on weekends and holidays. Trail maps are available at the Koke'e Museum (p239) in Koke'e State Park. Hiking poles or a sturdy walking stick will ease the steep descent into the canyon.

Make sure you know when the sun will set, and aim to return long before dark, as daylight inside the canyon fades well before sunset. Beware of rain, which creates hazardous conditions: red-dirt trails quickly become slick, and river fords rise to impassable levels.

Pack light, but carry enough water for your entire trip, especially the uphill return hike. Do not drink fresh water without treating it. Cell phones won't work, so hike with a companion if possible, or at least tell someone your expected return time.

Koai'e Canyon Trail   HIKING
(http://hawaiitrails.ehawaii.gov) To hike the Koai'e Canyon Trail, you must first descend the 2.5-mile Kukui Trail, then hike a half-mile upstream along the Waimea Canyon Trail. Only then do you meet this moderate trek, measuring 3 miles each way, which leads along the south side of Koai'e Canyon to swimming holes that are best avoided after rain, when flash floods threaten.

Beyond Wiliwili Camp, by the river at the bottom of the Kukui Trail, there are three further camps along this route. After you pass the first, Kaluaha'ulu Camp (per night $18), half a mile along from Wiliwili Camp, stay on the river's eastern bank – do not cross. Soon you'll reach the trailhead for the Koai'e Canyon Trail, marked by a brown-and-yellow sign. Look out for greenery and soil that conceal drop-offs alongside the path.

Next up, 1.25 miles along the Koai'e Canyon Trail, is Hipalau Camp (per night $18). From here on, the trail is hard to find. Keep heading north; don't veer toward the river, but keep ascending at roughly the same level, midway between the canyon walls and the river. Growing steeper, the trail enters Koai'e Canyon, recognizable by the red-rock walls rising to the left. The last camp, a total of 2.5 miles along the Koai'e Canyon Trail, is Lonomea Camp (per night $18). Soak up the best views at the emergency helipad before retracing your steps.

Check http:/camping.ehawaii.gov for details of trails.

POLIHALE STATE PARK

The endless expanse of Polihale Beach, which makes up **Polihale State Park** (https://hawaiistateparks.org/kauai; 📷), is as mystical as it is enchanting. The long slow drive here, along a rutted 5-mile dirt road, brings you to the edge of eternity. The wide virgin beach curls into dunes that climb into bluffs, while the foothills of the Na Pali cliffs rise to the north. Families come here to camp and picnic, surf and watch sunsets.

Polihale translates as 'home of the underworld.' According to traditional Hawaiian belief, this is where souls departed for the afterlife. The cliffs at the end of the beach still hold ancient ruins, constructed over the ocean to serve as the jumping-off place for spirits.

To reach the park, fork right at the end of Kaumuali'i Hwy, 6 miles beyond Kekaha, then turn left onto a dirt road a few hundred yards along. Most car-rental companies forbid customers to drive to the beach, especially without a 4WD, but the road is generally passable in an ordinary vehicle. You have to go slow; the 4.8 miles typically take half an hour.

The park has restrooms, outdoor showers and a picnic area, but no lifeguards – be very careful if you go swimming, and only enter the water during calm conditions.

For surfers, Polihale has some good beach breaks that tend to shift with the winds. Currents can be strong. Toward the south end, look for a reef break at Queen's Pond. To the north, hit up the beach peaks or head for Echo's, at the start of the Na Pali cliffs (advanced riders only). Skilled boogie boarders will have fun here.

Want to spend the night? Make advance reservations to sleep at the rustic **campsites** (https://camping.ehawaii.gov/camping; per tent site $18, for up to 6 people), perfect for weekends at the edge of the world. You'll be rewarded with beautiful sunsets, late afternoons and early mornings without a soul in sight, and mind-blowing views of Ni'ihua and the Na Pali Coast. There are showers and toilets, but campfires are not allowed.

Kukui Trail
HIKING

(http://hawaiitrails.ehawaii.gov; off Waimea Canyon Dr) The narrow, switchbacking Kukui Trail drops 2000ft in its 2.5-mile course down to the river, but offers little in the way of sweeping panoramas. The steep climb back out of the canyon means it's only advisable for seriously fit and agile hikers. Alternatively, just hike the first mile down to reach a bench with an astonishing view.

The trail starts from the Iliau Nature Loop trailhead, just before Mile 9 on Hwy 550. Look out for a small sign directing hikers to turn left and descend the steep slope, with the hill at your back. When you hear the sound of water, you're near the picnic shelter and Wiliwili Camp (p238), where overnight camping – mostly used by hunters – is allowed with an advance permit.

The sun can be unrelenting on this exposed trail, so bring a hat and sunblock.

Pu'u Ki-Wai'alae Trail
HIKING

(https://hawaiitrails.org) This remote trail branches away northeast from the Waimea Canyon Trail, around 5 miles up from the rivermouth, and heads for 11 miles (one way) to the Wai'alae Cabin, where you can camp by permit.

Iliau Nature Loop
HIKING

(https://hawaiitrails.ehawaii.gov; off Waimea Canyon Dr) This easy, level, 0.3-mile nature loop makes a good leg-stretcher if you're itching to escape the car but lack the time, energy or equipment for a big trek. *Iliau*, a plant endemic to Kaua'i's Westside, grows en route. It grows up to 10ft tall, and blossoms in May/June. The trailhead is a quarter-mile before Mile 9 on Hwy 550. For a top-notch panorama of Waimea Canyon and its waterfalls, simply walk for around three minutes beyond the bench on your left.

Waimea Canyon Trail
HIKING

(http://hawaiitrails.ehawaii.gov) Either pick up the relatively flat, 11.5-mile (one way) Waimea Canyon Trail at the foot of the Kukui Trail, then follow it along the bottom of Waimea Canyon to Waimea town, or hike upstream in reverse. En route, you'll repeatedly have to cross the river. An

LAZY DAYS IN WAIMEA CANYON & THE WEST SIDE

Kaua'i's western shoreline fronts a dry, sunny world of red-dirt hills and long sunsets. A combination of magnificent landscapes, deserted beaches and welcoming towns makes for a destination where every visitor craves to linger.

WALKS

From the red-dirt trails that wind through Waimea Canyon (p233) – 'the Grand Canyon of the Pacific' – and the upland rainforests, to an art walk in charming Hanapepe, there are tons of ways to access the beauty of the Westside on foot. Yes, intense hikes explore Waimea Canyon and Koke'e State Park, but casual strolls also offer windows into that natural wonderland.

SHOPPING

Over the years, Hanapepe (p224) has grown into what has to be the westernmost bohemian artist enclave in the USA. As a result, this tiny town is packed with art galleries that throw their doors open on Friday evenings. You can also find various artisans, jewelers and craftspeople trading their wares any day of the week.

PICNIC

Head to Hanapepe or coastal Waimea, stock up on some grinds (you can't go wrong with *poke*, unless of course you forget to bring a cooler) and head to Salt Pond Beach, Waimea Canyon, or anywhere along the western coast. Consume delicious food, wash it down with fresh fruit juice and watch the sun dip into the Pacific. Bliss.

CLOUDIA SPINNER/SHUTTERSTOCK ©

1. Hanapepe (p220)
2. Waimea Canyon State Park (p233)
3. Fruit at smoothie stand, Waimea (p226)

entry permit is required (available at self-service trailhead registration boxes). Bring mosquito repellent. You might see locals carrying inner tubes on the upstream hike, so they can float home the easy way.

Cycling

Mountain bikers are allowed to follow 4WD hunting-area roads off Waimea Canyon Dr, even when the yellow gates are closed on non-hunting days. The one exception is Papa'alai Rd, which is closed to non-hunters.

Outfitters Kauai   CYCLING
(☑888-742-9887, 808-742-9667; www.outfitterskauai.com; 2827a Po'ipu Rd, Po'ipu; 4½hr tours adult/child 12-14yr $109/89; ⊘tour check-in usually 6am) For lazy two-wheeled sightseeing, it's hard to beat this 13-mile downhill glide along Waimea Canyon Dr. Participants cruise down the highway at a gentle pace, with a comfy, wide saddle and high-rise handlebars. Note that you'll see little of the canyon proper, as the ride begins lower down the road. Tours include snacks and drinks. Reservations required.

🛏 Sleeping

Only backcountry camping is allowed in Waimea Canyon State Park. All four backcountry campgrounds (per night $18) along the canyon's trails are on forest reserve land. They have open-air picnic shelters and pit toilets, but no other facilities; all fresh water must be treated before drinking. Advance permits are required; get them online from http:/camping.ehawaii.gov, or in person at the Lihu'e state parks office.

Wiliwili Camp   CAMPGROUND $
(http:/camping.ehawaii.gov; per night $18) This backcountry camp is located beside the Waimea River at the foot of the Kukui Trail, a 2.5-mile hike down from the highway.

❶ Getting There & Away

The southern boundary of Waimea Canyon State Park is 6 miles up from Waimea. Two roads access the park. Highway signs direct traffic up Koke'e Rd (Hwy 552), which climbs from Kekaha, because it's broader and safer for tour buses. Car drivers, however, should take the more scenic Waimea Canyon Dr (Hwy 550), which starts beside the visitor center in Waimea and meets Koke'e Rd between Miles 6 and 7. Either way, with its steep gradients and sweeping curves, it's a long, slow drive.

KOKE'E STATE PARK

Sprawling across the summit of Kaua'i's original volcano, Koke'e (ko-*keh*-eh) State Park encompasses some of the island's most precious ecosystems and extraordinary landscapes. Even a brief visit is hugely rewarding, thanks to the two end-of-the-road lookouts perched atop the highest cliffs of the Na Pali Coast. Koke'e is also arguably the single best hiking destination in Hawaii; if possible, hike at least one of its wondrous trails, either out to further dramatic coastal overlooks or into the depths of the mysterious Alaka'i Swamp. Botanists will revel in the range of endemic species, while birders will have their binoculars full.

Although the rainy season lasts from October through May, you'll likely need a waterproof layer year round. With much of the park over 4000ft above sea level, you should also bring a fleece jacket, or something heavier if you're camping in winter, when temperatures dip below 40ºF (4ºC).

◉ Sights

★ **Koke'e State Park**   PARK
(https://hawaiistateparks.org/kauai; $5 per day parking fee, covers all overlooks in Koke'e & Waimea Canyon state parks) `FREE` Besides the two Na Pali lookouts at the end of the paved highway, Koke'e State Park is the starting point for almost 50 miles of outstanding hiking trails. Some lead to perilous clifftop eyries, others inland to the woods overlooking Waimea Canyon, and yet more into the Alaka'i Swamp, home to Hawaii's largest surviving concentration of native bird species.

Not only is the swamp inhospitable to exotic species, but mosquitoes, which transmit avian diseases, have never thrived here thanks to its high elevation. Ancient Hawaiians never established a permanent settlement in these chilly highlands. They only ventured here to collect feathers from forest birds and cut koa trees for canoes, using a precipitous and long-vanished trail that ran down the mountain ridges into Kalalau Valley.

★ **Awa'awapuhi Lookout**   VIEWPOINT
Right at the end of the 3.1-mile Awa'awapuhi Trail, this incredible overlook affords hard-earned views over a tortuous, sheer-walled valley that snakes into the Na Pali cliffs.

MORE HAWAIIAN ISLANDS

If you find yourself staring out to sea imagining that Kaua'i and its neighbor, Ni'ihau, mark the end of the Hawaiian islands, think again – there's more! The Northwestern Hawaiian Islands begin more than 150 miles northwest of Kaua'i and stretch for another 1200 nautical miles. They represent an enormous area of some 582,578 sq miles of ocean known as **Papahanaumokuakea Marine National Monument** (www.papahanaumokuakea.gov), the largest protected marine reserve in the world.

This 'other Hawaii' is grouped into 10 clusters, containing both atolls and single-rock islands. From east to west, the clusters are Nihoa Island, Mokumanamana (Necker Island), French Frigate Shoals, Gardner Pinnacles, Maro Reef, Laysan Island, Lisianski Island, Pearl and Hermes Atoll, Midway Atoll and Kure Atoll. The total land mass is less than 6 sq miles, however, which is why they remain so little known. Managed by the **US Fish & Wildlife Service** (FWS; www.fws.gov/refuge/Midway_Atoll/), and scene of the famous World War II naval battle, Midway Atoll is normally the only island open to visitors.

Amazingly, Nihoa and Necker islands, the two closest to Kaua'i, were home to a small permanent population between around 1000 and 1700 CE. More than 135 archaeological sites have been identified there. As many as 175 people of Hawaiian origin lived on Nihoa, while Necker was used for religious ceremonies. The fact that anyone at all could survive on these rocks is remarkable. Nihoa juts from the sea like a broken tooth, with 900ft sea cliffs, and is little more than a quarter of a square mile in size. Necker is one-sixth that. What some folks will do for a bit of sun.

★**Pu'u o Kila Lookout**   VIEWPOINT

A mile beyond the Kalalau Lookout, the paved park road dead-ends at the Pu'u o Kila Lookout. The views of Kalalau Valley, plummeting 4000ft below, are similarly spectacular, but it's usually less crowded. This is also the trailhead for the Pihea Trail (p240). It's well worth hiking a short way along, though beyond the first half-mile it gets physically challenging.

Kalalau Lookout   VIEWPOINT

(Mile 18, Koke'e Rd) Shortly before the end of the highway, the Kalalau Lookout gives a fabulous overview of Kalalau Valley, sweeping around its towering green-swathed walls and down to the ocean. Conditions tend to be clearest in early morning. Even if the valley is concealed by clouds, stick around; at any moment the mists may swirl away, unveiling mighty waterfalls and splendid rainbows. Rather incongruously, the parking lot is overlooked by a 'golf ball' installation belonging to the Pacific Missile Range.

Kilohana Lookout   VIEWPOINT

The reward for hikers who make it all the way through bog and forest to the far end of the Alaka'i Swamp Trail (p240), the Kilohana Lookout (4022ft) has phenomenal views across steepling Wainiha Valley and Hanalei Bay to the ocean. There's no shelter at all.

Koke'e Natural History Museum   MUSEUM

(☑ 808-335-3353; www.kokee.org; Mile 15, Koke'e Rd; donation $3; ☉ 9am-4pm; ⊕) This two-room museum doubles as the visitor center for Koke'e State Park. Helpful staff provide detailed current hiking advice, and sell useful, albeit schematic, trail maps; call for real-time weather reports.

Museum displays include larger-scale topographical maps, exhibits on flora and fauna, and historic photographs, plus botanical sketches of endemic plants and taxidermic representations of some of the park's wildlife.

Lolo Vista Point   VIEWPOINT

This staggering viewpoint perches high above the Na Pali Coast at the far end of the 3.8-mile Nu'alolo Trail (p240). The last few hundred yards of the hike run atop a bare, sheer-sided red-earth ridge.

Pihea Lookout   VIEWPOINT

Sitting at 4284ft, atop a ludicrously steep and slippery little hillock, this high-arching lookout provides great views down across the valleys.

To reach it, you have to hike a mile from the Pu'u o Kila Lookout along the Pihea Trail (p240). Especially after rain, it can be a seriously squelchy and slippery trek.

WAIMEA CANYON & THE WESTSIDE KOKE'E STATE PARK

Kumuwela Lookout VIEWPOINT

This overlook marks the end of the Canyon Trail. Enjoy epic canyon and waterfall views as you rest at the picnic table.

🏃 Activities

Koke'e Resource Conservation Program VOLUNTEERING

(☎ 808-335-0045; www.krcp.org) 🌿 If you're so entranced by Koke'e's spectacular beauty that you want to contribute your time and energy into keeping it beautiful, get into the backcountry with this ecological restoration organization. Programs aim to eradicate invasive species and restore the island's native habitat.

Hiking

Koke'e State Park's extraordinary trails range from swampy bogs to wet forest to knife-edge, red-dirt canyon rims capable of causing vertigo in the hardiest mountain goat. You could easily do three separate day hikes in entirely different terrains, with abundant opportunities to spot endemic species including endangered rainforest birds. While many of the finest trails start along the main highway, other scenic hikes set off from Halemanu Rd, which leaves Koke'e Rd just north of Mile 14. Whether it's passable in a non-4WD vehicle depends on recent rainfall. In any case, most rental agreements forbid off-road driving.

Bring plenty of food and water, and be prepared for wet, cold weather at any time. You may also be glad of hiking poles, or at least a stout stick, on the many steep descents. For trail information, stop at Koke'e Museum or visit the Na Ala Hele website (p275; http://hawaiitrails.ehawaii.gov).

★ Awa'awapuhi Trail HIKING

Arguably the best trail in Koke'e, measuring 3.1 miles one way, the Awa'awapuhi Trail (p210) culminates in unsurpassable vistas from the Awa'awapuhi Lookout (p238), 2500ft above the Na Pali Coast. While demanding considerable stamina, it's less steep or technical than the Nu'alolo Trail nearby, and makes a better fit for families. It starts alongside Koke'e Rd, 1.7 miles uphill beyond the lodge.

★ Nu'alolo Trail HIKING

The Nu'alolo Trail (p210), which drops down to the stunning Lolo Vista Point (p239) from just south of Koke'e Lodge, is 3.8 miles each way, a little longer than the Awa'awapuhi Trail to which it's linked via the Nu'alolo Cliffs Trail.

It's also significantly steeper, with stretches of almost-sheer muddy scrambling and an alarming ridge walk at the very end.

★ Pihea Trail to Alaka'i Swamp Trail HIKING

For sheer scenic splendor, you can't beat the first mile of the Pihea Trail. Setting off from Pu'u o Kila Lookout (p239), at road's end, it follows a bare ridge, slick with mud, with huge views over Kalalau Valley to one side and dense rainforest to the other. Continue onto the Alaka'i Swamp Trail to create a strenuous 7.5-mile round-trip trek.

Beyond the initial half-mile, the Pihea Trail grows ever more challenging, with very steep sections where you effectively have to climb miniature waterfalls. Persist if you can to reach Pihea Lookout (p239), perched atop the highest peak (4284ft). Shortly before that, the Pihea Trail proper drops inland, down wooden stairways, to enter a magical, moss-laden mountaintop forest.

Head left onto the Alaka'i Swamp Trail at a clearly marked intersection, 0.75 miles along. This too starts by descending a rickety stairway, at the foot of which you have to either wade or rock-scramble across a small stream. A 4-mile round-trip hike, mostly along an unstable wooden boardwalk, will take you across eerie, misty boglands to breathtaking Kilohana Lookout (p239).

If you choose to stay on the Pihea Trail rather than following the Alaka'i Swamp Trail, you'll end up at Kawaikoi Campground instead.

★ Cliff & Canyon Trails HIKING

(♿) For some of the best family hiking in the park, set off along the straightforward 0.1-mile Cliff Trail (p211), which starts 0.8 miles down Halemanu Rd. Enjoy the canyon views, then keep going on the forested, 1.7-mile Canyon Trail, which descends steeply before reaching a vast red-dirt promontory, poised above stark cliffs.

Just beyond, some huff-and-puff climbing brings you to Waipo'o Falls.

Hike Kaua'i Adventures HIKING

(☎ 808-639-9709; www.hikekauaiadventures.com; half-/full day for 2 people $280/380) Longtime resident Jeffrey Courson has hiked every trail on Kaua'i and will tailor an ideal bespoke itinerary to meet your needs. An expert on local flora, fauna and history, he includes door-to-door service too. You'll have a blast.

ALAKA'I SWAMP

Nothing provides an out-of-the-ordinary hiking experience quite like the Alaka'i Swamp. Designated a wilderness preserve in 1964, this soggy wonderland is crossed by a hiking trail that to protect its unique plantlife consists largely of wooden boardwalk. In the swamp's waterlogged conditions, the planks rot at an alarming rate; sometimes they sag underfoot, at others they seesaw into the ooze, and for long stretches they're missing altogether. Add the usual persistent rain and the need to cross a small stream, and you're almost certain to get soaked.

Nevertheless, the trail traverses some truly fantastic terrain, including misty bogs peppered with knee-high trees and tiny, carnivorous plants. On a clear day, it culminates with outstanding views from Kilohana Lookout, across Wainiha Valley to the distant ocean. If it's raining, don't fret: search for rainbows and soak up the eerie atmosphere. Queen Emma was so moved by the tales of this spiritual place that she ventured out here herself, chanting in reverence.

The swamp has its own biological rhythms, and unlike almost everywhere else in Hawaii it's home to far more endemic birds than introduced species. Many of these avian survivors are endangered, however, and in some cases fewer than 100 birds now remain.

Halemanu–Koke'e Trail   HIKING

(🚶) This 1.2-mile route starts off Halemanu Rd, along from the Cliff and Canyon Trails (p211). A gentle recreational nature hike, it passes through a native forest of koa and ohia trees, which provide habitat for endemic birds. It ends near YWCA Camp Sloggett, a half-mile from Koke'e Lodge.

Black Pipe Trail   HIKING

A potential add-on at the start or end of the popular Canyon Trail, this half-mile trail is a good spot to see native hibiscus and *iliau* (an endemic tall-stemmed plant similar to the silversword found on Maui).

Pu'u Ka Ohelo Berry Flat Trail   HIKING

Looping out for 0.6 miles from Camp 10–Mohihi Rd, this trail leads past redwood, sugi pine and koa, and has a high canopy alive with native birds. Several small, rough hunting trails pass through here, so only leave the main trail if you know your way.

Po'omau Canyon Ditch Trail   HIKING

Accessed from the Berry Flat Trail, this strenuous 4-mile round-trip hike takes you along an irrigation ditch, past verdant forests and meadows. Combining two separate named trails, the Ditch Trail and the Po'omau Canyon Trail, it provides good overviews of two waterfalls.

Kawaikoi Stream Trail   HIKING

This easy, 1.8-mile loop sets off upstream from Sugi Grove Campground on Camp 10–Mohihi Rd (4WD only). Starting by following Kawaikoi Stream through a grove of Japanese cedar and California redwood trees, it climbs a bluff, then loops back down to the stream before returning to the trailhead. It also connects with the southern end of the Pihea Trail.

To reach the trailhead from the Koke'e Museum (p239), turn left onto Hwy 550, then left again at the first dirt road. You'll reach a picnic area after 3.7 miles. Park there, ford the stream, and continue up to Sugi Grove Campground.

🎉 Festivals & Events

Banana Poka Round-Up   ART, MUSIC

(☑ 808-335-9975; www.kokee.org; Mile 15, Koke'e Rd; ⊙ late May; 🚶) 🕊 This unique festival strips Koke'e of an invasive pest from South America, the banana *poka* vine, then weaves baskets from it. Come for live music, a rooster-crowing contest and the 'Pedal to the Meadow' bicycle race.

⭐ Eo e Emalani I Alaka'i   DANCE, MUSIC

(☑ 808-335-9975; www.kokee.org; Mile 15, Koke'e Rd; ⊙ Oct) Commemorating Queen Emma's 1871 expedition to the Alaka'i Swamp, this one-day outdoor dance festival takes over the meadows outside the Koke'e Natural History Museum for a Saturday in mid-October. The highlight is the arrival of the queen on horseback, to be greeted by hula troupes from all over the island.

WAIMEA CANYON & THE WESTSIDE KOKE'E STATE PARK

🛏 Sleeping & Eating

Koke'e State Park Cabins
CABIN $

(☎808-652-6852; www.westkauailodging.com; Mile 15, Koke'e Rd; cabin $91-148) There's an undeniable thrill to sleeping in these basic mountain cabins, set in a clearing just down from Koke'e Lodge. Bare-floored and spacious, each holds a double bed plus twin beds, a kitchen, hot shower, linens and blankets. Prepare yourself for cold, damp nights at any season, though the wood-burning stove (the only heating source) warms things up nicely.

There's no phone or wi-fi connection. Check-in is down in Waimea across from the visitor center; buy firewood there and pick up other supplies before driving up.

Kawaikoi & Sugi
Grove Campgrounds
CAMPGROUND $

(http:/camping.ehawaii.gov; tent site per night $18, for up to 6 people) Roughly 4 miles east of Koke'e Lodge, off the 4WD-only Camp 10–Mohihi Rd, these primitive campgrounds have pit toilets, picnic shelters and fire pits. There's no water source, so you'll need to bring your own or treat the stream water. Three-night maximum stay; advance camping permits required.

Koke'e State
Park Campground
CAMPGROUND $

(http:/camping.ehawaii.gov; Mile 15, Koke'e Rd; tent site per night $18, for up to 6 people) The park's most accessible camping area, Koke'e State Park Campground, is alongside the highway just north of the meadow, a few minutes' walk from Koke'e Lodge. The campsites sit in a grassy area beside the woods and have picnic tables, drinking water, restrooms and outdoor showers. There's a five-night maximum stay. Book online in advance.

YWCA Camp Sloggett
CAMPGROUND, CABIN $

(☎808-245-5959; www.campingkauai.com; tent sites $15, cottage, lodge or bunkhouse $120-200) Choose basic cottage, lodge or bunkhouse accommodations at this extremely rustic (even run-down) facility, or camp on the grass; hot showers available throughout. The cottage has a king-sized bed, kitchen and wood-burning fireplace, while the bunkhouse and lodge are outfitted for large groups, with kitchen/kitchenette. Bring sleeping bags and towels. Reservations seldom needed for camping, but call to check.

To get here, turn right off Koke'e Rd, just past the lodge, at the YWCA sign and follow the dirt road for around 0.5 miles.

Koke'e Lodge
AMERICAN $

(☎808-335-6061; www.kokeelodge.com; Mile 15, Koke'e Rd; mains $9-12; ☺9am-4pm) This log-cabin restaurant overlooks a large meadow that's stalked by marauding wild roosters. The one dining option in the park – and there's nothing else within a half-hour's drive – it's open in daytime only, serving egg-or-pancake breakfasts followed by island-style lunches including *loco moco*, burgers and a tasty Portuguese bean soup. A gift counter sells sundries, souvenirs and a few snacks.

ℹ Getting There & Away

The southern boundary of Koke'e State Park lies beyond Pu'u Hinahina Lookout as you climb Koke'e Rd. After Mile 15, you come first to its rental cabins, then the large meadow that holds its restaurant and museum, and then its campground.

The road ends another 4 miles along, at Pu'u o Kila Lookout. That's a total of 19 miles up from Waimea, a drive that takes at least 45 minutes. There's no gas en route, and only minimal food or supplies, at Koke'e Lodge.

Understand Kaua'i

History

As with most islands, the history of Kaua'i is charted by arrivals. The arrival of plants and animals, the arrival of humans, the arrival of European explorers, the arrival of disease, the arrival of missionaries, the arrival of sugar, the arrival of the tourist horde.

Historic Sites

....

Nu'alolo Kai
(p232;
Na Pali Coast)

....

Grove Farm
Homestead
(p85; Lihu'e)

....

Makauwahi
Cave Reserve
(p192; Po'ipu)

....

Kilauea Lighthouse
(p143; Kilauea)

....

Russian Fort
Elizabeth State
Historical Park
(p226; Waimea)

Like other Hawaiian Islands, Kaua'i grew up in relative isolation. That is, until Captain Cook first landed in Waimea on the island's Westside in 1778. This transformational point in the island's history brought disease, new commerce, new technology, new religions and new ways of doing things. And while the broad strokes of Kaua'i's history connects with that of the other islands, it has a fiercely independent streak that goes back to the days of the Hawaiian kings. In some ways this independence remains a common denominator for life on the island today. Under the leadership of *mo'i* (island king) Kaumuali'i, Kaua'i and Ni'ihau were the last of the Hawaiian Islands to join Kamehameha I's kingdom in 1810. Unlike the other islands, they did so peacefully, more than 15 years after the rest of the islands were bloodily conquered.

But Kaua'i was slow to grow. It remained a sugar-plantation island into the 20th century – with notable migrations of Chinese, Japanese and Filipino workers. It only became iconic as a tropical paradise after WWII, when Hollywood glamorized Lumaha'i Beach in Mitzi Gaynor's *South Pacific* (1958) and the long-gone Coco Palms Resort in Elvis Presley's *Blue Hawaii* (1961). In 1982 Kaua'i was hit by Hurricane 'Iwa. Just 10 years later, it was again devastated by Hurricane 'Iniki, the most powerful hurricane to ever strike Hawaii; it left six people dead, thousands of people homeless and caused $1.8 billion dollars of damage statewide.

First Beginnings

Around six to 10 million years ago, volcanoes formed the islands of Kaua'i and O'ahu, the oldest of the Hawaiian Islands in geological time – the surrounding islands popping above the Pacific Ocean only in the last million years or so. From this remarkable birth, the air, wind

TIMELINE	6–10 million BCE	1000– 1200 CE	1200– 1400 CE
	Violent volcanic activity forms the islands of O'ahu and Kaua'i. Borne by wind, wing and wave, plants, insects and birds colonize the new land.	Polynesian colonists traveling thousands of miles across open seas in double-hulled canoes arrive in Hawai'i.	The Tahitian Long Voyages bring new gods to the islands.

and currents transformed the land from volcanic rock to the tropical paradise you see today.

The beginnings were slow. Seeds borne on currents, in logs or on bird feathers found their way to the island. Each new introduced species changed the islands' ecology forever. And it happened far less frequently than you would imagine. Given the isolation of the archipelago, many experts postulate that successful introductions of species only occurred once every 20,000 or 30,000 years.

Walk the Koloa, Waimea and Maha'ulepu heritage trails to connect with Kaua'i's history.

The First Settlers

Exactly how and when Kaua'i was first settled remains a controversy. Most archaeologists agree that the first humans migrated to the Hawaiian Islands from the Marquesas Islands. This settlement marked the end of a 2000-year period of migration by ancient seafarers, originally from Southeast Asia, that populated Polynesia.

Most original scholarship places the date of the first Hawaiian settlers around 500 CE. More-recent radiocarbon dating, combined with tracking of linguists, culture and other factors, places the date closer to 1000 to 1200 CE. The last migrations likely started from Tahiti. Known as the Long Voyages, they lasted from 1000 to 1400 CE and were likely voyages of discovery and not settlement.

The Tahitians also brought with them their own gods, like Kāne, lord of creation, and his opposing force, Kanaloa; Lono, the god of peace, and Ku, the god of war.

These new dates offer an almost revolutionary perspective to Hawaiian history. What was considered a thousands-year-old culture may have developed in a much shorter time. Some point out that the original settlers could have been subdued by more powerful later migrations, thus justifying the mythology of the *menehune* ('little people' who were forced to live in the mountains).

The original settlers made their journeys in double-hulled canoes 60ft long and 14ft wide, without any modern navigational tools. Instead they relied on the 'star compass,' a celestial map based on keen observation (and perfect memory) of star paths. They had no idea what, if anything, they would find thousands of miles away across open ocean, though many scholars now indicate that they brought with them the tools and resources they would need to populate a new world (seeds, women and children, plants and animals, gods and mythology). Amazingly, experts estimate that Hawai'i's discoverers sailed for four months straight without stops to restock food and water.

By and large, the consensus is that Kaua'i was the first island in the archipelago to be settled. These first settlers likely lived in caves, later building more substantial structures and small villages.

Check out *Paradise of the Pacific* by Susanna Moore for interesting storytelling on ancient Hawai'i.

1300	1778	1810	1815–17
Na Pali Coast settled at Nu'alolo Kai. Settlement survives 600 years.	Captain James Cook lands at Waimea; Hawai'i will never be the same again.	Kamehameha I unites the major Hawaiian Islands under one kingdom, called Hawai'i after his home island.	Georg Scheffer fails to conquer Hawai'i for Russia; he departs before finishing Fort Elizabeth on the southwest coast.

The Ancient Way of Life

Ancient Hawaiians had a hierarchical class system. At the top were the *ali'i nui* (high chiefs, descended from the gods), who each ruled one of the four major islands (including Kaua'i). A person's rank as an *ali'i* was determined by their mother's family lineage, making Hawai'i a matrilineal society.

The second class comprised *ali'i 'ai moku* (district chiefs) who ruled island districts and *ali'i 'ai ahupua'a* (lower chiefs) who ruled *ahupua'a*, pie-shaped subdistricts extending from the mountains to the ocean. Also ranked second were the kahuna (priest, healer or sorcerer), experts in important skills such as canoe building, religious practices, healing arts and navigation.

The third, and largest, class were the *maka'ainana* (commoners), who were not chattel of the *ali'i* and could live wherever they pleased but were obligated to support the *ali'i* through taxes paid in kind with food, goods and labor.

The final *kaua* (outcast) class was shunned and did not mix with the other classes, except as slaves. No class resented their position, for people accepted the 'natural order' and based their identity on the group rather than on their individuality.

Although the hierarchy sounds feudal, Hawaiian society was quite different because *ali'i* did not 'own' land. It was inconceivable to the Hawaiian mind to own land or anything in nature. Rather, the *ali'i* were stewards of the land – and they had a sacred duty to care for it on behalf of the gods. Further, the ancients had no monetary system or concept of trade for profit. They instead exchanged goods and services through customary, reciprocal gift giving (as well as through obligations to superiors).

Strict religious laws, known as the *kapu* (taboo) system, governed what people ate, whom they married, when they fished or harvested crops, and practically all other aspects of human behavior. Women could not dine with men or eat bananas, coconuts, pork and certain types of fish.

Surfing in Hawaii goes back to the beginning, when early Polynesian settlers brought the practice of bodyboarding to the islands. It was on Hawai'i that the practice of standing on boards really took hold and surfing held a central part in local culture with surf competitions, prized breaks that only the royalty could ride (and plenty of leftovers for the commoners), and intricate cultural traditions that guided the selection, creation and storage of surfboards made from koa, *wiliwili* and breadfruit wood.

The rise of consumerism presented by the introduction of money and Western goods was a substantial factor in the demise of the *kapu* system.

In *Legends and Myths of Hawaii*, King David Kalakaua (1836–91) captures the nature of ancient Hawaiian storytelling by seamlessly mixing history (of Kamehameha, Captain Cook, the burning of the temples) with living mythology.

1819	1820	1835	1848
King Kamehameha I dies and the Hawaiian religious system is cast aside.	Samuel and Mercy Partridge Whitney establish a mission at Waimea. Without the *kapu* system, Hawaiians prove ready to convert.	First successful commercial milling of sugar in Hawaii begins on Koloa.	Under the influence of Westerners, the first system of private land ownership is introduced.

Captain Cook

When British naval captain James Cook inadvertently sighted the uncharted island of O'ahu on January 18, 1778, the ancient Hawaiians' 500 years of isolation were lost forever. This new arrival transformed Hawai'i in ways inconceivable at the time.

Strong winds on that fateful day pushed Cook away from O'ahu and toward Kaua'i, where he made landfall on January 20 at Waimea Bay. Cook promptly named the islands the Sandwich Islands, after his patron, the Earl of Sandwich.

Cook and his men were enthralled with Kaua'i and its inhabitants, considering them to be robust and handsome in physical appearance, and friendly and generous in trade dealings. Meanwhile the Hawaiians, living in a closed society for hundreds of years, found the strange white men to be astounding. Some historians believe that they regarded Cook as the earthly manifestation of the great god Lono.

After two weeks, Cook continued to the Pacific Northwest for another crack at finding the elusive Northwest Passage across North America. Searching in vain for eight months, he returned south to winter in the Hawaiian Islands. In November 1778, Cook sighted Maui for the first time, but did not land, choosing instead to head further south to explore the nearby island of Hawai'i with its towering volcanic mountains. After landing in picturesque Kealakekua Bay in January 1779, Cook's luck ran out. An escalating series of conflicts ensued. When one of his ship's boats was stolen, Cook attempted to kidnap the local chief as ransom and was driven back to the beach. A battle ensued, and Cook, four of his men and 17 Hawaiians were killed.

The Hawaiian Kingdom

Among the Hawaiian warriors that felled Captain Cook was a robust young man named Paiea. Between 1790 and 1810, this charismatic leader, who became known as Kamehameha the Great, managed to conquer the islands of Hawai'i, Maui, Moloka'i and O'ahu.

To make his domain complete, Kamehameha tried to conquer Kaua'i too, but was thwarted by the formidable chief Kaumuali'i. An attack was thwarted when a case of plague wiped out a number of his warriors and chiefs. Kamehameha did, however, negotiate a diplomatic agreement with the chief, which put the island under Kamehameha's new kingdom, but gave Kaumuali'i the right to rule the island somewhat independently.

Kamehameha is credited with unifying all of the islands, establishing a peaceful and solidified kingdom. He was widely acknowledged as being a benevolent and just ruler, much loved by his people until his death in 1819.

In *Blue Latitudes: Boldly Going Where Captain Cook Has Gone Before*, Tony Horwitz examines the controversial legacy of Captain Cook's South Seas voyages, weaving amusing real-life adventure tales together with bittersweet oral history.

Of Hawai'i's eight ruling monarchs, only King Kamehameha I had children, who eventually inherited the throne. His dynasty ended less than a century after it began with the death of Kamehameha V in 1872.

1864	1890	1893	1900
Sugar baron-to-be George Norton Wilcox takes over the lease for Grove Farm in Lihu'e.	Lihu'e Hotel opens with emphasis on sunbathers; it's the first fully fledged tourist hotel in Kaua'i.	The Hawaiian monarchy, under Queen Lili'uokalani, is overthrown, ending 83 years of rule.	Hawaii becomes a US territory.

Enter the Missionaries

When Kamehameha died, his 23-year-old son Liholiho (Kamehameha II) became *mo'i* and his wife, Queen Ka'ahumanu, became *kuhina nui* (regent) and co-ruler. Both of them were greatly influenced by Westerners and eager to renounce the *kapu* system. In a shocking blow to tradition, the two broke a strict taboo against men and women eating together and later ordered many heiau (temples) and *ki'i* (idols) destroyed. Hawaiian society fell into chaos. Thus when the first missionaries to Hawai'i arrived in April 1820, it was a fortuitous moment for them. The Hawaiian people were in great social and political upheaval and many, particularly the *ali'i*, found the Protestant faith an appealing replacement.

The Hawaiians had no written language, so the missionaries established a Hawaiian alphabet using Roman letters and taught them how to read and write. This fostered a high literacy rate and publication of 100 Hawaiian-language newspapers. Eventually, however, missionaries sought to separate the Hawaiians from their 'hedonistic' cultural roots. They prohibited hula dancing because of its 'lewd and suggestive movements,' denounced the traditional Hawaiian chants and songs that honored 'heathen' gods, taught women to sew Western-style clothing, abolished polygamy and even banned the language they had taught them to write.

Many missionaries became influential advisors to the monarch and received large tracts of land in return, prompting them to leave the church altogether and turn their land into sugar plantations.

Big Sugar

Foreigners quickly saw that Hawaii was ideal for growing sugarcane and established small plantations using Hawaiian labor. But by then the native population had severely declined, thanks to introduced diseases. To fill the shortage, workers were imported from overseas starting in the 1860s, first from China, and soon after from Japan and the Portuguese islands of Madeira and the Azores.

The influx of imported foreign labor and the rise of the sugar industry had a major impact on the islands' social structure. Caucasian plantation owners and sugar agents rose to become the elite upper economic-and-political class, while the Hawaiians and foreign laborers became the lower class, without much of a middle class in between. Labor relations became contentious, eventually resulting in the formation of unions and strike action.

The plantation era provides the best artifacts of Kaua'i's short history. You can see old mills, plantation-era houses and other artifacts in places like Koloa (p187), Waimea (p228) and the Kaua'i Museum (p85) in

1924	1925	1934	1941
Hanapepe Massacre leaves 20 dead as Filipino strikers confront police.	The first air flight between the mainland and Hawaii is made. Eleven years later, Pan American launches the first commercial mainland–Hawaii flights.	First movie, *White Heat*, shot on Kaua'i.	Japanese attack Pearl Harbor; Japanese sugar workers are spared internment camp.

PROMISED LAND

Ancient Hawaiians had no concept of land ownership. The gods owned the land and people were stewards. In practical terms, the king controlled the land and foreigners had no means to own any.

In the 1840s, Americans sought to secure long-term property rights. In 1848 they convinced the Hawaiian government to enact the Great Mahele, a revolutionary land reform act that redistributed all kingdom lands into three parts: crown lands, chief lands and government lands (for the benefit of the general public).

Two years later the government went further and allowed foreign residents to buy land. Sugar growers and land speculators bought huge parcels for minimal sums from chiefs lured by quick money and from commoners ignorant of deeds, taxes and other legal requirements for fee-simple land ownership.

Native Hawaiians lost much of their land and struggled with ensuing economic problems. In 1920 Kaua'i's native son Prince Kuhio (congressional delegate for the Territory of Hawaii) convinced the US Congress to pass the Hawaiian Homes Commission Act, which set aside almost 200,000 acres of government land for Native Hawaiians to lease for $1 per year. It sounds terrific, but there are problems. Much of this land is remote and lacks basic infrastructure, such as roads and access to water and electricity. Lessees must build their own homes, which many applicants cannot afford. And applicants end up waiting for years, even decades. At the end of 2018 there were around 23,000 residential applicants waiting across the state, including 1684 on Kaua'i. Only about 9900 leases have been granted statewide since 1920.

Lihu'e, while the McBryde and Allerton Gardens (p63) preserve some of the pomp and circumstance of the era.

Overthrow of the Monarchy

In 1887 the members of the Hawaiian League, a secret antimonarchy organization run by sugar interests, wrote a new constitution and by threat of violence forced King David Kalakaua to sign it. This constitution, which became known as the 'Bayonet Constitution,' limited voting rights and stripped the monarch's powers, effectively making King Kalakaua a figurehead.

When Kalakaua, Hawai'i's last king, died in 1891, his sister and heir, Princess Lili'uokalani, ascended the throne. She tried to restore the monarchy, but on January 17, 1893, the leaders of the Hawaiian League, supported by both John L Stevens (the US Department of State Minister to Hawaii) and a 150-man contingent of US marines and sailors, forcibly arrested Queen Lili'uokalani and took over 'Iolani Palace in Honolulu – a tense but bloodless coup d'état. The Kingdom of Hawai'i was now the Republic of Hawai'i.

For a history of Hawaii you can finish on the flight over, *A Concise History of the Hawaiian Islands* by Phil Barnes captures a surprising amount of nuance in fewer than 90 pages.

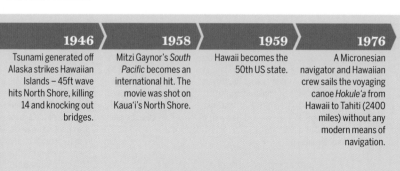

1946	1958	1959	1976
Tsunami generated off Alaska strikes Hawaiian Islands – 45ft wave hits North Shore, killing 14 and knocking out bridges.	Mitzi Gaynor's *South Pacific* becomes an international hit. The movie was shot on Kaua'i's North Shore.	Hawaii becomes the 50th US state.	A Micronesian navigator and Hawaiian crew sails the voyaging canoe *Hokule'a* from Hawaii to Tahiti (2400 miles) without any modern means of navigation.

In *Strangers from a Different Shore,* Ronald Takaki tells the story of the USA's Asian immigrant communities, from Hawaii's plantation laborers to the effects of WWII on racial discrimination and modern attitudes toward multiculturalism.

Annexation, War & Statehood

American interests pushed hard for annexation, while Hawaiians fought to prevent this final acquisition. In 1897 more than 21,000 people (almost half the population of Hawaii) signed an anti-annexation petition and sent it to Washington. In 1898 President William McKinley nevertheless approved the annexation, perhaps influenced by the concurrent Spanish–American War, which highlighted Pearl Harbor's strategic military location.

Statehood was a tough sell to the US Congress, but a series of significant historical events paved the way. In 1936 Pan American Airways launched the first commercial flights from the US mainland to Hawaii, thus launching the trans-Pacific air age and the beginning of mass tourism. A wireless telegraph (and later telephone) service between Hawaii and the mainland alleviated doubts about long-distance communication. Most importantly, WWII proved both the strategic military role of Pearl Harbor and the loyalty and heroism of Japanese immigrants.

During WWII the Japanese were initially banned from joining the armed forces, due to great suspicion about their loyalty. In 1943 the US government yielded to political pressure and formed an all-Japanese combat unit, the 100th Infantry Battalion. While only 3000 men were needed for this unit, more than 10,000 men volunteered.

By the war's end, another all-Japanese unit, the 442nd Regimental Combat Team, composed of 3800 men from Hawaii and the mainland,

EYE OF THE STORM

Almost three decades after Hurricane 'Iniki blasted Kaua'i, residents can still give blow-by-blow accounts of their survival on September 11, 1992. 'Iniki blew in with sustained winds of 145mph and gusts of 165mph or more (a weather-station meter in mountainous Koke'e broke off at 227mph). It snapped trees by the thousands and totally demolished 1420 homes (and swept over 60 out to sea). Another 5000 homes were severely damaged, while over 7000 sustained minor damage. Most of the island lacked electricity for over a month, and some areas lacked power for up to three months. Thirty-foot waves washed away entire wings of beachfront hotels, particularly those in Po'ipu and Princeville.

During the immediate aftermath, residents were remarkably calm and law-abiding despite the lack of power, radio or TV. Communities held parties to share and consume perishable food. Looting was minor and when grocers allowed affected residents to take what they needed, they insisted on paying.

Miraculously, only four people died, but the total value of the damage to the island was $1.8 billion. While locals notice the changed landscape, newcomers would never realize the havoc wreaked almost 30 years ago.

1976	1982	1992	1994
The grassroots organization Protect Kaho'olawe 'Ohana files a lawsuit in the Federal District Court to halt the US Navy's use of Kaho'olawe island as a practice bombing site.	Hurricane 'Iwa strikes Kaua'i – 1900 homes damaged or destroyed, 44 boats sunk, resorts wrecked.	Hawaii's most powerful hurricane ever, 'Iniki, destroys 1420 houses; four people are killed. Kaua'i declared a disaster area.	The Po'ipu Bay Golf Course hosts the annual PGA Grand Slam of Golf from 1994 to 2006. Tiger Woods takes first place for five consecutive years, from 1998 to 2002, and then two more in 2005 and 2006.

had received more commendations and medals than any other unit. The 100th Infantry also received special recognition for rescuing the so-called 'Lost Battalion,' stranded behind enemy lines in France.

While still a controversial candidate, the islands were finally admitted as the 50th US state in 1959.

The Hawaiian Renaissance

After WWII, Hawaii became America's tropical fantasyland. The tiki craze, surfer movies, aloha shirts and Waikiki were all Westernized, commercial images, but they made Hawaii iconic to the masses. Simultaneously, Hawaiians were increasingly marginalized by Western social, political and economic influences. The Hawaiian language had nearly died out, land was impossible for most Hawaiians to buy, and many of the traditional ways of life that had supported an independent people for over 1000 years were disintegrating. Without these, Hawaiians lost much of their own identity and even felt a sense of shame.

The 1970s introduced a cultural awakening, due largely to two events: in 1974 a small group called the Polynesian Voyaging Society (www.hokulea.com) committed themselves to building and sailing a replica of an ancient Hawaiian voyaging canoe, to prove that the first Polynesian settlers were capable of navigating the Pacific without the use of Western technology such as sextants and compasses. When the *Hokule'a* made its maiden 4800-mile round-trip voyage to Tahiti in 1976, it instantly became a symbol of rebirth for Hawaiians, prompting a cultural revival unparalleled in Hawaiian history.

The same year, a small grassroots group, the Protect Kahoʻolawe 'Ohana (PKO), began protesting against the treatment of Kahoʻolawe, an island the US military had used as a training and bombing site since WWII. The PKO's political actions, including the island's illegal occupation, spurred new interest in reclaiming not only Kahoʻolawe (which the US Navy relinquished in 2003) and other military-held lands, but also Hawaiian cultural practices, from hula to *lomilomi* massage.

Public schools started teaching Hawaiian language and culture classes, while Hawaiian immersion charter schools proliferated. Hawaiian music topped the charts, turning island-born musicians into now-legendary superstars. Small but vocal contingents began pushing for Hawaiian sovereignty, from complete secession from the USA to a nation-within-a-nation model.

The community website www.hawaiihistory.org offers an interactive timeline of Hawaii's history and essays delving into every aspect of ancient Hawaiian culture, with evocative images and links.

HISTORY THE HAWAIIAN RENAISSANCE

Surfing was falling out of favor in the early 20th century in Hawaii, but was resurrected when Jack London wrote about it in 1907 in an article titled 'A Royal Sport.'

2006	2007	2009	2018
Torrential rainstorms for over 40 days in February and March cause Kaloko Dam on the North Shore to break, causing a flash flood of 300 million gallons of water into the ocean. Seven people are swept to their deaths.	Protesters prevent the Superferry from entering Nawiliwili Harbor on its inaugural voyage, ending service to Kauaʻi.	Age of sugar ends on Kauaʻi with closure of Gay & Robinson mill in Kaumakani.	Kauaʻi is subjected to another significant natural disaster when flash floods severely impact the island's northern coast, closing roads and cutting off villages.

People of Kaua'i

The people of Kaua'i are diverse in many ways, but most share a few common characteristics. Sure, they know how to spread the love, but being a small island, they also know how to mind their own business. One of the central concepts here is *aloha 'aina* (love of the land). Head out to a community market or local beach and you will probably also witness a love for the sea, a love for family and tranquility, a love for community, a love for isolation and a love for spirit.

Kaua'i Identity

Family

In Hawaii, locals define 'family' much more inclusively than most mainlanders. Here, the *'ohana* (family) can extend beyond bloodlines to friends, teammates, coworkers and classmates. If people demonstrate the *'ohana* spirit, it means that they are generous and welcoming, like family should be.

Hanai (adopted or foster) children are common in Hawaiian families. To be a *hanai* child or to *hanai* a child is not odd or pejorative in Hawaii. Instead, *hanai* children are fully accepted into the family.

Locals might refer to a 'calabash cousin,' meaning a close friend akin to a cousin but not a blood relation. More commonly, you'll hear locals refer to 'aunty' or 'uncle' even if the person is not related at all. These elders are beloved community members, and calling them aunty or uncle connotes respect and affection.

Local Versus Transplant

Born-and-raised Kauaians tend to be easygoing and low-key for the most part, preferring the unpretentious small-town life. Multigenerational locals take pride in their roots and enjoy knowing and being known within their community – which is a good thing since anonymity is a short-lived state, thanks to the 'coconut wireless.'

Stereotypes of an unwelcoming local contingent do exist and there is some justification for that – after all, the infamous Wolfpak Surf Gang got its start on the North Shore. Resistance has been one of Kaua'i's strong suits throughout its history and the way that this still manifests itself today is in an insider-outsider mentality that can linger beneath the surface of everyday interactions. However, we find that if you give aloha, you get aloha.

The pace of island life is a few gearshifts down from that of the modern get-it-done-yesterday world. For most island-folk, tradition trumps change. Locals can be resentful of the influx of mainland transplants and their progressive ideals diluting traditional communities, especially on the North Shore. Yet other transplants seem to quickly find their feet: befriending neighbors, immersing themselves in the culture and simply slowing down and respecting local ways. As the saying goes, 'Kaua'i will either suck you in or spit you out.'

Typical transplants include post-college wanderers, surfer dudes, wealthy retirees or middle-aged career switchers seeking idyllic seclusion.

WHAT'S IN A NAME?

Haole White person (except local Portuguese). Translates as 'shallow breather.' Often further defined as 'mainland haole' or 'local haole.'

Hapa Person of mixed ancestry, most commonly referring to *hapa haole*, who are part-white and part-Asian.

Hawaiian Person of Native Hawaiian ancestry. It's a faux pas to call any Hawaii resident 'Hawaiian' (as you would a Californian or Texan), thus ignoring the existence of an indigenous people.

Kama'aina Literally defined as 'child of the land,' refers to a person who is native to a particular place. In the retail context, '*kama'aina* discounts' apply to any resident of Hawaii (ie anyone with a Hawaii drivers license).

Local Person who grew up in Hawaii. Locals who move away retain their local 'cred,' at least in part. But longtime transplants never become local. It is an inherited, elite status. To call a transplant 'almost local' is a welcome compliment, despite its emphasis on the insider-outsider mentality.

Neighbor Islander Person who lives on any Hawaiian Island other than O'ahu.

Transplant Person who moves to the islands as an adult.

Prince Kuhio Celebrations (p27)

Regional Differences

Despite the island's compact size, each geographical location has its own distinct vibe. Lihuʻe, the county seat, is a functional town where people go to work, not to play. Wailua's Upcountry remains a favorite residential area, while coastal Kapaʻa has taken on a burgeoning hippie front. Hanalei is a surf town, dominated by suntanned blonds and affordable only to multimillionaires. Poʻipu's sun-splashed beaches serve as a perennial summer camp for retirees, and the Westside – more so than any other region – has retained an echo of its multiethnic plantation-history traditions.

Lifestyle

Most residents focus on the outdoors. With the ocean as the primary playground, surfing is the sport of choice, along with fishing, free diving, hunting and 'cruisin' as popular pastimes. The workday starts and ends early, and most find a comfortable work/home balance.

The vast majority of residents work in fields related to tourism or the service industry. There are smaller groups of farmers and fishers, craftspeople and, of course, like anywhere else, there are doctors and lawyers and time-share salespeople.

Head to the beach at sunset and you'll see the balance at work. Locals, visitors and businesspeople all stop to take a last sunset surf session or just watch the sun dip below the horizon.

Not surprisingly, many Kauaʻi locals follow traditional lifestyle patterns. They often marry early and stick to traditional male and female roles. The easy lifestyle, especially in surf towns like Hanalei, seems to squelch ambitions to travel the world or attend mainland universities.

Locals and transplants tend to diverge in their careers and ambitions. Locals tend toward more conventional, 'American dream' lives, meaning marriage, kids, a modest home, stable work and free nights and weekends. Mainland transplants are here for other reasons: retirement, a dream B&B or organic farm, waves, art, or youthful shenanigans. All are free to be unconventional on Kaua'i.

In many ways you still see the remnants of ancient Hawaiian faiths both at home and in the church. It's not a hugely religious society, but you will find people of all faiths, with a strong Christian contingency and notable populations focusing on Eastern philosophies.

Multiculturalism

The overwhelming majority of Kaua'i's current immigrants are white, so the island's diversity is due to historic migration: Native Hawaiians and plantation immigrants (predominantly Filipino and Japanese).

During plantation days, whites were wealthy plantation owners and many streets and institutions were named after them (for example, Wilcox Memorial Hospital and Rice St). Their privilege is one reason why some resentment toward haole lingers. As time passes and the plantation era fades, the traditional stereotypes, hierarchies and alliances have softened.

That said, no ethnic group in Hawaii ever remained exclusive; instead, they freely adopted and shared cultural customs, from food to festivals to language. Folks of all backgrounds dance hula, craft hardwood bowls, play the ukulele and study the Hawaiian language.

Today there is no ethnic majority in the Hawaiian Islands. Due to this multiculturalism, you will find a blend of cultural influences and names. Many local Hawaiians have Caucasian or Asian surnames, for example.

Generally, locals feel bonded with other locals. While tourists and transplants are usually welcomed with open arms, they must earn the trust and respect of the locals. It is unacceptable for an outsider to assume an air of superiority and try to 'fix' local ways. Such people will inevitably fall into the category of 'loudmouth haole.'

The Hawaiian language is not widely spoken, though with the rise of immersion schools and renewed interest in 'everything Hawaiian' you'll probably hear it more today than 50 years ago. What you get instead is an island patois that combines surfer lingo, Hawaiian words and plenty of colorful metaphors.

Hawaiian Words

aloha – love, hello, welcome, goodbye

hale – house

kane – man

kapu – taboo, restricted

mahalo – thank you

makai – a direction, toward the sea

mauka – a direction, toward the mountains (inland)

pau – finished, completed

pono – goodness, justice, responsibility

wahine – woman

PEOPLE OF KAUA'I MULTICULTURALISM

ISLAND ETIQUETTE

➡ Practice acquiescence, be courteous and 'no make waves' (don't make a scene).

➡ Try to use basic Hawaiian words.

➡ Treat ancient Hawaiian sites and artifacts with respect.

➡ Dress casually as the locals do.

➡ Remove your shoes before entering homes and B&Bs.

➡ Give a thank-you *shaka* ('hang loose' hand gesture, with index, middle and ring fingers downturned) if a driver lets you merge or stops before a one-lane bridge.

➡ Don't assume being called a haole is an insult (but don't assume it's not either).

➡ Tread lightly with locals when surfing; it can quickly become unpleasant if you do otherwise.

➡ If you give aloha, you'll get aloha.

LOCAL PHRASEOLOGY

brah – shortened form of *braddah* (brother)

chicken skin – goose bumps from cold, fear, thrill

coconut wireless – the 'grapevine'; local gossip channels

cruisin' – refers to going with the flow, dating, roaming about, driving around, sitting still in one place, and many other active or passive activities or states of being

da kine – whatchamacallit; used whenever you can't think of the appropriate word

fo' real? – Really? Are you kidding me?

high makamaka – stuck-up, snooty, pretentious; literally high 'eyes,' meaning head in the air

howzit? – Hey, how's it going? As in 'Eh, howzit brah?'

rubbah slippahs – literally 'rubber slippers'; flip-flops

talk story – chitchat or any casual conversation

to da max – used as an adjective or adverb to add emphasis, as in 'da waves was big to da max!'

Social Issues

Among social issues on Kaua'i, three stand out: education, substance abuse and homelessness. With only three public high schools on the island, education remains a weak point. North Shore students, for example, can average three hours a day commuting to and from school. And with an 'us versus them' mentality often present between the student body and the faculty, public school can end up being more of a containment facility than an institution of learning. Parents, especially if they're mainland transplants, often try to get their kids into private schools.

Substance abuse on the island ranges from overuse of alcohol to the extremely damaging effects of crystal methamphetamine (or 'ice,' as it's known locally), and rapidly growing problems with opiates. Thanks to Kaua'i's reliance on imported goods, drugs can often make their way onto the island with ease, and in recent years the amount of black tar heroin reaching the island has increased.

In 2018, Kaua'i County became the first county in Hawaii to take legal action against the makers, marketers and distributors of opioid pain medications, marking progress in an ongoing battle against opioid addiction. The island's Adolescent Treatment and Healing Center opened in 2019 on former sugar plantation land near Lihu'e donated by Grove Farm. It provides inpatient rehabilitation facilities for 12 to 18 year olds struggling with addiction.

Homelessness was identified as one of Kaua'i's top three problems (along with traffic and drug use) in a 2017 survey of the island's residents. In 2019, a report estimated the island had a total of 443 homeless people, up from 293 in 2018. Some county campgrounds (especially Lucy Wright Park and Anahola) are used by homeless campers, and a significant number of people live in their cars along an undeveloped strip of Wailua's beachfront real estate between the Aston Islander on the Beach and Sheraton Kauai Coconut Beach Resort. A planned 'Ohana Zone' of specialist services and public housing especially designed for the homeless was announced in late 2019.

Hawaiian Arts & Crafts

E komo mai (welcome) to these unique Polynesian islands, where storytelling and slack key guitar are among the sounds of everyday life. Contemporary Hawaii is a vibrant mix of multicultural traditions and underneath it all beats a Hawaiian heart, pounding with an ongoing revival of Hawaii's indigenous language, artisanal crafts, music and the hula.

Hula

In ancient Hawai'i, hula was sometimes a solemn ritual, in which *mele* (songs, chants) were an offering to the gods or celebrated the accomplishments of *ali'i* (chiefs). At other times hula was lighthearted entertainment, in which chief and *kama'aina* (commoner) danced together, including at annual festivals. Most importantly, hula embodied the community – telling stories about and celebrating itself. Hula still thrives today, with competitions and expositions across the islands.

Gifted ukulele player Eddie Kamae is also a talented and prolific filmmaker. Among his documentaries, look for *Keepers of the Flame* (1988), which profiles three revered Hawaiian cultural experts: Mary Kawena Pukui, 'Iolani Luahine and Edith Kanaka'ole.

Island Music

Hawaiian music is rooted in ancient chants. Foreign missionaries and sugar-plantation workers introduced new melodies and instruments, which were incorporated and adapted to create a unique local musical style. *Leo ki'eki'e* (falsetto, or 'high voice') vocals, sometimes just referred to as soprano for women, employs a signature *ha'i* (vocal break, or split-note) style, with a singer moving abruptly from one register to another. Contemporary Hawaiian musical instruments include the steel guitar, slack key guitar and ukulele.

But if you tune your rental-car radio to today's island radio stations, you'll hear everything from US mainland hip-hop beats, country-and-western tunes and Asian pop hits to reggae-inspired 'Jawaiian' grooves. A few Hawaii-born singer-songwriters, most famously Jack Johnson, have achieved international stardom. To discover new hit-makers, check out this year's winners of the Na Hoku Hanohano Awards (www.nahokuhanohano.org), Hawaii's version of the Grammies.

Ukulele

Heard all across the islands is the ukulele, derived from the *braguinha,* a Portuguese stringed instrument introduced to Hawaii in 1879. Ukulele means 'jumping flea' in Hawaiian, referring to the way players' deft fingers swiftly move around the strings. The ukulele is enjoying a revival as a young generation of virtuosos emerges, including Nick Acosta, who plays with just one hand, and genre-bending rockers led by Jake Shimabukuro, whose album *Peace Love Ukulele* (2011) reached number one on Billboard's world music chart.

Both the ukulele and the steel guitar contributed to the lighthearted *hapa haole* (Hawaiian music with predominantly English lyrics) popularized in the islands after the 1930s, of which 'My Little Grass Shack' and 'Lovely Hula Hands' are classic examples. For better or for worse, *hapa haole* songs became instantly recognizable as 'Hawaiian' thanks to Hollywood movies and the classic *Hawaii Calls* radio show, which broadcast worldwide from the banyan-tree courtyard of Waikiki's Moana hotel from 1935 until 1975.

Cowboy Heritage

Spanish and Mexican cowboys introduced the guitar to Hawaiians in the 1830s. Fifty years later, O'ahu-born high-school student Joseph Kekuku started experimenting with playing a guitar flat on his lap while sliding a pocket knife or comb across the strings. His invention, the Hawaiian steel guitar *(kika kila),* lifts the strings off the fretboard using a movable steel slide, creating a signature smooth sound.

In the early 20th century, Kekuku and others introduced the islands' steel guitar sounds to the world. The steel guitar later inspired the creation of resonator guitars such as the Dobro, now integral to bluegrass, blues and other genres, and country-and-western music's lap and pedal steel guitars. Today Hawaii's most influential steel guitarists include Henry Kaleialoha Allen, Alan Akaka, Bobby Ingano and Greg Sardinha.

Slack Key Guitar

Since the mid-20th century, the Hawaiian steel guitar has usually been played with slack key *(ki ho'alu)* tunings, in which the thumb plays the bass and rhythm chords, while the fingers play the melody and improvisations, in a picked style. Traditionally, slack key tunings were closely guarded secrets among *'ohana* (extended family and friends).

The legendary guitarist Gabby Pahinui launched the modern slack key guitar era with his first recording of 'Hi'ilawe' in 1946. In the

Ukulele and feather rattles

1960s, Gabby and his band Sons of Hawaii embraced the traditional Hawaiian sound. Along with other influential slack key guitarists such as Sonny Chillingworth, they spurred a renaissance in Hawaiian music that continues to this day. The list of contemporary slack key masters is long and ever growing, including Keola Beamer, Ledward Ka'apana, Martin and Cyril Pahinui, Ozzie Kotani and George Kuo.

Traditional Crafts

In the 1970s, the Hawaiian renaissance sparked interest in artisan crafts. The most beloved traditional craft is lei-making, stringing garlands of flowers, leaves, berries, nuts or shells. More lasting souvenirs include wood carvings, woven baskets and hats, and Hawaiian quilts. All of these have become so popular with tourists that cheap imitation imports from across the Pacific have flooded into Hawaii, so shop carefully and always buy local.

Fabric Arts

Lauhala weaving and *kapa* (cloth made by pounding the bark of the paper mulberry tree) making are two ancient Hawaiian crafts practiced only by a small number of experts today.

Traditionally, *lauhala* was stripped and woven to serve as floor mats, canoe sails and protective capes. Weaving the *lau* (leaves) of the *hala* (pandanus) tree requires skill, but preparing the leaves, which have razor-sharp spines, is messy work that takes real dedication. Today the most common *lauhala* items are hats, placemats and baskets. Most are mass-produced, but you can find handmade pieces at specialty stores like the Big Island's **Kimura Lauhala Shop** (☑808-324-0053; 77-996 Hualalai Rd; ⊙9am-5pm Mon-Fri, 9am-4pm Sat) ✔ near Kailua-Kona.

Feather lei (p262)

Making *kapa* (called *tapa* elsewhere in Polynesia) is no less laborious. First, seashells are used to scrape away the rough outer bark of the *wauke* (paper mulberry) tree. Strips of softer inner bark are cut (traditionally with shark's teeth) and pounded with mallets until thin and pliable; they are soaked in water between beating to let them ferment and further soften.

Once soft enough, the bark strips are layered atop one another and pounded together in a process called felting. Large sheets of finished *kapa* are colorfully dyed with plant materials and hand-stamped or hand-painted with geometric patterns before being scented with flowers or oils.

In ancient times, *kapa* was fashioned into everyday clothing and used as blankets for everything from swaddling newborns to burying the dead. Today authentic handmade Hawaiian *kapa* cloth is rarely seen outside of museums, fine-art galleries and private collections.

Island Writings

For traditional myths and legends of Kaua'i, you can't go wrong with master storyteller Frederick B Wichman's anthologies, including *Touring the Legends of Koke'e* and *Touring the Legends of the North Shore,* both published by the Kaua'i Historical Society (www. kauaihistoricalsociety.org). Talk Story (p224) in Hanapepe is the best bookstore on the island.

Kaua'i's Contemporary Art Scene

Most artwork by Kaua'i artists is highly commercial: colorful, representational works that appeal to the tourist eye. Unique pieces that go beyond the stereotypes do exist, but they're harder to find and

KAUA'I ON SCREEN

Kaua'i has an extraordinary cinematic history; when Hollywood wants paradise, this is its first stop. Stop by the Kaua'i Visitors Bureau in Lihu'e for a free map of all films and locations. Also see www.filmkauai.com. The most important cinema and television productions filmed on the island include:

➡ *White Heat* (1934)

Set on a sugar plantation, the first movie shot on the island addresses the issue of cross-cultural relationships.

➡ *Pagan Love Song* (1950)

Actually set in in Tahiti, Esther Williams and Howard Keel launch Kaua'i's history of movie musicals.

➡ *South Pacific* (1958)

Standing in for the mythical island paradise of Bali Hai, Kaua'i's beaches suddenly became world famous.

➡ *Blue Hawaii* (1960)

It's Elvis baby, as the emerging rock-and-roll superstar tears it up at the Coco Palms Resort and on the Wailua River.

➡ *King Kong* (1976)

A remake of everybody's favorite giant-ape movie kicks off Kaua'i's ongoing role in Hollywood blockbusters.

➡ *Fantasy Island* (1977)

Stunning Wailua Falls grabs the limelight in the TV series' opening credits.

➡ *Raiders of the Lost Ark* (1983)

Harrison Ford and Steven Spielberg combine for Indiana Jones' first big-screen outing.

➡ *Jurassic Park* (1993)

Giant dinosaurs run amok, and blockbusting sequels follow in 1997 (*The Lost World: Jurassic Park*), 2001 (*Jurassic Park 3*), and 2015 (*Jurassic World*).

➡ *The Descendants* (2011)

George Clooney nixes a real-estate development on the island, and Hanalei has its moment in the sun. A killer soundtrack of traditional Hawaiian music too.

are displayed mainly in Honolulu museums and galleries. On Kaua'i, try the Kaua'i Society of Artists (p86) and the cluster of galleries in Hanapepe.

Notable fine artists (to name only a few) include the following:

Carol Bennett (www.carolbennettart.com) Meditative paintings of underwater movement.

A Kimberlin Blackburn (www.akimberlinblackburn.com) Uninhibitedly colorful, stylized sculptures and paintings.

Liedeke Bulder (www.liedekebulderart.com) Classic botanical paintings and skyscape watercolors.

Margaret Ezekiel Pastel drawings of cloudscapes or the human figure.

Mac James (www.macjamesonkauai.com) Nature paintings and drawings with contemporary environmental themes.

Bruna Stude (www.brunastude.com) Elegant B&W underwater photography.

To keep in touch with contemporary issues that are important to the Hawaiian community, both in the islands and in the global diaspora, browse the independent news and culture magazine *Mana* (www.welive mana.com).

Lei

Greetings. Love. Honor. Respect. Peace. Celebration. Spirituality. Good luck. Farewell. A Hawaiian lei – a handcrafted garland of fresh tropical flowers – can signify all of these meanings and many more. Lei-making may be Hawaii's most sensuous and transitory art form. Fragrant and ephemeral, lei embody the beauty of nature and the embrace of 'ohana (extended family and friends) and the community, freely given and freely shared.

The Art of the Lei

In choosing their materials, lei makers express emotions and tell stories, since flowers and other natural artifacts often embody Hawaiian places and myths. Traditional lei makers use feathers, nuts, shells, seeds, seaweed, vines, leaves and fruit, in addition to fragrant flowers. The most common methods of making lei are by knotting, braiding, winding, stringing or sewing raw materials together.

Worn daily, lei were integral to ancient Hawaiian society. They were important elements of sacred hula dances and given as special gifts to loved ones, as healing medicine to the sick and as offerings to the gods, all practices that continue today. So powerful a symbol were they that on ancient Hawai'i's battlefields, a lei could bring peace to warring armies.

Today, locals wear lei for special events, such as weddings, birthdays, anniversaries and graduations. It's no longer common to make one's own lei, unless you belong to a hula *halau* (school). For ceremonial hula, performers are often required to make their own lei, gathering raw materials by hand, never taking more than necessary and always thanking the tree and the gods.

You can find lei across the island. Keep your eyes out for eye-catching Ni'ihau shell lei.

Modern Celebrations

For visitors to Hawaii, the tradition of giving and receiving lei dates back to 19th-century steamships that brought the first tourists to the islands. Later, disembarking cruise-ship passengers were greeted by vendors who would toss garlands around the necks of *malihini* (newcomers).

In 1927 the poet Don Blanding and Honolulu journalist Grace Tower Warren called for making May 1 a holiday to honor lei. Every year, Lei Day is still celebrated across the islands with Hawaiian music, hula dancing, parades, and lei-making workshops and contests.

The tradition of giving a kiss with a lei began during WWII, allegedly when a hula dancer at a USO club was dared by her friends to give a military serviceman a peck on the cheek when offering him a flower lei.

On the 'Garden Island,' leathery, anise-scented *mokihana* berries are often woven with strands of glossy, green maile vines. Mokihana trees thrive on the rain-soaked western slopes of Mt Wai'ale'ale.

Landscapes & Wildlife

The Hawaiian Islands are the most isolated landmasses on earth. Born of barren lava flows, they were originally populated only by plants and animals that could traverse the Pacific – for example, seeds clinging to a bird's feather or fern spores that drifted thousands of miles through the air. Most flora and fauna that landed here didn't survive. Scientists estimate that new species became established maybe once every 20,000 years – and these included no amphibians, no browsing animals, no mosquitoes and only two mammals: a bat and a seal.

Above Alaka'i Swamp Trail (p241)

The wildlife that did make it here found a rich, ecologically diverse land to colonize. Developed in isolation, many of these species became endemic to the islands, meaning that they're found nowhere else in the world. Unfortunately, Hawaii has the highest rate of extinction in the nation and nearly 25% of all federally listed threatened and endangered species in the US are endemic Hawaiian flora and fauna. Only time will tell how climate change will affect the islands' unique species.

Animals

Kaua'i's main attractions for wildlife enthusiasts are resident and migratory birds, as well as myriad ocean creatures.

Ocean Life

Up to 10,000 migrating North Pacific humpback whales come to Hawaiian waters for calving each winter, and whale-watching can be excellent off Kaua'i's South Shore. Pods of spinner dolphins, with their acrobatic spiraling leaps, regularly approach boats cruising in Kaua'i's waters and can also be seen from the shoreline off Kilauea Point.

Threatened *honu* (green sea turtles) are traditionally revered by Hawaiians as an *'aumakua* (protective deity). Snorkelers often see *honu* feeding on seaweed along rocky coastlines or in shallow lagoons. Endangered Hawaiian monk seals also occasionally haul up on shore, which is a thrill for beachgoers who by law must observe turtles and seals from a distance.

Birds

Kaua'i is a birder's dream, with copious creatures soaring over its peaks and down its valleys. Lowland wetlands feature four waterbirds that are cousins of mainland species: the Hawaiian duck, Hawaiian coot, Hawaiian moorhen and Hawaiian stilt. The best place to view all four species is the North Shore's Hanalei National Wildlife Refuge. Although public access to the refuge is strictly limited, an overlook opposite Princeville Center provides a great view of the birds' habitat, with a serene river, shallow ponds and cultivated taro fields.

The nene, Hawaii's state bird, is a long-lost cousin of the Canada goose. Nene once numbered as many as 25,000 on all the islands, but by the 1950s only 50 were left. Intensive breeding programs have raised their numbers to around 2500 on three main islands: Maui, Kaua'i and Hawai'i (Big Island). You might see them in Hanalei wetlands, around golf courses and open fields, and at Kilauea Point National Wildlife Refuge.

SWIMMING WITH DOLPHINS

Hawaiian spinner dolphins are some of the most amazing, intuitive and curious creatures on earth. A highlight of many a trip is the chance to see these cetaceans up close. However, according to the National Oceanic and Atmospheric Administration (NOAA), the dolphins are facing increased pressure from humans, meaning you should think carefully about how you engage with dolphins while visiting.

There are a number of factors to consider. The number of dolphin-focused tours has grown across the islands, from about 10 in 2006 to over 70 today. Furthermore, dolphins hunt at night and then come into the shallows during the day to rest. NOAA argues that swimming with them during these resting periods affects their natural life cycles. In 2016 NOAA proposed a rule to clarify the Marine Mammal Protection Act and prohibit swimming with and approaching Hawaiian spinner dolphins within 50yd. The proposed rule was a sticking point for many people on Kaua'i and as of press time, the rule still hadn't been finalized. See https://www.fisheries.noaa.gov/action/enhancing-protections-hawaiian-spinner-dolphins for further information.

There are a few noteworthy exceptions to the rule. Persons who inadvertently come within 50yd, or who are approached by dolphins would be exempt. Vessels that are underway and approached, but make no effort to change course to intercept dolphins would also be exempt from the rule. This logic is designed to stop the practice of leap-frogging (less common on Kaua'i than the other islands), where boats take turns intercepting dolphin pods.

MARINE WILDLIFE 911
• •
Federal and state laws protect all of Hawaii's wild marine mammals and turtles from harassment. Legally, this usually means you may not approach them closer than 50yd (100yd for whales, or 20ft for turtles) or do anything that disrupts their normal behavior. The most important actions for island visitors to avoid are disturbing endangered monk seals and sea turtles that have 'hauled out' and are resting on beaches. If you see a fellow beach-goer hassling one of these sand-lounging beasts, feel free to get righteous on them.

Native forest birds are more challenging to observe, but the keen-eyed may spy eight endemic species remaining at Koke'e State Park, especially in the Alaka'i Wilderness Preserve. The *'apapane*, a type of honeycreeper, is the most abundant: a bright-red bird the same color as the *lehua* flowers from which it takes nectar.

Today, two-thirds of all endemic Hawaiian birds are extinct, the victims of aggressive introduced birds and infectious diseases. In 1992 Hurricane 'Iniki also contributed to this catastrophic decline: it was the last time three species were seen on Kaua'i. The Hawaii Audubon Society (www.hawaiiaudubon.org/kauai-birding) has comprehensive information on the island's birdlife and SoundsHawaiian (www.soundshawaiian.com) is a real treat for the ears, offering crisp recordings of island birdsong.

Plants

Ancient Hawaiians would scarcely recognize Kaua'i, having never encountered the tropical flowers, fruit trees and lush landscape that today epitomize the island. Mangoes came from Asia, macadamia nuts from Australia and coffee from Africa. Today many botanists and farmers advocate biodiversity, so alien species aren't necessarily bad. But, of Hawaii's 1300 endemic plant species, over 100 are already extinct and 273 are endangered.

Native Forest Trees

Over 90% of Hawaii's 1000-plus plant species are endemic to the islands. To see native forest trees, visit Koke'e State Park and the 10,000-acre Alaka'i Swamp Wilderness Preserve. Along the Pihea and Alaka'i Swamp trails you'll see the most abundant rainforest tree, *'ohi'a lehua*, a hardwood with bright-red or orange pompom-like flowers that provide nectar for forest birds. Another dominant forest tree (or shrub) is *lapalapa*, with long-stemmed leaves that flutter in the slightest breeze. Among the best-known tree species is koa, an endemic hardwood that is Hawaii's most commercially valuable tree for its fine woodworking qualities, rich color and swirling grain. You can identify koa trees by their distinctive crescent-shaped leaves.

Coastal Plants

Despite the rampant development along some parts of Kaua'i's coast, the shoreline is also a good place to find endemic plants. The harsh environment – windblown, salt-sprayed, often arid land with nutrient-poor, sandy soil – requires plants to adapt to survive, for example, by growing flat along the ground, becoming succulent or developing waxy leaf coatings to retain moisture. You can see many endemic coastal plants at Kilauea Point National Wildlife Refuge on the North Shore.

National, State & County Parks

About 30% of Kaua'i is protected as state parks and nature reserves. For hiking, don't miss Waimea Canyon State Park and Koke'e State Park, with their spectacular elevated views and numerous trails and campsites. On the Eastside, Nounou Mountain, with three steep but scenic hiking trails, is well-maintained forest-reserve land.

Ha'ena State Park is another favorite, as it has Ke'e Beach, a fantastic snorkeling spot, and the nearby Kalalau Trail leading into Na Pali Coast Wilderness State Park. The miles of sandy beach at Polihale State Park offer an escape from crowds, but beware two potential threats: hazardous ocean conditions and the bone-rattlingly rough 5-mile unpaved road to get there. Most of Kaua'i's best easy-access beaches are designated as county parks, such as sunny Po'ipu Beach Park (South Shore), serene 'Anini Beach Park (North Shore), calm Salt Pond Beach Park (Westside) and family-friendly Lydgate Beach Park (Eastside).

There are no national parks on the island, but there are three federal refuges, including the accessible Kilauea Point National Wildlife Refuge, which has spectacular wildlife watching, including migratory whales in winter and the only diverse seabird colony on the main Hawaiian Islands.

The Land

Kaua'i is the oldest and fourth largest of the major inhabited Hawaiian Islands, with volcanic rocks dating back over five million years and most of the island boasting the tropical trifecta of ocean, beach and mountain. Unlike the shiny black terrain seen on much of the lava-spewing Big Island (a baby at less than 500,000 years old), Kaua'i displays the effects of time and erosion, with weathered summits, mountaintop bogs and rainforests, deeply cut valleys and rivers, extensive sandy beaches, coral and algal reefs, and rust-colored soil indelible from both memory and your white sneakers.

KAUA'I'S TOP PARKS & PROTECTED AREAS

NATURE AREA	FEATURES	ACTIVITIES
Alaka'i Wilderness Preserve	rainforest, bogs, forest birds	boardwalk hiking, bird-watching
'Anini Beach Park	sandy beach, calm waters	swimming, windsurfing, picnicking
Ha'ena State Park	sandy beach, historic Hawaiian sites, marine life	swimming, snorkeling
Hanalei Bay	scenic circular bay, sandy beaches, winter waves	surfing, swimming
Hanalei National Wildlife Refuge	river, endangered waterbirds	bird-watching (limited access)
Kilauea Point National Wildlife Refuge	seabirds, coastal plants, nene (native Hawaiian geese), historic lighthouse	bird-watching, whale-watching
Koke'e State Park	trails, waterfalls, forest birds & plants, interpretive center	hiking, camping, bird-watching
Maha'ulepu Coast*	trails, waterfalls, forest birds & plants, interpretive center	hiking, camping, bird-watching
Na Pali Coast State Park	challenging trails, coastal flora, seabirds, archaeological sites	walking, windsurfing, surfing
Polihale State Park	coastal dunes, state's longest beach (dangerous currents)	walking, sunset watching, camping
Waimea Canyon State Park	colossal gorge, forestland	hiking, camping

*Private property not under governmental protection

Sea turtle

Volcanic Origins

Because its volcanic origins lie hidden under a carpet of forests, ferns and shrubland, Kauaʻi's landscape, particularly along the North Shore, is overwhelmingly lush and strikes many as the ultimate tropical beauty – which partly explains the frequency of visitors showing up for a week or two and staying a lifetime. Many folks' lives have shifted as a result of just driving down the hill from Princeville to Hanalei.

Perhaps duped by its round shape, scientists for decades believed that a single volcano formed Kauaʻi. But on the basis of evidence collected since the 1980s, scientists now think that Kauaʻi's entire eastern side 'slumped' along an ancient fault line, leaving a steep *pali* (cliff) along Waimea Canyon's western edge. Then, lava from another shield volcano flowed westward to the *pali* and pounded against the cliffs. The black and red horizontal striations along the canyon walls represent successive volcanic eruptions; the red color shows where water seeped through the rocks, oxidizing the iron inside.

Highs & Lows

Now shrunken by age, Kauaʻi is also slowly subsiding into the ocean floor. Don't worry though, the rate is less than an inch per century. Still, over eons those inches have cost the island 3000ft in elevation, making today's high point the 5243ft Kawaikini. Among the most visually spectacular valleys is Kalalau, with its curtain-like folds and knife-edge ridges, topping out just above 4000ft at lookouts where the road ends in Kokeʻe State Park. Views of the Na Pali sea cliffs are spectacular, but can only be seen from the deck of a boat, the windows of a helicopter – or, for the fit and eco-conscious, from the Nuʻalolo or Awaʻawapuhi trails in Kokeʻe State Park, or the grueling 11-mile Kalalau Trail in Na Pali Coast Wilderness State Park.

Survival Guide

Directory A–Z

Accessible Travel

Accommodations Hotels are required to be accessible under the Americans with Disabilities Act (ADA). Major hotels are equipped with elevators, phones with telecommunications device for the deaf (TDD) and wheelchair-accessible rooms (which must be reserved in advance). These services are unlikely in B&Bs and small hotels.

General Information Kaua'i County can be a resource, though its website (www.

kauai.gov/visitors) is clunky. If you have specific questions about traveling with a disability on Kaua'i, call the American Disability Act (ADA) Coordinator at the Office of the Mayor (808-241-4921). The **Disability and Communication Access Board** (%808-586-8121; http://health.hawaii. gov/dcab) also provides a tip sheet specifically for Kaua'i at https://health.hawaii.gov/dcab/ files/2018/07/Kauai-2018.pdf. Also worthwhile, with good links to other information, is www. gohawaii.com/trip-planning/ accessibility.

For an independent take on accessible travel on Kaua'i, see **Accessible Kauai** (www. accessiblekauai.com), an excellent online resource detailing helpful information on which adventure and activity operators are experienced and confident catering to visitors with disabilities. It also offers a good directory of accessible restrooms, restaurants with accessible facilities and recommended accommodations choices.

Guide & Service Dogs These dogs are not subject to the general quarantine rules for pets if they meet the Department of Agriculture's minimum requirements; see http://hdoa.hawaii.gov/ai/ aqs/guide-service-dogs for more details. All animals must enter the state via Honolulu International Airport.

Mobility There are currently no car-rental agencies with lift-equipped vehicles. Gammie HomeCare (www.gammie. com) rents portable ramps, wheelchairs, hospital beds, walking aids and other medical equipment. **Wheelchair Getaways of Hawaii** (☑800-638-1912; www. accessiblevans.com) rents wheelchair-accessible vans. Kaua'i County provides a Landeez all-terrain wheelchair at lifeguard stations at Po'ipu, Lydgate and Salt Pond Beach Parks. All **Kaua'i county buses** (☑808-246-8110; www. kauai.gov/bus; 3220 Ho'olako St, Lihu'e; one-way fare adult/

Climate

Lihu'e

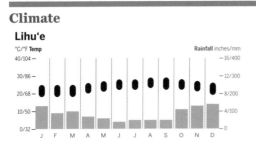

Princeville

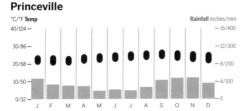

Koke'e State Park

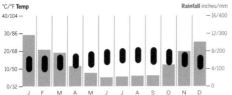

Electricity

Voltage is 110/120V at 60 cycles, with a standard US plug.

Type A
120V/60Hz

Type B
120V/60Hz

---

senior & child 7-18yr $2/1) are wheelchair-lift equipped.

Download Lonely Planet's free Accessible Travel guides from https://shop. lonelyplanet.com/products/ accessible-travel-online-resources-2019.

Customs Regulations

Non-US citizens and permanent residents may import the following duty free:

➡ 1L of liquor (if over 21 years)

➡ 200 cigarettes or 50 non-Cuban cigars (if over 21 years)

➡ $100 worth of gifts

Hawaii has strict restrictions against bringing in any fresh

fruits and plants, to prevent entry of invasive species. The rabies-free state enforces strict pet quarantine laws, though you can cut the time to five days if you meet specific requirements. For complete details, contact the **Hawaiian Department of Agriculture** (http://hdoa. hawaii.gov).

Discount Cards

On arrival at Kaua'i airport, pick up brochures and tourist information from near the baggage carousels. If you're planning on taking in part in multiple experiences like ziplining, ATV driving and mountain tubing, good multi-adventure discount coupons are included in these publications.

Food & Drink

Dining on Kaua'i tends to be quite casual – even when it is elegant. Top tourist restaurants require reservations (sometimes several days in advance).

EATING PRICE RANGES

The following price ranges refer to a main course.

$ less than $15

$$ $12–25

$$$ more than $25

Fish Markets Taking a *bentō* box, *poke* or sushi roll to go is a local tradition and most towns have a worthwhile fish market – and rotating farmers markets – worth checking out.

Joints Be they taco stands, noodle spots, hamburger places or juice bars, the small-time joints of the island are the lifeblood of island cuisine. Look for lines out the door at lunchtime to pick a top spot.

Restaurants There are plenty of fancy tourist restaurants, often with live entertainment.

Health

➡ For emergency medical assistance anywhere in Hawaii, call 911 or go directly to the emergency room (ER) of the nearest hospital.

➡ For nonemergencies, consider an urgent-care center or walk-in medical clinic.

➡ Some insurance policies require you to get pre-authorization for medical treatment from a call center before seeking help. Keep all medical receipts and documentation for claims reimbursement later.

Health Insurance

Kaua'i is a long way from everywhere. Having a good travel health-insurance plan if you are not on a US policy is advisable. US policies work here, but you may find you are out of network for much of your needs.

Availability & Cost of Health Care

➡ Health-care costs are the same or slightly higher than mainland US. This means it's expensive.

➡ The best hospital is the **Wilcox Memorial Hospital** (☏808-245-1100; www.wilcoxhealth.org; 3-3420 Kuhio Hwy) in Lihu'e.

➡ There is currently no hyperbaric chamber on Kaua'i.

Infectious Diseases

The best ways to prevent the spread of infectious diseases is to listen to public-health advise, wash your hands, use a condom and avoid being bitten by mosquitoes.

DENGUE FEVER

➡ There was a small outbreak of dengue fever on the Big Island in 2015–16, with no known cases on Kaua'i (http://health.hawaii.gov).

➡ Dengue is transmitted by aedes mosquitoes, which bite preferentially during the daytime and breed primarily in artificial water containers.

➡ Dengue usually causes flu-like symptoms, including fever, muscle aches, joint pains, severe headaches, nausea and vomiting, often followed by a rash.

➡ If you suspect you've been infected, do not take aspirin or NSAIDs (eg ibuprofen), which can cause hemorrhaging. See a doctor for diagnosis and monitoring; severe cases may require hospitalization.

GIARDIASIS

➡ Symptoms of this parasitic infection of the small intestine include nausea, bloating, cramps and diarrhea, and may last for weeks.

➡ To protect yourself, don't drink from untreated water sources (eg waterfalls, ponds, streams, rivers), which may be contaminated by animal or human feces.

➡ Giardiasis is diagnosed by a stool test and treated with antibiotics.

HEPATITIS A

There was an outbreak of Hepatitis A on Kaua'i and O'ahu in 2016. The outbreak was related to scallops being served at a sushi restaurant.

HIV & AIDS

➡ Out of 1.43 million, there were a total of 2393 reported cases of HIV on the Hawaiian Islands in 2016.

➡ HIV is primarily spread in the US through sex and shared needles.

LEPTOSPIROSIS

➡ Leptospirosis is acquired by exposure to untreated water or soil contaminated by the urine of infected animals, especially rodents.

➡ Outbreaks often occur after flooding, when overflow contaminates water sources downstream from livestock or wild animal habitats.

➡ Initial symptoms, which resemble a flu, usually subside uneventfully in a few days, but a minority of cases involve potentially fatal complications.

➡ Diagnosis is through urine and/or blood tests and treatment is with antibiotics.

➡ Minimize your risk by staying out of bodies of freshwater (eg pools, streams, waterfalls); avoid these entirely if you have open cuts or sores.

➡ On hiking trails, take warning signs about leptospirosis seriously. If you're camping, water purification and good hygiene are essential.

STAPHYLOCOCCUS

➡ Hawaii leads the nation in antibiotic-resistant staphylococcus infections. Staph infections are caused by bacteria, which often enter the body through an open wound.

➡ To prevent infection, practice good hygiene (eg wash your hands thoroughly and frequently; shower or bathe daily; wear clean clothing). Apply antibiotic ointment (eg Neosporin) to any open cuts or sores and keep them out of recreational water; if cuts or sores are on your feet, don't go barefoot, even on sand.

➡ If a wound becomes painful, looks red, inflamed or swollen, leaks pus or causes a rash or blisters, seek medical help immediately.

ZIKA

➡ Hawaii has had no locally acquired Zika cases and no mosquitoes transmitting the disease within the state since 2016.

➡ There were a total of 10 cases of Zika imported to the state in 2016, with two coming to Kaua'i.

➡ Zika is spread mostly by the bite of an infected aedes mosquito. These mosquitoes bite during the day and night.

➡ Zika can be passed from a pregnant woman to her fetus. Infection during pregnancy can cause certain birth defects.

➡ Zika can be passed through sex from a person who has Zika.

➡ There is no vaccine or medicine for Zika. Learn more at www.cdc.gov/zika.

Environmental Hazards
BITES & STINGS

➡ Any animal bite or scratch – including from unknown dogs, feral pigs etc – should be promptly and thoroughly cleansed with soap and water, followed by application of an antiseptic (eg iodine, alcohol) to prevent wounds from becoming infected.

➡ Hawaii is currently rabies-free. The state has no established wild snake population, but snakes are occasionally seen, especially in sugarcane fields.

INSECTS

➡ The most effective protections against insect bites are common-sense behavior and clothing: wear long sleeves and pants, a hat and shoes.

➡ Where mosquitoes are active, apply a good insect repellent, preferably one containing DEET (but not for children under two years old).

➡ Some spider bites (eg from black widows or brown recluses) contain toxic venom, which children are more vulnerable to; for anyone who is bitten, apply ice or cool water to the affected area, then seek medical help.

➡ Centipedes also give painful bites; they can infiltrate buildings, so check sheets and shoes.

➡ Leeches found in humid rainforest areas do not transmit any disease but their bites can be intensely itchy, even for weeks afterward.

MARINE ANIMALS

➡ Marine spikes, such as those found on sea urchins, scorpion fish and lionfish, can cause severe localized pain. If this occurs, immediately immerse the affected area in hot water (as hot as can be tolerated). Keep topping up with hot water until the pain subsides and medical care can be reached. Do the same for cone-shell stings.

➡ Stings from jellyfish and Portuguese man-of-war (aka bluebottles) also occur in Hawaii's tropical waters. Even touching a bluebottle hours after it's washed up onshore can result in burning stings. Jellyfish are often seen eight to 10 days after a full moon, when they float into Hawaii's shallow near-shore waters, often on the islands' leeward shores. If you are stung, douse the affected area in vinegar, or carefully peel off the tentacles with a gloved hand, then rinse the area well in sea water (not freshwater or urine), followed by rapid transfer to a hospital; antivenoms are available.

VOG

➡ Vog, a visible haze or smog caused by volcanic emissions from the Big Island, is often (but not always) dispersed by trade winds before it reaches other islands.

➡ Short-term exposure to vog is not generally hazardous; however, high sulfur-dioxide levels can create breathing problems for sensitive groups (eg anyone with respiratory or heart conditions, pregnant women, young children and infants). Avoid vigorous physical exertion outdoors on voggy days.

TAP WATER

The tap water on Kaua'i is drinkable, though in some places it might not taste great. One good tip is to fill a large bottle with tap water and let it sit in the fridge overnight with a few slices of lime.

Insurance

Ensure your policy covers theft, loss and medical problems. Some policies specifically exclude designated 'dangerous activities' such as scuba diving, surfing or even hiking. Make sure the policy you choose fully covers your planned (and perhaps unplanned and spontaneous) activities.

Check also that the policy covers ambulances and emergency evacuation by air. Access to medical treatment in the United States can be very expensive, and these costs are potentially magnified if evacuation off the island to Honolulu or mainland-US medical facilities is necessary.

Worldwide travel insurance is available at www.lonely-planet.com/travel-insurance. You can buy, extend and claim online anytime – even if you're already on the road.

Internet Access

Wi-fi is available at many accommodations. Smaller accommodations (eg B&Bs) typically provide free wi-fi; larger hotels will often charge $12 to $15 per day for in-room access, but that can often be negotiated out of the bill. Make sure to handle that ahead of time, or simply use the lobby wi-fi.

Most towns have at least one cafe with wi-fi. It's free at Starbucks (Lihu'e's Kukui Grove Shopping Center and Waipouli's Kauai Village Shopping Center).

Laundry

Most condos, B&Bs, inns and vacation-rental homes include free or inexpensive use of washers and dryers; hotels typically offer coin-operated laundry facilities.

Legal Matters

➡ You are entitled to an attorney from the moment that you are arrested. The **Hawaii State Bar Association** (📞808-537-9140; http://hawaiilawyerreferral.com; Suite 1000, 1100 Alakea St, Honolulu; ⏲8:30am-4:30pm Mon-Fri) is one starting point to find an attorney. If you can't afford one, the state is obligated to provide one for free.

➡ Driving with a blood alcohol level of 0.08% or higher constitutes driving under the influence (DUI).

➡ Possessing marijuana and narcotics is illegal, although smoking a joint rarely leads to arrest unless other crimes are involved. Still, better not to get spotted doing so.

➡ Hitchhiking and public nudity (eg at nude beaches) are illegal but the laws are rarely enforced.

➡ Smoking cigarettes is prohibited in all public spaces, including airports, bars, restaurants and businesses and, as of 2015, state parks and beaches.

➡ While the Department of Commerce & Consumer Affairs (www.cca.hawaii.gov) deals primarily with residents' issues, visitors who want to lodge a complaint against a business should contact the Department's Office of Consumer Protection.

LGBTQ+ Travelers

Sexual preference on Kaua'i is basically a non-issue. The island culture here is very welcoming and diverse. Hawaii has strong legislation which protects minority groups, and there is also a constitutional guarantee of privacy regarding sexual behavior between consenting adults. That said, there's neither a gay scene nor any public displays of affection on the island, as locals tend to keep their private lives to themselves.

Maps

Franko's Maps (www.frankosmaps.com) Outstanding full-color, fold-up, waterproof maps ($8 to $11) that pinpoint snorkeling, diving, surfing and kayaking spots, and also identify tropical fish.

Kaua'i Island Atlas & Maps (www.envdhawaii.com) Like a land version of the Franko map ($10), with all sorts of info on climate, geology and culture, along with town insets. Available at Koke'e Natural History Museum.

Kaua'i Official Guide Map Nice fold-out tourist freebie available from Kaua'i Visitors Bureau, Lihu'e. Identifies locations used in feature films.

MINIMUM LEGAL AGE TO...

ACTIVITY	AGE
Drink alcohol	21
Buy tobacco	18
Vote in an election	18
Drive a car	16

Na Ala Hele (http://hawaiitrails.
ehawaii.gov) This interactive
website is a tremendous resource
for information on the island's
public-access trails, including
maps and directions to trailheads.

TopoZone (www.topozone.
com) If you're a geographer,
backcountry explorer or map
fiend, TopoZone has general
topographical maps.

Money

ATMs are available in all
major towns. Visa and MasterCard are widely accepted.
American Express and Dis-
cover hit or miss.

ATMs

ATMs are available at banks,
supermarkets, convenience
stores, shopping centers
and gas stations. Expect a
surcharge of about $2 per
transaction, plus any fees
charged by your home bank.

Credit & Debit Cards

Major credit cards are widely
accepted at larger businesses, and they're necessary to
rent a car, order tickets by
phone and book a hotel room.
But smaller businesses such
as B&Bs may not accept
credit cards. In those cases,
a PayPal or Venmo account
may suffice if you'd rather not
deal in cash. Cash can be a
better option when shopping
at farmers markets, but most
food trucks on the island
accept credit cards.

Tipping

Leaving no tip is rare and
requires real cause.

Bars $1 per drink ordered.

Hotel bellhops $1 to $2 per bag.

Housekeeping staff $2 to $4
daily.

Parking valets At least $2 when
handed back your car keys.

Restaurants Tip 15% to 20%,
unless gratuity is included.

Taxi drivers Tip 10% to 15% of
metered fare.

Opening Hours

Banks 8:30am–4pm Monday to
Friday, some to 6pm Friday, and
9am–noon or 1pm Saturday

Bars & Clubs To midnight
daily, some to 2am Thursday to
Saturday

Businesses 8:30am–4:30pm
Monday to Friday, some post
offices 9am–noon Saturday

Restaurants Breakfast 6–10am,
lunch 11:30am–2:30pm, dinner
5–9:30pm

Shops 9am–5pm Monday to
Saturday, some also noon–5pm
Sunday

Post

➡ The US Postal Service
(www.usps.com) delivers
mail to and from Kaua'i.
Service is reliable but
slower than within
continental USA. First-class
airmail between Kaua'i and
the mainland takes up to
four days.

➡ First-class letters up
to 1oz (about 28g) cost
55¢ within the USA, $1.15
internationally.

➡ You can receive mail c/o
General Delivery at most
post offices on Kaua'i, but
you must first complete an
application in person. Bring
two forms of ID and your
temporary local address.
The accepted application
is valid for 30 days; mail
is held for up to 15 days.
Many accommodations will
also hold mail for incoming
guests.

Public Holidays

New Year's Day January 1

Martin Luther King Jr Day
Third Monday in January

Presidents' Day Third Monday
in February

Kuhio Day March 26

Good Friday Friday before
Easter Sunday

Memorial Day Last Monday
in May

King Kamehameha Day June 11

Independence Day July 4

Statehood Day Third Friday in
August

Labor Day First Monday in
September

Election Day Second Tuesday in
November

Veterans Day November 11

Thanksgiving Fourth Thursday
in November

Christmas Day December 25

Safe Travel

Kaua'i can be a safe and
easy-to-navigate destination
for seasoned travelers, but
however beautiful, nature
can pose a threat.

➡ Drownings happen in
high surf and in sheltered
coves. Always be aware of
currents, swell and tides,
and when in doubt, don't
go out.

➡ Roads can be dark
at night, which can
be disorienting and
intimidating for big-city
drivers.

➡ Keep valuables out
of sight when parked at
beaches and trailheads.

Visitors who become acci-
dent or crime victims can
contact the **Visitor Aloha
Society of Hawaii** (VASH;
☎808-926-8274; http://visit-
oralohasocietyofhawaii.org), a
traveler's aid organization,
for short-term assistance.

> **SURF REPORTS**
> Online reports are
> available at www.
> kauaiexplorer.com/
> ocean_report and www.
> surfline.com.

Hiking & Swimming

The major risks on Kaua'i lie here. In 2018 nine people drowned on the island, and tragically this number increased to 15 in 2019.

The climate, while idyllic in one sense, can bite back if you venture onto trails without ample food, water or bad-weather gear. Rivers can rise fast too. Make sure you are prepared for the elements and your level of activity before you venture out.

Theft & Violence

Kaua'i is a pretty quiet place and there's virtually no nightlife. Populated areas, such as towns and major sights, are relatively safe. Having said that, the island has its issues, like everywhere else.

➡ There's a drug problem, generally involving ice (crystal methamphetamine) or *pakalolo* (marijuana), which fuels petty crime. Be on guard at deserted beaches and parks (eg Nawiliwili Beach Park, Keahua Arboretum) after dark.

➡ Car break-ins occur mainly in remote areas, including roadside parks, campgrounds and parking lots, but not always.

➡ There's a deep insider/outsider mentality, with racial overtones. Certain beaches, surf spots, swimming holes and rural neighborhoods are unofficially considered locals only. In these places haole (white) tourists might encounter resentment or worse. The key is to avoid confrontation. Be careful in places where that bright new aloha shirt makes you stand out. Be aware when driving that this is not downtown Manhattan. When in doubt, drive slow, and don't use that horn.

Trespassing

➡ Heed *kapu* (no trespassing) signs on private property.

➡ Like the rest of the US, Hawaii does not have the open-access laws found in certain European countries.

Tsunami

During the 20th century, Kaua'i was hit by two major tsunamis. Both ravaged the North Shore, causing 14 deaths in 1946, and demolishing 75 homes and washing out six essential bridges in 1957. Today, new homes built in tsunami-prone areas (flood zones) must be built high off the ground.

➡ If you're at the coast when a tsunami occurs, immediately head inland.

➡ The front section of local telephone books has maps of areas susceptible to tsunamis and safety evacuation zones.

➡ Kaua'i has four civil defense sirens that can be used to issue a tsunami warning.

Telephone

Cell Phones

Cell reception is good except in remote locations. All multiband GSM phones will work in the US.

You need a multiband GSM phone to make calls in the USA. If your phone doesn't work, pop in a US prepaid rechargeable SIM card (with an unlocked multiband phone) or buy an inexpensive prepaid phone.

Network Coverage

Verizon has the best cellular network across the state, but AT&T and Sprint have decent coverage. While coverage on Kaua'i is good in major towns, it's spotty or nonexistent in rural areas.

Phone Codes

➡ Domestic long-distance calls must be preceded by 1.

➡ Toll-free numbers (area codes 800, 866, 877 or 888) must be preceded by 1.

➡ For all Kaua'i calls from a local landline, dial only the seven-digit number. For interisland calls, dial 1-808 and then the seven-digit number; long-distance charges apply.

➡ For Kaua'i, Hawaii and all out-of-state calls from a cell phone, dial the 10-digit number beginning with the 808 area code.

➡ For direct international calls, dial 011 plus the country code, area code and local number. An exception is Canada, where you dial 1 plus the area code and local number, but international rates still apply.

➡ If you're calling from abroad, the US country code is 1.

Phonecards

Prepaid phonecards are sold at convenience stores, supermarkets and other locations.

Time

➡ Hawaii has its own time zone and does not observe daylight saving time.

➡ During standard time (winter), Hawaii time differs from Los Angeles by two hours, from New York by five hours, from London by 10 hours and from Tokyo by 19 hours. During daylight saving time (summer), the difference is one hour more for countries that observe it.

➡ In midwinter, the sun rises around 7am and sets around 6pm. In midsummer, it rises before 6am and sets after 7pm.

➡ Upon arrival, set your internal clock to 'Hawaiian time,' meaning slow down!

Tourist Information

Tourist information kiosks aren't really a thing on Kaua'i, but the local tourist board, **Kaua'i Visitors Bureau** (Map p94; ☑808-245-3971; www.gohawaii.com/kauai; 4334 Rice St, Suite 101, Lihu'e; ☺8am-4:30pm Mon-Fri), does have a useful website and their office in Lihu'e is worth visiting for maps and information.

Division of Forestry & Wildlife (Map p94; ☑808-274-3433; http://dlnr.hawaii.gov/ dofaw/; 3060 Eiwa St, Room 306, Lihu'e; ☺8am-3:30pm Mon-Fri) For remote backcountry camping on the Westside, the Division of Forestry & Wildlife issues permits for four campgrounds in Waimea Canyon, three campgrounds (Sugi Grove, Kawaikoi and Waikoali) in and around Koke'e State Park, and the Wai'alae Cabin campground near the Alaka'i Wilderness Preserve.

Division of State Parks (Map p94; ☑808-274-3444; www. hawaiistateparks.org; 3060 Eiwa St, Room 306, Lihu'e; ☺8am-3:30pm Mon-Fri) Office issues camping and hiking permits for Na Pali Coast Wilderness State Park and camping permits for Koke'e State Park and Polihale State Park.

Division of Parks & Recreation (Map p94; ☑808-241-4463; www.kauai.gov; 4444 Rice St, Suite 105, Lihu'e Civic Center, Lihu'e; ☺8am-4pm Mon-Fri) For tourist information.

Visas

Rules for entry to the US keep changing. Confirm current visa and passport requirements for your country at the US Department of State website (www.travel. state.gov).

Upon arriving in the US, all foreign visitors must have their two index fingers scanned and a digital photo taken, a process that takes under a minute. For more information, see the Travel Security section of the US Department of Homeland Security (https://www.dhs. gov/how-do-i/for-travelers) site.

Visitor Extensions

To remain in the US longer than the date stamped on your passport, you must go to the Honolulu office of the **US Citizenship & Immigration Service** (www. uscis.gov; 500 Ala Moana Blvd, Bldg 2, Room 400, Kaka'ako) before the stamped date to apply for an extension.

Volunteering

Although paid work on Kaua'i can be hard to find, volunteers are often welcome, especially in the botanic gardens and state parks.

Hui O Laka (☑808-335-9975; www.kokee.org) Work around Koke'e State Park to eradicate invasive species, plant endemic species and participate in a bird count.

Kaua'i Habitat for Humanity (☑808-335-0296; http:// kauaihabitat.org/volunteer) ✐ Join a team of volunteers to build affordable homes for families in need.

Koke'e Resource Conservation Program (☑808-335-0045; www.krcp.org) ✐ Accepts short-term and long-term volunteers and interns to help with weed-control projects in and around Koke'e, Waimea Canyon and Na Pali Wilderness Coast state parks. It involves strenuous hiking and use of herbicides. Bunk-bed housing is provided at the historic Koke'e Civilian Conservation Corps (CCC) Camp.

Malama Kaua'i (☑808-828-0685; www.malamakauai.org) Volunteers needed for half-day shifts at Kilauea's community gardens.

National Tropical Botanical Garden (NTBG; ☑North Shore 808-826-1668 ext 3, South Shore 808-332-7324 ext 232; https://ntbg.org/support/ volunteer) Apply in advance to work in two of the most astonishingly beautiful botanical gardens in the world.

Sierra Club (https://sierra clubhawaii.org) Apply to volunteer with the island chapter of the age-old environmental group founded by the legendary John Muir.

Surfrider Foundation (☑808-635-2593; http://kauai.surf rider.org) Join a beach clean-up and help mitigate marine plastic pollution.

Waipa Foundation (Map p144;☑808-826-9969; www. waipafoundation.org; 5-5785 Kuhio Hwy, Hanalei) Volunteer opportunities include sessions on the fourth Saturday of each month, when visitors join hands-on community activities such as clearing invasive plants from waterways, or working in the taro fields. Sign up in advance and they'll prepare lunch for you.

Work

➡ US citizens can legally work in Hawaii, but considering the high unemployment rate, opportunities are limited. Short-term employment will probably mean entry-level jobs in the service industry. Specific outdoor skills (eg scuba diving) might land you a job with an activity outfit.

➡ Check the listings in newspaper classifieds and also the Kaua'i Craigslist website (https://honolulu. craigslist.org/kau/).

Transportation

GETTING THERE & AWAY

Getting here is easy, especially from the mainland USA and Canada, with numerous flights daily. Often, flights will get here with layovers in Honolulu. There are no ferry services here.

Air

Roughly 99% of visitors to Hawaii arrive by air. Hawaii's major interisland carrier – reliable Hawaiian Airlines – offers frequent flights linking Kaua'i to O'ahu, Maui and the Big Island.

Interisland airfares vary wildly, from $50 to $130 one way. Round-trip fares are typically double the price without any discounts. Usually the earlier you book, the cheaper the fare.

While it's often possible to walk up and get on a flight among the four biggest islands (particularly to/from Honolulu), advance reservations are recommended, especially at peak times.

DEPARTURE TAX

Departure tax is included in the price of a ticket.

Airline regulations concerning surfboards, bicycles and other oversized baggage vary and can be restrictive, not to mention expensive – ask before booking.

Airports & Airlines

The vast majority of incoming flights from overseas and the US mainland arrive at **Honolulu International Airport** (HNL; ☑808-836-6411; www.airports. hawaii.gov/hnl; 300 Rodgers Blvd; ☏), where travelers can catch an interisland flight to Kaua'i. In Honolulu, you will pass through customs. Airlines flying directly to **Lihu'e Airport** (LIH; Map p90; ☑808-274-3800; http://airports.hawaii.gov/lih; 3901 Mokulele Loop) from the US mainland and Canada include Alaska Airlines, American Airlines, Hawaiian Airlines, United Airlines and WestJet.

You pass through agricultural inspection on departure from Kaua'i.

TRANSPORT OPTIONS

Book ahead for rental cars. Major car-rental agencies have booths outside Lihu'e Airport's baggage-claim area, with complimentary shuttles to off-airport parking lots. Taxis wait curbside, or you can use an airport courtesy phone to call one. Average fares

---

from Lihu'e Airport include Kapa'a ($28), Lihu'e ($12) and Po'ipu ($43 to $53). For families or groups, it may be more economical to book an airport shuttle with **Speedi Shuttle** (☑877-242-5777; www.speedishuttle.com).

TICKETS

Hawaii is a competitive market for US domestic and international airfares, which vary tremendously by season, day of the week and demand. Competition is highest among airlines flying to Honolulu from major US mainland cities, especially between Hawaiian Airlines and Alaska Airlines, while Allegiant Air serves smaller US regional airports.

The 'lowest fare' fluctuates constantly. In general, return fares from the US mainland to Hawaii cost from $400 (in low season from the West Coast) to $800 or more (in high season from the East Coast).

Sea

The only commercial passenger vessels docking at Nawiliwili Harbor in Lihu'e are cruise ships, mainly **Norwegian Cruise Line** (NCL; ☑855-577-9489; www. ncl.com) and **Princess Cruises** (☑800-774-6237; www.princess.com).

CLIMATE CHANGE & TRAVEL

Every form of transport that relies on carbon-based fuel generates CO_2, the main cause of human-induced climate change. Modern travel is dependent on airplanes, which might use less fuel per kilometer per person than most cars but travel much greater distances. The altitude at which aircraft emit gases (including CO_2) and particles also contributes to their climate change impact. Many websites offer 'carbon calculators' that allow people to estimate the carbon emissions generated by their journey and, for those who wish to do so, to offset the impact of the greenhouse gases emitted with contributions to portfolios of climate-friendly initiatives throughout the world. Lonely Planet offsets the carbon footprint of all staff and author travel.

GETTING AROUND

Bicycle

Cycling all the way around the island isn't much fun, due to heavy traffic and narrow road shoulders. But it's a convenient way of getting around beach resorts, and the Eastside has a recreational paved bicycle path running through Kapa'a. The best bike ride on the island is down the winding road of Waimea Canyon.

Bicycles can be rented in Waipouli, Kapa'a, Po'ipu and Hanalei. Tourist resort areas and specialty bicycle shops rent beach cruisers, hybrid models and occasionally high-end road and mountain bikes. Rental rates average $25 to $40 per day (easily double that for high-tech road or mountain bikes).

Generally, bicycles are required to follow the same rules of the road as cars. Bicycles are prohibited on freeways and sidewalks. State law requires all cyclists under the age of 16 to wear helmets. For more bicycling information, including downloadable cycling maps, search the website of the Hawaii Department of Transportation (http:// hidot.hawaii.gov/highways).

Bus

The county's **Kaua'i Bus** (Map p90; ☑808-246-8110; www.kauai.gov/bus; 3220 Ho'olako St, Lihu'e; one-way fare adult/senior & child 7-18yr $2/1) stops approximately hourly on weekdays in towns along major highways, with limited services on Saturdays, Sundays and holidays. Routes run island-wide, but don't reach the Na Pali Coast Wilderness, Waimea Canyon or Koke'e state parks. Schedules are available online. Check the website for where to buy monthly passes ($40).

Buses are air-conditioned and equipped with bicycle racks and wheelchair ramps. A few caveats: drivers don't give change; surfboards (except for boogie boards), oversized backpacks and luggage aren't allowed on board; stops are marked but might be hard to spot; and schedules do not include a map.

Car & Motorcycle

Major international car-rental companies have booths at Lihu'e Airport, with free shuttle buses running to off-airport parking lots nearby. Locally owned rental agency **Rent-A-Wreck Kauai** (☑808-245-7177; www. rentawreckkauai.com; 3148 Oihana St; ☺8am-5pm) is located in Lihu'e, while **Rent**

a Car Kauai (☑808-822-9272; www.rentacarkauai. com; 4-1101 Kuhio Hwy), based in Kapa'a on the Eastside, offers free airport pickups and drop-offs.

Arriving on the island without reservations usually leaves you subject to higher rates and limited availability. Rental cars may be entirely sold out during peak travel times, so book ahead.

Mix it up by renting a VW Westfalia Camper through **Kauai Camper Rental** (☑808-346-0957; www. kauaicamperrental.com; per day $165). Also worth considering are 4WD overland expedition vehicles (with rooftop tents and compact kitchens) from **Kauai Overlander** (☑808-651-4952; www.kauaioverlander.com; per day $150).

Kaua'i has a belt road running three-quarters of the way around the island, from Ke'e Beach in the north to near Polihale State Park in the west.

Driving Licenses

➡ An International Driving Permit (IDP), which must be obtained before you leave home, is necessary only if your country of origin is a non-English-speaking one.

➡ You need a valid motorcycle license to rent one, but a standard driving license will suffice for mopeds. The minimum age for renting a car is generally 25, though some agencies make

STREET ADDRESSES

Street addresses on Kaua'i might seem long, but there's a pattern. The numerical prefix in street addresses along Kaua'i's highways (eg 3-4567 Kuhio Hwy) refers to one of five districts: 1 refers to Waimea and vicinity, including Ni'ihau; 2 is Koloa and Po'ipu; 3 is Lihu'e to the Wailua River; 4 is Kapa'a and Anahola; and 5 is the North Shore.

exceptions; for motorcycles it's 21, for mopeds it's 18.

Insurance

With the exception of remote areas such as Waimea Canyon Rd and the North Shore beyond Princeville, fuel is available everywhere, but expect to pay 20% more than on the mainland. Towing is also very expensive. Fees start at around $70, plus $7 per mile.

Renting

➡ Renting a car often costs more on Kaua'i than on the other major Hawaiian Islands. Normally, a rock-bottom economy car from a major rental company will cost you around $250 per week, with rates doubling during the peak periods. Rental rates will generally include unlimited mileage.

➡ To minimize costs, comparison shop; differences of 50% between suppliers are not unheard of.

➡ Another strategy for cost saving is to use a local rental agency. These mom-and-pop firms, which generally operate from home, rent used vehicles that may be 10 years old, but can be had for around $25 per day.

➡ For motorcycle rentals, the go-to place is **Kaua'i Harley-Davidson** ((☎808-212-9495; www.kauaiharley.com; 3-1878 Kaumuali'i Hwy; ⊗8am-5pm), which has a 20-bike fleet in Puhi, just outside Lihu'e. For smaller scooters and mopeds contact **Kauai Mopeds** (☎808-652-7407; www.kauai-mopeds.com; per day from $90).

➡ Rates for 4WD vehicles average $70 to $100 per day (before taxes and fees). Agencies prohibit driving off-road; if you get stuck they'll slap a penalty on you.

➡ Cars are sometimes prohibited by contract from traveling on dirt roads. That said, most roads are passable by regular car, if you go slow.

Road Conditions, Hazards & Rules

➡ Kaua'i remains very rural, with only one coastal highway connecting all major destinations. It's hard to get lost for long.

➡ Highway congestion has been lessened by road-widening, but there is still rush-hour traffic, especially between Lihu'e and Kapa'a. To help combat this, a 'contra-flow' lane is created from 5am to 10:30am

---

HIGHWAY NAMES

Locals call highways by their names rather than their numbers.

HIGHWAY	NICKNAME
Hwy 50	Kaumuali'i Hwy
Hwy 51	Kapule Hwy
Hwy 56	Kuhio Hwy
Hwy 58	Nawiliwili Rd
Hwy 520	Maluhia Rd (Tunnel of Trees)
Hwy 530	Koloa Rd
Hwy 540	Halewili Rd
Hwy 550	Waimea Canyon Dr & Koke'e Rd
Hwy 560	Kuhio Hwy (continuation of Hwy 56)
Hwy 570	Ahukini Rd
Hwy 580	Kuamo'o Rd
Hwy 581	Kamalu Rd & Olohena Rd
Hwy 583	Ma'alo Rd

ROAD DISTANCES & TIMES

Average driving distances and times from Lihu'e are as follows. Allow more time during morning and afternoon rush hours and on weekends.

DESTINATION	MILES	TIME
Anahola	14	25min
Hanalei	31	55min
Hanapepe	18	30min
Kapa'a	11	20min
Ke'e Beach	39	1¼hr
Kilauea Lighthouse	25	40min
Koke'e State Park	42	1½hr
Po'ipu	14	25min
Port Allen	17	30min
Princeville	30	50min
Waimea	23	40min
Waimea Canyon	37	1¼hr

weekdays on Kuhio Hwy (Hwy 56) in the Wailua area; this turns a northbound lane into a southbound lane by reversing the flow of traffic.

➡ Stay alert for one-lane-bridge crossings. Whenever there's no sign on one-lane stretches, downhill traffic must yield to uphill traffic.

➡ While drivers do tend to speed on highways, in-town driving is courteous and rather leisurely. Locals don't honk (unless a crash is imminent), they don't tailgate and they let faster cars pass. Do the same.

➡ State law prohibits more than one rider per moped, as well as requiring that they be driven in single file at a maximum of 30mph. Also, mopeds are not to be driven on sidewalks or freeways, but rather on roads with lower speed limits or on the highway shoulder.

➡ The state requires helmets only for motorcycle or moped/scooter riders under the age of 18. Rental agencies provide free helmets for all riders: use them.

Hitchhiking & Ride-Sharing

Hitchhiking is technically illegal statewide and hitchhiking anywhere is not without risks. Lonely Planet does not recommend it. Hitchers should size up each situation carefully before getting in cars and women should be wary of hitching alone. People who do choose to hitchhike will be safer if they travel in pairs and let someone know where they are planning to go.

Hitchhiking is not a common practice among locals. You're most likely to find a ride along the North Shore.

Taxi

The standard flag-fall fee is $3, plus 30¢ per additional 0.1 miles or up to 45 seconds of waiting; surcharges may apply for luggage, surfboards, wheelchairs and bicycles. Cabs line up at the airport during business hours,

but they don't run all night or cruise for passengers. Elsewhere, you'll need to call ahead in advance. Most taxi companies operate island-wide, but it's usually faster to call one that's closer to your location. Uber is available on the island, but there are a very limited number of drivers, mainly focused around Lihu'e and the Eastside.

➡ **Kauai Taxi Company** (☑808-246-9554; http://kauaitaxico.com) Based in Lihu'e.

➡ **North Shore Cab** (☑808-639-7829; www.northshorecab.com) Based in Kilauea.

➡ **South Shore Cab** (☑808-742-1525) Based in Po'ipu.

DIRECTIONS

Makai means 'toward the ocean'; *mauka* means 'toward the mountain.' Refer to highways by common name, not by number.

Behind the Scenes

SEND US YOUR FEEDBACK

We love to hear from travelers – your comments keep us on our toes and help make our books better. Our well-traveled team reads every word on what you loved or loathed about this book. Although we cannot reply individually to your submissions, we always guarantee that your feedback goes straight to the appropriate authors, in time for the next edition. Each person who sends us information is thanked in the next edition – the most useful submissions are rewarded with a selection of digital PDF chapters.

Visit **lonelyplanet.com/contact** to submit your updates and suggestions or to ask for help. Our award-winning website also features inspirational travel stories, news and discussions.

Note: We may edit, reproduce and incorporate your comments in Lonely Planet products such as guidebooks, websites and digital products, so let us know if you don't want your comments reproduced or your name acknowledged. For a copy of our privacy policy visit lonelyplanet.com/privacy.

WRITER THANKS

Brett Atkinson

A big Kauài mahalo to the following people. Thanks to Lisa Nakamasu and Christy Lagundino at the Kauài Visitors Bureau in Lihu'e, and also to Darragh Walshe in Auckland. Tubing, sailing, eating and drinking our way around the island in the name of research was brilliant fun with Carol, and my co-author Greg Ward was a witty and thoroughly professional writing partner. Final thanks to Victoria Smith at Lonely Planet for the opportunity to explore the Garden Island.

Greg Ward

Greg Ward would like to thank all those who made working on Kaua'i such a joy, especially my dear wife and traveling companion Samantha Cook; my co-author Brett Atkinson and project editor Vicky Smith; and everyone out there on the beaches and hiking trails, and in the restaurants and bars.

ACKNOWLEDGEMENTS

Climate map data adapted from Peel MC, Finlayson BL & McMahon TA (2007) 'Updated World Map of the Köppen-Geiger Climate Classification', *Hydrology and Earth System Sciences*, 11, 1633–44.

Cover photograph: Wailua Falls/Ignacio Palacios/Getty Images ©

THIS BOOK

This 4th edition of Lonely Planet's *Kaua'i* guidebook was researched and written by Brett Atkinson and Greg Ward. The previous three editions were written by Greg Benchwick, Adam Skolnick, Adam Karlin, Luci Yamamoto and Amanda C Gregg. This guidebook was produced by the following:

Senior Product Editors
Vicky Smith, Sandie Kestell

Regional Senior Cartographer
Corey Hutchison

Assisting Cartographer
Valentina Kremenchutskaya

Product Editors
Claire Rourke, Amy Lynch

Book Designer
Catalina Aragón

Assisting Editors
Janet Austin, Sarah Bailey, Bailey Freeman, Anne Mulvaney, Anna Tyler

Cover Researcher
Brendan Dempsey-Spencer

Thanks to
Dan Bolger, Fergal Condon, Sasha Drew, Sandie Kestell, Amy Lysen, Genna Patterson, James Smart, Gabrielle Stefanos, Kristy Uddin

Index

Map Legend

Sights

- Beach
- Bird Sanctuary
- Buddhist
- Castle/Palace
- Christian
- Confucian
- Hindu
- Islamic
- Jain
- Jewish
- Monument
- Museum/Gallery/Historic Building
- Ruin
- Shinto
- Sikh
- Taoist
- Winery/Vineyard
- Zoo/Wildlife Sanctuary
- Other Sight

Activities, Courses & Tours

- Bodysurfing
- Diving
- Canoeing/Kayaking
- Course/Tour
- Sento Hot Baths/Onsen
- Skiing
- Snorkeling
- Surfing
- Swimming/Pool
- Walking
- Windsurfing
- Other Activity

Sleeping

- Sleeping
- Camping
- Hut/Shelter

Eating

- Eating

Drinking & Nightlife

- Drinking & Nightlife
- Cafe

Entertainment

- Entertainment

Shopping

- Shopping

Information

- Bank
- Embassy/Consulate
- Hospital/Medical
- Internet
- Police
- Post Office
- Telephone
- Toilet
- Tourist Information
- Other Information

Geographic

- Beach
- Gate
- Hut/Shelter
- Lighthouse
- Lookout
- Mountain/Volcano
- Oasis
- Park
- Pass
- Picnic Area
- Waterfall

Population

- Capital (National)
- Capital (State/Province)
- City/Large Town
- Town/Village

Transport

- Airport
- BART station
- Border crossing
- Boston T station
- Bus
- Cable car/Funicular
- Cycling
- Ferry
- Metro/Muni station
- Monorail
- Parking
- Petrol station
- Subway/SkyTrain station
- Taxi
- Train station/Railway
- Tram
- Underground station
- Other Transport

Routes

- Tollway
- Freeway
- Primary
- Secondary
- Tertiary
- Lane
- Unsealed road
- Road under construction
- Plaza/Mall
- Steps
- Tunnel
- Pedestrian overpass
- Walking Tour
- Walking Tour detour
- Path/Walking Trail

Boundaries

- International
- State/Province
- Disputed
- Regional/Suburb
- Marine Park
- Cliff
- Wall

Hydrography

- River, Creek
- Intermittent River
- Canal
- Water
- Dry/Salt/Intermittent Lake
- Reef

Areas

- Airport/Runway
- Beach/Desert
- Cemetery (Christian)
- Cemetery (Other)
- Glacier
- Mudflat
- Park/Forest
- Sight (Building)
- Sportsground
- Swamp/Mangrove

Note: Not all symbols displayed above appear on the maps in this book

OUR STORY

A beat-up old car, a few dollars in the pocket and a sense of adventure. In 1972 that's all Tony and Maureen Wheeler needed for the trip of a lifetime – across Europe and Asia overland to Australia. It took several months, and at the end – broke but inspired – they sat at their kitchen table writing and stapling together their first travel guide, *Across Asia on the Cheap*. Within a week they'd sold 1500 copies. Lonely Planet was born.

Today, Lonely Planet has offices in the US, Ireland and China, with a network of over 2000 contributors in every corner of the globe. We share Tony's belief that 'a great guidebook should do three things: inform, educate and amuse'.

OUR WRITERS

Brett Atkinson

Brett is based in Auckland, New Zealand, but is frequently on the road for Lonely Planet, covering areas as diverse as Vietnam, Sri Lanka, New Zealand, Morocco, California and the South Pacific. He's a full-time travel and food writer specialising in adventure travel, unusual destinations and surprising angles on more well-known destinations. Craft beer and street food are Brett's favourite reasons to explore places, and he is featured regularly on the Lonely Planet website and in newspapers, magazines and websites across New Zealand and Australia.

Greg Ward

Since youthful adventures on the hippy trail to India and living in Spain, Greg Ward has written guides to destinations all over the world. As well as covering the USA from the Southwest to Hawaii, he has ranged on recent assignments from Corsica to the Cotswolds and Dallas to Delphi. Visit his website, www. gregward.info, to see his favourite photos and memories.

Published by Lonely Planet Global Limited
CRN 554153
4th edition – Apr 2021
ISBN 978 1 78657 855 6
© Lonely Planet 2021   Photographs © as indicated 2021
10 9 8 7 6 5 4 3 2
Printed in China